COLLECTED ESSAYS IN LAW

Law's Premises, Law's Promise

The Collected Essays in Law Series
General Editor: Tom D. Campbell

The Jurisprudence of
Law's Form and Substance

Robert S. Summers

ISBN: 0 7546 2024 7

Constitutional Interpretation

Frederick Schauer

ISBN: 0 7546 2039 5

Regulation, Crime, and Freedom

John Braithwaite

ISBN: 0 7546 2005 0

Legal Rules and Legal Reasoning

Larry Alexander

ISBN: 0 7546 2004 2

Thomas Morawetz

Law's Premises, Law's Promise

Jurisprudence after Wittgenstein

LONDON AND NEW YORK

First published 2000 by Ashgate Publishing

Reissued 2019 by Routledge
2 Park Square, Milton Park, Abingdon, Oxon, OXl 4 4RN
52 Vanderbilt Avenue, New York, NY 10017

Routledge is an imprint of the Taylor & Francis Group, an informa business

A Library of Congress record exists under LC control number:

ISBN 13: 978-1-138-71130-3 (hbk)
ISBN 13: 978-1-138-71127-3 (pbk)
ISBN 13: 978-1-315-20047-7 (ebk)

Contents

Introduction vii

Series Editor's Preface xvi

PART I: ESSAYS IN ANALYTICAL JURISPRUDENCE

1 The Rules of Law and the Point of Law 3
University of Pennsylvania Law Review, **121**, 1973, pp.859–873

2 The Concept of a Practice 19
Philosophical Studies, **24**, Kluwer Academic Publishers, 1973, pp. 209–226

3 Understanding, Disagreement and Conceptual Change 37
Philosophy and Phenomenonological Research, **41**, 1980, pp.46–63

4 A Utilitarian Theory of Judicial Decision 55
Arizona State Law Journal, **1979**, 1979, pp.339–365

5 The Epistemology of Judging: Wittgenstein and Deliberative Practices 83
Canadian Journal of Law and Jurisprudence, **3**, 1990, pp. 35–59

6 Understanding Disagreement, the Root Issue of Jurisprudence 109
University of Pennsylvania Law Review, **141**, 1992, pp.371–456

7 Law as Experience: The Internal Aspect of Law 195
SMU Law Review, **52**, SMU Law Review Association, 1999, pp. 27–66

PART II: ESSAYS ON LIBERALISM

8 Persons Without History: Liberal Theory and Human Nature 237
Boston University Law Review, **66**, 1986, pp.1013–1037

9 Liberalism and the New Skeptics 263
In Harm's Way: Essays in Honor of Joel Feinberg, ed. J.L. Coleman and A. Buchanan, Cambridge University Press, 1994, pp122–138

PART III: ESSAYS ON CRIMINAL RESPONSIBILITY

10 Retributivism and Justice 283
Connecticut Law Review, **16**, 1984, pp. 803–820

11 Reconstructing the Criminal Defenses: The Significance of Justification 301
The Journal of Criminal Law and Criminology, **77**, 1986, pp. 277–307

Name Index 333

Introduction

1. On Method: Games, Rules, Practices

Anyone writing philosophy in the shadow of Wittgenstein is likely to be preoccupied by the metaphor of games. Wittgenstein seems to recommend that we look at familiar subjects of philosophical scrutiny, such as knowledge claims and moral judgments, on the model of games. Judgments and claims are analogous to moves within games (practices) whose rules are mutually understood and taken for granted. Accordingly, what appear to be philosophical conundrums are, it is suggested, misunderstandings of the contextual nature of the subject.

The metaphor has been influential and controversial. Philosophical writers following Wittgenstein find the metaphor inescapable and inexhaustible. And they may find it as intriguing and seductive for what it conceals as for what it illuminates.

The phrase 'language game' is associated with Wittgenstein. The phrase is misleading if it implies that his interest is primarily with moves in language. To be sure, language is our main medium of communication, and Wittgenstein draws our attention to the publicity of language. But the shared practices that involve language are shared practices of understanding, interpreting, and experiencing. Thus, the shared practices that a philosopher, following Wittgenstein's example, must explicate are habits or modes of cognition, behavior, and feeling as much as they are dispositions to use language.

It is obvious that we use language to speak about language. On such occasions, we are both inside and outside a particular language, inside insofar as we are practitioners or users of it, outside insofar as we make it the object of scrutiny. This inside/outside circumstance may be complex, but it is hardly puzzling or paradoxical.

Philosophical investigations embody a problematic form of this situation. Our modes of understanding and experience are practices that we come to identify with our nature. They are so familiar that we may appropriately be bewildered if asked to describe them. And yet philosophy is the activity of giving just such descriptions. Indeed, the philosophical task is hard for several reasons.

First, we tend to see our values and modes of understanding as marks of our individuality, elaborations of our nature, features of a private domain of thought and feeling. In considering the extent to which the things we say and think are practices bounded by rules, we are forced to rethink the private/public relationship. We learn from others what counts as a 'move' in discourse, what counts as evidence or justification for a knowledge claim or for an assertion of value. How we think about these matters is mirrored by what we are disposed to say, and what we are disposed to say constitutes a learned practice that is public and shared with others.

Such practices are describable as rule-governed. But the notion of a rule in this context is itself complex and problematic. We can set down the rules of chess or baseball with some hope of objectivity and completeness. But any similar hope vis-a-vis the 'rules' of value discourse and inquiry is likely to seem illusory.

A second reason that the philosophical task is daunting is the complexity of the relevant practices. Once we concede the relevance of the metaphors of games and rules, we begin to appreciate how many and varied are the moves that must be explained. For example, an account of the 'game' of value discourse-and-thinking must not only describe the criteria of good and bad acts, of good and bad persons, and of rightness and wrongness. It must not only describe relations among these notions. It must also, in tacit acknowledgment of the controversial character of these matters, explain the 'rules' for agreeing and disagreeing about such matters. It must account for instances of both closure and unresolvability in such disagreements. It must distinguish between unintelligible judgments, intelligible and disputable judgments, and uncontroversial ones. And it must explain the scope and nature of disagreements about these second-order questions.

Besides all this, it must give an account of how we think and talk about value systems that are not our own, those of other times and cultures. It must explain when and why such 'alien' systems sometimes lead us to change our own way of proceeding and sometimes do not. And it must explain debates about the very nature and purpose of value inquiry and judgment insofar as such debates are events in the practice itself.

In brief, the 'game' or practice of value discourse-and-thinking is fluid, multi-leveled, and self-reflective. It is fluid insofar as different players may play by somewhat different rules but are capable of recognizing and addressing the fact that they are doing so. Virtually every situation of moral judgment can give rise to disagreement. Thus, 'players' are playing the same game not because they are playing by the same rules but because they are capable of recognizing and acknowledging the variations among their individual styles of play.

The practice is multi-leveled insofar as rules for making judgments coexist with rules for examining the process of making judgments. Rules for disagreeing coexist with rules for understanding such disagreements and the existing strategies for resolution, and so on. The practice is self-reflective insofar as moves within the practice meld indistinguishably with moves in discourse *about* the practice. We make moral judgments often in full awareness of our disagreements about both the methods and the point of making moral judgments. We discuss moral judgments prepared to slip into a defense of and a debate about those methods, that point.

It follows that the third reason philosophy is hard is that our practices are works in progress, moving targets. These practices themselves – making value judgments, gaining knowledge – are constantly under re- and deconstruction. Each of us as player/practitioner inhabits a place within these practices. Each of us is prepared to carry out a particular way of playing, assessing evidence, drawing conclusions, trying to resolve disagreements, and each of us is prepared to defend our way of playing even as we are also prepared, ordinarily, to reexamine it.

We leave none of this behind when we are asked to do philosophy. Derrida says that 'we inhabit the structures that we deconstruct.' The window through which the philosopher looks when asked to address a domain of understanding, thought, experience, and discourse is the window of her own spontaneous practice. To be sure, she must be self-conscious about the window, scrutinizing it for partiality and preference. And yet, she remains in tension: she is at once inside and outside the practice. Or rather she is inside but has the task of examining it self-consciously, questioning as much as possible the biases that come with insideness.

Therefore, games are defective and misleading, if indispensable, metaphors for practices. Standard examples of games have discrete rules and assign players defined goals. Instances of games begin and end, and one is a player as long as the game lasts. There is no conceptual tension between the roles of player of a game and describer of the game from outside.

2. Law

Philosophers of law are understandably seduced by the metaphor of games. More than most practices, law is identified with rules. When we talk about rules of morality or rules of cognitive or scientific understanding, the notion of a rule is used metaphorically. But talk about rules of law is hardly metaphorical; rules are a familiar, arguably essential, aspect of the practice.

Accordingly, schools of jurisprudence are marked by the lessons they draw from the metaphor of games. Positivism identifies law with social order imposed and maintained through rules. H.L.A. Hart's model of rules distinguishes primary rules, rules that impose obligation on all citizens, from secondary rules that define law's institutions and instruct officials about making, interpreting, and applying primary rules. Hart and Joseph Raz emphasize the game-like ways in which law makes certain kinds of behavior significant and non-optional and the availability of game-like formal criteria for law's rules. Their account implies that among the most interesting ways in which law differs from a game are that, from birth to death, we never cease playing and that the game's rules are constantly changed and reconceived (in accord with formally prescribed procedures) as the process goes forward.

For positivists, the relationship between the internal and external perspectives in law is analogous to such relationships in games or languages. One may be a player qua citizen (or lawyer or judge) and, assuming a different role, one may describe law in its generality qua theorist. Positivists see little tension between these roles.

Such tension becomes apparent when one takes law seriously as a vehicle, perhaps the primary vehicle, for realizing shared social aspirations, for applying social morality. Raising this possibility involves questioning the point of law. This is a much more problematic issue in regard to law than it is with regard to games or languages. Games such as chess or basketball have an internal point, namely whatever it takes to win, and an external point, such as the pleasure of playing or the thrill of victory. Language has the point of communication, along with such secondary points as self-realization. But the point of law, and the controversies that envelop it, occupy the players of the game, the participants of the practice, at many points. Legislators who create law, judges who apply it, and officials who execute it shape their decisions around their conception of the purposes law serves. And they are not likely to agree.

Critical theorists echo the positivists' insight that the rules of law meet formal rather than normative criteria. They, like positivists, claim to speak as theorists from outside legal systems looking in. But, unlike positivists, they are concerned with the relationship between the roles of participant and theorist and with its implications for normative choices. Embracing the positivistic insight that the legal system has 'open texture,' that its rules are under construction as the game proceeds, they radicalize that insight in two ways. First, they examine various internal decisions – interpretive decisions of judges, legislative choices, strategies of attorneys – as reflecting individual predilections and agendas. Such decisions may reflect personal histories and perspectives or the orientations of classes and interest groups that such individuals represent. In either case, legal decision-making is 'politics all the way down.' And second, critical theorists abandon the positivist distinction between a core of settled law and a periphery of law-in-the-making. Political choices and fluidity pervade the system.

Critical theorists seem to assume that as theorist/outsiders, they are in a position to correct the perspective of the legal insiders, the players. Even if players think of themselves as disinterested and aperspectivally objective, the critical theorists' gloss is that they are wrong.

But this conclusion is itself paradoxical. It ignores the truism that all theorists are also participants in some legal system and the fact that *all* theoretical postures are abstracted from the experiences of participants. In any case, the conscientious and self-critical insider is more than the instantiation of a political agenda. As we have seen, she inhabits the 'game' at many levels. She is prepared to defend a set of interpretations and goals. She anticipates disagreements and has strategies for seeing choices from multiple perspectives. She strives to distinguish bias and partiality from disinterest and objectivity, and she has ways of assessing her own decisions in light of such distinctions. At the same time, she appreciates that critical theorist's skepticism. The tension between participant and theorist is expressed in the (potential or actual) awareness that her aspirations toward disinterest and objectivity will be realized only partially and provisionally.

Liberalism and legal naturalism are theories of law that take account of such aspirations. Unlike positivism and critical theory, they proceed from the insider's tentative confidence that the point of law can be harmonized with human aspirations, that, in Ronald Dworkin's terms, it makes sense to think of law as 'working itself pure.' Liberalism, as John Rawls suggests, begins with the hope that some systems of social order are self-evidently superior to others. We can rise above or put aside the interests of class and personal disposition to construct the rules of a game in which we all have a better chance of flourishing. Law becomes the quest for such rules.

The mystery at the heart of the process is whether the quest is a delusion. It may be a delusion in two senses. On one hand, there may be no possible consensus about social ideals or about the conditions that support human flourishing. Both within and between cultures, we may ever be at the mercy of warring visions. On the other hand, whether or not there are such conditions, persons may be incapable of distinguishing them from more parochial interests and agendas. The notion that each of us makes decisions from her own perspective and in light of her own experience may take an invidious turn. It may imply that claims *about* our practices and their implicit values are not just colored but tainted by the fact that they are made from *within* such practices, by theorists who are also players.

3. Essays in Jurisprudence

Philosophy, as exemplified in the essays that follow, requires humility and candor in two respects. First, the distinctive Wittgenstinian gesture is to focus on practices as collective inventions and conventions. Claims to know and understand are moves within practices. Such moves are meaningful to ourselves and others only when they conform to shared conventions that determine such practices.

Second, we must be mindful of the lesson of hermeneutics. Each of us participates in the practice in his own distinctive way. In the light of an idiosyncratic personal history, each of us has a unique 'take' on our shared experiences, a unique way of understanding and of giving voice to that understanding. The bounds of intelligibility mirror the fact that we are playing the same game; the nuances of variation and disagreement in our play reflect the fact that we each appropriate the 'game' in our own way.

Legal philosophy is the intersection of two practices, the practice defined by law and legal institutions and the philosophical practice of scrutinizing law. One can look at *both* of these practices in the light of the distinction just made. Thus the practice of law as carried out by various role players – judges, legislators, attorneys, citizens – comports with certain rules; there is a degree of uniformity of conduct that allows us to identify the practice. On the other hand, each legislator, judge, and so on, has a personal way of carrying out the role.

And the same goes for those who look at law philosophically. Certain observations are common currency and reflect a shared conceptual understanding. And yet each asks different questions, weighs relevant evidence differently, reaches different conclusions.

The essays in Part I of this collection fall within analytical jurisprudence. They discuss the concept of law and the roles of actors within the practice. In doing so, they assess the various understandings of law and legal decision-making offered by legal positivists, legal naturalists, and critical theorists in the light of Wittgenstein's notion of a practice and the insights of hermeneutics.

The first three essays ('The Rules of Law and the Point of Law,' 'The Concept of a Practice,' and 'Understanding, Disagreement, and Conceptual Change') are about the usefulness and limitations of the metaphor of games. In particular, they make clear the oddness and significance of the fact that law is a 'game' in which the point – the goals, the purpose, the ideals – of the practice is itself an element of scrutiny and disagreement by the players.

Two other essays in Part I apply ethical theories and hermeneutical understanding to the role of judging. Utilitarianism can be invoked as a general theory of moral value and as a possible theory of judicial decision. With regard to both kinds of applications, many writers oppose utilitarian decision-making to decisions based on rights. 'A Utilitarian Theory of Decision-Making' argues that these two strategies can be reconciled and locates utilitarian aspirations within a system that takes rights seriously. A more recent article, 'The Epistemology of Judging: Wittgenstein and Deliberative Practices,' examines the link between a judge's predilections in deciding cases and the judge's implicit commitment at a jurisprudential level to views about the point of the practice.

The last two articles in Part I ('Understanding Disagreement, the Root Issue of Jurisprudence' and 'Law as Experience: The Internal Aspect of Law') explore the consequences for theory of seeing law as a deliberative practice, a practice in which both the rules and the point of the practice undergo constant internal examination and redefinition. One consequence is jurisprudential, the conclusion that different schools of theory about law offer partial views. Positivitic, naturalistic, and critical approaches to law reflect useful but limited aspects of a practice that remakes itself through self-reflection by its participants. A second consequence is that what Hart calls 'the internal aspect of law' is dauntingly complex and, at the same time, the key to unpacking law as a practice. Traditional antinomies in legal theory can be bridged by an understanding of these complexities.

The essays in Part II take up liberalism in legal theory. Liberal political theory has had an uneasy coexistence with naturalistic legal theory. In the work of Jeremy Bentham and John Austin, liberalism coexisted with a positivistic characterization of law. The ideals of liberalism guided legal reform, while law itself was a malleable product of collective institutional acts. For contemporary theorists such as Ronald Dworkin, by contrast, law has at its core a conception of rights that evolves over time through refinement of such liberal ideals as autonomy and respect. For Dworkin, positivism offers an inadequate picture of the place of such natural values at the core of the law, values that give the practice its point.

For critics of liberalism and naturalism, the notion of an evolving consensus about such values being realized through law is a disingenuous myth. Generalities about autonomy realized through rights lack content until they are informed by political conceptions. These conceptions in turn are informed by interests. The essays in Part II ('Persons without History: Liberal Theory and Human Nature' and 'Liberalism and the New Skeptics') defend liberalism against such criticisms. They describe it not so much as a shared system of value but rather as a shared framework of discourse-and-thought through which conflicting values and goals can be acknowledged and within which such conflicts can be bridged.

The essays in Part III examine noteworthy links between law and morality in criminal law. Arguably, criminal law is special in three ways. It addresses the problem of social disorder and personal security directly. Whatever other purposes law serves, its minimal aspiration is to secure social order.

Second, criminal prohibitions seem, to a significant extent, to reflect the coincidence of law and morality. The most serious crimes are often violations of fundamental moral norms. Positivists are likely to concede that criminal law offers the natural law theorist's best case for a moral core in law, and critical theorists are likely to admit that the most serious criminal offenses show a consensus of shared interest that transcends race, class, and gender.

Third, criminal law forces us to examine the boundaries of will and responsibility. Whatever purposes or cross-purposes they serve, most participants in the practice (citizens, judges, legislators, and lawyers) are assumed to be capable of rule-following, of governing and ordering their conduct. Criminal law tests the limits of that assumption, at least for some actors in some situations.

The essay 'Retributivism and Justice' looks at a pervasive disagreement in the theory of punishment. The disagreement seems to be about the point of the practice of punishing. The disputants adopt, respectively, the rhetoric of rights-and-retribution and the rhetoric of utilitarianism. The essay argues that the conflict is something of a mirage. Our shared goals, as represented in any persuasive utilitarian theory, incorporate a prior understanding of the rights of individuals and the deserts of offenders. Thus, notions about desert, retribution, and rights do not stand in opposition to utilitarian thinking about punishment but inform it.

The more recent essay 'Reconstructing the Criminal Defenses: The Significance of Justification' is about the limits of moral responsibility. The vexed distinction in criminal law between excuses and justifications reflects the infusion of moral distinctions in law. Specifically, it requires us to distinguish judgments about the results of conduct from judgments about motives and judgments about actors' capacities. In other words, it demands that we clarify the terms and beliefs under which persons participate in joint practices in all their moral and psychological complexity.

***

A theme that runs through these essays is that theoretical polarities often reflect distortions of understanding. The theoretical wars between naturalists and positivists, between critical theorists and liberals, between utilitarians and rights theorists are often shadow-boxing, often collisions (in Wittgenstein's famous and felicitous image) between the fly and the walls of the fly-bottle. They can be criticized as examples of theory untethered to the complex awareness and strategies of the insider to the practice. Recognition of the priority of the insider as participant and attention to the insider's options for self-reflection can often bridge the austere oppositions of theory and thus yield insight.

Thomas Morawetz is currently Tapping Reeve Professor of Law and Ethics at the University of Connecticut School of Law. He taught formerly in the Philosophy Department at Yale University. His many publications are primarily on topics in jurisprudence, ethics, law and literature, criminal law, and legal professionalism.

Series Editor's Preface

Collected Essays in Law makes available some of the most important work of scholars who have made a major contribution to the study of law. Each volume brings together a selection of writings by a leading authority on a particular subject. The series gives authors an opportunity to present and comment on what they regard as their most important work in a specific area. Within their chosen subject area, the collections aim to give a comprehensive coverage of the authors' research. Care is taken to include essays and articles which are less readily accessible and to give the reader a picture of the development of the authors' work and an indication of research in progress.

The initial volumes in the series include collections by Professors Frederick Schauer (Harvard), *Constitutional Interpretation*, John Braithwaite (ANU), *Regulation, Crime and Freedom*, Tom Morawetz, *Law's Premises, Law's Promise*, Robert Summers (Cornell), *Law's Form and Substance*, and Larry Alexander (San Diego), *Legal Rules and Legal Reasoning*. These collections set a high standard for future volumes in the series and I am most grateful to all of these distinguished authors for being in at the start of what it is hoped will become a rich and varied repository of the achievements of contemporary legal scholarship

Part I

Essays in Analytical Jurisprudence

[1]
The Rules of Law and the Point of Law

H.L.A. Hart's book, *The Concept of Law*,[1] is a description of the kinds of rules which are characteristic of a legal system and which give it its structure. Ronald Dworkin has argued that such an account of the concept of law is, in important ways, mistaken because law encompasses "standards that do not function as rules, but operate differently as principles, policies, and other sorts of standards."[2]

I shall attempt to evaluate Dworkin's criticism, but I shall not do so directly. I shall first ask what would count in a very general way as a satisfactory analysis of a rule-structured activity like law—what kinds of questions such an analysis must answer. Such an investigation, if carried forward with moderate success, would allow us to ask whether Hart's analysis satisfactorily answers these questions. If it is not satisfactory, we can ask how it can be made satisfactory and whether these changes are of the sort that Dworkin recommends.

I. The Nature of Open and Closed Practices

According to John Rawls, a practice is any "form of activity specified by a system of rules . . . which gives the activity its structure."[3] To say this is to distinguish between activity which merely occurs regularly or *as a rule*, and activity which is governed by rules. Hart's example is that if most members of a community go to the movies on Friday night, it is proper to say that they go to the movies on Friday as a rule, or that they are in the habit of going to the movies. But it is not the case that they are following a rule in going to the movies, nor is it the case that their activity constitutes a practice. Stopping cars at red lights, on the other hand, may be something individuals do as a rule, or are in the habit of doing, but to say this is ordinarily inadequate or, worse, misleading. It is misleading because they are also *following* a rule and thereby are involved in a practice.[4]

This distinction can be clarified as follows. An external observer

[1] H.L.A. Hart, The Concept of Law (1961).

[2] Dworkin, *Is Law a System of Rules?*, in Essays in Legal Philosophy 25, 34 (R. Summers ed. 1968).

[3] Rawls, *Two Concepts of Rules*, 64 Philosophical Rev. 3 n.1 (1955).

[4] *See* H.L.A. Hart, *supra* note 1, at 9-13.

may record the frequency of movie-attending behavior and the frequency of stopping-at-red-light behavior. He may, moreover, record the kinds of reactions which follow deviations from set patterns, and he may be able to anticipate sequences of behavior and response with a fair degree of accuracy. What he cannot do from an external standpoint is to invoke a conceptual distinction between mere irregularities in behavior and violations of rules. This distinction *may* be reflected only in the attitudes participants take (internally) to deviations. Participants within a practice invoke the rules as standards to describe behavior which conforms to the rules and to criticize deviation. Failure to go to the movies on Friday night is an irregularity which is not usually described or criticized as a violation of a rule; failure to stop at a red light will be seen not as a mere irregularity but as a violation of a rule.[5] *One* kind of rule violation is a mistake; mistakes are attributable only in a context in which behavior is seen as rule-governed. For example, one can be said to move the bishop wrongly (rather than unusually) and thereby make a mistake in chess only when the behavior of playing is seen as governed by the rules of chess.[6]

Thus, the idea of a practice cannot be understood without the idea of a rule. The idea of a rule introduces a distinction between mere irregularities of behavior and violation of rules, and it allows us to refer to rules as standards which participants themselves employ.

I would like to distinguish between two kinds of practices, open and closed practices. Chess and baseball are closed practices. Roughly, a closed practice is one in which each instantiation (each *game*, for example) has an explicit beginning and end. Participants qualify as participants when they are familiar with all the rules of the practice which define moves, positions, goals, etc., rules which can be given more or less exhaustively and are *constitutive* of the practice. During a game, these rules are fixed. Without having violated rules, the participants are ordinarily in an adversary situation, and the constitutive rules specify, among other things, the goal or goals of the participants. I do not want to say, however, that all games are closed practices or that all closed practices are games.

An open practice, and I shall argue that law is an open practice, has none of these features. Participation is ordinarily open-ended, and the rules of the practice are standing rules which govern on-going activity. Participants are not required to know the particular rules which

[5] *Id.*

[6] This distinction parallels Rawls' distinction between the summary conception of rules and the practice conception of rules. A rule exists in the example of movie-going only as a description of regular behavior. Rawls, *supra* note 3, at 19-30.

define permissible moves and positions in order for them to qualify as participants, and in fact they may not do so. Moreover, it may be impossible in principle to give an exhaustive and complete account of the rules of the practice, either because they are unlimited in number or, more importantly, because the set of rules is constantly evolving. The practice may provide institutional ways in which rules can be changed. Ordinarily in an open practice participants are not adversaries, although an adversary situation may be created when a rule is violated.

Examples of open practices are particular legal systems and particular languages. Traffic rules and rules of grammar and usage are standing rules. Stopping at a red light or using "table" in successful communication are not moves within a game which has a formal beginning and end. Further, no citizen and no user of English is expected to know all the particular rules which govern behavior within the practice in order to be regarded as a participant. No exhaustive account of the first-order rules of a legal system or of English can be given. Even if such a listing could be given, the rules in their application would be unlike those of chess or baseball because they have, as Hart has argued, *open texture*. Rules of law have open texture if no statement of them can anticipate every possible problematic application.[7] Similarly, no statement of the rules of English can be anything but an approximation of usage. Laws change, and there are even *rules within the practice* which instruct officers of the practice how to make such changes. Furthermore, law and language are both cooperative enterprises, at least as long as the rules are followed.

Using the rough distinction between closed and open practices, I shall argue that certain features of closed practices are not present in all practices, as Rawls seems to suggest. Rawls says that "the rules of practices are logically prior to particular cases."[8] By this, he means that the intelligibility of the very terms with which we describe an activity presupposes the rules. "[G]iven any rule which specifies a form of action (a move), a particular action which would be taken as falling under this rule given that there is the practice would not be *described as* that sort of action unless there was the practice."[9]

[7] *See* H.L.A. HART, *supra* note 1, at 123:

> Particular fact-situations do not await us already marked off from each other, and labelled as instances of the general rule, the application of which is in question; nor can the rule itself step forward to claim its own instances. In all fields of experience, not only that of rules, there is a limit, inherent in the nature of language, to the guidance which general language can provide.

[8] Rawls, *supra* note 3, at 25.

[9] *Id.*

Rawls draws examples from baseball; among them are "striking out," "stealing a base," "balking."

Rawls concludes that a player within a practice, *qua* player, can have no authority to question

> the propriety of following a rule in particular cases. To engage in a practice, to perform those actions specified by a practice, *means* to follow the appropriate rules. If one wants to do an action which a certain practice specifies then there is no way to do it except to follow the rules which define it. Therefore, it doesn't *make sense* for a person to raise the question whether or not a rule of a practice correctly applies to *his* case where the action he contemplates is a form of action defined by a practice. If someone were to raise such a question, he would simply show that he didn't understand the situation in which he was acting.[10]

Rawls' example is again drawn from baseball. During a game a player cannot ask to be permitted four strikes. Being at bat is a situation defined by the practice, and it does not make sense for the player to question whether the rules governing batting correctly apply to his case. He can question the rule only when he is *not* a participant by suggesting that the rules in general be *changed* to allow batters four strikes.

In a closed practice the constitutive rules anticipate all situations. No situation can arise in which it is unclear whether a player ought to be permitted four strikes. In other words, the rules of a closed practice do not have open texture.[11] Moreover, the constitutive rules of a closed practice make no provision for change, or, a fortiori, for criticism, of the rules themselves within the practice. Thus, the suggestion that a player be permitted four strikes cannot be made by a player within the context of the practice and is meaningful only as a recommendation for new constitutive rules.

In open practices none of this is true as a matter of course. Any question whether a move is permitted in chess has an easy answer, presupposes the rules, and is obviated by a knowledge of the rules. On the other hand, a question whether a move is permitted in law (for example, whether an ordinance forbidding mechanized transportation in a park forbids pogo sticks) may have no easy answer. What is called for is an interpretation of the rules, and whatever guidelines

[10] *Id.* 26 (emphasis added).

[11] *See* note 7 *supra*. Throughout the discussion of closed and open practices, note the distinction between *a* game of baseball and *the* game of baseball. A game of baseball is an activity which is an instance of a closed practice. The game of baseball can be regarded as an evolving institution over time in which the rules change, in which a commissioner makes quasi-judicial decisions, etc. In this sense, it is like an open practice. In referring to baseball as an example of a closed practice, I have in mind the former sense. It is clear that only the former sense is at issue in Rawls' article.

are relevant to interpretation are also relevant to criticism and change. To say that a participant may appeal, in questioning the traffic ordinance, to guidelines other than the rules themselves, is to say that rules are not constitutive of moves within law as they are of moves within closed practices.

Rawls recognizes that a practice may provide for the change of rules, but his analysis seems incomplete. He first says that "if one holds an office defined by a practice then questions regarding one's actions in this office are settled by reference to the rules which define the practice."[12] Here, "officer" apparently designates anyone whose behavior is governed by the rules; questions regarding pitchers, batters, and chess players *are* settled by reference to the rules. Rawls continues, "If one seeks to question these rules, then one's office undergoes a fundamental change: one then assumes the office of one empowered to change and criticize the rules, or the office of a reformer, and so on."[13] Here, Rawls acknowledges that there may be practices more complex than chess, practices within which some rules confer a special kind of authority on certain players—the authority to change and to criticize the rules.[14]

But who are these officers and what is the nature of their authority? They are not like umpires since umpires administer the rules but do not change or criticize them. Are they like judges? A judge's role seems to be both to administer and to interpret rules. Legislators too are empowered to change and to create laws. But the substantive exercise of such authority cannot consist of moves defined by existing rules. In this sense, the reformer works *in vacuo*. At most, the rules which empower him and define his role set limitations and guidelines for his conduct, such as acting in the public interest. But they do not inform his behavior, as do the rules of a game; they do not determine what counts as implementation of the public interest.

To summarize, I have tried to identify the nature of a practice and to distinguish closed and open practices. A closed practice, like chess or baseball, is adequately explicated in a full statement of its constitutive rules. The rules do not change within the game and are definitive for the evaluation of moves within a game. To criticize the rules is to stand outside the practice and to recommend a new practice.

By contrast, within an open practice rules may be evaluated and changed, and the considerations relevant to evaluation and change do

---

12 Rawls, *supra* note 3, at 28.

13 *Id.*

14 Rawls is clearly not referring to such decisionmaking officers of baseball as umpires. Umpires are empowered only to apply rules, not to criticize or question them.

not emanate from other rules. I shall next argue that these considerations can be understood only as grounded in what I shall call the "point" of the practice.

If we ask a chess player what the point of the game is, he *may* say that the point is to checkmate the other player's king. Similarly, the point of baseball is to score more runs than the other team. In each case a rule of the game instructs the players how one wins. If we ask a player to *justify* a move he has made, he may do one of two things. If he thinks we are unfamiliar with the rules, he may cite the rule which allows him to make his move. If he thinks we are familiar with the rules, he may explain his strategy; he may explain the move in relation to the rule which specifies the point of the game for players in their roles as adversaries. The specification of the rules of chess or baseball is at the same time the specification of the point of the game *in this sense.*

On the other hand, the point of chess or baseball may be said to be the exercise of skill, the enjoyment of playing, etc. This point is nowhere specified in the rules. Described in this way, the point of the game is a justification for playing. It is not a constitutive feature of the game since a game of chess or baseball can be carried forward even if the players do not enjoy it and even if they exercise little or no particular skill.

What I wish to suggest about law as a practice, and about open practices generally, is that the point (or goal) of the practice is, on the one hand, not given in a specification of the rules, and yet must be taken into account before the application of rules to moves can be explained. The point of an open practice is *like* checkmating in chess in that it determines the strategy with which particular moves are made; it gives them their *raison d'être.* In what follows I shall use the example of law to illustrate that an account of an open practice is not complete once the rules are given; the point of the practice must be given as well.[15]

II. The Point of Law

I suggested initially that an account of what is required for the satisfactory analysis of a practice would help us evaluate Hart's analysis of law. I shall try to show that law, as an open practice, can be understood—and specifically that the features which Dworkin identi-

[15] The following section is an attempt to qualify and restrict the very general notion of the point of law. It is irrelevant whether one holds that there is one point of law or several complementary ones.

fies can be understood—only if both the rules of law and the point of law are taken into account. But what is the point of law? I shall not defend a particular formulation of it, but I shall suggest how it might be understood.

There is general agreement among legal philosophers that law is (at least) a system of rules for ordering behavior and that *some* legal rules are coercive and backed by sanctions.[16] Behavior which would go unpunished in the absence of a legal order is punishable within the legal order. Obvious examples are the taking of life and driving beyond a certain speed. Of course, not all legal rules are of this sort.[17] Insofar as it is coercive, law is different from such other practices as the English language, chess and baseball. In all of these practices the existence of the practice increases behavioral options; certain forms of behavior—verbal communicating, playing baseball—become possible *ipso facto* by virtue of the existence of the practice.

To say that the very existence of a practice creates new behavioral options is to give a very rough justification of the practice, which is not immediately available for coercive rules. It is available only if one can say that by limiting a certain range of behavioral options, a greater general good, otherwise unattainable, is made available to those whose behavior is limited. Only the minimal limitation needed to secure the greater good can be justified in this way.

The notion of justification in terms of the greater good encompasses not only material benefit but such values as justice and fairness. The suggestion here, which I shall discuss more fully below, is that any justification of a legal decision is *formally* justification in terms of the general good. The enhancement of a special interest is justified only insofar as it redounds to the general good.

It is now possible to formulate tentatively the point of law. The point is to limit permissible human activity in a general way so as to attain a greater general good that would otherwise be unattainable. Law can be justified only if it is admitted that this kind of justification can arise and that individuals *can* be benefited by limiting their options —when such a limitation is general.[18]

Even if a justification of law will be of this sort, why *must* a characterization of law include *any* justification at all? Why not say

---

16 *See* H.L.A. HART, *supra* note 1, chs. II-V.

17 Rules which empower individuals to make contracts or wills are not properly regarded as coercive rules. *See id.* 27-41.

18 One who holds that there can be no justification for any infringement on human freedom would hold that all legal systems are unjustified. *See* Rawls, *Justice as Fairness*, 67 PHILOSOPHICAL REV. 164 (1958). Rawls argues that rational, self-interested individuals will recognize that a general limitation of the sort contemplated by law will be in their best interest.

that law is simply a system of rules, some of them coercive? The reason is that this leaves unexplained the strategy of the players, the reasons and justifications that they themselves give for moving as they do. It is important to recall the difference between closed and open practices. In closed practices, the strategies of the players, their reasons and justifications for moving, can be understood in terms of the rule which specifies the point; for example, checkmating. In open practices there is no such rule.

The point of law is reflected in the strategies of players, in the reasons and justifications which are given. This may be seen by looking briefly at the actual practice of citizens, legislatures and courts. Consider the citizen obeying a traffic light. Under ordinary circumstances, he might explain his act by saying, "That's the law." If asked to *justify* his act, he might say that without such a rule, highway safety (an ingredient of social order) could not be realized. By the restriction of a personal option, the general benefit of safe driving is made possible. This justification is a justification *both* of the general rule *and* of each particular act which falls under it.[19] Thus it is possible for someone who is seeking urgent medical aid to argue that the traffic law ought not to apply in his case because its point is not served. This argument *makes sense* and it is very different from the suggestion of a baseball player that he be permitted four strikes. (To say that the argument makes sense is not to say that the law does not apply or ought not to apply. It is to say that *whether* the law applies is for those empowered to administer the law to decide, taking the point of law as relevant to their decision.)

Secondly, consider a legislature passing on a statute which regulates the sale of firearms. A basic justification of the law is that by limiting the option of individuals to own firearms without regulation, a greater good is secured for the whole community. A showing that the community is in some way better off without such regulation, or a showing that such a limitation goes beyond the minimal restriction needed to secure the good, is tantamount to a showing that the law is unjustified.

Finally, if we consider the arguments which lawyers and courts use to support, challenge and defend decisions, we will find them invoking what Dworkin calls "principles, policies and other sorts of standards." In one of Dworkin's examples, a decision limiting the ability of automobile manufacturers to limit their own liability by warranty

19 This is not to say that every feature of the law will stand in need of justification. Some features may be arbitrary, as is the color at which one stops or the date on which tax returns are due.

in case of defect is justified by the argument that, on the whole, consumers and public interests must be fairly treated.[20] An option created within law itself, the freedom of manufacturers to contract, is limited because such a limitation is necessary for the general good.

My argument should be qualified in five ways.

(1) The suggestion that the point of law is to limit permissible human activity in a general way so as to bring about greater general good than would otherwise be attainable should be tested as an attempt to represent the general character of the reasons which are given—by citizens, legislatures, lawyers, courts—to justify and criticize laws and their applications. Regardless of whether my particular formulation requires qualification, I am suggesting both that some characterization *can* be given, *i.e.* that there is a point of law, and that the role of principles as reasons can be understood only if there is a point of law which they instantiate.

(2) I am not suggesting that every citizen would be able or likely to justify law-obeying behavior in terms of the general good. But to give no justification at all ("that's the law") is to open oneself to the criticism that one has failed to consider for what justifiable reason one is acting. Further, I am not suggesting anything about the relation between the relevant justifications participants might give and their *motivation* for acting as they do. A fortiori, I am not saying anything about motivation or individual purposes at all. The point of the law and one's own point (or purpose) in following the law (helping one's family or keeping out of trouble) may be different matters entirely.

(3) The general principle which I have called the point of law is compatible with the existence of conflicting views about the general good. Most disagreements about what ought to be law and about how a particular law ought to be interpreted are *framed* as arguments about what kinds of acts would secure the general good. Even laws which seem hostile to the general principle (for example, Nazi expropriation laws, laws of apartheid) are defended or justified in terms of some such principle. Thus, the principle is an attempt to account for what counts as justification or criticism of *any* law in any system; in that sense what I have called "the point of law" belongs to the concept of law.

(4) Can there be a legal system in which laws are not justified in this way, in which, for example, they are simply oracular pronounce-

20 *See* Dworkin, *supra* note 2, *passim*. For purposes of argument, I take for granted that Dworkin is correct on these points. The case in question is Henningsen v. Bloomfield Motors, Inc., 32 N.J. 358, 387, 161 A.2d 69, 85 (1960).

ments? If so, the so-called point of law is not really a necessary feature of the concept of law.

This criticism mistakes the nature of the present discussion, which is not to give necessary features in the absence of which a practice *cannot* be called "law." There may be practices with coercive rules about which there is no satisfactory answer to "Is it law?" The suggested hypothesis is one example. Another would be a system having coercive rules but no rules specifying how to recognize valid law or how to administer it.[21] In this sense, the concept of law is itself a concept with open texture. There are no hard and fast rules for its application to penumbral cases.

(5) It is important that the same kind of considerations are usually relevant in determining the application and interpretation of particular rules and in determining what rules the practice ought to include. Law in its character as an open practice is different from a game, in which moves are justified by appeal to rules, and the set of rules (the game itself) is justified, if at all, by appeal to such different considerations as display of skill, entertainment, etc., all of which are general utilitarian considerations.

III. Hart's Analysis of Law

Hart's analysis of law is an analysis in terms of rules. As we have already seen, and as Hart argues, any analysis of a practice must begin with the notion of rule-governed behavior, which is to be distinguished from merely regular behavior.[22] Moreover, Hart notes that law is a practice in which at least some of the rules are coercive; they are rules whereby "human beings are required to do or abstain from certain actions, whether they wish to or not."[23] Hart calls these rules "primary rules of obligation."

Hart recognizes that law includes more than coercive rules, in part because legal coercion requires machinery for administration and enforcement, and he discusses the importance of "secondary" rules which empower some participants to administer the law. "[T]hey provide that human beings may by doing or saying certain things introduce new rules of the primary type, extinguish or modify old ones, or in various ways determine their incidence or control their operations."[24] Rules about making contracts, the formation of legislatures, and the

[21] *See* H.L.A. Hart, *supra* note 1, at 114-20. In Hart's terminology this is the question whether a legal system may have primary rules of obligation and no secondary rules. Primitive systems of coercive social organization may be of this form. *See also id.* ch. I.

[22] Text accompanying notes 3-6 *supra*.

[23] H.L.A. Hart, *supra* note 1, at 78-79.

[24] *Id.* 79.

conduct of courts are all of this sort. Since the set of primary rules changes over time, there must be a criterion for the primary rules of the practice. The special secondary rule which gives this criterion is "the rule of recognition." A primary rule is *valid* if it meets the criterion of the rule of recognition. The rule of recognition is what Dworkin calls a "master rule" which distinguishes laws from other social standards.

Finally, Hart notes that the application of primary rules to situations is sometimes uncertain because laws have open texture. Those empowered to interpret rules in these cases cannot merely have recourse to the rules themselves in making their interpretation; they must also make determinations with recourse to other (extralegal) considerations.[25] To say that judges have this power is simply to say that they have discretion.

In general, Hart seems to analyze law as if it were a closed practice, since closed practices are adequately analyzed when their constitutive rules are exhaustively given. Hart gives what he regards as an adequate account of the *kinds* of rules that are distinctive of law. Yet this is an incomplete portrait of law, while an account of chess in terms of its rules would not be incomplete, because it fails to answer why the players make the moves they make, what goals guide them, what reasons and justifications they might give for their moves, and in what way these reasons and justifications make sense. In chess an account of the rules includes an account of the point of the activity so that these questions are answered. In law, by Hart's own admission, these questions involve considerations not specified in the rules.

To analyze law as a closed practice is to analyze it as an oddly defective closed practice—defective because its rules generate hard cases. The wheels of the machine get stuck as they cannot get stuck in baseball. Therefore, special technicians must be called in; their expertise cannot be specified within the practice of law and consists in something extralegal. They have discretion to exercise their delegated powers. In regarding law as an open rather than a closed practice, we consider the possibility that it is not defective at all. The possibility is that at all levels of the on-going practice participants have recourse not only to rules but to relevant purposes and goals of the practice.

This is not to say that Hart's analysis is incorrect as an analysis of the kinds of rules that comprise law. But an adequate account of legal rules is not necessarily an adequate account of the concept of law. In particular, I am not suggesting that a rule which is valid by the rule

[25] For Dworkin's discussion of this point, see Dworkin, *supra* note 2, at 44-54.

of recognition must meet some further test, specified by the point of the practice. Valid laws may be said to violate the point of the practice, and this gives the impetus for reform. The vulnerability of existing law to criticism and modification inherently prevents law from becoming the fixed system that is a closed practice.

IV. Dworkin's Response to Hart

Dworkin's objections to Hart's theory are framed as objections to positivism. I shall discuss Dworkin's objections before considering briefly whether they are also objections to positivism.

The first of three challenged tenets of positivism is "that the law of a community is distinguished from other social standards by some test in the form of a master rule."[26] Dworkin notes that policies and principles belong to law and that they have no place in Hart's system of primary and secondary rules. This challenges the theory that the rule of recognition is a criterion for all standards properly called "law."

I shall assume with Dworkin that principles cannot be brought under the rule of recognition,[27] and that principles play a role at all levels of legal reasoning.[28] But nothing in Hart's analysis precludes supplementation by the notion of the point of law and the principles that flow from it. The rule of recognition is the criterion for legal rules rather than for law. This recommendation does not greatly alter Hart's program, a large part of which is to show that analyses of law as a *homogeneous* set of primary rules are inadequate. In this he succeeds.[29]

Dworkin suggests that principles—unlike legal rules—"are controversial . . . [and] numberless, and they shift and change so fast that the start of our list would be obsolete before we reached the middle."[30] This leaves their origin and character unintelligible and leaves mysterious just why they count as justification. The mystery evaporates if principles are seen as instantiations of the point of the practice, relevant in legal decisions as vectors pointing to the common purpose for which law exists.

Dworkin's second objection is derived from the first. He challenges the theory of judicial discretion as a theory that once a judge has exhausted all relevant legal rules, there are no further considerations

---

26 *Id.* 59.

27 It seems clear that Hart would agree that principles cannot be brought under the rule of recognition.

28 *See* text accompanying note 20 *supra*.

29 For Hart's critique of John Austin's theory of jurisprudence, see H.L.A. Hart, *supra* note 1, at 1-76. Austin suggests that legal rules are homogeneous and may all be seen as coercive rules; Hart's account of secondary rules corrects this defect in Austin's theory.

30 Dworkin, *supra* note 2, at 58.

binding upon his decisionmaking. If what I have argued is correct, principles which represent the point of law are binding in the sense Dworkin requires. He makes two points in support of this argument:

> [N]ot any principle will do to justify a change, or no rule would ever be safe. There must be some principles that count and others that do not, and there must be some principles that count for more than others. It could not depend on the judge's own preferences amongst a sea of respectable extra-legal standards, any one in principle eligible, because if that were the case we could not say that any rules were binding. We could always imagine a judge whose preferences amongst extra-legal standards were such as would justify a shift or radical reinterpretation of even the most entrenched rule.
>
> Second, any judge who proposes to change existing doctrine must take account of some important standards that argue against departures from established doctrine, and these standards are also for the most part principles. They include the doctrine of 'legislative supremacy,' a set of principles and policies that require the courts to pay a qualified deference to the acts of the legislature. They also include the doctrine of precedent . . . .[31]

We have already seen that the relevance and importance of a principle—the extent to which it is binding—cannot depend on the judge's preferences. They depend on the relation of the principle to the point of the practice, minimal coercion for the greater general good. Such doctrines as stare decisis have general relevance because it can always be argued that reliance on established practice is in the general interest.[32]

The third untenable tenet of positivism, according to Dworkin, is the theory of legal obligation whereby "a legal obligation exists when (and only when) an established rule of law imposes such an obligation. . . . [I]n a hard case—when no such established rule can be found—there is no legal obligation until the judge creates a new rule for the future."[33] This tenet follows from the identification of law with a system of rules and from the identification of obligation with the existence of particular primary (coercive) rules of obligation.

Again it is difficult to evaluate Dworkin's argument as a criticism of Hart, even if the argument itself is granted. It is possible to agree

[31] *Id.* 51-52.

[32] The point of the practice can be seen as a criterion of relevance for suggested principles just as the rule of recognition is a criterion of validity for suggested primary rules. To show that a principle is relevant is to show that it refers to a social order in which coercive (and other) rules exist only for the sake of the greater general good. It seems that the point of the practice is a substantive limit on possible reasons and justification, while the rule of recognition is a formal criterion.

[33] Dworkin, *supra* note 2, at 59.

with Hart that existing legal rules do impose obligations and still to hold that law is not simply a matter of rules. Valid rules may be criticized as bad law, as misrepresenting the point of law. To argue this may be to suggest that the obligatory nature of an unjustified rule is eroded, and that only justifiable rules impose obligations. If this is true, the obligatory nature of rules does not follow simply from their validity, as Hart suggests, but from their justifiability. On the other hand, if Hart is saying merely that prima facie obligation and justifiability attach to valid rules, this more cautious and tentative position is not vulnerable to criticism in the same way.

To decide whether Dworkin's argument is a refutation of Hart, one must decide how strong a position Hart takes. Let us call "strong" the position that the rule of recognition is a master rule for all law, that judges in hard cases cannot resolve cases by rule and are left to their own preferences, and that any valid legal rule determines obligation. Dworkin refutes this position. But if Hart holds that the rule of recognition is the criterion for legal rules (rather than for all of law), that judges in hard cases must appeal to principles (not to their own preferences) rather than to legal rules which are themselves ambiguous, and that legal rules are prima facie rules of obligation (but not necessarily obligatory if they are bad law), then none of Dworkin's three criticisms seems relevant to his position.

V. Positivism

Dworkin identifies the stronger position with positivism. If we assume *arguendo* that Hart holds the weaker position, and argue that this analysis of legal rules must be supplemented by an account of the point of the practice to compose an adequate account of the practice, is this composite account still a kind of positivism?

In an explanatory note in *The Concept of Law*, Hart lists five views, all of which appear in contemporary Anglo-American jurisprudence, as "positivism."[34] With regard to each, I shall ask whether either Hart's view or the composite view is positivism.

(1) "Laws are commands of human beings." This view, according to Hart, presupposes that rules are homogeneous and fails to give an adequate account of the role of secondary rules.[35] Hart's view and the composite view are not positivism in this sense.

(2) "There is no necessary connexion between law and morals, or law as it is and law as it ought to be." A law may be valid law

---

[34] H.L.A. Hart, *supra* note 1, at 253.
[35] *See id.* 1-76.

even if criticized as bad law, as betraying or undercutting the point of the practice. In this sense, both Hart's view and the composite view are positivistic.

(3) "The analysis or study of meanings of legal concepts is an important study to be distinguished from (though in no way hostile to) historical inquiries, sociological inquiries, and the critical appraisal of law in terms of morals, social aims, functions, &c." In this fairly trivial sense, Hart's view and the composite view are both positivistic, insofar as they are attempts to provide a study of meanings.

(4) "A legal system is a 'closed logical system' in which correct decisions can be deduced from predetermined legal rules by logical means alone." Neither view is positivistic in this sense. Hart recognizes open texture, and the composite view explains open texture by the fact that law is an open and not a closed practice.

(5) "Moral judgments cannot be established, as statements of fact can, by rational argument, evidence or proof." Neither theory takes a stand on this question.

It follows that the composite or amended theory is neither more nor less positivistic than Hart's theory. The composite theory, moreover, explains those features of law which Hart's analysis, taken only as an analysis of legal rules, leaves inchoate. Dworkin correctly objects that these features require explanation.

[2]
The Concept of a Practice

(1) "Practice", as used by John Rawls, is "a sort of technical term meaning any form of activity specified by a system of rules which defines offices, roles, moves, penalties, defenses, and so on, and which gives the activity its structure."[1] Using this definition, I shall argue that practices are of different kinds and I shall attempt to distinguish and characterize three kinds. The importance of doing so lies in the fact that games, language, legal systems, morality, and even cognition may be analyzed by philosophers as rule-structured activities, and therefore as practices, with little attention to what, *qua* practices, they do or do not have in common. I shall attempt to set a framework within which this can be done.

(2) A first kind of practice is represented by such games as chess and baseball. Such games are often held to be paradigms of practices in general.[2] I shall argue that games like chess and baseball represent only one kind of practice and have determinate features which practices of other kinds lack. The features to which I shall call attention are not features of all games, nor of games exclusively, but they are characteristic features of *some* games, and therefore of some practices.

(2.1) One feature of chess and baseball is that the rules which define "offices, roles, moves, penalties, defenses, and so on" are constitutive rules. In calling them "constitutive rules" I mean that the rules of such a practice can be given more or less exhaustively, and that each participant in the practice must be familiar with the rules as a logical condition of participation. I shall explain these points below.

(2.1.1) The constitutive rules of chess, for example, identify the pieces in the game, the kinds of moves that each player can make, the goal of the game, and what constitutes termination of a game. Chess can be identified with the set of its constitutive rules: chess is a game in which the bishop is moved diagonally, in which the object is to checkmate the king, etc.

This example must be qualified in four ways. First, to say that a game has constitutive rules is not to deny that, in addition to its constitutive rules, a game may have other rules. For example, some rules may be added at the option of the players. A rule which limits the time a player can take between moves is one example. Secondly, several determinate versions of a game may exist; for example, the number of innings in a complete game of Little League baseball is different from the number of innings in a major league game. Thirdly, the determinate set of constitutive rules of chess or baseball may change over time but may not change within a particular instance of the practice (a game of chess or baseball). Finally, in addition to the constitutive rules, there may be (and usually will be if the game is an interesting one) principles of strategy which the good player will follow.

(2.1.2) I would like to claim that in games like chess and baseball constitutive rules are easily distinguishable from optional rules or strategic principles. To make good this point, and to make good the more general point that chess and baseball have constitutive rules at all, we need a more rigorous characterization of the notion of a constitutive rule. Rawls' account is too inclusive. For example, some moves which represent defensive moves, such as a rule that outfielders must shift position when bases are loaded, is a strategic principle. We need a characterization which distinguishes constitutive rules within the larger class of rules which define "offices, roles, moves, penalties, defenses, and so on."

I shall attempt a rough intuitive characterization. Given the larger class of rules, the constitutive rules of a game are the rules which an individual must learn before he can be a participant in the game. (In other words, to regard someone as a participant is to regard him as having learned or in some way mastered the constitutive rules.) This is so because being a participant in a game or practice involves more than behaving in a certain way; it also involves having a critical reflective attitude toward one's own behavior and that of others. In particular, it involves the ability to criticize one's own behavior and that of others by appealing to the rules of the practice. It is only *qua* participant, moreover, that one is capable of making mistakes. Only if we regard someone as a participant do we describe irregularities in his behavior as, possibly, mistakes.[3]

In chess, a player must not only know how to move the bishop and the pawn, but he must be able to move all the other pieces, must know that the point of the game is to checkmate the king, etc. To say that the constitutive rules of chess or baseball may be given exhaustively is only to say that at some point instruction will terminate with "But you don't need to know that yet" or "But that's just a matter of strategy", etc. I assume that there will be general agreement among players when that point is reached. But general agreement is consistent with particular disagreement. When players disagree whether a particular rule *must* be taught to a prospective player, the question whether the rule is or is not a constitutive rule has no answer. The line of demarcation between constitutive rules and other rules may be indefinite or hazy.

One further qualification is needed. To say that a player must have a critical reflective attitude, and must be able to criticize his behavior and that of others, is not to say that he can or will reproduce the constitutive rules of the game on demand. Rather, having a critical reflective attitude is one aspect of having an internal rather than an external point of view.[4] One who has the internal point of view, who has learned the constitutive rules, will ordinarily describe an instance of the game in its own terminology ("Then Jones struck out.") and may be able to interpret the game to noninitiates ("He is allowed to swing at the ball and miss only three times. That's called 'striking out'."). A noninitiate will be able to do neither of these things; he will describe events within the game as he would events outside it, with no reference to the constitutive rules which give the activity its structure.

(2.2) The constitutive rules of chess and baseball are characteristically simple and unambiguous. They do not have "open texture"; that is to say, there are no relevant situations in which their application is undetermined.[5] The success of the game as a game depends on these features. In chess, for example, it is clear at any time what moves are permissible for the bishop and what moves are not, whether the king is checkmated or whether it isn't, etc. In baseball, a player is always 'out' after three strikes, and a half-inning is always over after three 'outs'. It would be a defect in the game if this were not so.

The simplicity of the rules, and of the structure, of chess and baseball consists in this. At each point in the game, which proceeds by discrete steps ('moves', 'at bats'), some player has a finite and describable set of alternatives moves. A chess player must move one of a finite number of pieces, and each piece can be moved in only a prescribed way. A pitcher will throw either a 'strike' or a 'ball'; a batter either will be 'out' or will 'get on base'. The game proceeds only when all prior moves have been completed unambiguously. A pitch is thrown only after the last pitch has been (definitively) called. There are no intermediate moves; a chess piece is moved to one square or another but not in between. The way in which the move is made – hesitatingly, aggressively, absent-mindedly – is irrelevant to the significance of the move and the progress of the game. In other words, moves do not admit relevant degrees or qualifications.

An officer within the game may have the particular role of determining what kind of move has been made. Chess has no such arbiter. Baseball has umpires. The arbiter exercises final judgment in applying standards prescribed in the constitutive rules of the game. The umpire determines whether a pitched ball is a 'strike' or a 'ball' by its location in flight.[6] An arbiter is needed when the determination is difficult and players would be likely to disagree, and because a definitive determination is needed for the progress of the game. The arbiter, in making a decision, has no discretion to use standards other than those prescribed by rule.

(2.3) The constitutive rules, including the standards which an arbiter applies, are arbitrary. Why is a player out after three strikes rather than after four or two? Why does the bishop move diagonally? It is not clear how one can answer these questions. One appropriate response is that the rules say so. Another is an historical account of how the game came to be. If the question is a request for a justification of the rule, perhaps none can be given ("That's just how the game is played."). A tentative justification ("The game works well, is fun, etc., with these rules.") can be rebutted with the suggestion that the game would work better with altered rules with two strikes or a zig-zagging bishop. It is not clear how (or whether) such a disagreement can be resolved. In other words, to say the rules are arbitrary is to say that no justification can be given for them, taken individually. A justification offered for the game *in toto* might justify alternative games as well.

The question, "What is the point of the game?", is ambiguous. It may mean "What, according to the rules, is the goal that the players seek?" ("How do you win?") .The answer is that the point is to checkmate the other player's king, or to score more runs than the other team. Or it may mean "Why do people play?", "How do they justify playing?" and "What is their purpose in playing?" An answer here makes no reference to the rules of the particular kind of game. The answer may be "to have fun", "to kill time", "to develop skills", etc. Moreover, the point in this sense may be irrelevant to the progress of any particular instance of the game of chess or baseball, which can proceed whether or not the players are having fun, developing skills, etc.

(2.4) In summary, a practice of the first kind is not only an activity structured by rules but is like a game in more particular ways. Each instance of the activity (each game of baseball) is a series of discrete moves structured by rules, and the duration of each instance is the duration of the series of moves which comprises it. Participation by players begins with the first move and ends with the last.[7] A game can only begin when all participants are capable of being players (have learned the game), although it may be possible to "learn by playing".

A practice of the first kind has identifiable constitutive rules, familiarity with which is a condition of engaging in the activity. Rawls claims no less than this when he says that

> the mark of a practice [is] that being taught how to engage in it involves being instructed in the rules which define it, and that appeal is made to those rules to correct the behavior of those engaged in it.... It is essential to the notion of a practice that the rules are publicly known and understood as definitive.[8]

Participants, in other words, must have an internal point of view toward the activity.

If we regarded games as paradigmatic of practices in general, we would have certain expectations about their constitutive rules. The rules would be unambiguous, or at least ambiguity would be a defect. The practice would proceed by discrete stages, at each of which the alternative moves open to players would be limited and clearly delineated. Moreover, the rules, taken individually, would be arbitrary. A question about the point of the practice would ordinarily be a question about what the constitutive rules specify as the goal of the players.

(3) In a second sense, a practice is still an activity "specified by a system of rules... which gives the activity its structure", but it is in specific ways unlike the kind of game I have been concerned with. I shall suggest that legal systems and languages are practices of this second kind, not only because they *lack* certain features which games have, but because they *have* certain features which games do not have. I shall make passing reference to Hart's analysis of law as a practice and Wittgenstein's remarks about language.[9] I shall not take issue at all with Wittgenstein's

suggestion that it is useful to emphasize that language is a practice by referring to it as if it were a game.

(3.1) Before examining ways in which practices of the second kind differ from practices of the first, I would like to discuss one way in which they are alike. To say that a practice is an activity structured by rules is to say that relevant behavior of participants can be evaluated by applying the rules as norms. Behavior may conform or fail to conform, and behavior which fails to conform may be called a 'mistake'. This is equally true whether the activity is a game of chess and the mistake is moving the bishop sideways, whether it is a conversation and the mistake is using 'imply' for 'infer', or whether it is driving and the mistake is going through a red light. In each case behavior which violates the rules *may* be called a mistake if certain further conditions (inadvertance, etc.) are satisfied. In each case, also, only an initiate, one who is familiar with the fact that there is a rule and with its content, can be regarded as making a mistake. One who doesn't know English can't be making a mistake in English just as one who doesn't know chess can't be making a mistake in it.[10]

(3.2) One who violates the rule for the use of 'infer' and 'imply' is violating a rule of English. But is this a constitutive rule? If not, what is a constitutive rule for English? Are there any constitutive rules for English or, alternatively, for the American legal system? I have identified the constitutive rules of a practice of the first kind as the rules a player must learn before he is able to play the game. But are there any particular rules a user of the English language must have learned before he is able to use English?

(3.2.1) I shall consider language before turning to law. First, it may be improper to ask whether a user of English must learn certain rules because becoming a user of English (learning English) may not be a matter of learning rules at all, but a matter of acquiring a way of behaving.[11] *A fortiori*, there can be no constitutive rules, no rules which must be learned before one becomes a participant. To say that becoming a user may be a matter of acquiring a way of behaving is not to deny that a user of English will have an internal point of view. Being an English speaker involves more than emitting appropriate sounds regularly (*i.e.*, behaving *as if* one were following a rule); it is also a matter of being able to criticize misuse by others and to ask appropriate questions. For example, becoming a user of color language consists not merely in applying 'red', etc., correctly but also in criticizing incorrect use and in being able to ask, "What color is that?"[12]

Secondly, the status of rules of English in justifying moves by speakers is different from the status of rules of practices of the first kind in justifying moves by players. Of course, there is similarity as well difference. Since language is a practice, rules relevant to a particular instance of usage can always be cited. Assume an instance of correct or incorrect usage, an easy case ("The banana is yellow.") One who is asked to defend his usage *may* appeal to a dictionary or a manual of correct usage; one who accuses him of a mistake will appeal to the same kinds of sources. What both draw upon are rules of usage. In this way, speaking English is like playing chess. In both cases, participants will defend or criticize particular moves by appeal to rules. In both cases, it is possible that the participants *may* appeal not to authoritative documentation but simply to the fact that that's how the 'game' is played.

But the difference here is greater than the similarity. The rule-book of chess is definitive and will determine correctness; the dictionary or the manual is in no way definitive, is at best a rough account of usage. The dictionary rule can always be rebutted with "But I was speaking in dialect", "Usage has changed", or simply "You understood me, didn't you?" A rule-book of chess is authoritative and gives the constitutive rules of chess; a dictionary or manual is not authoritative and is an *approximate* description of the practice as it is carried on. In chess, one goes from the particular move to the rule which it instantiates; the process of justification and criticism stops there. In language, one can defend the particular move in terms of the rule it instantiates, but the rule is itself of uncertain status. It stands as a rule, paradoxically, not because it belongs to a finite set of interlocking constitutive rules, but because it represents what speakers, in practice, actually do.

The suggestion here is that in practices of the second kind rules codify and structure the actual practice, but no set of rules is definitive or constitutive of the practice. In these practices, and not in games, the practice evolves, the rules change, through the participation of the participants themselves. While the rules of chess or baseball may evolve or change, they do so of necessity outside and not within particular instances of the game. The rules of practices of the second kind are in a sense malleable and change with usage. I have already pointed to the fact that rules of language are not definitive when codified, that any codification is an approximation of actual usage. Although the situation is more complicated with regard to law, I shall attempt to show that the rules of a legal system are also malleable, also change within the ongoing practice.

(3.2.2) Again, assume an instance of compliance with or violation of the law. Compliance (or violation) is compliance with a specifiable rule, and the rule can be documented in a judicial decision, a statute, or some other source. Such rules are what Hart calls "primary rules of obligation". They are rules which structure the behavior of ordinary players (citizens) and correspond to the constitutive rules of baseball or chess. But, unlike chess or baseball, law has other players who are specially empowered to change particular rules of the ongoing practice and to administer and interpret them. Thus a legal system, unlike a language, has rules which specify what counts as a primary rule, how primary rules can be changed, etc. Hart calls these "secondary rules".[13]

The status of an alleged primary rule may be challenged in two ways. The first challenge is that it doesn't meet the criterion set by the secondary rules and is therefore invalid, *e.g.*, it has been overruled by a later decision, or it has never been voted into law by the legislature, etc. The second challenge is of a different sort and does not make appeal to rules. It is that the alleged rule does not conform to the principles and policies which underlie and justify the law, to the usages and relationships which inform the legal system. I take this to be part of Ronald Dworkin's amendation of Hart's analysis of law.[14] Without evaluating Dworkin's argument as a whole, I take it to be correct in this: when a primary rule is challenged, the challenge is often not of the form that the rule has improper credentials (is invalid) but rather of the form that it undercuts principles which the usages of the law are intended to implement and safeguard.[15]

The importance of this point is that primary rules of a legal system are, within the ongoing practice, not definitive, just as the rules of a language are not definitive. Any attempt to freeze them in a legal code or a dictionary will fail. In spite of all the differences between language and law as practices, they are alike in that they are both in a sense organic, as games are not. Moves that are made within the practice have the power to erode the rules of the practice.

(3.2.3) Why is this so? A difference between practices of the first kind and practices of the second kind is that games cannot be seen as tools whereas law and language can be seen as tools.[16] Men communicate by way of language; although language is not the only way in which men communicate, it is the primary way. Men secure order in society by law; again, although law is not the only way order is secured, it is the primary way. Men communicate in infinite and infinitely varied situations, and men seek social order in infinite and varied situations. Only a finite variety of situations can arise in games, and the rules of games anticipate all possible moves in all possible situations. Since this cannot be the case for the rules of a language or a legal system, it follows that such rules cannot be formulated once, for all. A language or a legal system cannot have constitutive rules in the sense in which a game does. A consequence, as we shall see, is that the rules of law and language have "open texture".

(3.3) The rule for moving the bishop is unambiguous and clear. In every case in which we can move the bishop we know what moves are permitted and what moves are forbidden. The same is not true in speaking. Wittgenstein argues that attaching meaning to a word is not a matter of being "equipped with rules for every possible application of it."[17] It is not a defect but a feature inherent in language that words have this character. Wittgenstein is careful to distinguish actual language from "ideal" language, defined on the model of games: "We often *compare* the use of words with games and calculi which have fixed rules, but cannot say that someone who is using language *must* be playing such a game."[18]

H. L. A. Hart has argued that legal rules also have this "penumbral" character, and have it necessarily. The penumbrum of a legal rule is the range of hypothetical situations in which its application is indeterminate.[19] The hypothesis of an ideal language is analogous to the provision of legal rules determinate for all occasions, which would generate a "mechanical jurisprudence". "If the world in which we live were characterized only by a finite number of features, and these together with all the modes in which they could combine were known to us, then provision could be made in advance for every possibility .... Plainly this world is not our world."[20] The limited conditions that are realized in games are not realized in law, as they are not realized in language.

(3.4) The internal point of view of the player of a game is that of someone who has learned the constitutive rules, who knows how the game is played. What appears as random activity to the noninitiate is seen as ordered moves by the initiate. The internal point of view of a speaker of English or a legal subject cannot be defined in the same way. A speaker does not have at hand a finite arsenal of directives which inform every relevant move that he might make. And yet, as speaker, he is able to apply rules to identify mistakes or unintelligibility, to criticize others, etc.

I would like to distinguish the internal point of view of a language user, *per se*, from the internal point of view of a speaker of English. The former can best be characterized not as having at hand a particular set of rules but as having at hand the notion that certain kinds of behavior are within the domain of activity governed by rules and can be judged normatively (as conforming or failing to conform with rules). In brief, the internal point of view of the language user consists not in knowing a definitive set of rules but in having the *notion* of a rule of language. To one who lacks the notion all languages have the character of noise. To one who has the notion of language, particular languages are examples of practices. Thus a language user may be able to identify a totally unfamiliar language *as* language.

Beyond this, no further specification can be given of the internal point of view of the speaker of English. There are varying kinds and degrees of facility in English, from that of the young child, through that of the foreign speaker, to that of the native speaker; among native speakers, endless variations occur. Just as there is no set of constitutive rules for English, there is no particular kind of facility which can be identified with the internal point of view of the English speaker.

Hart draws an analogous distinction with regard to law. The external observer of a legal system is "content merely to record the regularities of observable behavior",[21] just as an observer of language might record regularly emitted sounds.

> His description of their life [of participants in the legal system] cannot be in terms of rules at all, and so not in terms of the rule-dependent notions of obligation and duty. He will miss out a whole dimension of the social life of those whom he is watching, since for them the red light is not merely a sign that others will stop; they look upon it as a *signal* for them to stop, and so a reason for stopping.... To mention this is to bring into the account the way in which the group regards its own behavior. It is to refer to the internal aspect of rules seen from their internal point of view.[22]

In contrast to the external observer, the internal observer has the notion of a social rule, and therefore of a practice.

(3.5) One who has the internal point of view, who has the notion that verbal behavior is a rule-governed activity or practice, has some notion of the point of the practice. Roughly the point of the practice, the English language, like that of any language, is communication. Here I am not concerned to specify exactly what the point of a language is. I am concerned only to argue that insofar as we see language as a tool, it makes sense to ask for its point. Nor am I concerned to argue that every utterance in language has the same point or that a given utterance has only one point. J. L. Austin has shown that any particular utterance may have various uses and each use may well be called a 'point' of the utterance.[23] Notwithstanding this, it can also be argued that language has various uses insofar as it is a vehicle of communication. Thus, Austin's analysis underscores the teleological character of such practices (or tools) as language, because what Austin calls illocutionary forces are the uses language serves.

To ask, therefore, for the point of a practice of the second kind is to make a different kind of inquiry than to ask the point of a game. The point of a game is defined by a particular constitutive rule. There is no equivalent rule of usage for language which tells a player what constitutes final success. There can't be, because there is no final success in language. There is no notion of victory or defeat. For the point of language, we must ask what kind of tool it is, what job or jobs it does. Success is a matter of doing that job.[24]

The point of a legal system is not to be found in any of the particular rules of the system, but in the role that the system plays. I cannot here define the exact nature of that role or job. It may roughly be characterized as preserving social order by making certain forms of behavior non-optional, by creating and enforcing coercive rules.

(3.6) The fact that the point of a legal system is not posited in any primary rule is relevant to explaining the role of decision makers within the system. Games have decision makers who apply prescribed standards. They apply them to determine which of several alternative moves has been made. The umpire determines whether a pitched ball is a 'ball' or a 'strike'. Although the umpire's determination may affect which team scores the most runs, the point of the game (scoring the most runs) must not play any part in his determination. For it to do so would be to undercut his neutrality.

Judges and other arbiters in the legal process do not have this kind of role. In considering this, Dworkin argues that their discretion is not discretion in the "umpire" sense, or weak sense, as it would be in a system of mechanical jurisprudence. Indeed, a judge does not have discretion at all when a clear, established rule is applicable. The characteristic situation in which a judge has discretion is one which is not anticipated by the primary rules of law. It is one with regard to which either the rules of law have "open texture" or no rule seems suitable. Dworkin argues that the discretion that judges have here signifies that they are not bound by rules but are bound other legal standards. Judges, in hard cases, are bound by principles, such principles as "No man may profit from his own wrong."[25]

I shall not consider Dworkin's argument that such principles are binding and are part of the law. Assuming that the argument is successful,[26] where do the principles come from? They are not rules of the practice, as are the standards which umpires apply; they come to bear when no rules are available. I suggest that they come rather from the point of practice and represent the judge's conception of the job that legal systems exist to do. The judge who affirms the principle that precedent is not to be overturned lightly appeals to the point of law as an ordering of expectation and of behavior. The judge who invokes the principle that no man may profit from his own wrong appeals to the point of law as securing justice. It is clear that at this level various principles can count as representing the point of law, but it is equally clear that not just any principle will do.[27]

A related description can be given of language. Here too there is no "mechanical jurisprudence". Here there are no institutionalized arbiters at all. But when the attempt is made to arbitrate, what is set down as correct usage is also determined by the point of the practice, by what succeeds in communication. The manuals and dictionaries of a language change to reflect changes in writing and speech. A lexicographer's decision about the rules of a language is a decision about how people succeed in using language.

(3.7) I argued above that the rules of a game are arbitrary. I am tempted to say that the rules of language are also arbitrary, and the arbitrariness of both is limited only by practicability. A batter could 'walk' after three rather than four 'balls' but not after thirty because this would extend the game inordinately. The word 'chair' could play the part of the word 'table', but a nine-syllable substitute would be impracticable. Similarly, the law could require three instead of two witnesses to a valid will, but twenty would be impracticable. I am not suggesting, of course, that it doesn't matter which of various practicable alternatives occur in rules; good reasons related to the point of the law of wills can be given for expanding the number of required witnesses or for reducing it. I am merely suggesting that we can imagine alternative systems of rules. We not only can *imagine* them; we have at hand different languages and different legal systems.

The suggestion that legal systems are arbitrary must be qualified. All legal systems have some substantive features in common, and these features inform the content of its rules. They are psychological and sociological facts which are the general conditions of human interactions. They are the general conditions within which any legal system functions. Hart emphasizes the "distinctively rational connexion" between natural facts and the content of legal rules, and he numbers among such natural facts human invulnerability, approximate equality, limited altruism, limited resources, and limited understanding and strength of will.[28] One way of expressing the point of law might be that the law employs coercive rules to meet these conditions and satisfy the needs to which they refer.

The arbitrariness of language must be similarly qualified. The rules which describe linguistic transformations refer to conditions within which particular languages are possible. Whether such rules merely represent psychological facts or whether they are grounded differently in human activity is controversial.[29]

(3.8) I have not attempted to give either a general account of practices of the second sort or a specific account of the nature of a language or a legal system as a practice. Rather, I have attempted to show that features characteristic of games (but not all games) are not characteristic of other practices which have been analyzed on the basis of the paradigm of games. I have also shown that these practices have features of their own. Practices as different as the social phenomena of language and law seem to share such features, which characterize a second kind of practice. This kind of practices evolves and therefore has no constitutive rules which are primary (in Hart's sense) and at the same time definitive. It evolves because it embraces an unforeseeable range of situations in which its rules have employment for social ends. The rules must have open texture and allow indefinite application. The point of the practice, what it is a tool *for*, determines the evolution of the rules.

(4) There is a third kind of activity "specified by a system of rules... which give the activity its structure", but which I hesitate to call a 'practice' at all. I would like to introduce this difficulty by indicating the kind of rule I have in mind.

Wittgenstein, in *On Certainty*, considers two hypotheses. (1) "Imagine that [a pupil] questioned the truth of history (and everything that connects up with it) – and even whether the earth had existed at all a hundred years before." (*OC*, 311) (2) "Imagine that the schoolboy really did ask 'and is there a table there even when I turn round, and even when *no one* is there to see it?' Is the teacher to reassure him – and say, 'Of course, there is!' ?" (*OC*, 314) Wittgenstein observes that "it would be the same if the pupil cast doubt on the uniformity of nature, that is to say on the justification of inductive arguments.... This pupil has not learned how to ask questions. He has not learned the game that we are trying to teach him." (*OC*, 315) In other words, he is treating a rule of how men think about history (that it is continuous, not systematically delusive, etc.) as if it were an empirical proposition *within* history. The truth of physics cannot be regarded as a truth *within* physics. Wittgenstein says, "I am inclined to believe that not everything that has the form of an empirical proposition *is* one." (*OC*, 208)

To say that the truth of history or of physics (as a practice) is grounded in rules and not empirical propositions is to say that we don't know what it would be like to find evidence which falsifies them, or evidence which confirms them. And this is not because no evidence is available but because these are not the sorts of considerations which we speak about as falsified or established. Rather, they are the framework of the activity (activities) within which we speak of propositions (historical facts, physical descriptions) as falsified or established.[30] The individual who is able to carry on investigations within history or physics – or simply any individual who makes reference to the past or to physical objects – operates within a structure of rules which the hypothetical schoolboy lacks. These rules are rules which have expression *within* language, as in the proposition that nature is uniform, but they are not rules of language any more than the rules of chess are rules of language.

(4.1) What is the practice or activity which is structured by rules of this sort? One possible response is that it is the activity of being reasonable (or rational) or of understanding. What distinguishes Wittgenstein's recalcitrant schoolboy from the student of history is that the former is not being reasonable. Wittgenstein says that "the reasonable man does not have certain doubts", (*OC*, 220) and

> the existence of the earth is rather part of the whole *picture* which forms the starting-point of belief for me. (*OC*, 209).... It gives our way of looking at things, and our researches, their form. Perhaps it was once disputed. But perhaps, for unthinkable ages, it has belonged to the *scaffolding* of our thoughts. (*OC*, 211)
>
> If I say "*we assume* that the earth has existed for many years past" (or something similar), then of course it sounds strange that we should *assume* such a thing. But in the entire system of our language-games it belongs to the foundations. The assumption, one might say, forms the basis of action, and therefore, naturally, of thought. (*OC*, 411)

In these passages Wittgenstein seems to be doing what P. F. Strawson has called "descriptive metaphysics". He seems "to describe the actual structure of our thought about the world."[31] To see metaphysical propositions as rules of our thought about the world is to explain a characteristic feature of metaphysical argument, as Strawson has argued. This is that sceptical arguments presuppose their falsity because "we must accept [the truth of induction, for example] in order to explain the conceptual scheme in terms of which the sceptical problem is stated. But once the conclusion is accepted, the sceptical problem does not arise. So with many sceptical problems: their statement involves the pretended acceptance of a conceptual scheme and at the same time the silent repudiation of one of the conditions of its acceptance."[32]

(4.2) To call the activity in question "our thought about the world" and the search for its rules 'metaphysics' or (perhaps) 'philosophy', is to explain my hesitation about calling the activity a 'practice'. I don't know what it would mean to ask whether the rules are arbitrary, or what the point of the practice is. And yet, what Wittgenstein calls "the basis of action, and therefore, naturally, of thought" is a basis within which practices properly so-called exist.

One example of this is that law as a practice invokes blame, choice, responsibility as central concepts. But these concepts are not defined in the rules of law but in "our thought about the world", in particular our thought about persons. Only if one of the rules in the 'scaffolding' of our thought is that persons are capable of autonomous choice is moral reasoning possible, and by derivation do the moral categories of law become meaningful. But the relation between such practices as law and language on the one hand, and the rules of thought (moral, metaphysical, psychological), if there are any, is a different topic.

NOTES

[1] John Rawls, 'Two Concepts of Rules', *The Philosophical Review* LXIV (1955), 3.

[2] See Rawls, 'Two Concepts of Rules', and H. L. A. Hart, *The Concept of Law* (Oxford 1961).

[3] It is incorrect to suppose that knowing or having learned a game is tantamount to, not making mistakes. The correct view is contained in Wittgenstein's remarks on mistakes. "When someone makes a mistake, this can be fitted into what he knows aright." *On Certainty* (Oxford, 1969), § 74.

[4] The distinction between an internal and an external point of view is elaborated by Hart in *Concept of Law*, Chap. V. What I call a "critical reflective attitude" on the part of participants is what Hart refers to as "the way in which the rules function as rules in the lives of those who normally are the majority of society". *Concept of Law*, p. 88.

[5] The notion of open texture is also drawn from Hart. In discussing legal rules, he notes the following: "Whichever device, precedent or legislation, is chosen for the communication of standards of behaviour, these, however smoothly they work over the great mass of ordinary cases, will, at some point where their application is in question, prove indeterminate; they will have what has been termed an *open texture*." *Concept of Law*, p. 124.

[6] Ronald Dworkin calls this the 'weak sense' of the term, 'discretion'. Cf. Dworkin, "Is Law a System of Rules?" in Robert S. Summers, *Essays in Legal Philosophy* (Oxford, 1968), p. 45.

[7] Of course, a game may have rules which permit or require a player to terminate his involvement in the game before the game itself ends.

[8] Rawls, *op. cit.*, p. 24.

[9] Cf. Hart, *op. cit.*; Ludwig Wittgenstein, *Philosophical Investigations* (New York, 1953), passim.

[10] Just as a violation of a constitutive rule may be, but is not necessarily, a mistake, by the same token a mistake is not necessarily a violation of a constitutive rule. A violation of a strategic principle may also be called a 'mistake' by players.

[11] Although one may learn rules by example, one ordinarily learns the rules of a game through verbal instruction. Such instruction is possible only for one who already has mastered a language. Such instruction is not possible for one who has mastered no language, i.e., for one who is learning his first language. In using the inadequate phrase, "acquiring a way of behaving", for the process of acquisition of one's first language, I intend to refer in a general way to Wittgenstein's remarks on language acquisition in *On Certainty*, passim. E.g., "The child knows what something is called if he can reply correctly to the question 'what is that called?' Naturally, the child who is just learning to speak has not yet got the concept *is called* at all." (*OC*, 535, 536).

It must also be noted that learning a second language may not have this character at all and may be a matter of learning rules in the strict sense.

[12] Cf. Wittgenstein, *On Certainty*, 524–544. (Note: All references to works of Wittgenstein employ citations of paragraph numbers, not pages.)

[13] Hart, *op. cit.*, Chap. V.

[14] Dworkin, *op. cit.*

[15] An example is the principle that no man ought to profit from his own wrong.

I am not contending that Dworkin would accept this description of the principles relevant to legal decisions. My description anticipates my discussion of the 'point' of law below.

[16] Cf. Wittgenstein, *Philosophical Investigations*, Pt. 1.

[17] *Ibid.*, 80.

[18] *Ibid.*, 81.

[19] Hart, *op. cit.*, p. 124.

[20] *Ibid.*, p. 125.

[21] *Ibid.*, p. 87.

[22] *Ibid.*, pp. 87–88.

[23] Cf. J. L. Austin, *How to Do Things with Words* (Oxford, 1962), Lectures VIII–X. Austin himself uses the phrase "uses of language" to characterize the class within which illocutionary and perlocutionary acts are included. The uses or purposes of language in his and my discussion are to be distinguished from the uses or purposes of particular speakers. An utterance may have a use which the speaker did not intend (which was not to the speaker's purpose).

[24] In this sense, enjoyment or the exercise of skill is not the point of chess because a game can be regarded as a successful game even if it was not enjoyed or was not an exercise of skill.

[25] Cf. Dworkin, *op. cit.*, p. 48.

[26] In support of the argument it is noted that a judge could not (acceptably) cite the principles that every man or some men may profit from their wrongs. In this sense, at least, the given principle is binding.

[27] Cf. n. 26 above. I am assuming for purposes of my argument that all relevant principles can be subsumed under a single *point* of law. This assumption is not at all self-evident.

[28] Hart, *op. cit.*, pp. 189–195.

[29] Cf. Noam Chomsky, *Language and Mind* (New York, 1968); Sidney Hook (ed.), *Language and Philosophy* (New York, 1969).

[30] In spite of the content of the quotations which follow (section 4.1), it is not at all clear to me that Wittgenstein would accept this account. In many passages Wittgenstein suggests that *no* propositions have the character of belonging to the framework of the activity in general. Rather, he suggests that it is the case that in any particular instance of judging, some proposition must serve as a rule or be beyond doubt, not subject to confirmation or falsification. "... it seems impossible to say in any *individual* case that such-and-such must be beyond doubt if there is to be a language-game – though it is right enough to say that *as a rule* some empirical judgment or other must be beyond doubt." (*OC*, 519). This is true, for example, of the proposition that one's apparatus is not illusory in a scientific emperiment. The proposition is beyond doubt only in this context. In others, e.g., if one has taken drugs or if one's hand passes through air in seeking to touch the apparatus, one may well argue that the apparatus is illusory.

Nonetheless, many passages suggest that Wittgenstein takes a stronger position.

226

This would be the position that some propositions, for example a proposition about the truth of induction, are beyond doubt in so wide a range of contexts that we identify following them *as* rules with rationality.

> So rational suspicion must have grounds?
> We might also say: "the reasonable man believes this".
> Thus we should not call anybody reasonable who believed something in despite of scientific evidence. (*OC*, 323, 324)

[31] P. F. Strawson, *Individuals* (London, 1959), p. 9. As discussed in n. 30, many passages in Wittgenstein suggest that he would reject the intelligibility of the project of descriptive metaphysics.

[32] Strawson, *op. cit.*, p. 106.

[3]
Understanding, Disagreement, and Conceptual Change

The idea of a conceptual scheme is elusive. It is notoriously difficult to define criteria for marking one conceptual scheme from another or to explain how it is possible to apprehend a conceptual scheme from within a particular and different one. Nor is it clear that such questions are intelligibly formulated. Wittgenstein, in *On Certainty,*[1] reformulates relevant issues in an illuminating way. He considers shared language-games (or, as I shall call them, shared practices), the conditions of mutual understanding, and the conditions for disagreement. His remarks are fragmentary, but I shall try to elicit and evaluate his insights to show how they clarify the idea of a conceptual scheme. In doing so, I shall offer an informal analysis of the notions of understanding and disagreement.

As in earlier writings, Wittgenstein seems to suggest that A and B can be said to disagree about p only if claiming p is a move in a shared language-game, or practice. To have a shared practice is not only to have a shared vocabulary but also shared assumptions about what sorts of grounds are relevant to what sorts of claims and shared criteria of judgment. This does not mean that all understandable disagreement is resolvable disagreement. Resolution will not occur when there is disagreement about what particular matters are relevant to particular conclusions, or about how much weight to assign particular pieces of evidence, or whenever parties have inconclusive evidence. The notion of a shared practice is elastic and inexact, and necessarily so. It is the notion that persons may have shared critical standards and yet use them differently to some extent. A determination of what is a shared standard used differently and what is a different standard can only be made case by case.

However elastic it is, the notion may be attacked on other grounds than vagueness. It may be said that we understand persons and disagree with them in many situations in which we do not have shared practices, shared ways of assessing evidence, and so forth. In fact, one of the things we typically claim to understand is precisely this: that others have practices in which we do not participate and/or practices the premisses of which we reject. Some examples can be

[1] Ludwig Wittgenstein, *On Certainty,* edited by G.E.M. Anscombe and G.H. von Wright (Oxford, 1960).

drawn from the history of thought, for example history of science. We claim to understand Aristotle and Newton, and part of what we say we understand is that their conceptions of what counts as evidence, and even of what it means to seek evidence, are irreconcilably different from each other's and from our conceptions. Further, the understanding involved is not reciprocal; we say we understand them but make no assumption that they would understand us. (We may be quite convinced of the opposite.)

Another set of difficult counterexamples does not involve change in critical standards over time or the absence of reciprocity. We claim to understand systems of moral practice and belief and religious systems which coexist with our own practices, but in which we do not participate or believe. We recognize mutually incompatible alternative practices. What I use as a *basis* for judgment may be rejected by others as nonsense. Even more importantly, what is a criterion of judgment for me here-and-now may not be a criterion for me in the future and may not have been so in the past.

I shall distinguish two questions. First, if my ability to understand is coextensive with my own usages (my practice), how can I say (truthfully) that I understand practices which I reject and in which I do not participate? Second, if one can recognize and understand such alien practices, how may one regard them? Do we have criteria of evaluation which entitle us to say that some practices are better than others, or truer than others, or more advanced that others?

1. *The Limits of Understanding*. The first problem is one of setting limits. Not every odd saying is understandable; not all aberrant behavior, including aberrant verbal behavior, can be understood as part of a coherent, if different, way of thinking. How do we delimit the set of experiences which are evidence of alien practices? Consider some examples.

> 333. I ask someone "Have you ever been in China?" He replies "I don't know." Here one would surely say "You don't *know*? Have you any reason to believe you might have been there at some time? Were you for example ever near the Chinese border? Or were your parents there at the time when you were going to be born?" – Normally Europeans do know whether they have been in China or not.

> 257. If someone said to me that he doubted whether he had a body I should take him to be a half-wit. But I shouldn't know what it would mean to try to convince him that he had one. And if I had said

something, and that had removed his doubt, I should not know how or why.

67. Could we imagine a man who keeps on making mistakes where we regard a mistake as ruled out, and in fact never encounter one?

E.g. he says he lives in such and such a place, is so and so old, comes from such and such a city, and he speaks with the same certainty (giving all the tokens of it) as I do, but he is wrong.

But what is his relation to this error? What am I to suppose?[2]

Each of these examples shows how much stage-setting is needed before one can fit a verbal claim (or more generally, any piece of behavior) into a framework of procedures and assumptions attributable to the claimant. The various examples are not indisputably nonsense, but they are nonsense until a context is offered, until we know what kind of experience would be regarded as counting for or against the claim.

236. If someone said "The earth has not long been ... " what would he be impugning? Do I know?

Would it have to be what is called a scientific belief? Might it not be a mystical one? Is there any absolute necessity for him to be contradicting historical facts? or even geographical ones?

237. If I say "an hour ago this table didn't exist" I probably mean that it was only made later on.

If I say "this mountain didn't exist then," I presumably mean that it was only formed later on — perhaps by a volcano.

If I say "this mountain didn't exist half an hour ago," that is such a strange statement that it is not clear what I mean. Whether for example I mean something untrue but scientific. Perhaps you think that the statement that the mountain didn't exist then is quite clear, however one conceives the context. But suppose someone said "This mountain didn't exist a minute ago, but an exactly similar one did instead." Only the accustomed context allows what is meant to come through clearly.

Cases in which we despair of understanding show how special are those cases which we recognize as claiming, doubting, or making a

---

2 See also passages 106, 108, 255, 258.

mistake in different practices from our own. We need a hypothesis about what is being doubted or about how such mistakes arise and can be corrected. It seems we can form and apply such hypotheses about moral, scientific, religious, or other beliefs which we do not share, but this is not yet so in the passages quoted above. I can, for example, understand how a medieval psychologist may doubt and confirm claims about personality based on a theory of humors.

Thus, the naked claim that "we don't know how one gets to the moon, but those who get there know at once that they are there" does not challenge and offer an alternative to "our whole system of physics." An alternative physics would explain how such things were possible in a system which explained the more ordinary events of experience as well. The explanation would not (we are assuming) be one which we would accept or which would be familiar to us, but it would (as in the case of the psychology of humors) have to be recognizable as an explanation in a system. We feel less "distant" from medieval cosmologists (from whose theories we can predict their conclusions and observations) that we do from the person whose claims and other behavior seem simply inchoate.

We would be bewildered by someone who denied the law of induction or denied that there were physical objects.[3] This is so because such assertions cannot be fitted into unfamiliar practices; they are incompatible with proceeding in any intelligible way.

2. *Evaluating Others.* We can now turn to cases of very general systems of belief which we recognize as coherent practices which are not our own.

> 132. Men have judged that a king can make rain; *we* say this contradicts all experience. Today they judge that aeroplanes and the radio, etc. are means for the closer contact of peoples and the spread of culture.

> 608. It is wrong for me to be guided in my actions by the propositions of physics? Am I to say I have no good ground for doing so? Isn't precisely that what we call a 'good ground'?

> 609. Supposing we met people who did not regard that as a telling reason. Now, how do we imagine this? Instead of the physicist, they consult an oracle. (And for that we consider them primitive.) Is it wrong for them to consult an oracle and be guided by it? – If we call this "wrong" aren't we using our language-game as a base from which to *combat* theirs?

[3] See passages 35, 500.

605. ... What if the physicist's statement were superstition and it were just as absurd to go by it in reaching a verdict as to rely on ordeal by fire?

To confront *these* alien practices is to recognize them *as* practices with understandable and predictable procedures. Oracles and ordeal by fire are recognizable as systematic resources used to find things out. What is involved in saying that these practices are more or less "correct" than our own? Are we entitled to say that they are wrong?

I shall argue that two very different (and incompatible) responses to these questions can be found in Wittgenstein. The first response, which is popularly identified with Wittgenstein, and correctly so, leads to unsatisfactory conclusions, as I shall try to show in the rest of this section. It is easily sketched, as follows. We can call matters "right" and "wrong" insofar as we have shared procedures for determining what is right and what is wrong. This does not mean that in sharing a practice we will be able to resolve all disagreement or agree about the weight of every piece of evidence, but it does mean that we must share general criteria for what counts as evidence. Where there are significant differences between different persons' criteria, different but internally consistent systems of reaching conclusions, there is no ground for claiming that one way of proceeding is right in itself or closer to being right than another. At most one can reject a different system and adhere to one's own system but to do so is not to make a grounded decision. If, for example, I try to offer grounds by showing that the oracle or the rain-making dance is statistically unreliable, the adherent of these practices will reply that this is irrevelant. He will say that I have not proved that there is no connection between the oracle and events, etc., but only that the gods are capricious. Both I and the tribesman claim to derive our ways of proceeding from experience, and neither of us can ground his preference by appeal to independent criteria of decision.

130. But isn't it experience that teaches to to judge like *this*, that is to say, that it is correct to judge like this? But how does experience *teach* us, then? *We* may derive it from experience, but experience does not direct us to derive anything from experience. If it is the *ground* of our judging like this, and not just the cause, still we do not have a ground for seeing this in turn as a ground.

If the rainmaker and I have such different practices, I cannot give him grounds (which he will see as grounds) for abandoning his beliefs. I may convert him to my beliefs and procedures, but I cannot do so by giving grounds.

> 611. Where two principles really do meet which cannot be reconciled with one another, then each man declares the other a fool and heretic.
>
> 612. I said I would "combat" the other man, — but wouldn't I give him *reasons?* Certainly; but how far do they go? At the end of reasons comes *persuasion*. (Think what happens when missionaries convert natives.)
>
> 92. ... May someone have telling grounds for believing that the earth has only existed for a short time, say since his birth? — Suppose he has always been told that — would he have any good reason to doubt it? Men have believed that they could make rain; why should not a king be brought up in the belief that the world began with him? And if Moore and this king were to meet and discuss, could Moore really prove his belief to be the right one? I do not say that Moore could not convert the king to his view, but it would be a conversion of a special kind; the king would be brought to look at the world in a different way.[4]
>
> Remember that one is sometimes convinced of the correctness of a view by its simplicity or symmetry, i.e. these are what induce one to go over to this point of view. One then simply says something like: "*That's* how it must be."

According to passage 92, I may try to convert another (and succeed) by saying that my picture of the world is simpler or more comprehensive, but this is not a reason why my picture is "right." Nor is there an independent standard of simplicity or comprehensiveness. The rainmaker's notion of a capricious god may be simpler than my meteorological determinations; the concept of *materia universalis* may be as comprehensive as any concept in my picture. Nonetheless, it may be the case that *when* conversion occurs, it occurs because the adopted theory is *thought* by the convertee to have one or another such advantage as greater comprehensiveness, greater simplicity, etc.

Individuals use oracles, believe in capricious gods, or disbelieve in beings which they cannot perceive because they have been taught to make judgments in certain ways. Judgments are possible, we have seen, insofar as certain judgments are held fast.

> 142. It is not single axioms that strike me as obvious, it is a system in which consequences and premises give one another *mutual* support.

---

[4] See also passages 262, 264.

144. The child learns to believe a host of things. I.e. it learns to act according to these beliefs. Bit by bit there forms a system of what is believed, and in that system some things stand unshakeably fast and some are more or less liable to shift. What stands fast does so not because it is intrinsically obvious or convincing; it is rather held fast by what lies around it.[5]

The judgment that there are capricious gods and that they must be placated is the kind of principle which governs action and thought in a general way and is generally held fast.

Let's stand back from this argument and evaluate it. It is obviously true that I may discover and recognize internally consistent ways of thinking and investigating which are incompatible with my own practices. I may or may not be able to offer arguments which the other person will recognize as reasons for preferring my practices. If our ways are very different, many of my reasons will predictably be rejected. It is also true that he and I proceed as we do and believe in the reliability of our practices in part because we learned to do so. (But to say that this is the cause is not to say it is the reason we follow our practices.) There is no independent standpoint available to either of us from which to evaluate competing practices: "experience does not direct us to derive anything from experience." (130) Experience is not an independent ground from which to judge practices.

These observations, let us assume, are uncontroversial, but do they support the following conclusions? One conclusion is that I am not entitled to call the oracle-consulter unreasonable or to claim that his practice is wrong. He is reasonable insofar as he follows his practices as scrupulously as I follow mine. Accordingly, his practice is not wrong but only different; to be entitled to call him "wrong" I must be able to show that he misapplies shared and accepted procedures, but clearly he and I do not share relevant procedures. Thus, divergent on-going practices are generally not to be called more or less reasonable. Just as this is true of me and the oracle-consulter, it is *pro tanto* true of Aristotle and Einstein, a Buddhist and a Christian, a theist and an atheist, and an egalitarian and an elitist. The question of justifying one way of proceeding in the face of the other cannot arise because there is no shared framework in which the activity of judging and justifying can proceed.

These conclusions fly in the face of ordinary usage and experience. From the fact that I "inherited" my practices it does not

[5] See also passages 140, 141.

follow that I cannot have and give compelling grounds for my "preference." The naming of a cause does not preclude my having reasons. My being able to justify my rejection of oracle-consulting does not seem to depend on whether the mistaken oracle-consulter can or cannot understand my justification. Moreover, when the consulter abandons his practice and is converted to the practices of modern science, such "conversion" or "persuasion" does not seem altogether different from the outcome of reasoning from some common ground. In fact, given the divergence that the argument assumes, conversion would (implausibly) seem to be an altogether capricious event.

Can we say that the diversity between the theist and the atheist, the egalitarian and the elitist, the Buddhist and the Christian is genuine disagreement, and that each comes to understand and reject the other's position by using a shared practice which makes possible such understanding? To answer this, we must reconsider what counts as a shared practice. There seem to be three possibilities. If we accept the general argument (which we are in the process of evaluating), we must say *either* that the theist and the atheist, etc., share the same practices and can judge each other *or* that they do not share the same practices and cannot judge each other. If, however, we find grounds for rejecting the general argument, we may be able to say that they do not share the same relevant practices but can judge comparatively nonetheless. This third possibility is attractive insofar as (1) the divergences at issue seem to be paradigm cases of practices which are not shared and (2) it seems correct to say that a preference for, say, experimentation over oracle-consulting is reasoned, defensible, and justifiable.

If we reject the proferred general argument, we may also try to accomodate some other complications which do not seem accountable by the general argument. For example, I regard Newton as reasonable, but would regard a Newtonian in the twentieth century as reasonable. I regard certain moral positions with which I disagree as reasonable and reject others as unreasonable. On occasion, I will question whether *I* have proceeded reasonably. Thus, the view that, if I am to make judgments of reasonableness, I must hold my own practices as the norm, is betrayed by experience.

I shall consider in the next section a more satisfactory analysis of divergences in thought and practice. Before doing so, I shall summarize the experiences which such an analysis must explain.

(1) If someone in my own society believes that he can read his

future in tea leaves I will say he is wrong and offer him reasons which I expect him to recognize as reasons and which may or may not persuade him to give up his practice. If he persists and gives no reasons which *I* can recognize as reasons, I will say that he is unreasonable. If I find someone in an alien culture who has exactly the same belief, I will have exactly the same reasons for saying he is wrong, reasons which may or may not be intelligible to him. Whether he understands my reasons and whether many others in his society do what he does are irrelevant to my belief that his way of going about things is wrong and to my conviction that I have good reasons for thinking this.

(2) I will, let us assume, think of an alien practice as one in which certain *kinds* of reasons which I offer will be rejected out of hand because of beliefs which are held fast. One example is that of an "ultimate" belief in a capricious god. But if I ascribe this kind of closure to an alien practice, how can I imagine such a practitioner *ever* recognizing recalcitrant experiences and changing his ways of proceeding? And if I do not conceive of him changing in understandable ways, how do I account for "conversion"? More importantly, what right do I have for claiming that my practices can change and that I can recognize recalcitrant experiences when I deny these capacities to others? How is it that *I* ever come to reject some of my inherited beliefs and claim to do so in reasoned ways? The fact of change suggests that the model of practices as closed must be rejected in principle.

(3) I can imagine myself converting an oracle-consulter into a man of modern science by introducing him to methods and resources (technologies, terms, etc.) which I have and he lacks. Such examples of conversion can be documented. I call him primitive because I have these resources which are unfamiliar to him and because, let us suppose, he has no resources which are unfamiliar to me. I cannot imagine he will convert me into a consulter of oracles, and, as a matter of sociological fact, this kind of conversion rarely happens. It is not impossible, but it is more than unlikely, that he will be able to introduce me to matters which can be explained by appeal to his resources and not by mine. It is not at all unlikely (there is ample precedent) that I will be able to introduce him to such matters. If he insists that his scheme explains more, he will offer either *explananda* which I cannot explain or dismiss, and I will then no longer regard him as primitive, or *explananda* which I can explain and dismiss, in which case I will fail to understand the grounds of his insistence.

I regard very differently the prize-winning chemist who insists that the wine is the blood of Christ than I do the oracle-consulter. I do not think that the chemist will give up his claim if I can show him what I know. The suggestion that we must treat all nonshared practices indifferently and nonevaluatively cannot take account of our different attitudes to primitive and to sophisticated practices, nor does it explain our expectations in encounters with so-called primitive ones. I shall now sketch a view of divergent practices which takes account of these expectations.

3. *The Perspective of One's Own Practice.* We have seen that in some instances of divergence in practice-and-belief, the divergence is irreducible and attempts at conversion will be unavailing. Here are some examples, drawn from *On Certainty.*

> 239. I believe that every human being has two human parents; but Catholics believe that Jesus only had a human mother. And other people might believe that there are human beings with no parents, and give no credence to all the contrary evidence. Catholics believe as well that in certain circumstances a wafer completely changes its nature, and at the same time that all evidence proves the contrary. And so if Moore said "I know that this is wine and not blood," Catholics would contradict him.
>
> 336. But what men consider reasonable or unreasonable alters. At certain periods men find reasonable what at other periods they found unreasonable. And vice versa.
>
> But is there on objective character here?
>
> *Very* intelligent and well-educated people believe in the story of creation in the Bible, while others hold it as proven false, and the grounds of the latter are well known to the former.

In these cases all "facts" known to one party are known to the other, but *some* facts and procedures affirmed by one are denied by the other. The Catholic who believes in transubstantiation does not deny the chemist's facts about wafers and wine, but he holds some facts to be true on the basis of resources which the chemist rejects. Each knows the nature of the other's grounds and the other's conception of evidence, and each believes that the other can offer him no troublesome arguments why he is wrong. Coexistence and interaction of the Catholic with the chemist are possible to the extent that there is much that they share in the face of this disagreement. Indeed, their shared conception of ordinary genetics and ordinary chemistry makes it possible for them to understand and express their disagreement, its nature and limits. The disagreement is "fixed" and any change of position involves not so much a weighing of new evidence but an alteration of a conception of evidence, i.e., a conversion.

> 645. I can't be making a mistake, — but some day, rightly or wrongly, I may think I realize that I was not competent to judge.[6]

To what extent is the relationship between the chemist and the Catholic generalizable to other examples of conflicting practices? Note that in this case there is a stable impasse because each understands all claims and procedures of the other. Rejection of one another's views presupposes understanding. It misrepresents the situation to say that the two *mean* different things by what they say simply because they have different beliefs and procedures; they share meanings insofar as they share usages. When one affirms and the other denies that *this* is blood, they are *using* words in the same way and they mean the same things by them.

(Note that there is ambiguity in the claim, "If the Catholic and the chemist have different practices, they must mean different things by the word 'blood.' " The claim is true insofar as one and not the other will apply "blood" to the wine in some contexts. It is not true insofar as they both apply the word to the wine in the same context when one affirms and the other denies that *this* is blood.

The same ambiguity haunts these passages.

> 63. If we imagine the facts otherwise than as they are, certain language-games lose some of their importance, while others become important. And in this way there is an alteration — a gradual one — in the use of the vocabulary of a language.

> 65. When language-games change, then there is a change in concepts, and with the concepts the meanings of words change.

If I become converted to Catholicism and begin to affirm what I now deny, do the meanings of my words change so that what I now affirm has a different meaning than what I then denied? To say this seems needlessly paradoxical; it implies wrongly that the chemist is not denying what the Catholic affirms.)

The situation of the Catholic and the chemist is atypical among examples of so-called different "conceptual frameworks." If we con-

---

[6] See also passages 646, 647.

sider the situation of the oracle-follower vis-a-vis the modern scientist, or of the Ptolemaic astronomer vis-a-vis the modern astronomer, we have a different situation, more clearly asymmetrical in understanding.[7]

> 286. What we believe depends on what we learn. We all believe that it isn't possible to get to the moon; but there might be people who believe that that is possible and that it sometimes happens. We say: these people do not know a lot that we know. And, let them be never so sure of their belief — they are wrong and we know it.
>
> If we compare our system of knowledge with theirs then theirs is evidently the poorer by far.
>
> 288. 'We are quite sure of it' does not mean just that every single person is certain of it, but that we belong to a community which is bound together by science and education.

To say in particular cases that "their system of knowledge is poorer by far" and that we are "bound together by science and education" is to say that whenever I can say what they believe I am in a situation in which my usages (my meanings) embrace and include theirs. Understanding and evaluating their beliefs *presuppose* that I can say what they believe, and say it (of course) in my own words, with my own concepts. Once I have said what *they* think, I will either recognize in their observations recalcitrant data for my own ways of thinking, or I will use what I think about the same matters as a measure of what is wrong or right in their thought. In this sense their system is poorer: what I hold true is inevitably my measure for what is true in what they hold.

It is obviously not an objection to passage 286 that we learn from others; learning requires and presupposes that within our own way of thinking we can recognize recalcitrant or unexplained experience. Perhaps the Ptolemaic astronomer cannot learn directly from the

[7] I have been assuming without argument that the nonreligious person who denies that the wine is the blood of Christ can be said to understand the religious claim. I think we must reject any analysis of "understanding x" such that the criterion for understanding x is believing that x is true, for this would preclude the possibility of understanding a claim and holding it to be false. More generally, an adequate analysis of understanding will show how it is possible for two persons to understand a proposition and disagree on its truth value. The blood/wine passage in *On Certainty* suggests that Wittgenstein's analysis of understanding would be unsatisfactory in this way.

modern astronomer because he cannot experience the same things as data. But perhaps he can learn through intermediaries, in effect recapitulating the history of astronomy. Accordingly, Wittgenstein says that we learn only from someone to whom we are bound together by science and education, who knows what we know and more. This means that the teacher shares all of the relevant usages of the learner and has other usages as well, and that he can display a relationship between the old (shared) ones and the new. To the extent that one learns one comes to adopt a system. The reason we call certain people and systems "primitive" is that we cannot learn from them in this sense. We can represent their beliefs and procedures to ourselves, while they cannot apprehend our own. (They *may* of course think about us in precisely the same way as we think of them, if they think of our ways as understandable at all. Passage 286 says that insofar as I see their – or they see my – system as *different*, I (or they) will also see it as poorer in this sense.)

What significance do these reflections about the relation of understanding to evaluation in regard to alien systems have for my attitude toward my own system?

> 595. "But I can still imagine someone making all these connexions, and none of them corresponding with reality. Why shouldn't I be in a similar case?"
>
> If I imagine such a person I also imagine a reality, a world that surrounds him; and I imagine him as thinking (and speaking) in contradiction to this world.
>
> 599. ... One could describe the certainty of the proposition that water boils at circa 100° C. That isn't e.g. a proposition I have once heard (like this or that, which I could mention). I made the experiment myself at school. The proposition is a very elementary one in our text-books, which are to be trusted in matters like this because ... – Now one can offer counter-examples to all this, which show that human beings have held this and that to be certain which later, according to our opinion, proved false. *But the argument is worthless. To say: in the end we can only adduce such grounds as we hold to be grounds, is to say nothing at all.*
>
> I believe that at the bottom of this is a misunderstanding of the nature of our language-games. (emphasis added)
>
> 606. That to my mind someone else has been wrong is no ground for

> assuming that I am wrong now. – But isn't it a ground for assuming that I *might* be wrong? It is *no* ground for any *unsureness* in my judgment, or my actions.

Here Wittgenstein is clearest about the consequences of the asymmetry between one's own way of thinking about one's own procedures and one's ways of thinking about the ways of thinking of others. In referring to asymmetry as a fact I do not mean simply that my ways of thinking are mine, which is tautological, nor that I will see alien ways as "poorer by far," which *may* be false – as in the case of the confrontation with the Catholic. I mean rather that, in the absence of a recognition of recalcitrant experience, I will use what I hold true as the measure of what is true in the beliefs of others. To understand the oracle-consulter or the Catholic each of us employs his own ways of thinking and judging. To regard the oracle-consulter as thinking in contradistinction to this world is *the same thing as* regarding him as thinking in contradistinction to my way of thinking. I cannot ask and make a coherent judgment about whether my own "connexions" "correspond with reality" (595). For me to question my world-picture in this way is *already* for me to disown it in the face of a new conviction about how things are. (Of course another person *can* regard me as thinking in contradistinction to this world.)

Presented with what others offer as grounds, I can give reasons which satisfy me for rejecting grounds of this kind, whether or not they satisfy (or are intelligible to) those particular other persons. The fact that others proceed differently (to my mind, wrongly) is no *evidence* at all that I am wrong; it is not the sort of thing which counts as evidence. In the same way, the *possibility* of coming upon recalcitrant experiences is not the sort of thing which can dislodge my confidence.

> 513. What if something *really unheard-of* happened? – If I, say, saw houses gradually turning into steam without any obvious cause, if the cattle in the fields stood on their heads and laughed and spoke comprehensible words; if trees gradually changed into men and men into trees. Now, was I right when I said before all these things happened "I know that that's a house" etc., or simply "that's a house" etc.?

> 558. We say we know that water boils and does not freeze under such-and-such circumstances. Is it conceivable that we are wrong? Wouldn't

> a mistake topple all judgment with it? More: what could stand if that were to fail? Might someone discover something that made us say "It was a mistake"?
>
> Whatever may happen in the future, however water may behave in the future, — we *know* that up to now it has behaved *thus* in innumerable instances.
>
> This fact is fused into the foundations of our language-games.

The point here is not psychological but logical. A condition of thinking about any, alien ways of thinking, or about possible recalcitrant experiences, is to have a way of thinking which is not alien and within which one is confident that such recalcitrant experiences will not occur. One's own way of thinking is one's only resource for recognizing the behavior of others as "giving grounds" or as "making judgments," and it is one's only measure for truth and falsity. To say that p is true for someone else, someone who makes judgments in a recognizably different way, is no basis at all for my saying that it is true, partly true, or something I cannot judge. The concepts one uses to describe alien ways of thinking are one's own concepts; one's attitude toward the truth and falsity of the beliefs of others is determined by one's own criteria for what is true. The question whether one's own point of view *ought* to have this role is really the nonsensical question whether what *I* call judgment and evidence are *really* judgment and evidence.

The hypothesis that I can assess (from some independent standpoint) my own practices (my own ways of thinking and judging), that I can hold them in abeyance, and that I *ought* to do so, involves two misconceptions about the asymmetry between one's own practices and those of others.

(1) We never say of others, from colleagues to aborigines, that what they say or claim to know *must* be the case insofar as they claim to know.

> 137. Even if the most trustworthy of men assures me that he *knows* thus and so, this by itself cannot satisfy me that he does know. Only that he believes he knows ...
>
> 69. I should like to say: "If I am wrong about *this*, I have no guarantee that anything I say is true." But others won't say that about me, nor will I say it about other people.[8]

[8] See passages 13, 14, 22.

With others I can always demand grounds and in principle assess whatever grounds are proferred. I inevitably see the claims of others as *personal* testimony and I can always ask why I should believe what another person believes.

> 174. I act with complete certainty. But this certainty is my own.

It is a fallacy to say that because my claims as seen by others are "merely" personal and because "my certainty is my own," I ought to (or can) subject my own ways of proceeding to the same kind of scrutiny and evaluation as I do the claims of others. This is nonsense: what could I use to check my picture of world and my practices as a whole but my picture of the world and my practices? The recommendation that I treat my own claims as *merely* personal is incoherent. In involves the misconception that I can stand impartial between my own ways of proceeding and those of others. (Of course, I may well question whether I have grounds for particular empirical beliefs within my system, but doing so presupposes that I do not question whether what I am looking for are the sorts of things which *count* as grounds.)

Accordingly my attitudes toward my own practices are unavoidably these:

> 436. Is God bound by our knowledge? Are a lot of our statements *incapable* of falsehood? For that is what we want to say.
>
> 607. A judge might even say "That is the truth – so far as a human being can know it." But what would this rider achieve? ("beyond all reasonable doubt").
>
> 623. What is odd is that in such a case I always feel like saying (although it is wrong): "I know that – so far as one can know such a thing." That is incorrect, but something right is hidden behind it.
>
> 578. But mightn't a higher authority assure me that I don't know the truth? So that I had to say "Teach me!"? But then my eyes would have to be opened.

We "want to say" that "God is bound by our knowledge" because the possibility of higher authority is one which *cannot* count in our reasoning. I can admit the possibility that I will come to think differently (that "my eyes" will be "opened") but I cannot accomodate this standing possibility ("so far as one can know such a thing") by disclaiming my own certainty.

Saying "I cannot be wrong" and "That cannot be false" does not and cannot have the consequence that I or others will *never* abandon what is claimed.

> 652. Now can I prophesy that men will never throw over the present arithmetical propositions, never say that now at last they know how the matter stands? Yet would that justify a doubt on our part?

And this yields a philosophically important general conclusion about practices: we claim, *not wrongly,* that some of our beliefs are universal (or universally true) and yet we cannot anticipate whether these beliefs will themselves be given up.

> 559. You must bear in mind that the language-game is so to speak something unpredictable. I mean: it is not based on grounds. It is not reasonable (or unreasonable).
>
> It is there - like our life.
>
> 440. There is something universal here; not just something personal.

The possibility of radical contingency cannot be expressed by "I might be wrong," which has its use when a mistake can be fitted with other things about which I am not mistaken. My attitude that my own notions of judgment and evidence (my own ways of proceeding) are universally applicable and that alien notions (Aristotelian scientific befiefs and procedures, mystical beliefs and procedures, etc.) are matters to be evaluated to determine whether they offer experiences recalcitrant to my way of understanding, is not *merely* an attitude. It is (as we saw) a "logical" condition of making judgments and using "true" and "false."

> 404. I want to say: it's not that on some points men know the truth with perfect certainty. No: perfect certainty is only a matter of their attitude.
>
> 405. *But of course there is still a mistake even here.* (emphasis added)

Men do not "know the truth with perfect certainty" because there remains a series of impotent possibilities – possibilities because they cannot be discounted, because life is unpredictable; impotent because the awareness of their possibility is not the sort of thing I can weigh as evidence for or against any grounded beliefs.

> 642. But suppose someone produced the scruple: what if I suddenly as it

> were woke up and said "Just think, I've been imagining I was called L.W.!" – well, who says that I don't wake up once again and call *this* an extraordinary fancy, and so on?
>
> 223. For mightn't I be crazy and not doubting what I absolutely ought to doubt?

New and recalcitrant experiences will make me alter my ways of thinking and judging to accommodate them before I admit incoherence. Even seeing myself as crazy is, as a last resort, a way of attributing coherence through a universal world-picture; I do so in this case by abdicating from my own ways of judging altogether and deferring to those whom I hold to be sane and whose judgments can be trusted. "If that is wrong then I am crazy" is not an argument that I am not crazy, but it describes the nature and depth of my conviction; it is said perhaps to persuade but more importantly to characterize the consequences for me of conceding error.

(2) The first misconception is that we can (and ought to) take the same critical posture toward our own ways of judging and our own world-picture as we take to those of others and as others take toward ours. A second relevant misconception is that since we can doubt and justify some of our beliefs, we ought to be able to doubt and justify all of them indiscriminately. Doubting and being wrong occur within practices, and doubting requires that some beliefs (which are constitutive of the practice) not be doubted, not be the sort of thing which can be doubted. To have a practice which involves judgment is to apply the same standards of judging to all that is understood, including the alien practices and criteria of others.

To conclude, my encounters with the oracle-follower, the Catholic and the Ptolemaic astronomer involve matters which I will understand, if at all, through my own concepts and which I will judge by my own criteria of judging truth and falsity. My tools of understanding may be used badly or well; there is good and bad history of science, good and bad philosophy, but I cannot judge that my tools are *inherently* inadequate for the task. The oracle-follower and the Ptolemaic astronomer will, it is likely but not certain, offer no experiences which I cannot comfortably accommodate (or think so, which comes to the same thing). I may convert them to my way of thinking, and they may convert me to theirs; that is unpredictable. But in applying my concepts to understand their behavior and thought, I hold those concepts to be universally applicable.

[4]
A Utilitarian Theory of Judicial Decision

I. Introduction

The nature of judicial decision-making is a major preoccupation of contemporary jurisprudence. Prominent and influential writers like Ronald Dworkin and John Rawls[1] have taken the position that no utilitarian account of judicial decision-making, or of moral decision-making in general, can work. My main purpose in this article is to outline and explain the main features of a plausible utilitarian account. In doing so, I shall rebut some of the most common criticisms but I shall not try to offer a full defense of utilitarianism against its most sophisticated critics. Rather, this can be seen as a preparatory study for such a defense.

The question "What is the nature of judicial decision-making?" is ambiguous. It may be a question in pursuit of a *description* of what constrains judges or one seeking criteria for what counts as *justification* for judicial decisions. I shall take it as the latter, as a question about the criteria by which judicial decisions are to be assessed. Even so, the question is still ambiguous. It may be a question about the criteria of what is *permissible* in judging or about the criteria of what is *desirable* (or optimal). One can argue that a positivistic account of decision-making,[2] like that offered by H.L.A. Hart,[3] includes an account of what is permissible. Accordingly, Hart's account implies that it is impermissible for a judge to violate the formal rules which instruct him how to carry out his job and which limit his power. Within his delegated duties, he may use discretion to decide hard cases by appeal to relevant moral and factual considerations.[4] Al-

---

1. *See* R. Dworkin, Taking Rights Seriously vii-xv (1977); J. Rawls, A Theory of Justice 60-65 (1971).

2. In general, positivists define law as a system of rules or general commands backed by the threat of enforceable sanctions. H.L.A. Hart, The Concept of Law 20-25 (1961). Hart's sophisticated description of the structure of a legal system stresses the interrelation of two kinds of rules, primary rules which prescribe restrictions on the actions of citizens generally and secondary rules which instruct officials how to make, change, and administer the primary rules of the system. *Id.* at ch. V.

3. *Id.* at chs. IV - VI.

4. I am using the term "discretion" here in the uncontroversial sense in which the judge is asked to bring forth reasons in exercising his judgment to decide hard cases. The question whether a judge has discretion in a stronger sense than this is controversial between Dworkin and Hart.

though the distinction between what is permissible and what is optimal is sometimes hard to draw and sometimes controversial,[5] I offer utilitarianism as a theory of the second kind. It is a theory of optimal decision-making, a theory about criteria for evaluating judicial decisions within the range of what is permissible.

II. LEGAL REASONING AS MORAL REASONING

A. Theory of Moral Decisions

A moral decision, as I shall use the term, is any decision which can reasonably be expected to affect persons in a beneficial or harmful way. Judicial decisions are moral decisions because they affect persons by benefiting or harming them. A theory of judicial decision will therefore be a theory about moral decisions which gives special attention to the position and power of judges. Our job is to locate the very general moral standards which judges are expected to deploy and which are deployed in the criticism of judges. To find such standards is to put forward a theory about justification, an analysis of what it is that counts as justification for a judicial decision and as justification in criticism.

Any search for critical standards, whether for legal reasoning or for moral reasoning, presupposes that two extreme views are untenable. These are the views (1) that a simple decision procedure exists for every case that may come up for decision, i.e., that there are no hard cases, and (2) that "anything goes" in legal or moral reasoning, that there are no critical standards to be found.

(1) It is easily seen why we are not likely to find a decision procedure for moral problems. Suppose, for example, that a president or legislator must decide whether to recommend using particular funds to improve a defensive missile system rather than to raise price supports for farmers. A moral debate about this decision will have to take into account many things: the likelihood that new defense systems will be needed for security, predictions about how such systems will be used, the economic circumstances of farmers, the effect on food prices, and many others. Such decisions are characteristically hard for two reasons. The first is that such factual determinations are complicated and uncertain. The second is that, even if such factual predictions could be made with certainty, different persons would weigh their moral importance (and strategic relevance, etc.) differently. This is not only true in a complex governmental decision. It is equally true in the case of a simple decision to break a promise to A (to

5. Dworkin, for example, often says that in saying that a judge must emulate a judicial Hercules, he is describing the judge's duty. *See* R. DWORKIN, *supra* note 1, at 105-30. If this is so, the judge has a duty to do what is optimal and the distinction between what is permissible for him and what is optimal for him vanishes. I am assuming the distinction does not vanish.

meet A for lunch, for example) to help friend B (who needs help moving furniture). This is a fairly trivial case because the moral consequences of breaking or not breaking the promise are likely to be small, but even here the same difficulties are present. I cannot anticipate the results of my acts with certainty, and I am not likely to weigh the expected consequences of either action exactly as another person would. To suppose that there is a decision procedure for moral problems which *eliminates* these difficulties and to seek that procedure is to pursue a chimera.[6]

Notice that the difficulties are not relieved if one believes that morality consists in following rules which are strict and unqualified, rules like, "Always tell the truth," "Never take the property of another without permission," "Keep your promises," and so forth. There is still the problem of what to do when the rules conflict. What if telling the truth *involves* breaking a promise? One may argue that there are other rules which specify which rules have priority over others. An example would be, "Keep promises unless they involve lying because truth-telling has priority." But surely this is not very persuasive. There are some cases, easily imagined, in which a lie is justified because the adverse effects of breaking a promise would be very dire and other cases in which this is not so. It will now be suggested that this only shows that the rules need to be refined further. But counter-examples will always be available; the task of refinement can never be completed.

(2) If it seems plausible that there cannot be a moral decision procedure which prevents real dilemmas from arising, it is also plausible that not anything goes, that not all *ostensible* moral opinions about situations are intelligible *as* moral opinions or, if intelligible, are capable of being seriously entertained. For example, someone who said that in general it is morally good to break promises or to maim philosophers would simply not be understood as holding a permissible and interestingly original moral view. Instead, he would lead us to think either that he was misspeaking (did not say what he meant or didn't understand how to use the language) or that he could offer a special ulterior justification, e.g., that promise-breaking tests the mettle of the would-be promisee, benefiting him by making him self-reliant and tolerant of disappointment.[7] Such a reason may still be unpersuasive and we may dismiss it, but it is intelligible while the bare original claim is not. Similarly one who argues for the moral merits of a policy which is said both to increase the likelihood of war and

6. Kant, among others, claims that such a procedure exists, and that it generates clear solutions, at least with regard to promise-keeping. I. KANT, FOUNDATIONS OF THE METAPHYSICS OF MORALS (L.W. Beck trans. 1959). [Originally published in German in 1785.] In discussing objections to utilitarianism in Section 2 of this chapter, I discuss the view that to take promise-keeping seriously as a moral commitment is to be committed to keep all promises. I criticize this view, and the criticisms are relevant to Kant's position.

7. A third possibility is simply to regard the speaker as crazy.

decrease the availability of goods, puts us on notice that he will offer a special reason why such consequences are to be sought.

There are two ways in which a moral claim, a claim that an act would be morally good or bad, can seem unintelligible. The first, as we have just seen, is a claim that endorses an act which is prima facie bad, and does so for no redeeming ulterior reason. The second is a claim to which moral considerations simply seem irrelevant. The claim that it is good, in itself, to clap hands or make objects blue is a claim of this kind. Again, the claim can be redeemed as a moral claim only if a special kind of second-level justification is given, for example, that clapping is healthful exercise or that blue is an especially pleasing color.[8]

These very general remarks suggest some general conclusions about moral reasoning because they lead us to ask what feature of moral claims makes them understandable *as* moral claims. The examples suggest that there is *some* connection between the judgment that an act is morally good and the judgment that someone or other is benefited by it. What is peculiar about the claim that maiming or clapping hands is good is that there is no connection to benefit, and the criterion for a relevant explanation is that it establishes some connection of this kind. I am using "benefit" in the very general sense of "affecting someone in a positive way." The examples above illustrate this point. The person affected positively may in some cases be the actor himself. It may be commended to me as morally good to cultivate my talents not because others will gain but because I will be better as a result.[9] Just as there is a connection between goodness and benefit, there is a parallel connection between the judgment that an act is morally bad and the judgment that someone is harmed by it. So far I have not tried to *examine* the connection beyond suggesting that it is a necessary minimal condition of sincerely calling an act "good" to think that someone is benefited by it, etc.

I am not at all suggesting that there is a decision procedure for determining what things are benefits or for weighing benefits. I cannot expect that another person will agree with me on all my claims about what is beneficial or on my judgments about relative benefit, but I *can* expect that the reasons I give will tend to be understandable to him and vice versa. I can also expect that various particular and general differences in factual belief will often underlie and be available to explain our differences when they arise. I may believe, for example, that it is bad to discipline children

8. This argument is elaborated and defended in my paper, *Goodness and Benefit*, 9 J. VALUE INQUIRY 1 (1975). *See also* Foot, *Moral Beliefs*, in THEORIES OF ETHICS 83 (Foot ed. 1967).

9. Note that not all consequences which are morally significant when A brings them about for B are also morally significant when A brings them about for himself. It may be morally praiseworthy to feed a hungry child but not to have a meal when one is hungry oneself. Significantly moral self-regarding acts require a special account.

by locking them into rooms; someone else may defend it on moral grounds. The difference between us may well turn to be a difference in our beliefs about the psychology of children. I may believe that such punishments create unresolved anger and mistrust between parents and children and are not effective in bringing about greater responsibility. A contrary belief about psychological facts will most likely lie beneath a contrary moral judgment.

We can also see why there is *rough* congruence in moral judgment.[10] Each person's notion of benefit has two components, some sense of the ways in which all persons are benefited in similar ways because they have similar needs, wants, and pleasures, and some awareness of the range of different personal ways in which persons are benefited—and of the reasons for those idiosyncracies. The fact that we successfully anticipate and understand the reasons which others give when benefit is discussed, whether we agree in our conclusions or not, is evidence that we have a shared sense of what benefit is.[11] To say that terms like benefit and harm (and goodness and badness) refer to a range of factually specifiable consequences for persons in general is to give a *naturalistic* account of them.[12] It is naturalistic because it says that certain substantive things or kinds of things are essentially good things to bring about and because it thus ties the moral notion of goodness to a particular factual content. By contrast, a non-naturalistic account would expalin the use of a term like goodness by a formal feature, for example, by saying it is the expression of a strong preference.

To summarize, I have suggested by example why there is not likely to be a decision procedure for moral reasoning and why, at the same time, there are some substantive standards for what counts in moral

---

10. What is the community of moral judges to which "our" refers? That community is certainly not defined by or limited to those who share a particular language. Rather, it is characterized by those who can recognize and understand moral situations and dilemmas, whether they appear in daily life, in Plato, Rousseau, Proust, Kierkegaard, Kawabata, or a contemporary mystery novel. The members of such a community will decide moral cases differently but will share criteria for the relevance of moral reasons and will grasp the sources of their disagreement. Obviously, this notion begs many questions about criteria of membership in such a community, about reciprocal understanding, and so on.

11. This is not a special feature of the notions of harm and benefit but a feature of all notions, from such concrete ones as that of chair or food to such abstractions as happiness or liberty. I am here making a *logical* point: for terms to have common usage they must be understood in more or less the same way by users. Related arguments are to be found in L. WITTGENSTEIN, PHILOSOPHICAL INVESTIGATIONS (1953).

12. The first step of a naturalistic account of our criteria for benefit would be to examine shared desiderata of survival. But an account of survival is only a minimal account of benefit. Note also that a naturalistic account of benefit would attend to differences among persons as well as similarities; A may naturally be benefited by X while B may naturally be benefited by Y. These are facts which they may understand about themselves and about each other, facts which can then be a basis of moral action.

reasoning ("*not* anything goes"). This analysis depends on the link between goodness and benefit and on the *relative* determinateness of the notion of benefit. While there is no objective measure for benefit, those who discuss benefit reach mutually understandable conclusions on the basis of shared criteria.

B. Responses and Objections

Before pursuing this argument further, I want to anticipate some responses and objections. (1) A possible response to my analysis is this: "If there is no decision procedure for moral reasoning, so much the worse for moral reasoning. Lacking a decision procedure, it is a defective form of reasoning." This response imposes an unreasonable Procrustean demand. There may be imagined advantages to a decision procedure for moral judgment just as there may be such advantages to knowing the future with certainty. (It takes little imagination to see there may be disadvantages as well.) But the envisaged form of life is not *our* form of life nor is it a form of life which persons have ever had or can ever expect to have.

(2) A variation on the first response is that if no decision procedure exists, moral and legal reasoning are not worth serious study. The investigation becomes a topographic survey of the terrain, an account of what persons happen to do when they make moral or legal judgments, and of whether they happen to agree or disagree. If we *could* generate a decision procedure, this would give a test for determining when judges (moral or legal) do their job badly or well. In the absence of one, we have no such test.

This objection rests on a misunderstanding. The misuse of the metaphor of topography shows this clearly. The "terrain" is not just surveyed and described. The moral and legal judgments made in particular cases are the philosopher's raw material, not his end product. He uncovers not only the judgments persons make but the *standards* which they use to arrive at judgments and to criticize the correctness of judgments.

This is a general point about practices in which judgments can be made by using objective standards but in which there is, nonetheless, no decision method of deciding hard cases unequivocally. Just as there are standards for judging satisfactory moral decisions, there are standards for judging satisfactory cars, good cuisine, outstanding football playing, and good driving. None of these involve a decision procedure which yields the same judgment by all judges or in all contexts. There will be unresolved controversies about all these matters. None, on the other hand, involves license on the part of the judge to say anything he pleases on whatever grounds he may choose at random. It would not make sense to judge football by the standards of ballet. A different way of making my point is that it is wrong to say that judgments are *either* objective or subjective if "objective" means "made according to a decision procedure" and "subjective" means "made without recourse to publicly shared standards." Judgments which are involved in most activities are neither.

(3) Still another objection says that unless I can claim that there exists a decision procedure (that moral and legal judgments are "objective") I can neither expect nor demand that others will share my views or my conclusions. This objection is in fact very similar to the second objection. What we have seen is that while I cannot expect others to reach all the same specific judgments that I reach, I inevitably expect them to have the same standards of judgment. I will, in particular, expect others to have the same criteria for what kinds of reasons are relevant, to weigh reasons in anticipatable ways, and to justify odd-sounding conclusions in anticipatable ways. This expectation is not coercive. It is not a "demand." Rather, it is a fact that *unless* they act in this way, they will not be participating in a shared activity ("practice") of judging. We will not be talking about the same activity.[13]

(4) A point to remember about legal and moral reasoning is that we expect decision-makers to act in a disinterested way. This means that in making a moral judgment, one must put aside one's own particular interest in the result and attend to benefits and harms for others.[14] When we talk about moral reasoning and moral action, we presuppose that individuals have the capacity to lay their own immediate interest to one side; a psychological theory which denies this will deny the possibility of moral judgment.[15] This matter is particularly clear in the judicial context. The fact that a decision may help or hinder a judge in his personal or professional interests must be irrelevant to his decision. (This is a basic standard, whether or not judges in fact lapse in this way.)

13. There is a sense in which certain odd-sounding claims about benefit, harm, and value may be intelligible as pathology. For example, the claim that clapping hands is harmful and dangerous, and therefore morally bad, may have to do with the particular significance that clapping has for the victim of a psychological disturbance. But this is not to understand the claim as a debatable moral claim made on the basis of criteria.

14. To choose disinterestedly is to choose without any particular or *special* regard for oneself. This is not to say that effects on oneself must be discounted completely. Rather, they must be treated with the same regard as benefits to others. Kant makes the general point about disinterest, saying that moral action involves treating others as ends in themselves and not as means toward achieving one's own interests. I. KANT, FOUNDATIONS OF THE METAPHYSICS OF MORALS 56-57 (L.W. Beck trans. 1959). [Originally published in German in 1785.] A form of the basic imperative of morality is to treat others in accord with a rule which one can will universally as a rule of behavior.

15. Note the distinction between the deterministic view that individuals must always act in their own interest and the recommendation that individuals always act in their own interest even though they have the choice of not doing so. A variation of the latter view is the theory that it is always in one's interest to act morally and that one serves self-interest (at a second level) by being moral (on the first level).

C. Summary

I have tried to lay a foundation for a theory of judicial decisions by sketching the outlines of a theory about moral decisions. My assumption in doing so is that a judicial decision is a kind of moral decision, that what makes a hard case hard for a judge is that it presents a moral dilemma, or at least a difficult moral determination. If this is so, a judge can ignore the moral dimensions of his role only at his peril.

The moral theory we have considered has its beginnings in some simple observations. It says that there is a logical connection between moral judgments and factual judgments about benefit and harm, and that the moral goodness of an action or decision depends on its beneficial and harmful consequences. The theory formulated in this way will provoke contradictory responses. One response is that it is obvious and empty. Who would have thought that judges ought to function in any other way than to bring about benefit and prevent harm? It will be said that this is true and absurdly uninformative. A second, and very different, response is that the theory is radical and preposterous. Surely judges are constrained by standards other than the injunction to do good by maximizing benefit and minimizing harm. The result of judges following *this* rule would be chaos, the collapse of the institutions of law.

Clearly, the theory needs elaboration as an informative account of the standards which underlie moral and legal judgment. The theory is best explained by uncovering and answering various objections to it. I shall approach this job in three steps. First, I will fill out some of the details and applications of the theory by showing something of its pedigree. That is, I will show why it is a kind of utilitarian theory. But utilitarian theories are a family of different theories about moral reasoning and I shall show how our theory is related to other utilitarian theories. Second, I will look at some general objections which have been raised against utilitarianism and see which objections are relevant to our account. I will consider how those objections can be met. Third, and most important, I shall discuss the application of a utilitarian theory of moral reasoning to judicial decision-making.

III. UTILITARIANISM: CRITICISMS AND CORRECTIONS

The motive behind nineteenth-century utilitarian theories is altogether different from our own motive. Jeremy Bentham, the "inventor" of utilitarianism, tried to devise a decision procedure for moral judgment, an intellectual strategy which would generate uniform objective solutions for moral problems and which would reduce all factors in a moral question to a common measure.[16] The present theory makes no such claims. It is

16. J. BENTHAM, PRINCIPLES OF MORALS AND LEGISLATION (1948). [Originally published in 1789.]

not a mechanism for reforming the practice of moral reasoning; it is intended instead as a reminder and a perspicuous rendering of the standards which already inhere in the practice of moral reasoning as it is generally carried on. The notion of benefit is a notion we already have and employ. Let me explain these matters by raising particular points of difference.

In classical Benthamite utilitarianism, the goal of morality is to maximize pleasure and minimize pain.[17] Pleasure and pain are taken to be the common denominators of all morally relevant experiences. For other utilitarians influenced by Bentham, maximizing happiness ("the greatest happiness for the greater number"[18]) is the goal. It was quickly pointed out that there were difficulties in the Benthamite strategy since (a) pleasure, pain, and happiness are not measurable and (b) there are other moral goals besides pleasure, happiness, and the avoidance of pain. For example, it is easy to see that the pain of serious injury exceeds the pain of an unconvenient change of plans; an act which has the consequence of causing serious injury is therefore, for moral reasons, to be seriously avoided. But the question, how *much* worse is a serious injury, is unanswerable if it is a demand for a numerical answer. Much of Bentham's strategy seemed to presuppose that these factors can be quantified. The second objection can be illustrated by the moral value assigned to courage or self-sacrifice. Actions of this kind may benefit others and have altruistic motives, but they may do so by adding to the sum of dignity and self-respect in the world rather than to pleasure and happiness.[19]

Objections of these kinds are irrelevant to a theory based on benefit and harm. The theory does not claim to give a decision procedure and acknowledges that benefit and harm are not measurable. What degree of agreement may exist in moral judgment is a function of the way (independent of theory) persons experience benefit and harm and not a function of mathematical reforms in judgment generated by the theory. The theory meets criticism (b) by demonstrating that the notion of benefit encompasses the moral goals which happiness, pleasure, and the avoidance of pain leave out. For example, by teaching someone self-discipline we may be benefiting him and therefore performing a moral act whether or not there is a net increase in pleasure or happiness.[20]

17. *Id.* at chs. III - V.

18. 10 J. BENTHAM, WORKS 142 (1830). *See* J.S. MILL, UTILITARIANISM *passim* (1973). [Originally published in 1861.]

19. See R. BRANDT, ETHICAL THEORY ch. 15 (1959) for an account of these criticisms.

20. Two points. This argument can only be carried out piecemeal. As each particular moral goal is considered, it can be argued that that goal is compatible with a theory of benefit and not with a theory of pleasure. The possibility of a counterexample (a moral goal which is not beneficial) cannot be ruled out but the burden rests with those who would disprove the theory. Secondly, note that it is always possible to save a theory that happiness is the sole moral goal by *redefining* happiness to coincide with the sum of moral goals.

Modern critics of utilitarianism offer a criticism which is a variation of one just considered. Critics such as Richard Brandt and John Rawls argue that utilitarians advocate maximizing social welfare and that this leaves aside other important moral goals.[21] Brandt offers the example of an aged parent who is artificially kept alive at great expense and with a heavy emotional toll on his family. Brandt argues that the utilitarian would find no social welfare — and therefore no value — in keeping the parent alive.[22] Rawls argues, to the same effect, that a utilitarian would be committed by his theory to breaking his promises whenever some social welfare was to be attained by doing so.[23]

Such criticisms are not relevant to the theory of benefit and harm. Note first that the situations described or suggested by Brandt and Rawls in the examples are potentially very difficult. No adequate theory can generate easy answers and any adequate analysis will have to attend, more than Brandt and Rawls do, to the details of the particular situation. Where the prospect of survival, or of recovery of consciousness, or of diminution of acute pain is slight in the case of the aged parent, the dilemma will be hard. Analogously, there are cases in which promise-breaking is justified even though, in the absence of other considerations, there is likely to be harm to the promisee who has relied on the promise. For the utilitarian, promise-breaking will be justified only to the extent that the benefit to be derived through the breach overrides this harm. Thus, the first mistake that Brandt and Rawls make is supposing that the answers to such dilemmas are obvious (that one preserves life at all cost, that one keeps all promises) and that the utilitarian answer *obviously* is the opposite of the correct answer.

The criticisms involve a second mistake which is more general and more important. They presuppose that all utilitarian theories (a) say that the moral worth of an act is determined by its consequences for welfare *and* (b) assign a specific weight to the relevant consequences. But the theory of benefit and harm explicitly does (a) and not (b). The significance or weight given to each factor in any moral situation is informed by our intuitions and by the usages which exist independently of the theory. Thus, in Brandt's case of the aged parent, the theory alone tells nothing about whether the benefit to the parent (and to relatives) of extended survival does or does not outweigh the suffering, expense, etc. All it tells us is that when we *do* make a moral judgment, we must attend as carefully and disinterestedly as possible to considerations of benefit and harm, for what else is relevant? It is certainly possible and indeed likely that survival for

21. *See* Brandt, *Toward a Credible Form of Utilitarianism*, in MORALITY AND THE LANGUAGE OF CONDUCT 107 (1963); Rawls, *Two Concepts of Rules*, 64 PHILOSOPHICAL REV. 3 (1955).

22. Brandt, *supra* note 21, at 110.

23. Rawls, *supra* note 21, at 17.

one day may outweigh in benefit a great deal of suffering and long-term financial hardship; the utilitarian whose theory is based on benefit and harm would not necessarily say otherwise.

Having answered one set of criticisms, we must consider the objection that utilitarianism is an inadequate theory of moral reasoning in need of completion. On this view it is a vague or weak theory which instructs us to look for benefit and harm but which seems to allow almost *anything* to count as benefit and harm. Critics insist that it needs to be supplemented or replaced by a theory of rules (Rawls) or a theory of rights (Dworkin) which would identify particular kinds of moral consequences which would have priority over others. An example would be a set of moral rules which said that the benefits of liberty always have priority over material benefits.

I shall look in detail at theories of this kind but a general response is that my theory is only as elastic (or non-specific) as the notion of benefit and that the elasticity of the notion must not be exaggerated. The philosopher's job doesn't end with uncovering the utilitarian principle, the relation of goodness and benefit. It also involves doing what J. L. Austin calls "linguistic phenomenology"[24] on the notions of benefit and harm to determine what sorts of things count as benefit and how much divergence exists and can exist among those who use the notion. Those who find utilitarianism an inadequate theory seem to assume that this enterprise will yield little.

One form of this criticism is that unless we can say more about benefit we will have to give up making interpersonal comparisons. Unless there is an objective measure of moral worth, formulated in rules of justice as a theory of rights, we must concede that what benefits a person is only what he *thinks* benefits him. Once we concede this we are no longer able to make moral judgments which are anything more than judgments about preference satisfaction. Accordingly, Ronald Dworkin claims that utilitarian theories collapse into theories which determine moral goals by looking at the preferences of those affected by the action.[25] This, Dworkin argues, entails fatal difficulties which will affect *any* theory in which preferences are a criterion for determination of goals, for example, a theory which says that happiness is to be maximized. Surely not all happiness is to count; what about the happiness of the sadist who enjoys the suffering of others? The same objection affects a theory of social welfare as long as social welfare is measured by preferences, by what persons claim (or think) they want. A society which has never experienced free speech or self-government may not include aspects of liberty in its notion of welfare. This should not mean that we *must* leave it out of account in considering that

24. J. Austin, Philosophical Papers 130 (1970). G.E.M. Anscombe makes a similar point in *Modern Moral Philosophy*, 33 Philosophy 1-2 (1958).

25. R. Dworkin, *supra* note 1, at 233-38.

society's welfare. This criticism clearly indicts a theory of benefit *if* the theory *defines* benefit by appeal to preferences.

Obviously, it is a sound observation that a theory which would define moral action in terms of maximizing personal preferences *is* a defective theory. But a theory which talks of maximizing benefit is not subject to this objection. The theory makes clear that, even if we assume that most persons most of the time are good judges of what is beneficial or harmful to them, being benefited and thinking that one is benefited are different matters. It is always possible to be mistaken. To the extent that these are different matters, to the extent that someone's sense that something will benefit him is only one factor among others in my judgment about what will benefit him, the sort of objection Dworkin presents is irrelevant. But, at the same time, a theory which meets the objection in this way invites the criticism that it is paternalistic. When a moral or judicial decision-maker claims that a decision will benefit A and B in spite of what A and B happen to think or prefer, his claim is frankly paternalistic. But is it to be rejected *because* it is paternalistic?[26] In responding, we need to distinguish two points. One is that there are perfectly ordinary situations in which an external observer may be expected to know what is going to benefit or harm a person better than that person. The observer may, for example, have special expertise. He may be a doctor, lawyer, engineer, or psychiatrist who knows that if the agent proceeds as he intends the consequences will, by the agent's own *eventual* admission, be disastrous. Even if it is conceded that paternalism has this limited justification, it will be said that paternalism is easily abused and the moral or legal judge will be tempted to override the preferences of the person affected even when he does *not* know better. Even more importantly the procedure seems to ignore the important benefits of being able to choose for oneself even when one chooses wrongly.

A brief answer is that *any* theory may be abused; it is no part of a theory to preempt its abuse. But, if we put this aside, the objection is important because it is related to one of the most general and pervasive criticisms of utilitarianism, that no utilitarian theory can give proper attention to the moral importance of liberty and fairness.

So far, we have clarified the theory that moral reasoning is in fact a matter of reasoning about benefit and harm by contrasting it with other kinds of utilitarian theories. Thus, it does not reduce moral considerations to a common denominator like pleasure, happiness, or social welfare. In doing so, it exempts itself from the criticism that it oversimplifies moral dilemmas or that it leaves out of account certain intuitions about the moral importance of life or of promises. It is, in other words, not a strongly

26. *See* Feinberg, *Legal Paternalism*, 1 CANADIAN J. PHILOSOPHY 105 (1971).

revisionist theory which says that our ordinary moral intuitions are too complex and inconsistent; rather, it is a theory which takes up these intuitions and shows how they are to be reconciled. But if it is not an overly strong theory, it is also not a weak theory which says that the only justifiable goal identifiable in moral reasoning is the satisfaction of preferences (or want-satisfaction). The theory, in invoking the notion of benefit, uses a notion which is strong enough to be used in criticism of preferences. It is a part of the theory that we are able to explain those situations of moral judgment in which we say that, wants and preferences notwithstanding, it is in the interest of persons to be compelled, for example, to go to school or to confront their responsibility, etc.

IV. Utilitarianism and Liberty

Perhaps the most frequent and vigorous criticisms of utilitarianism say that no utilitarian can give a satisfactory account of the moral importance of liberty.[27] Such critics emphasize that this point is particularly important when we are concerned with the morality of political or legal decisions. It is argued that an overriding interest in maximizing benefit and minimizing harm will inevitably lead (a) to decisions in which liberty is undercut for the sake of so-called benefit and therefore (b) to a situation in which persons are treated unfairly. The utilitarian is said to be led to these unfortunate results in two ways. First, his method of resolving cases will be to weigh liberty — when he considers it at all — as just one of several benefits which, as a class, are to be maximized. A failure to secure liberty may be offset by beneficial gains of other kinds. For example, a curtailment of free speech may be justified by an increase in material wealth overall. Second, the practice represented in this method will be to impose a judgment about maximal benefit on others; this will inevitably undercut liberty to choose how one will live and even to choose to harm oneself. Thus, these critics say that a utilitarian approach undercuts liberty in two significant ways, by arrogating to the decision-maker unlimited decision-making power and by the particular decisions which he is likely to make. It follows that a theory which takes liberty seriously will have two features. It will place "jurisdictional" limits on decision-makers, limits which respect the inviolable liberties of individuals, and it will involve criteria for decision-making which will give special priority to liberty over and above consequences of benefit and harm.

The criticisms, as I have summarized them, are well-represented by Ronald Dworkin's *Taking Rights Seriously* and John Rawls's *A Theory*

27. *See, e.g.*, J. Rawls, *supra* note 1 at 22-33, 183-92 (1971); R. Dworkin, *supra* note 1, at 81-130, 266-78. Dworkin, unlike Rawls, opposes utilitarianism to theories of *rights* rather than to theories of liberty but the criticisms are similar.

of Justice.[28] Dworkin makes the first suggestion, that in a correct theory of moral/judicial decision-making, enjoying liberty is not just one kind of beneficial consequence among others. Rather the possession of rights by individuals is a kind of *veto* upon decision-making which individuals have implicitly and which decision-makers must respect.[29] Liberty, if it is understood to be the enjoyment of matured and concrete rights,[30] constitutes an outer bound on permissible interventions in persons' lives. Dworkin argues that this notion of a boundary limiting what decision-makers can and cannot alter is one which utilitarians cannot take seriously.

The second suggestion is made by Rawls when he offers criteria for just decision-making. One criterion is that considerations of liberty be "prior in lexical ordering" to considerations of welfare.[31] This means that the goal of insuring for each participant in a practice (e.g., each member of a society subject to a legal system) the most extensive liberty which is compatible with a like liberty for all[32] cannot be overridden in the pursuit of any allocation of wealth in the form of "primary goods" (largely material wealth), however abundant and however equitable the distribution may be. The point of both Dworkin's and Rawls's arguments is that a theory founded on liberty (or rights)[33] as *opposed* to a utilitarian theory accurately gives the standards implicit in moral judgments, particularly moral judgments relating to public affairs.

This indictment raises several independent questions. Do the critics represent utilitarianism correctly? Do their own theories yield clear alternatives? I shall argue that the critics misrepresent utilitarianism as it can be construed along the lines of the theory of benefit and offer alternatives which are themselves unclear, alternatives which *may* in practice give the same results as the utilitarian theory. Consider the following points.

(1) One assumption which may be implicit in these criticisms is that liberty is not the *sort* of good which a utilitarian can take seriously. This means that utilitarians characteristically attend to tangible and material ends and prefer ends which are quantifiable; the paradigm is the accumulation of property. It is clear that this accusation misfires. The notions of benefit and harm are neutral with regard to the tangibility of ends. (Even classical utilitarians spoke of pleasure and happiness, and what is less tangible than pleasure?)

There is a more subtle form of the criticism. Liberty, unlike pleasure or happiness, is not so much a *goal* of action as an aspect or condition of

28. R. DWORKIN, note 1 *supra;* J. RAWLS, note 1 *supra.*
29. "Individual rights are political trumps held by individuals." R. DWORKIN, *supra* note 1, at xi.
30. *Id.* at 90-94.
31. J. RAWLS, *supra* note 1, at 40-45, 60-65 (1971).
32. *Id.* at 60.
33. See note 27 *supra* for the difference between Rawls and Dworkin.

acting and living.[34] When we speak of liberty, we are thinking of the needs of persons as actors, as persons who make choices and are aware of doing so. This abstract conception stands in contrast to the equally abstract conception of persons as passive collectors of goods. A moral theory which has a place for liberty must be based on an active rather than a passive conception of persons.

Let's see how a utilitarian might try to meet this criticism. Obviously, he needs a rich conception of benefit and harm. Benefits are not just goods received and harm is not just material injury or deprivation of goods. One is benefited whenever one is allowed or encouraged to act in a way that furthers self-esteem, self-improvement, the development of capacities, and the expressing and testing of one's thoughts. To be provided with the conditions of living in this way is a benefit just as it is a benefit to have food, shelter, health care, and love.[35] I shall call benefits of the first kind "active benefits" and the second kind "goods." It seems clear that active benefits can be secured only indirectly, by setting conditions for living well in these respects. The initiative for living well lies with the individual.[36] This does not mean, however, that these benefits are secured only by governmental self-abnegation, e.g., by non-interference with speech, assembly, etc. They are also served by such affirmative interventions as compelling public education, providing mental health care, and preventing persons from interfering with the exercise of speech, etc., by others.

The critics are correct that it is an important feature of an adequate moral theory that benefit and harm be generalized in this way. But there is no reason to think that a utilitarian theory of benefit and harm cannot meet this challenge.

(2) The criticism may be made in a different form, drawing attention not to the *kinds* of benefits the utilitarian can include within his theory but to the way in which he says we *compare* benefits in moral reasoning. Even when critics concede that utilitarians allow *some* weight to be given to the exercise of liberty, to self-esteem, and so forth, they claim that utilitarians will not be able to give them enough weight to generate a satisfactory account of their place in moral reasoning. This, we have seen, leads Rawls to say that there is a lexical ordering among principles of justice and that liberty has priority over wealth.[37]

---

34. This is not to deny that securing liberty may be the goal of political activity. But it is a goal only in the sense that it is sought as a condition or aspect of other contemplated future activities. The notion of liberty which I am using combines, I think, what Isaiah Berlin calls negative liberty ("freedom from . . .") and positive liberty ("freedom to . . ."). Liberty as a way of acting is positive liberty; liberty as a condition of acting is negative liberty. *See* I. BERLIN, *Two Concepts of Liberty*, in FOUR ESSAYS ON LIBERTY 118 (1970).

35. I am not suggesting that the two kinds of benefits are commensurable. See the discussion which follows in the text.

36. Again, this is Berlin's notion of positive liberty. *See* note 34 *supra*.

37. J. RAWLS, *supra* note 1 at 42-45 (1971).

This objection is a variation of one we have already considered. The critic persists in attributing to the utilitarian a *particular* and a *counterintuitive* assignment of weights to benefits. Once it is conceded that the theory *describes* moral reasoning as the weighing of benefits but *imposes* no weighing of its own, the objection disappears. It is entirely compatible with utilitarian theory that the moral decision-maker have a deep-seated commitment to "active benefits" and regard the recognition and fostering of the conditions of liberty as an extraordinarily important, and ordinarily supervening, way of conveying benefits. A moral/judicial decision which ignored or undervalued this range of considerations would be objectionable not because it was any more or less an instance of utilitarian reasoning but because it would rest on a mistaken conception of benefit.[38] If Rawls or Dworkin were to fault utilitarianism for failing to *guarantee* that liberty will be a supervening consideration, they would be looking for the guarantee in the wrong place. Recognition of the importance of liberty will be part of an adequate analysis of benefit.

There is one way in which the more general notion of benefit fits moral judgment better than a set of rules which give priority to liberty. There will always be special situations which are counterexamples to such rules, situations in which material needs are so urgent that a curtailment of liberty is morally justified. Governments justifiably declare curfews in emergencies, censor newspapers during war, and appropriate private resources to prevent starvation. A general rule of thumb that active benefits are supervening over goods is compatible with the recognition that in exceptional cases active benefits may justifiably be suspended to secure survival or minimal welfare. (This is analogous to the observation that promise-breaking will generally be harmful, given the expectation of reliance on the promise, but in special cases will be justifiable.) In clearly exceptional cases it will *not* be justifiable on utilitarian grounds to adhere to the rule which gives priority to liberty, to allow starvation, or to keep promises come what may.

Rawls admits that his principles will not apply to all situations, particularly not those in which scarcity or extraordinary dangers would make the exercise of liberty a matter of no significance.[39] He admits that a theory which offers rules of priority in assessing benefits tends to be caught between insisting that liberty is in principle a prior and overriding matter and admitting that there are situations in which goods are of primary

38. Of course the line between (a) inadmissible, mistaken conceptions of benefit and (b) the admissible range of views about benefit is itself a fuzzy line. Anti-Utopian novels by Orwell [*1984* (1949)] and Zamiatin [*We* (1924)] illustrate that there are easy examples of inadmissible conceptions. Furthermore, disputants who hold different admissible views will each regard the other as mistaken and try to persuade the other of his mistake.

39. J. RAWLS, *supra* note 1, at 235-42 (1971).

importance.[40] Utilitarianism is not caught up by this seeming paradox since it rests only on the situationally variable notion of benefit. Exceptions to the liberty principle are just those cases in which the benefits to be gained by pruning liberty to prevent material harm are overriding.

(3) The problem with utilitarianism, according to a different criticism, is not that it ignores active benefits or that it undervalues them. Rather the problem is that a utilitarian decision-maker thinks of himself as *allocating* benefits, regardless of the nature of the benefits. To take liberty (or rights)[41] seriously is not to think of them as something dispensed but as a limitation on the kinds of allocations permitted to the decision-maker. They are a veto which individuals have over the range of possible decisions.

It is hard to see what difference this criticism suggests *either* in the way decisions would be made *or* in the way decision-makers would generally think of their powers. On either the recommended theory or utilitarianism the decision-maker intervenes to affect persons' lives. A decision to secure conditions for the exercise of freedom is still a situation which is affirmatively brought about. Respecting liberty or rights is not the same thing as refraining from a decision, not the same thing as refusing to make a decision. By refusing to act he may abet the infringement of liberty. If the practical point of the objection is not to recommend inaction by the decision-maker when rights are at stake, perhaps it is a point about the "demand" character of the decision. Perhaps it says that a decision to respect rights or secure liberty is incumbent on him in a way that the decision to maximize benefits is not. But this is a distinction without practical effect since the general principle of utilitarianism *already* makes it incumbent on the decision-maker to maximize benefit.

Lying behind the objection is a sound observation, but one which has little to do with the merits of utilitarianism. The point is not about alternative standards or points of view for the decision-maker, since on either theory he must not think of himself as inactive when rights are claimed and since (as I have argued) a utilitarian position may adequately capture his stance as a defender of liberty. Rather the point is about the attitude of the person affected by his decision. From this point of view, certain conditions which we call "rights" seem so clearly essential to the exercise of personality[42] that the decision-maker seems to have no choice but to

---

40. I do not mean to suggest that Rawls himself is either unaware of this possible dilemma or caught in it. He argues that limitations on liberty in societies that are not well-ordered are limitations which proceed from (and can be justified by appeal to) the principles of justice themselves. "Unfortunate circumstances and the unjust designs of some necessitate a much lesser liberty than tha' enjoyed in a well-ordered society." *Id.* at 243.

41. *See* note 27 *supra.*

42. I am using the notion of personality in Max Weber's sense of the "understandable motivations of the single individual." *See* H.H. GERTH & C. WRIGHT MILLS, FROM MAX WEBER: ESSAYS IN SOCIOLOGY 55 (1958). I do not intend to say that Weber subscribes to the view suggested about the

convey these benefits. But this is an illusion. In hard or easy cases, the decision-maker chooses. The question is not whether he chooses but how.

(4) A final objection which may be raised is a psychological point and not a philosophical one. The point is that decision-makers who think of themselves as weighing benefits are likely to undervalue liberty and that decision-makers who think of liberty or rights as an absolute veto over conflicting benefits will in fact appropriately weigh so-called active benefits and respect rights. It follows that the advocacy of a *self-conscious* utilitarian approach to decision will lead judges to make erroneous decisions.

This is a strange argument. On one level, it is irrelevant since we are investigating the proper standards which ought to govern decision-making, the standards which are implicit in moral reasoning.[43] The notion that a decision-maker may abuse those standards is irrelevant. We are not investigating whether false standards *ought* to be promulgated among decision-makers as a prophylactic against abuse. In other words, we are concerned with the standards themselves and not with an examination of the benefits and harms of promulgating those standards.

Beyond this, the psychological assumption is unconvincing. It presumes that we know more about how moral decisions are made than we really know and that we know how judges would use or abuse particular standards. Furthermore, if the assumption about how judges apply standards were true, it would go far to undermine confidence in the use of *any* standards in moral judgment, whether they were the standards of the liberty-theorist or the utilitarian.

V. UTILITARIANISM AND JUDICIAL DECISIONS

In discussing theories about liberty, we have noticed some special features of judicial decision-making. Unlike the ordinary person in moral situations, a judge's decisions frequently affect liberties and ostensible rights. The objections of the liberty-theorist are raised most interestingly with regard to the decisions of public officials. In this section, I shall apply our general account of a utilitarian theory based on the notion of benefit to the decisions of judges.

There are constraints on judging which are not moral constraints; among these are formal and procedural rules. But all judicial decisions affect persons in beneficial or harmful ways. Decisions affect not only petitioners before a court, but also persons who will have to modify their behavior in accord with law as it is set in specific decisions, and even

relation of liberty and personality.

43. We are investigating the proper standards which "ought" to govern decision-making, not from the particular point of view of the theorist's personal preferences, but from the point of view of what is implicit in the practice of moral discourse.

persons who merely have a general interest in the stability of government. In this sense, judicial decisions are necessarily moral decisions[44] and a general account of moral justification applies to them as well. And yet, at the same time, a judge's decisions have various kinds of beneficial and harmful effects which an ordinary person does not have to take into account. For example, a decision which may maximize benefit in a particular case may also (a) cause havoc in the legal system and (b) conflict with the formal criteria (Hart's secondary rules) of judicial decision-making. In addressing these distinctions, we must ask first how, in practice, a judge would go about making decisions in a utilitarian way.

First of all, note that in *every* moral decision some benefits and harms are direct while others are indirect. The direct effects are not necessarily weightier, and the indirect effects may be overriding in determining the merits of an action. For example, White's decision to break a promise to Brown in order to be available to perform a service for Green has the direct consequences of harm to Brown (detrimental reliance, loss of the object of the promise, etc.) and benefit to Green. Indirect consequences are of several kinds. Some are consequences for the immediate participants, others are not. The decision may damage the friendship between White and Brown, it may create a friendship between White and Green, or it may undermine White's trust among his friends generally. Other consequences are more remote. The decision, if widely known, may set a precedent for others in the community, may make persons generally aware of and responsive to the plight of persons like Green, and may weaken the institution of promise-keeping. Obviously, the claim that a particular consequence will be significant depends on the situation.[45] The general point is that each of an indefinite array of consequences, near and remote, are appropriately raised, evaluated, and perhaps dismissed. The appropriate array of consequences to consider is not defined as (a) the consequences of breaking promise X to Brown in order to, etc., but as (b) the consequence of White's breaking promise X to Brown in order to, etc. *Who* the decision-maker is and *how* he is situated are often critically important in an assessment of consequences.

The decisions of a judge in court necessarily have wider consequences than the moral decisions of a person who does not have an institutional role. A decision that Jones is liable in damages to Kramer is altogether different from the decision (and implementing action) of Robin Hood in taking a sum equal to the assessed damages from Jones and giving it to Kramer, even when the relationship and mutual claims of Jones and Kramer are in both cases the same. As a utilitarian, one is not concerned with

44. *See* section I *supra*.

45. For example, it is often implausible that breaking one's word will significantly damage the institution of making promises.

the consequences attributable to the abstraction "deciding to transfer a sum as reimbursement for injury from Jones to Kramer" but with the consequences in the concrete situations of (a) Judge Tuck deciding in the state court of appeals that . . . and (b) Robin Hood deciding to steal from Jones, etc. The difference in context necessarily means that what I have called the indirect consequences will make a significant and possibly decisive difference between the two decisions. Judge Tuck, like Robin Hood, will consider as one element the history of relations between Jones and Kramer, the harm caused by Jones to Kramer, and the probable effect on Jones and Kramer of an award of damages. But there are other important elements present in Judge Tuck's considerations and *not* in Robin Hood's. Among them are the effect in general on business practices of parties relevantly like Jones and Kramer, the effect on other jurisdictions and other kinds of cases, the effect on public perception of judges and confidence in the law, and so on.

Judges, like others who administer and determine the law, affect society in ways that private moral decision-makers cannot. Even a highly visible, well-publicized private moral decision has no direct effect on other decisions in similar cases. It is not binding on other decision-makers however much it may have the force of example. Most legal systems, however, follow a system of precedent whereby a decision, once made, is binding on similar cases (the doctrine of stare decisis). Consistency is not an inherent feature of the collection of private moral decisions by various decision-makers or even by a single one. Consistency is, on the other hand, required of a legal system; rules enforced on behavior in a particular system or jurisdiction must be mutually consistent. This does not mean that there are no lapses in consistency but that it is incumbent on judges to reconcile decisions with the body of existing law.

I shall assume without argument that there is a general benefit in having a system of some public rules which are highly predictable and applied consistently, rather than a system of ad hoc decisions without discernible guidelines for future behavior. In other words, I assume it is desirable to have a system of laws over and above a system of private moral decision and action.[46] The consequence for the role of judges is that they must regularly attend to two kinds of beneficial/harmful consequences of any decision. The first kind involves both direct and indirect benefit and harm to those who have relied on existing law in its consistency and stability. Whenever a judge contemplates a decision which changes the law, he is likely to impinge upon and damage the interests of those who have relied on standing law. There are many general doctrines in the law which are

46. Presumably an anarchist would disagree. Hobbesian arguments about the desirability of coerced order can be used to sustain the point.

designed to minimize this kind of dislocation. The *doctrine of precedent*, the doctrine that decisions should generally not be given ex post facto application (assuring that those affected by changes in law be in a position to be warned of the change), and the doctrine that a decision which represents a change be made on the narrowest available grounds are examples.[47] The generally beneficial consequences which are at stake when these doctrines are applied are reliance on settled law and consistency of treatment between parties to old and new cases.[48] The second group of beneficial and harmful consequences are the effects of a decision on the parties to the case, that is, direct and indirect benefits and harms to the petitioner and the defendant. In many cases, of course, a decision advances both groups of considerations at once; by adhering to settled law, a judge may benefit the parties to the case. In many hard cases, however, there is conflict; in these cases, considerations of justice to the parties to the case must be weighed against unsettling the law.[49]

The array of considerations of benefit and harm which a judge must consider is still more complicated than has been indicated. In every decision, a judge sets a rule of law to govern the case before him and relevantly similar cases. Among the benefits and harms which he affects and must weigh are not only (a) benefit and harm to parties at issue and (b) general considerations of predictability and reliance on settled law but also (c) benefit and harm to all subsequent parties likely to be affected directly or indirectly by the decision. Richard Wasserstrom, in his book, *The Judicial Decision*,[50] gives the example of a foreclosure proceeding by a wealthy mortagee against an improverished widow. From the perspective of Robin Hood, the widow's benefit seems to outweigh any possible benefit to the mortagee in allowing foreclosure. A judge, on the other hand, must consider the general effect of the practice which he is setting up by the rule of his decision. He must anticipate, for example, that mortgagees, knowing that enforcement of mortgage terms will be hampered in similar cases, will refuse to give such mortgages with the predictable consequence of great harm to the class of widows in similar straits.[51]

A judge will characteristically have to be more conservative than a

47. *See* A. Bickel, The Least Dangerous Branch (1962) and R. Wasserstrom, The Judicial Decision (1961).

48. R. Wasserstrom, *supra* note 47, at 66-69. Wasserstrom lists other purposes like certainty and efficiency, *id.* at 60-66, 72-74, but I find it unconvincing that certainty is a separate virtue, distinct from reliance, or that efficiency is an independent virtue at all. In other words, there may be some comfort in knowing where one stands vis-a-vis a stable but unjust law but no comfort at all in knowing it will be applied efficiently.

49. I am using "doing justice to the parties" as a synonym for "maximizing benefit among the parties." Thus, I assume the arguments of previous sections have been accepted. The dilemma I am describing is the main subject of Wasserstrom's book.

50. R. Wasserstrom, note 47 *supra*.

51. *Id.* at 141-45.

private moral agent since considerations of kind (b) will count against decisions to change existing law and thereby disturb expectations built upon existing law. Considerations of kind (c) will in many cases, but not all, also have the effect of standing in the way of change. For example, the effect of refusing to enforce the terms of the mortgage in Wasserstrom's example is to damage future widows. A judge will do so reluctantly and will have to find countervailing benefits. On the other hand, in a case in which corporations limit their warranty coverage on products so that consumers cannot recover for defects, a change in the law which extends greater protection to consumers by outlawing such limitations may be justified in terms of the interests of parties to the case *and* of others similarly situated.[52]

Wasserstrom's discussion of judicial decision-making is also concerned with the complexity of a judge's moral decisions. I shall clarify the theory I have been offering by comparing it with Wasserstrom's perceptive analysis.[53] Wasserstrom identifies two unsatisfactory procedures for judicial decision. The first is based only on considerations of stability and reliance. He calls it the model of precedent; it gives priority to those considerations which I have labelled kind (b). The second model is based on considerations of fairness and justice to the parties to the immediate case (considerations of kind (a)); Wasserstrom calls it the equity model. Wasserstrom concludes that a utilitarian committed to weighing benefits and harms in the *individual* decision will follow the second model. He argues that a modified two-level utilitarianism is needed to combine the virtues and avoid the defects of the two procedures: at the first level the judge consults established rules, and at the second he evaluates the rules in terms of their general effect in advancing the purposes of law.[54]

Wasserstrom's recommendation is ambiguous. Either he is proposing a procedure which will generate the same decisions as the straightforward utilitarianism advanced above because it will ultimately involve considerations of kinds (a), (b), and (c) or he means that *extra* deference should be paid to precedent considerations over and above whatever benefits are to be achieved by such deference. It is hard to see what can be said for the second position. By definition, no benefit overall can be gained by instructing a judge to follow such an injunction except on the theory, rejected above, that judges be *instructed* to follow a different theory from the sound procedure they are *expected* to follow.[55] It is easy to see where Wasser-

52. *See* Henningsen v. Bloomfield Motors, Inc., 32 N.J. 358, 161 A.2d 69 (1960), as discussed in R. Dworkin, *supra* note 1, at 23-24.

53. Wasserstrom's entire book is about the three models of judicial decision-making, the defects of the first two models, and the virtues of a "two-level" procedure.

54. R. Wasserstrom, supra note 47, at ch. 7.

55. *See* sections I and II *supra.*

strom goes wrong. He assumes that a utilitarian who simply considers the consequences of his decisions will be limited to considerations of kind (a), what he calls equity matters. But this is not so because the judge as utilitarian will be aware of his institutional role. As such, he will have to consider a range of benefits and harms beyond those which Wasserstrom calls equity matters, the range which includes (a), (b), and (c).

Therefore, a utilitarian theory of judging will not cause havoc because it will not involve ad hoc decisions made solely on the merits of claims by particular petitioners and effects on particular first parties. The misunderstanding that it would do so seems to be the basis of Wasserstrom's objection. A different criticism is suggested by Dworkin. It is that, whatever the merits of utilitarianism as a moral theory may be, it is not the job of judges to rectify misallocations of benefit and harm. This is the job of legislators. The job of judges, unlike that of legislators, is to apply laws and not determine policy.[56]

This argument has both a crude and a sophisticated form, although Dworkin offers only the latter. In its crude form, it is the theory we were able to reject above, namely that legislators have followed and should follow a strict decision procedure whereby correct answers are deduced from existing law. A sophisticated form is that it is not the job of judges to formulate and implement policies but only to safeguard principles of justice by making secure the rights of individuals. The distinction between policies and principles is at the heart of Dworkin's challenge to utilitarianism. A policy, for Dworkin, is a standard which sets out as a goal "an improvement in some economic, political, or social feature of the community."[57] A principle is a standard which sets forth "a requirement of justice or fairness or some other dimension of morality."[58]

> Principles are propositions that describe rights; policies are propositions that describe goals . . . . I shall distinguish rights from goals by fixing on the distributional character of claims about rights, and on the force of these claims, in political argument, against competing claims of a different distributional character . . . . A goal [unlike a right] is a nonindividuated political aim, that is, a state of affairs whose specification does not in this way call for any particular opportunity or resource or liberty for particular individials.[59]

I shall try to show that it is not obvious why this is offered as an alternative to utilitarianism[60] or why it would in practice generate different results. In the language of benefit and harm, we may say that the term

56. R. DWORKIN, *supra* note 1, at ch. 4.
57. *Id.* at 22.
58. *Id.*
59. *Id.* at 90-91.
60. *See id.* at vii.

"rights" identifies particular ways in which persons may be significantly harmed or benefited. These are harms and benefits so significant that (a) each person may think of them as conditions to which he is entitled and (b) only in exceptional cases can they outweigh other kinds of benefits and harms. Thus a utilitarian judge will give this class of benefits and harms a natural priority over others, not because they are expressed in principles rather than policies, but because they are weightier benefits.

One rebuttal to this argument is that the utilitarian practice does not guarantee that each person's rights will be protected while such a guarantee is an essential part of Dworkin's theory. While this seems true on its face, there is a fatal difficulty. According to Dworkin, the only guaranteed rights are institutional ones (as opposed to background rights) and concrete ones (as opposed to abstract rights).[61] What does this mean? Among other things, it means that whether one has a right which *must* be respected depends on an assessment of the particular situation in which the right is claimed. But this is no more of an assurance than the utilitarian was willing and able to give in saying that rights are labels for benefits of supervening weight prima facie but that they must be assessed in particular contexts against competing benefits of comparable weight.

A different argument for Dworkin's position is that the contrast between rights and other benefits is so great and so clear that the utilitarian notion of a weighing or balancing is a misrepresentation of the process of decision. But the contrast is least clear where it is most needed, in hard cases. To be sure, Dworkin is correct that in ordinary cases decision-makers ought not to prefer policy to principle since this seems to suggest that they may disregard rights of persons in effecting social or economic ends. But this is not a distinctive feature of the role of judges. It is the moral responsibility of all lawmakers. This is an abuse of proper decision-making no less when it is done by legislation than when it is done by a judge, and for the same reason. Thus, both legislators and judges must attend to principles as weightier considerations than policies, in general, because principles tend to reflect more important benefits. But when we attend to hard cases, the distinction between policies and principles does not seem more helpful than the instruction to look for the most important benefits. In hard cases, how do we know what is a principle and what a policy? That is, how do we know what rights persons have? Is universal education a policy or principle? Is it a right? Is providing minimal subsistence a policy or a principle? Do persons have a right not to be allowed to starve? Indeed, it makes sense to say that the protection of rights is itself a kind of policy, is a supervening policy for legislators *and* for judges and, further, that cases are often ripe for judicial decision when that supervening policy has

61. *Id.* at 93.

not been properly respected by legislators.

To summarize these criticisms, it is hard to see how Dworkin's theory achieves clarification of issues that the utilitarian theory fails to achieve. If the distinction between policies and principles (between goals and rights) is to have a special use, it must give us a special identifying mark for rights so that we can recognize when a right demands recognition, i.e., just when a utilitarian weighing is said to be preempted by a right. But what makes a case controversial and difficult is precisely that we are unsure whether a benefit (usually an "active benefit") is so important that it overrides others and decide cases. Is, as we have said, the benefit of being educated at public expense through the age of seventeen a right supported by principle or a societal goal described by a policy? Is there a right to be considered for law school admission without consideration of one's race, or is it simply one goal among others to treat persons in this way?[62]

We must not leave Dworkin without noting and borrowing an important insight about judicial decision-making.[63] A useful definition of a hard case is that it is a case in which existing case law and statutes, the existing system of judicial precedents, and other immediately relevant rules of decision, tend to generate or fit a result which offends the judge's intuitions about benefit and harm. The legal system, as it comes down to the judge, is not merely a system of rules or a system of results, i.e., a system of particular allocations of benefit. It is also a system of reasons. The development of a legal system can be traced through the reasons which judges have given for particular determinations, reasons which embody many conceptions of human nature and therefore of the ways persons are benefited and harmed. The judge's matured decision must be informed by this history. His own determination of benefit and harm must be formed by consulting the justifications offered by other judges in other relevant opinions. He cannot (as a matter of logic) accept all mutually inconsistent arguments and all points of view, but he must mold his own consistent standards around those standards which embody for him the values of the legal system itself. As Dworkin says, this task is described as an ideal and demands a judicial Hercules.[64]

62. Dworkin discusses this situation. R. DWORKIN, *supra* note 1, at 223-39. Dworkin repeatedly concedes that the distinction between rights and goals is an elusive one:

> It is hard to supply any definition that does not beg the question. It seems natural to say, for example, that freedom of speech is a right, not a goal, because citizens are entitled to that freedom as a matter of political morality, and that increased munitions manufacture is a goal, not a right, because it contributes to collective welfare, but no particular manufacturer is entitled to a government contract. This does not improve our understanding, however, because the concept of entitlement uses rather than explains the concept of a right. *Id.* at 90.

63. DWORKIN, *supra* note 1, at 105-30. The ensuing discussion in the text is my gloss upon Dworkin's story of a judicial Hercules and I am not at all certain he would accept my version of it.

64. *Id.*

It is important to stress the magnitude and nature of the task for two reasons. First, the utilitarian principle must not be taken to license the judge's disregard of the history of decisions and opinions in his legal system. It does quite the opposite, since that history is the repository of conceptions of benefit and harm in the face of which he forms his own conception. The second reason is that a redirection of the law by a decision in a hard case is one which must be justified by appeal to reasons which meet commonly shared criteria of relevance, criteria developed and illustrated in that history. There is all the difference there could be between saying correctly that these standards are incumbent on a judge and saying that he is narrowly bound by past decisions.

VI. THE USES OF A THEORY OF DECISION

A theory which explains the nature of standards of decision-making, particularly moral standards, is not necessarily a theory which dissolves dilemmas. It may map the rough terrain which a decision-maker must cross but it does not make the terrain smooth. It would be fine, we might have thought, for philosophers of law to make hard cases easy — or at least easier, to tell us how to find right answers. Perhaps they can do so by telling us that judges exhaust relevant law at a certain point and have license beyond that point. Perhaps, on the other hand, they can tell us where to find natural law or how to identify those rights which decide cases and are formulated in principles of law.[65]

Utilitarianism not only disappoints all these expectations but explains why they must be disappointed. A decision about benefit and harm is a decision based on experience and ideally on wisdom, not a decision based on rules or license. A theory about decision cannot impart the stuff of experience, the appreciation of benefit and harm, any more than a philosophical theory about the nature of knowledge can impart knowledge about physics or history. Ironically (with some historical justification), utilitarianism is frequently criticized for having just such ambitions. We have seen that some forms of utilitarianism are vulnerable on those grounds.

The model of decision-making presented here allows us to give a synoptic account of well-known debates on constitutional theory. For example, such writers as Alexander Bickel and Felix Frankfurter, on one hand, and so-called judicial activists,[66] on the other, debate whether it is generally wise for judges to intervene when controversial rights seem to be at issue

---

65. Dworkin does not claim to make hard cases easy in this way. *See* note 61 *supra*.

66. Compare, in this regard, A. BICKEL, note 47 *supra*, with any of several sympathetic discussions of the practices of the Warren Court or with the judicial opinions of William O. Douglas and Hugo Black.

and when at the same time judicial vindication of such rights would significantly alter processes of social change. Bickel, following Frankfurter, commends what he calls the "passive virtues."[67] He means that courts should be reluctant to take upon themselves the responsibility for changing social practices in unforeseeable ways. He adds that the framers of the Constitution anticipated such risks.[68] One way of representing such debates (which the proponents may or may not find congenial) is to say that they are about what weight, as a general matter, is to be assigned to the benefits associated with the precedent model. Thcy involve disagreement about the indirect or secondary effects of judicial activism.[69]

It is incorrect to think that self-conscious awareness of utilitarianism as a theory of decision is useless in such debates and, a fortiori, in resolving hard cases. Its use is elusive and indirect. It makes the discussant or judge aware of the standards of debate and the criteria of evidence. It makes explicit the process of fitting a decision within a general and publicly defensible theory of benefit and therefore of human nature.

67. A. BICKEL, *supra* note 47, at 200.

68. *See id.* at 200-07.

69. A secondary effect is a kind of indirect effect on the institutions of law and society.

[5]
The Epistemology of Judging: Wittgenstein and Deliberative Practices

1. Introduction

Wittgenstein seeks to inoculate us against the lure of metaphors.[1] The conundrums of philosophy are, he implies, often the misbegotten offspring of abused metaphors. How many rooms are needed to house the "furniture of our mind"? With what key do others gain access to my "private" thoughts and feelings?[2]

Jurisprudence has its own syllabus of philosophical puzzles. One of the hardiest is the issue of judicial license and judicial standards. This issue has special fascination for American legal theorists because of the pivotal role played by the Supreme Court in exercising the power of judicial review by interpreting the Constitution.[3] American theorists have taken for granted,[4] and other theorists have seemed to acquiesce in this assumption,[5] that to understand the nature of law is to understand how appellate judges find and/or make law.[6]

An early version of this paper was prepared for the Seminar in Legal Philosophy, held at the University of Western Ontario in August 1989. I wish to thank the participants, and especially Jules Coleman, Dennis Patterson, and Donald Regan, for their helpful comments.

1. L. Wittgenstein, *Philosophical Investigations*, G. Anscombe, trans., (New York: Macmillan, 1968), 3d ed., cf. Part I, section 115: "A *picture* held us captive. And we could not get outside it, for it lay in our language and language seemed to repeat it to us inexorably." and Part I, section 193: "The machine as symbolizing its action: the action of a machine—I might say at first—seems to be there in it from the start. What does that mean?—If we know the machine, everything else, that is its movement, seems to be already completely determined."
2. Wittgenstein's own examples of abused metaphors are much richer and more layered. Consider his observation about the metaphor of expression: "Misleading parallel: the expression of pain is a cry—the expression of thought, a proposition.

   As if the purpose of the proposition were to convey to one person how it is with another; only, so to speak, in his thinking part and not in his stomach." (*Philosophical Investigations, supra* n. 1, Part I, section 317.)

   Consider also the following: "One might also say: Surely the owner of the visual room would have to be the same kind of thing as it is; but he is not to be found in it, and there is no outside." (*Philosophical Investigations, supra* n. 1, Part I, section 399.)
3. H.L.A. Hart remarks on this preoccupation and seeks to explain it in "American Jurisprudence through English Eyes" in *Essays in Jurisprudence and Philosophy* (Oxford: Clarendon Press, 1983).
4. The work of Ronald Dworkin best illustrates this central preoccupation with the question of how judges find law as the key to the understanding of the concept of law. This position was first sketched in "The Model of Rules I and II" in *Taking Rights Seriously* (Cambridge: Harvard Univ. Press, 1978), and remains the methodological basis of Dworkin's work in *Law's Empire* (Cambridge: Harvard Univ. Press, 1986).
5. In recent jurisprudence, the task of analyzing law is treated as the task of analyzing legal reasoning, and the main "official" reservoir of legal reasoning is judicial opinions. This was not the case for such earlier jurisprudential theorists as John Austin and Hans Kelsen, for whom the analysis of law was more or less the analysis of statutes. Thus, such British theorists as Neil MacCormick give as much centrality to judicial reasoning as does any American theorist. On the other hand, Joseph Raz continues in the older tradition that does not give precedence to judicial opinions over statutes as the main resource for speculation about the nature of law. See N. MacCormick, *Legal Reasoning and Legal Theory* (Oxford: Clarendon Press, 1978), and J. Raz, *The Concept of a Legal System* (Oxford: Clarendon Press, 1970).
6. Throughout this article, my references to judicial reasoning are intended to characterize appellate decisions. Even more restrictively, I am concerned largely with constitutional interpretation at the appellate level. I am prepared to generalize my description of "deliberate practices" to judicial decision-making on a broader scale, but do not do so in this article.

Judicial review and the power of judges receive scrutiny periodically. The last fifteen years have been one such period, distinguished by a splendid outpouring of articles and books.[7] Nonetheless, the issue remains largely unclarified notwithstanding the best efforts of inventive writers. Indeed, the most recent writings represent a scaling back of ambitions, in effect a tacit admission of failure.[8]

One Wittgensteinian explanation of such cycles in philosophy is that they involve the dogged pursuit of a metaphor. I shall argue that in the recent debates over constitutional interpretation the metaphor at issue has been the metaphor of a game, with its implications that judging is a rule-governed activity and judges are like the players of games.

In one respect this metaphor is special because it is the Wittgensteinian metaphor par excellence, the metaphor Wittgenstein himself is taken to have perpetrated.[9] Many writers take as one of Wittgenstein's signal contributions to philosophy the suggestion that discourse is to be understood on the model of "language games".[10] This suggestion is, as I shall argue, doubly misleading because Wittgenstein is not merely concerned with language and because his concern with discourse is not bounded by the metaphor of games.[11] In examining the metaphor of games, therefore, I shall be considering its merits as a general metaphor for discourse, as a representation of what concerns Wittgenstein himself, *and* as a metaphor for legal discourse, specifically judicial interpretation.

The trajectory of the debates over constitutional interpretation in the last fifteen years is relatively clear. The concern in this round of the perennial

7. Any attempt to list the main contributors to this movement risks offending by omission—and any adequate list would be formidably long. Even a partial and inadequate list would have to include Paul Brest, Ronald Dworkin, John Hart Ely, Owen Fiss, Stanley Fish, Thomas Grey, Richard Kay, Sanford Levinson, Michael Perry, Jefferson Powell, Lawrence Tribe, and Mark Tushnet.

8. The main argument of Mark Tushnet's recent *Red White and Blue* (Cambridge, Mass: Harvard Univ. Press, 1988) is that all attempts to formulate a standard for constitutional interpretation on the basis of "grand theory" have self-destructed and they have done so because they are grounded on the untenable assumptions of liberalism. The recent work of Michael Perry (*Morality Politics and Law* (New York: Oxford Univ. Press, 1988)) and Sanford Levinson (*Constitutional Faith* (Princeton, N.J.: Princeton Univ. Press, 1988)) is not so much a frontal attempt to develop criteria for constitutional interpretation as an oblique investigation of the nuances and implications of the idea of constitutionalism.

9. The term "game" does double duty in Wittgenstein's *Philosophical Investigations* and in his other works. The use of the word "game" (*Spiel*) is itself an example of a "language-game" (*Sprachspiel*). Wittgenstein uses it to demonstrate that using language (participating in the "language-game") is not a matter of following rules, in particular not a matter of following rules that specify the necessary or sufficient conditions for using particular words correctly, not in other words a matter of understanding the "essence" of, e.g., a game. Compare *Philosophical Investigations, supra* n. 1, part I, section 65: "For someone might object against me: 'You take the easy way out! You talk about all sorts of language-games, but have nowhere said what the essence of a language-game, and hence of language, is: what is common to all these activities, and what makes them into language or parts of language. . . .'
And this is true.—Instead of producing something common to all that we call language, I am saying that these phenomena have no thing in common which makes us use the same word for all,—but that they are *related* to one another in many different ways."

10. Wittgenstein himself uses the term (*Sprachspiel*) frequently in *Philosophical Investigations* and elsewhere but, as I argue below (text at n. 48), his own examples and questions (a) invite generalization to non-linguistic practices and (b) reject unequivocally the paradigmatic use of any particular conception of a game.

11. It cannot be emphasized too strongly that I am not referring to Wittgenstein's own use of the word "game" (*Spiel*) but to its use by those who see the essence of a game as a matter of acting in conformity with shared and mutually identifiable rules and sharing a conception of the point or goal to be achieved through participation. Wittgenstein argues persuasively against such essentialism; *supra* n. 9 and n. 48 below. Much post-Wittgensteinian philosophy, including contemporary jurisprudence, rests heavily on such essentialist assumptions.

debate, as in previous rounds,[12] is fear of judicial power and license. The first step in framing the issue is to note the failure of any purely formalistic account of decision-making.[13] To say that judges apply law cannot mean that they do so deductively or by appeal to a straightforward algorithm. Hard cases arise, and hard cases are by definition ones in which both outcomes and methods of resolution are endlessly controversial. If this is so, what is the boundary of judicial power? If judges may choose among methods of resolution that are their own invention, is their power to remake law without limit?[14]

The second step is to meet the challenge of describing standards and techniques of judicial interpretation. The task is simultaneously descriptive and normative. A theorist claims to make explicit the techniques that are generally implicit in the process of judicial interpretation.[15] But the theorist also claims thereby to be positing an ideal that is implicit in the role, an ideal that judges may or may not realize. The task is both hortatory and critical. The theorist speaks to judges in the hope of illuminating what they do and to critics of the judicial process in the hope of sharpening the critics' tools.

Implicit in the theorist's understanding of her task is the assumption that only one technique of interpretation is the correct way of proceeding, that only one set of rules characterizes judicial interpretation. To think otherwise, to concede that several acceptable techniques may coincide, is to readmit indeterminacy and license. If judges have the capacity to choose among several acceptable ways of proceeding, then the fear of license is well grounded and the critic is disarmed. The fear is not so much that *anything goes* in judicial interpretation, not that judges may appropriately consult astrological charts or their bias in favor of diminutive plaintiffs in making decisions.[16] The fear is rather that within the range of defensible strategies, judges may effect and justify almost any outcome.

The third step, then, is to defend a particular strategy as the unique strategy that informs and constrains judicial interpretation. The theorist must argue first that the strategy is practicable, that it can in fact be carried out, and that it determines solutions to problems.[17] The theorist must also argue that the

12. The trajectory of this phenomenon seems to have a twenty-five year or so cycle. Legal realism in the late 1920's and early 1930's revolutionized thinking about judicial decision-making. See L. Kalman, *Legal Realism at Yale, 1927-1960* (Chapel Hill: Univ. of North Carolina Press, 1986). In the late 1950's, the writings of Alexander Bickel and Herbert Wechsler, among others, marked another significant revival of interest.

13. The most influential critique of formalism in recent jurisprudence has been that of H. L. A. Hart, *The Concept of Law* (Oxford: Clarendon Press, 1961), chapter vii. An interesting recent example of the revival of formalism is E. Weinrib, "Legal Formality: On the Immanent Rationality of Law" (1988), 97 *Yale L. J.* 949.

14. The first half, chapters 1 through 5, of Tushnet, *Red White and Blue*, *supra*, n. 8, is a critique of formalist and anti-formalist theories of judicial decision-making. (Tushnet uses the term "formalism" more broadly than I do here or than Weinrib does, see n. 13. Formalism, for Hart and Weinrib, characterizes decision-making by recourse to the "internal logic" of legal propositions. Formalism, for Tushnet, refers to any theoretical attempt to prescribe standards for decision-making.)

15. For a discussion of the claim that this is, as a general matter, the task of philosophy, see A. Danto, *What Philosophy Is: A Guide to the Elements* (London: Cambridge Univ. Press, 1968); R. Rorty, *The Linguistic Turn* (Chicago: Univ. of Chicago Press, ed. 1967), introduction.

16. There is an important distinction here between the factors that affect judicial decisions and the reasons that are used by judges to justify opinions. Legal realism was concerned as much with the former as with the latter. The contemporary debate is primarily about the latter, about what counts as justification in "official" judicial reasoning. The term "reasoning" is, of course, ambiguous, referring both to the process of discovery (or of arriving at an opinion) and the process of justification.

17. To say that a standard *determines* a result is not to say that a particular result follows deductively from

strategy yields correct, or at least sound, answers.

This is not to say that all theorists share optimism about defining and defending a strategy of judicial interpretation. Counterpoised against such optimists are theorists who argue that the quest for a unique constraining strategy of judicial interpretation is doomed, and that the project itself is mired in contradiction.[18]

A diagnosis of the debate must begin with two observations. First, the very conception of the theoretical project is grounded on the metaphor of games. If we are to understand judges as constrained, we must understand the rules by which they must be playing. Such rules are both descriptive and normative.[19] In the absence of such rules, judges must be seen as unconstrained.

By the same token, judges' attempts to justify favored outcomes by writing opinions makes sense if they are playing by the same rules. In other words, they must recognize reasons as relevant or irrelevant to decisions in the same way, must have the same methods for assigning weight to relevant reasons, and so forth. Unless this is so, unless they are playing the same game by the same rules, the process of justification in opinion writing is empty rhetoric. The task of the theorist, then, is to identify the rules of the game whereby judicial interpretation, and its explication in opinion writing, takes place—so that the true constraints of the process can be made explicit, so that correct decisions and techniques can be identified, and so that deviants can be chastised and corrected.

The second preliminary observation is that this account of the theoretical task seems wildly at odds with judicial practice, now and in any foreseeable future. The untheoretical observer's view is that judges do and will continue to decide cases in different ways. They will continue to write justificatory opinions in which they genuinely speak to each other but with different commitments about what is relevant and with little hope that, over time, diversity will turn into consensus.

From the point of view of the theorist, the situation is paradoxical. A player of chess plays with a player of Chinese checkers, and they in turn play with

---

the standard or that application of the standard dictates one particular result in a particular case. Analogously, the rules of a game like chess determine the course of play but allow for many possible different moves. They constrain and order the results but allow for a range of alternatives.

With regard to judicial reasoning, the adoption of a standard has two consequences. First, it mandates the kinds of reasons that can be given in justification of particular results. Second, in doing the former, it limits the range of results that may be reached.

18. As indicated above, this is largely the argument of the first part of Tushnet, *Red White and Blue*. See also other writers in the Critical Legal Studies movement, especially R. Unger, *The Critical Legal Studies Movement* (Cambridge, Mass.: Harvard Univ. Press, 1986), and D. Kennedy, "The Structure of Blackstone's Commentaries" (1979), 28 *Buffalo L. R.* 205. Owen Fiss labels the practitioners of critical legal studies "nihilists" and defends the label in "The Death of Law?" (1986), 72 *Cornell L. R.* 1.

19. The rules of many activities are both descriptive and normative. The rules of driving or swimming characterize the activity and are implicated in any description. At the same time, they also characterize a standard of performance. One can carry out the rules in a marginal or an exemplary way, without or with skill and expertise.

Two qualifications. (a) To say there are rules for driving or swimming is not to prejudge whether there is a *single* way to carry out the activity or many alternative ways. Indeed the meaningfulness of that question may depend on the level of generality at which the rules are posed.

(b) The rules of games such as chess and baseball are in part purely descriptive. The rule that a team in baseball retires after three players are "out" is hard to construe as normative, i.e. as a basis for evaluating better or worse games.

a third who is playing bridge. Each justifies her moves by appealing to her particular game. And they persist. And yet they understand each other. How can this be so?

In Part 2 of this paper I shall examine the metaphor of games as a general philosophical strategy for analyzing discourse and human understanding. I shall look at some misapplications of the idea that the Wittgenstinian [author's preferred spelling, eds.] notion of a practice can best be understood as a "language game". I shall describe what I call "deliberative practices" to clarify the ways in which practices are not illuminated by the theoretical paradigm of a game.

Part 3 describes ways in which the metaphor of games gives a distorted view of judicial interpretation and it concludes that judicial interpretation is a paradigmatic case of a deliberative practice. Part 4 is a critique of the aims of recent theory about judicial, and particularly constitutional, interpretation insofar as the agenda of such theorists rests implicitly on the metaphor of games. My conclusion draws more general lessons for philosophical method in legal theory.

2. Games and Practices

a. Wittgenstein and Practices

The concept of a practice is at once among the most useful and most disputed tools of twentieth-century philosophy.[20] Many philosophers trace their use of it to Wittgenstein, and the Wittgenstinian concept, as a philosophical tool, is often assimilated to that of a "language game". After explaining the concept in Wittgenstein, I shall argue that, used in a certain way, the notion of a language game is doubly misleading.

An intuitive look at practices may begin with such nonlinguistic activities as driving or swimming. In each case, persons acquire skills or ways of proceeding that become habitual and unreflective. When we call such skills "second nature", we mean that, though they are socially and culturally acquired, such ways of proceeding become as much a part of us as our genetic endowment.

A habitual repertoire has distinctive features. Each technique involves ways of perceiving, feeling, and acting. A good driver makes judgments about road conditions and the disposition of other drivers, apprehends dangers, and acts accordingly. What she does unreflectingly can, however, be made conscious. Ordinarily the need to do so will not arise.[21]

20. Philosophers who have discussed Wittgenstein's use of the concept most illuminatingly are P. Hacker, *Insight and Illusion* (Oxford: Clarendon Press, 1972), S. Kripke, *Wittgenstein on Rules and Private Language* (Oxford: Basil Blackwell, 1982), S. Hilmy, *The Later Wittgenstein* (Oxford: Basil Blackwell, 1987), and R. Rorty, *Philosophy and the Mirror of Nature* (Princeton, N.J.: Princeton Univ. Press, 1979). The implications of the notion of a practice, and of the concomitant distinction between being inside and outside a practice, go far beyond the realm of Wittgenstein studies and are explored in contemporary philosophical movements from hermeneutics to neo-Kantianism and neo-Hegelianism. See, for example, H-G. Gadamer, *Truth and Method*, G. Baden and J. Cumming trans., (New York: Continuum, 1975) and *Hegel's Dialectic* (New Haven: Yale Univ. Press, 1976), Hoy, *The Critical Circle* (Berkeley: Univ. of California Press, 1978), G. Shapiro and A. Sica, *Hermeneutics: Questions and Prospects* (Amherst: Univ. of Mass Press, 1984), and R. Geuss, *The Idea of a Critical Theory* (Cambridge: Cambridge Univ. Press, 1981).

21. The need to do so will arise if one is instructing someone else or if one has to relearn the activity after, for example, an injury.

40

A characterization of what is involved in having such a skill, in being a good driver, will be at once descriptive and normative. The characteristics of a driver (in general) are distinguished only in degree from the characteristics of a good driver. To be able to identify driving is also to be able to detect good driving. Both thresholds are inherently vague. No clear and simple criterion distinguishes those who cannot drive from those who do so very badly. Similarly, not everyone will agree on the marks of very good driving. But the range of understandable disagreement is small.[22]

Some of our practices are primarily communicative (as driving obviously is not). And some of our communicative practices, by far the most important ones, are linguistic.[23] Wittgenstein attends to such aspects of language as color-descriptions and expressions of pain. Just as driving is a skill that individuals acquire because a public practice, a shared activity, already exists, so too perceptions of color and distinctions among kinds of pain manifest the acquired skills of those who have been initiated into certain practices. Persons identify colors and pains to the extent that a place exists for the recognition of color and the expression of pain in the relevant practices of a culture.[24]

Some philosophers have seen this suggestion as revolutionary and counter-intuitive. The philosophical assumption of most empiricists has been that the domain of private experience is fully configured and that the public arena of language is merely a set of conventions and labels attached to the distinct elements of private experience.[25] But Wittgenstein challenges this. He asks us to reflect on what it could be like to experience a color for which a place was not already prepared in the experiential realm shared with others.[26]

b. Deliberative Practices

These considerations about practices in general and about simple linguistic practices have implications for more complex practices that involve deliberation. I shall explain the ways in which deliberation about, say, judicial

22. This means merely that one can anticipate the range of variation in criteria for driving—and one can anticipate the kinds of criteria that simply make no sense (unless an exceptional context is created). One person may tend to favor careful drivers who obey speed limits, while another may favor accident avoidance even at excessive speed. But it would be hard to understand "crashing into as many red cars as possible" as a standard for good driving (unless the act is part of a contest, etc.).

23. Non-linguistic ones are waving and pointing. See Wittgenstein, *Philosophical Investigations, supra*, n. 1, part I, section 454.

24. In *Philosophical Investigations, supra* n. 1, Wittgenstein discusses color in Part I, sections 273 through 278. Consider, for example, section 275:

> Look at the blue of the sky and say to yourself "How blue the sky is!"—When you do it spontaneously—without philosophical intentions—the idea never crosses your mind that this impression of colour belongs only to you. . . .

See also Wittgenstein, *Remarks on Colour*, L.L. McAlister trans. (Oxford: Basil Blackwell, 1977). Wittgenstein's extensive discussion of pain in *Philosophical Investigations* is to be found in Part I at sections 283 to 304, 310 to 317, 350 to 351, 384, and 391 through 398. Consider section 384: "You learned the *concept* 'pain' when you learned language."

25. In the history of British empiricism, John Locke held a distinctive theory along these lines. See *An Essay on Human Understanding* (Oxford: Clarendon Press,1894). In the twentieth century, Bertrand Russell and A. J. Ayer clung to many of the traditional tenets of British empiricism.

26. *Philosophical Investigations, supra* n. 1, Part I, section 381: How do I know that this colour is red?—It would be an answer to say, "I have learnt English."

Two qualifications are relevant. (a) An individual may experience colors that have no *simple* name. One may say that one wants "a slightly pinkish shade of pale ochre" on one's wall. But the color one envisions is a color that one imagines others capable of envisioning. (b) The communal color language may change over time. Words like "indigo" and "cerise" may fall in and out of ordinary use.

decisions is more complex than deliberation about color or pain.

All practices allow the possibility, indeed the inevitability, of idiosyncracy within shared ways of proceeding. Even if it is true that persons have a shared conception of the nature of driving, each driver also has a personal style. Even good drivers differ in style. Each of us has a distinctive way of using color language. I may tend not to discriminate among various shades of red; a friend may tend to distinguish sharply between scarlet and crimson; another friend may use these two terms in a distinctively different way from the first friend.[27]

In deliberative activities this possibility of diversity within shared, and mutually understood, ways of proceeding is especially significant. A deliberative practice involves discourse with the shared purpose of forming and defending judgments. Examples of deliberative practices are esthetic debate, moral reasoning, historical discourse, and judicial decision-making. The subject may be the beauty of an object, or whether an action is right, or whether an event is a turning point in history, or whether a plaintiff has a right to a favorable judgment. All such debates have certain features in common. All refer to widely shared activities and/or institutions in civilized societies. All are realms of discourse that seem almost indispensable in the transactions of civilized persons. In all these domains, the main debates extend over the history of civilization and seem intractable.[28]

It is equally important to see what draws participants together as to see what separates them.[29] Even when they disagree, they recognize the argumentative strategies of others. They share a sense of what reasons are relevant to the common discourse. Discussing beauty, they may consider symmetry and asymmetry, balance and imbalance, representational aspects of the object, context, purpose. They will not consider relevant whether the artist had long or short life, whether her name began with a vowel or consonant, or whether the object or performance is privately or publicly financed. These observations may seem trivial, but only because they are so familiar, so much a part of what we do. They are "second nature". Each participant can anticipate[30] the moves that others will make. The practice consists in the recognition of a family of reasoning strategies that admit a spectrum of judgments.

But it is not the case that anything counts. To say that any move is permissible is to say that no move is permissible. Just as in driving or in identifying colors, the publicly shared understanding of what moves are

27. It is important that the question which of the three of us is *correct* in his use of color terms may be a meaningless question. All three ways of speaking may be appropriate in different contexts and there may be no general criteria, relevant to all contexts, for distinguishing scarlet from crimson. When and where they are needed, new conventions will be invented.

28. This point is true whether one is speaking of individuals, and saying that these subjects have concerned persons in all cultures and been richly debated over the course of history, or speaking of so-called schools of thought, and saying that distinctive points of view about these issues (objectivism vs. subjectivism, realism vs. idealism, relativism vs. absolutism) have recurred insistently over the history of human speculation.

29. For an extended discussion of this point see T. Morawetz, *Wittgenstein and Knowledge: The Importance of On Certainty* (Amherst: Univ. of Mass. Press, 1978).

30. That is to say, one can anticipate a range of intelligible moves and responses. If a response is wholly unexpected and seems unintelligible or nonsensical, one can construct the kinds of conversational bridges that would make it intelligible. Of course, conversations sometimes take surprising turns within the bounds of these constraints.

comprehensible ways of proceeding is what makes the practice possible.

If participants are able to discuss beauty, justice, and historical influence because they have learned what is relevant to such discourse, how is it that they do not all act the same, all reaching the same conclusions in the same way? In simpler practices, color identification for example, differences among individuals are usually treated as *de minimis*. In general, it is neither of philosophical nor practical interest to argue at length over whether a color sample is really midnight blue or indigo. This is another way of saying that color language is not really a deliberative practice.

Deliberative practices are characterized both by what binds participants together and what distinguishes them. No two persons have had the same history or the same characteristics. Some are more credulous than others, more perceptive, more doubtful, more hesitant. Much more importantly, each will have a characteristic way of reasoning that cuts across the several deliberative practices in which she participates and represents an interpretive orientation to the world, a way of sorting out the phenomena of experience and making sense of them.

This needs explanation. I shall first look at examples drawn from deliberative practices other than legal reasoning. In section 3, I shall look at judicial interpretation directly.

Consider first debates about beauty. How diverse may be the reasons given to justify and explain esthetic judgments? What kinds of different strategies may participants in the practice expect to meet? One person may offer psychological grounds for attributing beauty. Another may refer to inherent properties of the object itself. Yet another may look to the ways in which the object expresses the intentions of the artist, and/or the quality of those intentions. A fourth may appeal to the social and political role of the object as a basis for esthetic merit.[31]

A debate among such participants is complicated even further by the fact that these several strategies of reasoning are not independent of each other. Each participant will to some extent take account of the reasons offered by others by finding a place for them within her own favored strategy.[32] One may explain psychological response as a manifestation of inherent features of the object, while another may say that accounts of inherent features are reducible to psychological factors. Thus, a part of each participant's way of proceeding will be a strategy for incorporating or dismissing the favored strategies of others. And each in turn will recognize and anticipate such moves as part of the ongoing practice.[33]

Two observations. The diverse strategies that make up a deliberative practice compete insofar as there is no natural order of precedence among cate-

31. An anthology of historical approaches is A. Hofstadter and R. Kuhns, *Philosophies of Art and Beauty* (New York: Modern Library, 1964). A collection of recent diverse writings is C. Harrison and F. Orton, *Modernism, Criticism, Realism* (San Francisco: Harper and Row, 1984).

32. By using the word "strategy" for what others may call (and for what I call elsewhere) a "way of proceeding" and "way of reasoning", I do not imply that these strategies serve ulterior aims or that they involve strategic planning.

33. Compare *Philosophical Investigations*, *supra*, n. 1, Part I, section 241: "'So you are saying that human agreement decides what is true and what is false?'—It is what human beings *say* that is true and false; and they agree in the *language* they use. That is not agreement in opinions but in form of life."

gories of facts, among categories of reasons and justifications. For example, psychological explanations are not inherently more basic than political and economic explanations, nor is the reverse true. Appeals to the inherent features of a work of art are neither more nor less basic a mode of justification (in esthetic reasoning) than appeals to the creator's intentions.[34] In defending one's own judgment in a particular case, one is also defending one's *style* of judgment, one's way of ordering the data of experience to give some kinds precedence. The attempt to convince others is not only an attempt to make them agree with one's own conclusions but also to bring them around to deploying reasons in the same way.[35]

The second observation is that the persuasive attempts of each participant are not, as one might think, doomed.[36] To say that each participant has a particular way of proceeding in reasoning is not to say that he is condemned to repeat the same moves forever. Individual participants differ not only in judgments and in ways of reaching those judgments, but also in their susceptibility to persuasion, to considering and adopting other points of view and other strategies. Similarly, the practice itself, as a collection of strategies mutually recognized by participants, evolves. In retrospect[37] a theorist finds that some strategies gain currency while others go into temporary or permanent eclipse.[38]

Other deliberative practices can be analyzed similarly. One historian will use the influence of ideas as the *explanans* that unlocks historical change, another will look to economic motives and events, while still another will stress the charismatic influence of leaders.[39] In moral discourse, some theorists will see altruistic utilitarianism as offering the most coherent account of reasons relevant to moral judgment, another will see psychologistic or hedonistic utilitarianism as basic, while another will say that moral reasoning is essentially deontological.[40]

34. Reductionism was more widely discussed in the philosophy of science and of social science a generation ago that it is today. Compare E. Nagel, *The Structure of Science* (New York: Harcourt and Bruce, 1961) with H. Brown, *Perception, Theory and Commitment* (New York: Columbia Univ. Press, 1979).

35. This fact, I would argue, is what fuels debate within deliberative practices. Participants manifest and seek to validate their ways of thinking through participation. (This is a truism rather than a claim for empirical psychology.)

36. Wittgenstein is sometimes falsely charged with conservatism. The suggestion is that innovation and change are ruled out by a practice-based account of experience because individuals can only learn and do what others have done before them. This shows a misunderstanding of Wittgenstein and of practices. Part of what one learns in acquiring a practice is the constraints within which creativity and innovation are possible. See relevant discussion in D. Pole, *The Later Philosophy of Wittgenstein* (London: Athlone Press, 1958) and D. Bloor, *Wittgenstein: A Social Theory of Knowledge* (New York: Columbia Univ. Press, 1983), at pp. 160-173.

37. Hegel's familiar reference to the owl of Minerva implies that shifts in collective ways of thinking can only be appreciated and understood retrospectively. See G. Hegel, *The Philosophy of Right*, Knox trans. (Oxford: Clarendon Press, 1942), preface: "The owl of Minerva spreads its wings only with the falling of the Dusk." Thomas Kuhn's innovative work on scientific revolutions has the same implication. The nature and significance of a scientific revolution can only be appreciated after it has occurred and after a new way of thinking has came to inhabit "normal science". See below at n. 67.

Arguably, certain political and esthetic manifestoes are self-conscious attempts to alter prevailing practices. They are Janus-faced. Their contemporaneous intelligibility depends on their relationship to existing practices but they are prospective attempts to transform those very practices. Consider for example the esthetic manifestoes of Kandinsky, Apollinaire, Mondrian, and the futurists.

38. Examples in politics are the hierarchic presuppositions of feudalism and of Renaissance statecraft.

39. These ways of looking at history are attributable, respectively, to Max Weber, Friedrich Engels, and Thomas Carlisle (and their followers).

40. The philosophers most closely identified with these positions are, respectively, John Stuart Mill,

44

c. On Language Games

Wittgenstein does not give an account of deliberative practices. His examples of practices are simpler: discourse about color, communicative expressions of pain, and so on.[41] Nonetheless, certain themes of his account of knowledge, certainty and judgment seem fundamental to any general account of discourse. An individual's ways of reasoning and understanding, and arguing and judging, are spontaneous ways of organizing experience that reflect a shared practice. Reasoning and understanding are parts of a learned repertoire as much as are swimming and driving. Every practice is as simple and as complicated as it needs to be to serve as a tool for organizing experience and proceeding through it. If we have not invented a sharp distinction between crimson and scarlet, the reason is that we do not ordinarily need it. If we operate with different but related strategies in reaching legal decisions as judges, then an account of the practice must recognize and respect the diversity and relatedness of those strategies. Philosophy, Wittgenstein tells us, leaves everything as it is.[42]

The term "language game" is doubly misleading. The analogy of driving and swimming demonstrates that some practices are non-linguistic. Practices that *do* involve language are not exclusively linguistic. Necessarily, the experiences and expectations of color identification presuppose that there are linguistic conventions through which we have been taught and by which we communicate. But the skill of color recognition is no more reducible to skill in using words like "yellow" than the skills of driving are reducible to the skill of using terms like "stop" and "accelerate".

The same goes for deliberative practices. The patterns of reasoning involved in forming and justifying judgments are patterns expressed in language and described through language. But the intellectual strategy that leads someone to explain social and economic phenomena by reducing them to patterns of individual psychology is not adequately described by rules that instruct one in the use of words.[43] By focusing on the idea that practices are made up of shared linguistic rules, some followers of Wittgenstein imply that on-going practices are more homogeneous than they really are.[44] It is important to remember how diverse are the variant strategies of historians, or moralists, or judges that are expressed in the same shared lexicon.

Just as deliberative practices are not, or not merely or primarily, activities of language, so too they are not very much like games. Some similarities are obvious and explain the seductiveness of the metaphor. One must be initiated

---

Thomas Hobbes, and Immanuel Kant. Each has influenced ethical theorists through subsequent generations. In my references to ethical theory I am assuming that the positions of various theories bridge questions of metaethics and questions of normative ethics. In other words, theorists reach what John Rawls calls "reflective equilibrium" with regard to reconciling metaethical commitments and substantive ethical judgments. See Rawls, *A Theory of Justice* (Cambridge: Harvard Univ. Press, 1971), at 20.

41. *Supra*, nn. 26 and 27.

42. *Philosophical Investigations,supra* n. 1, Part I, section 124. "Philosophy may in no way interfere with the actual use of language; it can in the end only describe it.
For it cannot give it any foundation either.
It leaves everything as it is."

43. See I. Hacking, *Why Does Language Matter to Philosophy?* (Cambridge: Cambridge Univ. Press, 1975), chapters 11-13.

44. See articles in S. Holtzman and C. Leich, *Wittgenstein: To Follow a Rule* (London: Routledge and Kegan Paul, 1981).

through a period of learning. Once one has become a participant, one can make appropriate or correct moves and one can make mistakes.[45] As in games,[46] some rules are constitutive rather than regulative. This means that a participant gains a new way of looking at a domain of experience that is constituted by the concepts and conceptual relationships she has learned. For example, thinking and talking about strikes and runs is meaningless outside the domain of baseball. To learn the rules of baseball is to enter a new domain of experience. Similarly, to learn the concept of a tort or a privacy right is not merely to acquire a new way of thinking about the world; the experienced world itself acquires new characteristics. The idea of a tort only belongs in a world governed by law.[47]

Practices are not games. Games have beginnings and ends. Usually they proceed by discrete moves, rounds, or turns. Games[48] are at bottom reducible to rules and all players must play by the same rules. Moreover, some of the rules must specify the point of playing, the goal that gives purpose to the players' moves. Players may differ in strategy and technique but there is ordinarily a clear distinction between the rules, on which they must agree, and the strategies of play, on which they may well differ.[49]

In characterizing a relatively simple linguistic practice, such as color language or pain language, the game analogy is compelling. It makes sense to say that in identifying shades of blue or describing aches, a condition of the recognition of and communication about such experiences is that participants follow the same rules.[50] Either they follow the same rules and are participants in a shared practice, or they do not and the scope of their color and pain experience remains inaccessible and uncertain.[51] But even in these prac-

45. See Wittgenstein, *On Certainty* (Oxford: Basil Blackwell, 1969), section 614.

46. J. Rawls, "Two Concepts of Rules", (1955) 64 *Philosophical Review* 3.

47. The distinction between constitutive and regulative rules (and between constitutive and descriptive concepts) has unclear borders. Consider, for example, the economist's use of the term "preference satisfaction." The term has technical significance in economic theory but also refers to a phenomenon that lives outside the domain of economic theory. The same can be said of the sociologist's use of the term "charisma." The same, however, cannot be said of "run" or "strike" in baseball.

48. Wittgenstein, as noted above at n. 9, admonishes us to remember that if we "look and see whether there is anything common to all" games, we "will not see something that is common to all, but similarities, relationships, and a whole series of them at that." He goes on, "I can think of no better expression to characterize these similarities than 'family resemblances'; for the various resemblances between members of a family: build, features, colour of eyes, gait, temperament, etc. etc. overlap and criss-cross in the same way.—And I shall say: 'games' form a family." *Philosophical Investigations,supra* n. 1, Part I, sections 66 and 67.
My critique is of the use of a paradigm of games whereby all participants follow the same rules and have in mind the same point or purpose for engaging in the joint activity. Rawls and Kuhn use the paradigm to illuminate political and scientific activity.

49. In actual games and in the game-paradigm, the distinction is maintained between rules, by which all players must abide, and strategies, which players may devise on their own and which are likely to differ from player to player. It is relatively easy to sort out the activities of baseball players or chess players along these lines.
The use of the game-paradigm for judges presupposes that in judging as well one can distinguish the rules from strategies. One of my main criticisms of the use of the metaphor of games for deliberative practices is that this distinction cannot be made in the case of judging. In other words, the quest for shared rules of relevance for justificatory reasons must yield to the recognition of a plurality of competing strategies of justification.

50. This is not to say that Robinson Crusoe, alone on a desert island, cannot notice a particular color of fruit and then reidentify the color elsewhere on the island. But terms that he invents and uses are in principle terms that he can share with any subsequent visitors to the island; in principle his language can be a public language. The "private language" question is much debated in writings on Wittgenstein. See, for example, Kripke, *supra* n. 20.

51. Compare *Philosophical Investigations, supra* n. 1, Part I, section 250: "Why can't a dog simulate

46

tices, the game analogy breaks down. For one thing, the rules of the practice are not constitutive of pain experience *in the same way* that the rules of chess are constitutive of the experience of castling and checkmating. For another, color and pain recognition does not proceed in goal-directed moves.

The game metaphor breaks down altogether in accounting for deliberative practices. A basic constraint of the metaphor is that justificatory arguments make sense only among participants who are playing by the same rules who have the same standards of relevance for reasons. Among persons playing by different rules, justificatory moves are mere illusions and discourse proceeds at cross-purposes. Understanding this, participants must abandon their attempts or coerce (rather than persuade) others into playing by their rules.[52]

But in deliberative practices justificatory moves proceed in the face of differing strategies of reasoning. The practice consists in the recognition that these differing strategies exist and compete. From the standpoint of games, this characteristic of deliberative practices can only be a paradox. On discovering that others are playing by different rules, one will either bring them around to playing by the same rules or stop playing. Making further moves loses its point when others are playing a different game. The game itself loses its point.

And yet, the very point of deliberative practices seems to be to justify both a particular result and a particular *way* of reaching the result against those who reason differently. Participants have a stake not in a particular set of arbitrary rules but in a particular way of making sense of experience. A deliberative practice is a domain within which such different strategies compete. To give up or alter one's method of justification is not simply to decide to play by different rules but to decide to see the world differently.

Rather than saying that we can understand deliberative practices by seeing them as a kind of game, we might say rather that we can understand games as simplified, externalized, and therefore degenerate kinds of practices.[53] A justificatory response within a game ("Why did you move as you did?") may be a reminder of the shared rule or a reference to the player's strategy for winning.[54] The rules are fixed, arbitrary, and assumed to be known to all. But only the least important aspects of experience have this kind of simplicity. Only the least important aspects of life leave participants the option whether or not to play. In the more immediate and important practices—moral practices, psychological transactions, economic and professional judgments—we have

pain? Is he too honest? Could one teach a dog to simulate pain? Perhaps it is possible to teach him to howl on particular occasions as if he were in pain, even when he is not. But the surroundings which are necessary for this behaviour to be real simulation are missing."

52. In *On Certainty*, Wittgenstein says, in confronting those who reason differently, "we use our language-game to *combat* theirs," section 609. According to this assumption, reasoning and persuasion and justification are possible only among those who reason in the same way; otherwise, there is only competition and combat.

53. True games can be seen as mimicking the ordered or practice-like character of all conduct but in a form in which the goal is arbitrarily posited (and therefore bears no inherent relationship to human needs and desires) and in which moves and rules are simplified into relatively simple and rigid patterns.

54. See *supra* n. 49, for discussion of the distinction between rules and strategy in the context of a game—and for an argument that the distinction evaporates in a deliberative practice.

a stake unavoidably and the shared rules-and-strategies are endlessly controversial.

This conclusion about deliberative practices has implications for the role of theorists. Games afford a clear distinction between players and observers, insiders and outsiders.[55] Insiders play by the rules and justify their actions by resort to the rules. Outsiders are not bound by the rules. As observers, their questions about justification involve the justification of one set of rules in comparison with other variants of the game.

In considering deliberative practices, we lose the sharpness of this distinction. In part, the distinction remains in place. Practitioners inhabit a particular strategy of moral argument, historical interpretation, and so on, while theorists are occupied in noting and describing variant strategies. But part of one's understanding of deliberative practices *as a theorist* involves an interpretation, necessarily controversial, of the point of the exercise—of the point of esthetic activity, moral criticism, historical investigation. A theorist as well as a practitioner will therefore have a stake in a particular strategy and an attitude toward the point of the practice. This will color her account of the practice. A justification of the practice from a theoretical standpoint will look much like a justification given by a practitioner with a particular strategy within the practice.[56]

3. Legal Interpretation as a Deliberative Practice

a. Judges and Games

In this section I shall consider why the metaphor of games is a seductive tool for understanding constitutional interpretation,[57] why this metaphor can be said to confuse the analysis, and how the suggestion that judging is a deliberative practice, rather than a game, satisfactorily explains what judges do.

Three decades ago, political and legal philosophy in England and America were reborn.[58] A crucial ingredient of this renaissance was the idea that political and legal reasoning constitute practices and that the job of theorists is to

55. One of the most widely discussed aspects of Hart's jurisprudential writings is his distinction between an internal and an external point of view. This distinction has also occupied moral philosophy over the last forty years. See Hart, n. 13 *supra*, at 55-60; P. Soper, *A Theory of Law* (Cambridge, Mass: Harvard Univ. Press, 1984); K. Baier, *The Moral Point of View* (Ithaca: Cornell Univ. Press, 1958); B. Williams, *Ethics and the Limits of Philosophy* (Cambridge Mass: Harvard Univ. Press, 1985); and T. Nagel, *The View from Nowhere* (New York: Oxford Univ. Press, 1986).

56. Whether one is concerned with practitioners such as the justices of the U. S. Supreme Court or with theorists such as Tushnet, Ely, Bork, Fiss, and Dworkin, each propounds a controversial account of the point of the enterprise of judicial decision-making (and specifically constitutional interpretation). Although the position of pure outsider can, in principle, be adopted, it leaves the theorist with little to say. The reason philosophers are occupied with theories of law or morality or history but not with theories of baseball or chess is precisely because a theory of baseball would be uninteresting insofar as it would not pose controversial alternatives with regard to the point of the practice. A theorist of baseball *would* be a pure outsider, a pure describer, whereas a theorist of law or morality or history exists self-consciously in tension between commitment to a controversial justification of the practice and transcendence of that commitment.

57. *Supra* n. 6. The analysis need not be limited to constitutional decision-making or to appellate decision-making, but I do not try to generalize the argument here.

58. During the reign of logical positivism in the 1930's through the 1950's, moral, political, and legal philosophy were in eclipse. Such then-popular theories as emotivism and prescriptivism implied that moral and political discourse was not to be treated as a form of reasoning so much as a form of pure

48

uncover the constitutive rules[59] of these practices. This way of understanding the relevant methodology was common to self-described legal positivists and legal naturalists.[60] H. L. A. Hart described law as a complex game with two kinds of rules, those that instructed ordinary citizens on their obligations and rights and those that instructed officials in carrying forward institutional roles. To understand the task of judges is to understand the second-order rules that define their role.

The [illegible] of law as a practice becomes evident when we compare judges with the officials of real games. Ronald Dworkin reminds us that umpires in baseball exercise discretion in a different way from judges.[61] Umpires are entrusted with the task of making final judgments about particular actions and events[62] but the standards to be used are clearly and uncontroversially set for them. Even when umpires disagree about a result they do not and cannot disagree about the standards to be used in reaching the result.[63] Judges, on the other hand, disagree about method as well as result.

Judges and umpires differ in yet another respect. Umpires are not in any sense players in a second-order game since groups of umpires do not characteristically engage in deliberative moves and countermoves. They make spontaneous and final decisions and the game moves on. Panels of judges on the other hand engage in complex practices of interaction that are observed and analyzed. One level of analysis is the informal level of social and political maneuvering that is largely unrecorded and invisible, more guessed about than seen. Another level is the explicit dialogue whereby written opinions, including dissenting opinions, spell out both results and justificatory strategies. Although it is rare for a particular case to elicit written opinions (concurrences, dissents) from several members of the panel, judges quickly become identified with particular strategies and their dialogue persists over series of related cases. Thus, the implicit dialogue becomes explicit.

The second-order practice of judging is therefore unlike the activity of umpires because it involves moves and countermoves among participants who are responding to each other's strategies and are aware of doing so. The relevant moves are justificatory arguments. (With regard to judging, as with other deliberative practices, one may have the illusion that the interactive character of the activity is inessential. It seems as if one can make judicial decisions or write history or make moral judgments without taking into account and responding to the judgments—legal, historical, moral—of others.

---

expression or attempted coercion. See, for example, J. Urmson, *The Emotive Theory of Ethics* (London: Hutchinson Press, 1968) and T. Weldon, *The Vocabulary of Politics* (Baltimore: Penguin, 1953). Hart's *Concept of Law*, *supra* n. 13, and Rawls' *A Theory of Justice*, *supra* n. 40, are the most influential masterworks in the renaissance of political and legal philosophy under the rubric of linguistic analysis.

59. *Supra* n. 46.

60. The distinction sketched by Rawls in "Two Concepts of Rules" was elaborated and used both by Hart in *The Concept of Law* and by Dworkin in the essays in *Taking Rights Seriously, supra* n. 4, 13, and 46.

61. Dworkin, *Taking Rights Seriously,supra* n. 4, pp. 31-39. Here Dworkin distinguishes among several senses of discretion.

62. E.g. actions such as whether player x tagged up when he rounded second base, and events such as whether the ball was in the strike zone as it crossed home plate.

63. That is to say, they must abide by the rules of baseball as recorded and agreed-upon rules specifying what constitutes a strike, when a player must touch base, etc. The rules leave no effective room for ambiguity or interpretation.

This illusion parallels the illusion that it is inessential for the recognition of color or pain that there be a public practice of labeling and distinguishing among colors, or of identifying and diagnosing pains, into which persons are initiated. As with color and pain, one's awareness of what counts as a move in forming a legal and moral judgment or in defending an account of history presumes an established context in which there are justificatory moves and countermoves.)[64]

b. The Limits of a Kuhnian Account of Judging

Consider again the initial appeal of the metaphor of games as an idiom for the justificatory moves and countermoves of judging in general and constitutional interpretation in particular. The argument is straight-forward and exploits the comparison with color language. In describing color, we make sense and succeed in recognizing and communicating about color to the extent that we play by the same rules. What you call "red" is (more or less)[65] what I call "red". If we were to play by different rules we would have, at best, only the appearance of mutual understanding and communication. In that case, we would either bring others round to our way of speaking, adopt their rules, or decline to engage further with them.

The discovery that judges are playing by different rules seems to produce an impasse and a crisis. The considerable and imaginative efforts of recent theorists fall readily into place as attempts to address what they see as an impasse.[66] The impasse is explicable by noting two differences between the relatively simple game of color identification and the relatively complex one of judicial interpretation. The first difference is that discrepancies among players of the color game are immediately apparent. In the face of discrepancies, the game breaks down. Discrepant justificatory strategies among judges are less obvious. Decision making can proceed for some time under the public misconception that there are shared rules. The misconception may or may not be shared by the judges themselves.

The second difference explains the first. The practice of judging, unlike the practice of color identification, seems to call for a shared notion of the point of the activity which informs the rules governing reasoning and justification.[67] This shared notion is what Thomas Kuhn, in the context of analyzing scientific theory-building, calls a "paradigm". Judges, like historians and those engaged in moral reasoning, have a favored conception of the purpose served by their activity. In true games, the goal of play is easily and unambiguously

64. Just as one can imagine a single judge sitting in judgment, one can also imagine a person alone in the desert identifying colors. But in both cases, the event is imaginable because it is also imaginable as a collective enterprise, whereby several persons carry out judgments, argue among themselves, etc. Compare Wittgenstein's observations on this, *supra* n. 26 and accompanying text.

65. *Supra* n. 27.

66. Most of the theorists of the late 1970's and early 1980's speak eloquently about a sense of crisis and an impasse with regard to theorizing about judging. See, for example, J. Ely, *Democracy and Distrust* (Cambridge, Mass: Harvard Univ. Press, 1980), at 73-75; L. Tribe, *Constitutional Choices* (Cambridge, Mass: Harvard Univ. Press, 1985), at 3-21; and M. Perry, *The Constitution, The Courts, and Human Rights* (New Haven: Yale Univ. Press, 1982), at 9-36.

67. Kuhn's account of scientific discovery and change is explained in T. Kuhn, *The Structure of Scientific Revolutions* (Chicago: Univ. of Chicago Press, 1962). See also I. Lakatos and A. Musgrave, *Criticism and the Growth of Knowledge* (Cambridge: Cambridge University Press, 1970) and I. Hacking, *Scientific Revolutions* (Oxford: Oxford Univ. Press, 1981).

specified (checkmating the king, scoring the most runs). Kuhn argues that in shared activities of research and reasoning there must be a similar consensus, a shared understanding of the kind of knowledge sought and of the methods appropriate to seeking it. But in such activities as judging, and writing history, this shared understanding is problematic. Differing strategies of justification may be evidence, in Kuhn's terms, of differing paradigmatic understandings of the point of the activity.

This impasse yields a sense of crisis. Judges, unlike historians and individual moral agents, have a political role and wield institutional power. Any political actor becomes a threat to the security of the rule of law unless her power is constrained. Constraint for judges, in turn, seems to lie in the availability of a widely shared and uncontroversial conception of the purpose to be served by judges and of the rules for judging that flow from that conception. Some theorists prefer to say that such rules insure that judges will act objectively rather than subjectively.[68] If, on the other hand, every conception is controversial among both judges and theorists, then judges are in fact unconstrained, loose and potentially destructive actors within the political structure.[69]

This analysis remains within the metaphor of games. Paradigm-driven activities are sophisticated games in several senses. The success of the activity depends on a shared conception of the purposes of the activity and of the rules to be followed. For Kuhn, of course, scientific research is the main example. In the light of his account, the game metaphor must be relaxed only slightly. It must be rethought to take account of the fact that the "game" of scientific investigation and reasoning does not proceed by discrete moves, does not begin and end at predetermined and rule-determined times, and is not competitive in a zero-sum sense (whereby a win by one player entails an equal loss by another).

The Kuhnian idea of an investigative paradigm—the idea of reasoning as a modified game—is the missing link between the simple idea of a game and the search for a theory of judicial interpretation. The effort of theorists is directed not toward simple assimilation with games but toward eliciting a shared idea of constitutional interpretation from which uncontroversial rules, as constraints and as ideals, follow. The alternatives that have received the most attention have long been familiar. Many writers favor adherence to the structure and role of government as conceived by the founders of the constitution. Such "interpretivism" takes two forms, adherence to the intentions of the founders insofar as it is discoverable through all kinds of historical investigation and adherence to the text of the constitution and to its original meaning.[70] By contrast, other writers (noninterpretivists) look to the evolution of constitutional thought, in which the founders represent but one moment, and stress the continual rethinking of the role and structure of government

68. This notion of judicial objectivity is put forward by Owen Fiss in "Objectivity and Interpretation" (1982), 34 *Stanford L. R.* 739.

69. See sources listed, *supra* n. 66.

70. Ely follows many other writers in adhering to the term "interpretivism." Tushnet and Brest, in their influential and persuasive critiques, prefer the term "originalism." See Tushnet, *supra* n. 8, and P. Brest, "The Misconceived Quest for the Original Understanding" (1980), 60 *Boston University L. R.* 204. See also R. Kay, "Adherence to the Original Intentions in Constitutional Adjudication: Three Objections and Responses" (1988), 82 *Northwestern University L. R.* 226.

represented in our constitutional history.[71] Such theorists tend to see judges as spokespersons for a consensus of received values and ideals that may be loosely connected to the thought of the founders, uninformed as it is by the events of the last 200 years.

Theorists debate both the practicability and merits of such theories. Defenders of interpretivism must wrestle with the question whether the intentions of the founders are in fact retrievable in a way that dictates a discrete strategy of decision in hard cases. Defenders of non-interpretivism must wrestle with the equally intractable question whether any current and continuing social consensus exists about the issues raised by contemporary constitutional questions. Critics of both positions argue, often compellingly, that reference to original intent and reference to a pervasive social consensus mask the indiscipline of judges and that neither form of rhetoric proceeds from genuinely constraining rules.[72]

In the rest of this section, I shall address the question at a higher level of abstraction. If we grant that judges proceed and think of themselves as proceeding in all of the ways described by theorists, are we required by the metaphor of games and the Kuhnian requirement of a shared paradigm to admit that there is no shared practice, only the facade of one? How well indeed does the metaphor of games, as modified through Kuhn's model, really fit our deliberative practices?

c. Judging as a Deliberative Practice

The behavior of judges does not fit the metaphor of games. The simple metaphor of a game—with its discrete moves and static, written rules, with its clearly distinguished beginning and end—is clearly irrelevant. The more complex notion, the Kuhnian paradigm, is overtly metaphorical and says that communicative practices are game-like in an essential way—constituted by shared rules that define what counts as a move, what the point of communication is, and what counts as a relevant reason or relevant justificatory argument in discourse. Kuhn suggests that scientific investigation, like color identification, proceeds because we agree about what counts as a justificatory move, because we agree about what kinds of evidence are relevant in the process of making and debating judgments, and because we have a shared commitment to the point of the deliberative enterprise.

That's not how judges work. I have already looked at debates among historians, at moral discourse, and at judging, to suggest that in describing deliberative practices, even this more complex use of the game metaphor is unhelpful. According to the metaphor, the possibility of genuine deliberation presupposes common strategies of deliberation. Judges must have in common a conception of the point of the practice and of the rules of relevance that govern justificatory moves. The absence of shared rules is a defect; the more diverse the rules by which different participants operate, the more defective the practice is. The practice cannot proceed unless the defect is

71. Dworkin and Fiss are examples. *Supra* nn. 4 and 68.
72. Tushnet, among others, offers a compelling argument of this kind. *Supra* n. 8.

52

cured. Judges who proceed in the face of such diversity re-enact the drama of Babel. By assumption, they cannot recognize each other's arguments as having justificatory force because they do not share the same assumptions about what counts as justification.

The actual practice of judges seems to fly in the face of this account. What this account describes as a defect is a definitive and inevitable feature of deliberation. Judges characteristically disagree not only about the results in particular cases but about the method through which results should be derived and defended. The distinction between interpretivists and non-interpretivists marks only the first layer of disagreement about method. Within the first (interpretivist) group, judges will differ about the level of generality with which the founders anticipated and set in motion a determinate structure and about the kinds of resources relevant to debates over their actions. Within the second (non-interpretivist) group, judges will differ in their conception of the kinds of goals and values appropriate to judicial (rather than, say, legislative) action and in their conception of the kinds of data—political, economic, sociological, psychological, historical—that are the "bottom line" of legal deliberation.

If such diversity seems ineradicable and if judicial deliberation (as constitutional interpretation) is characterized by such diversity, then the game metaphor is not a tool but an obstacle to understanding. The idea of a deliberative practice, as outlined in Section 2, is the alternative tool. A deliberative practice embraces participants with different commitments to different argumentative strategies and conceptions of goals. They are bound together not by shared rules but by mutual recognition of an array of relevant ways of proceeding. Deliberation proceeds as an activity in which each reaches and justifies judgments *and* deploys his justificatory strategy in part to persuade others to adopt it but also to vindicate his own way of making sense of experience.

This account explains an otherwise curious aspect of deliberative activity. A distinguishing feature of both games and Kuhnian game-like investigative paradigms is that implicit in each is a clear distinction between insiders and outsiders. In both games and game-like activities, the rules are settled during play. The role of an insider, a participant in the practice, is to make moves in accord with the rules and in the light of the mutually understood point of the practice. These moves may take the form of justificatory arguments in the case of scientific investigation for example.[73] The role of an outsider—an observer, commentator, or theorist—is to take note of the rules and illuminate them in the light of the implicit point of the practice. The outsider herself is not committed to the rules, is not in a position to make justificatory arguments, and must see the rules in some sense as an arbitrary posit. Thus the

73. This point illustrates the way in which the example of game-like activity, on the Kuhnian model, is midway between a real game and a deliberative practice. On the one hand is the requirement that participants must play by the same rules and must agree about the shared point or aim of their activity. In this sense, the model is a variant of a game. On the other hand the moves themselves are justificatory arguments, reasons for judgment. In this sense, the activity is like a deliberative practice. The distinction between insiders and outsiders (participants and theorists) is clearer in Kuhn's model than it is in a deliberative practice.

outsider may contemplate the possibility of chess played, hypothetically, by different rules and the historical reality of scientific investigation proceeding under different paradigms.[74]

Deliberative practices do not yield so clear a distinction between the roles of insiders and outsiders. The so-called rules of the practice and the point served by them are inherently disputable. Justification within the practice means not merely justifying particular conclusions but particular ways of reaching those conclusions.

It may be said that the insider/outsider distinction can be transposed to deliberative practices with little modification. The outsider as theorist would thus have the role of describing the practice as a family of strategies of justification rather than as a single rule-governed strategy. But this may be too simple. A neutral or impartial standpoint is available to the outsider of a game because the point of a game is given and uncontroversial. The same is true of game-like investigative paradigms. But with deliberative practices like judicial reasoning, moral reasoning, or explaining history, the point of the enterprise is itself controversial. Even the outsider must, in this sense, choose sides.

Explaining why this is so requires a more general discussion of being inside and outside a practice. This, in turn, requires us to attend briefly to such abstract and intractable issues as the nature and limits of philosophy, and the nature and limits of self-awareness. Consider three steps in the development of these issues.

(1) A spontaneous general attitude toward knowledge and belief, ingrained both in ordinary attitudes and in the history of philosophy, is commonly called foundationalism. A foundationalist believes that all sorts of questions—about history, about the physical world, about psychology—have answers. Any issue is such that there is some truth about the matter, and the task of investigation is to discover that truth, to bring one's beliefs into accord with what is the case. This may be easy or difficult—easy if we wish to discover whether we are wearing shoes, difficult if we wish to discover the origin of the universe or the biography of an ancient prophet—but the task is to do what needs to be done to grasp what is true.

An insight of philosophers from Kant onward is that what we say we know about events, objects, persons, etc., is not simply the result of getting immediately in touch with how things "really are". What we know is conditioned by how we know, not only our physical capacities but also our conceptual frameworks.[75] Wittgenstein and Kuhn in different ways draw conclusions from this insight. The ways in which we organize experience, ask questions about experience, and weigh evidence in drawing conclusions (forming beliefs, deciding what we know) are social practices, often widely shared

74. Critics of Kuhn question whether a theorist can indeed be an outsider in this sense or whether the reconstruction of scientific paradigms involves an implicit notion of rationality that transcends paradigms, a notion that allows us to speak meaningfully of progress in science. See, for related issues, I. Lakatos, "History of Science and Its Rational Reconstructions", and K. Popper, "The Rationality of Scientific Revolutions", in Hacking, *supra* n. 67.

75. See general discussion of conceptual frameworks in D. Davidson, "On the Very Idea of a Conceptual Scheme", in *Inquiries into Truth and Interpretation* (Oxford: Oxford Univ. Press, 1984); R. Rorty, *Contingency Irony and Solidarity* (Cambridge: Cambridge Univ. Press, 1989); and H. Putnam, *Realism and Reason, Philosophical Papers, volume 3* (Cambridge: Cambridge Univ. Press, 1983).

54

but nonetheless variable over time.

(2) If no thinker can, in principle, extricate herself from her ways of knowing, from the social practices by which she has grown accustomed to organizing experience, then she can never claim that a particular way of knowing is privileged over others. Nor can she claim that one variant practice (one way of looking into history or thinking about the universe) gets closer than others to what is true.

Foundationalists must therefore yield to nonfoundationalists. The role of epistemology is not to show how it is that we are getting ever closer to the truth, getting from mediated knowledge to immediate knowledge, but to show how knowledge is mediated.[76] The philosopher as epistemologist is the quintessential outsider with regard to the social practices of knowing. The insider is the inhabitant of the practice to whom the rules of the practice are second nature. Thus we come full circle to the metaphor of games in the sophisticated version suggested by Kuhn.

(3) It is necessary, in turn, to impeach this nonfoundationalist model and the metaphor on which it rests if we are to understand deliberative practices and specifically the practice of legal interpretation. The crucial point can be made in two interdependent ways. One is to say that deliberative practices do not involve (temporarily) settled ways of proceeding, within which reasoning and justification become possible, but competing ways of proceeding of which the various participants are aware. The other way of making the point is that the participants are simultaneously insiders and outsiders, insiders insofar as they are committed to a way of organizing experience that seems inescapable, outsiders insofar as they know that any justificatory move they can make is yet another move elaborating their own strategy within a deliberative practice.

In other words, deliberative practices do not permit theorists or practitioners to be outsiders in the nihilistic sense required by the metaphor of games. The foundationalist aspires to the possibility of being outside particular ways of thinking to apprehend reality in itself. The nonfoundationalist aspires to the possibility of being outside practices as games to achieve a point of indifference or neutrality toward all particular configurations of rules. Neither way of being outside is available *vis-a-vis* deliberative practices.

I am putting forward judicial interpretation—and whatever general understandings about law and legal systems follow from our understanding of judicial interpretation—as a clear example of a deliberative practice. I have been assuming that moral deliberation and debates about history yield other examples and that much of our reasoning activity has the character of a deliberative practice. But I shall leave aside any claims about just which kinds of reasoning fit the Kuhnian model and are in fact game-like and which, on the other hand, can be assimilated to judicial reasoning.[77]

76. One of the main ideas in Wittgenstein's *On Certainty, supra* n. 45, is that recognition that knowledge claims and claims about what is true can only occur within practices (or language-games) does not license skepticism or disenfranchise persons from using terms like "know" and "true." This recognition merely describes the conditions under which such terms *are* appropriately used. See Morawetz, *supra* n. 29, chapters 4 and 5.

77. No doubt some theorists would assimilate scientific investigation, Kuhn's main area of concern, with

These distinctions help explain the failure of the most representative recent theories of constitutional interpretation. I shall use my critique of the metaphor of games and of the consequent distinction between insiders and outsiders to show how and why theorists have failed to appreciate that judicial interpretation is a deliberative practice.

4. Theories of Constitutional Interpretation

No overview can do justice to the rich literature on constitutional interpretation of the last fifteen years. My concern is not with the details of the debates but with their shared aims and motivations. The fear and goals of these theorists are grounded in the metaphor of a game gone awry.[78] Their goal is to clarify and stabilize the rules of the game. This goal makes sense only as long as judicial interpretation is seen not as a deliberative practice but as a game. I shall suggest therefore that, at its most abstract level, the debate over constitutional interpretation is based on a misunderstanding of the kind of practice constitutional interpretation is and can be.

We have seen that we may simplify the matter by grouping theorists into three categories: interpretivists, noninterpretivists, and nihilists.[79] Interpretivists and noninterpretivists are committed to the constructive goal implicit in the game metaphor, the goal of finding and defending constraining standards for judicial interpretation that may be regarded as the rules of the game. By "constraining" I mean three things. First, the standards define a method of justifying deliberative judgments so that judges may not do "whatever they wish". Second, the standards define a correct or distinctly preferable method of justifying deliberative judgments. Third, the standards are rigorous enough to produce answers to hard questions of judicial interpretation. Each of these three aspects of constraint needs explanation.

The first sense of constraint poses the alternatives of license and rule-following; either there are discoverable rules that define decisionmaking or there are none. If there are discoverable rules, they are the rules of the game, the same for all judges. The second sense of constraint implies that in the actual practice of judges one can discover several alternative (rule-like) ways of proceeding. Unless one can show that one way of proceeding is correct (or superior to others), the collection of alternatives is tantamount to license. In other words, there is no middle ground between license and univocal rules. Specifically, to say that judges do not have license because they may choose among a limited set of alternative constraining rules is nonsense. The third sense of constraint is addressed to the relationship between rules (or methods or ways of proceeding) and decisions. It says that if judges may properly choose among alternative ways of proceeding, the results of deliberation are not constrained, but if there is only one correct or superior way of proceeding,

---

a deliberative practice and would contest the existence of shared paradigms. Perhaps the best account of the matter would suggest that the two models are not mutually exclusive, and that some areas of investigation and deliberation come closer to one model while others approximate the other.

78. *Supra* text at n. 49 and *passim*.

79. These categories are explained above at text accompanying nn. 12-14, 70-71, and 81-83.

56

then results are circumscribed.[80]

Nihilists agree that the goal of theory is to undercover a constraining theory, one that is constraining is all three senses. But they attempt to show that the goal cannot be achieved. After looking briefly at interpretive, noninterpretive, and nihilistic theory, I shall conclude by arguing that the underlying three-part notion of constraint is appropriate to an analysis of games but not to deliberative practices.

(1) Interpretivists are preoccupied with the first sense of constraint. They fear that judges will use the power of interpretation to effect political and social choices of their own. And they see the only adequate answer to that fear in the claim that concrete political and social choices have been taken out of the hands of judges *ab initio*, i.e., by the drafters of the Constitution. They argue that unless the constitution-making process can be seen as anticipating and answering such questions with some specificity, constraint is a mirage.[81]

The underlying scheme of analysis for interpretivists rests on three assumptions.

(a) Judges either are constrained by shared rules or are not constrained. In the latter case they have license, may make up or vary the rules at will. ("Rules" in this context means "criteria for justificatory reasons".)

(b) For judges to be constrained by shared rules, they must have recourse to a decisional method that does not essentially require judgments about contemporary values, social and political evolution, or social needs. A method that bases decision making on these latter considerations allows judges recourse to a panoply of subjective opinions and is tantamount to license.

(c) On the other hand, structural and substantive determinations made by the authors and ratifiers of the Constitution anticipate answers to constitutional hard questions and the shared rules of decision making require deference to those determinations. The very idea of constitutionalism also mandates such deference.

The interpretive theory is both descriptive and normative. It claims to unpack the idea of decision making and to describe the rules that underlie the practice, properly understood. But in doing so, it describes a standard and an ideal. Also, most interpretivists would argue that their theory is doubly a theory of constraint. It strongly constrains the sort of resources appropriate to decision making. It also constrains results, but less strongly.[82] Players playing

80. The relationship between rules and results is a complex one (not unlike the relationship between theories of metaethics and theories of substantive ethics). Practitioners who follow the same rules will not necessarily get the same results. The rules do not function as a decision procedure, nor do they put in place a deductive method. Rather, they are a criterion of relevance and importance for reasons. Historians who stress economic factors are more likely to attend to similar kinds of facts, but will not offer identical explanations. Judges who consult original intent will be disposed, one imagines, to entertain certain arguments about federalism but will not apply these arguments in the same way, nor will they necessarily come up with the same results in hard cases. The constraining effects of the rules of a game like baseball or of an experimental process in, say, biochemical research also allow for differing ways of carrying out the activity—but one must not draw the analogy too closely.

81. Such assumptions seem to underpin the work of writers as diverse as Robert Bork, Richard Kay, and John Hart Ely. See, for example, R. Bork, "Neutral Principles and Some First Amendment Problems", (1971) 47 *Indiana L. J.* 1, and "The Impossibility of Finding Welfare Rights in the Constitution", (1979) *Washington University L. Q.* 695; R. Kay, *supra* n. 70; and J. Ely, *supra* n. 66.

82. *Supra* n. 80.

by the same rules will, nonetheless, play differently. Judges who attend to original intent may disagree about what the constitution requires in particular cases.

Beyond this, interpretivists vary in the details. Some proffer interpretivism reluctantly, as a measure of the limits on judicial power to benefit society. Others put it forth enthusiastically, as one component of a framework in which government interferes minimally in persons' lives.[83] Some describe interpretivism as the only alternative to judicial license. Others claim only that it is a firmer constraint, a clearer rule, than others and defend it in the interest of institutional stability and predictability.[84]

(2) Non-interpretivists accept the same first premise. They reject, however, the second premise.

(b_1) Judges may be constrained by rules directing them to adhere to an evolved consensus about social value. Such rules may take various forms. According to various subtheories, judges may be required to reconstruct the abstract relationship between the individual and the state embodied in the Constitution, or they may be required to develop the best theory of constitutional rights that interprets concern and respect for individual autonomy, or they may be required to adhere to "disciplining rules" that insure fairness and conscientiousness in respecting shared values.[85]

(c_1) Adherence to such rules assures that judges will not decide in accord with whim, license, or personal preference. In other words they will decide objectively rather than subjectively. Such a procedure is in fact mandated by (or at least altogether consistent with) the Constitution, which anticipates that judicial interpretation will be shaped to the needs of the present rather than the dead hand of the past.

If the sticking point of interpretivism is that it may require judges to frustrate the best interests of the public in the interest of constitutionalism, the sticking point of noninterpretivism is that it presumes that the best interests will generally be transparent. The important point that I have emphasized throughout my analysis is that this expectation is unrealistic, *not* simply because judges have different "values" but because they have different ways of giving order to experience. What they share is mediated by language and the ways in which they differ are also reflected in language. The issue is not, as some political philosophers say, that some favor liberty and others equality.[86] The issue is rather that the ways in which persons fit psychological, economic, political, social experiences together, the ways in which they make sense of their own lives and the lives of others, differ significantly and that hard questions of decision making fall prey to that diversity. The fact that some are libertarian and others egalitarian is merely a symptom of this more

83. This contrast is reflected, respectively, in the work of Richard Kay on the one hand and Robert Bork (and Edwin Meese) on the other.

84. In this instance, the *former* view is held by Bork (and perhaps by Ely) while the latter is held by Kay.

85. Arguably these views are held respectively by Thomas Grey, Owen Fiss, and Ronald Dworkin. See, for example, T. Grey, "Do We Have an Unwritten Constitution?" (1975), 27 *Stanford L. R.* 703; O. Fiss, *supra* n. 68; and R. Dworkin, *supra* n. 4.

86. The tension between liberty and equality remains one of the principal conceptual ways in which alternative political theories are cast. It is possible to argue that this opposition is epiphenomenal and rests, in most cases, on deeper commitments to psychological, sociological, and methodological

58

encompassing and greater diversity.

(3) The distinction between interpretivists and non-interpretivists, apparently so clear, depends on a naive epistemology. It presupposes that one can, at will, assume either of two cognitive positions. The first is a value-neutral self-transposition into the attitudes and opinions of historical actors. The other is an appropriation of the values of one's culture and one's political tradition. Both are distinguishable from the identification and deploying of one's own personal values.[87]

A special contribution of hermeneutics is to show how fragile and dubious these distinctions are.[88] One's understanding of history is mediated through, and expressed within, the techniques of understanding—the categorical distinctions, the assumptions about value, etc.—that one employs as a particular participant in particular practices at a particular time in human history. Even if one can identify particular instances of tension between personal value preferences and a social consensus, or between a putative preference attributable to the founders and current attitudes, one cannot distinguish among these positions systematically. How one understands the past is colored by one's personal experiences. How one understands one's contemporaries affects one's decisions about values and goals.

The distinction between (b) and (b1) rests largely on a mistake about epistemology. The mistake is the following. Assume that one can distinguish (i) what the founders would have said about situation x, (ii) what a contemporary social consensus would maintain about situation x, and (iii) how Judge J would prefer to resolve situation x. To distinguish these conceptually is not the same as saying that judges either do or can follow one of the three methods of decision to the exclusion of the others. Indeed any judge's particular way of deciding will be affected by all three kinds of considerations. All three kinds affect each other in ways that only the foolhardy would claim to disentangle.

Equally foolhardy is the epistemological assumption that a judge can choose the perspective from which to decide a case. The particular way in which these three kinds of consideration color a judge's way of proceeding is neither volitional nor optional, no more volitional than the capacity to find a melody in a song or to notice a logical inconsistency or to avoid an on-coming truck in driving. All are aspects of participating in practices and all, while subject to reflection and conditioned by learning, are spontaneous responses to situations.[89]

The flaw, therefore, in much constitutional theory is represented by

assumptions made by the theorists who deploy various views about the relationship between liberty and equality. See, for example, A. Ryan, *The Idea of Freedom: Essays in Honour of Isaiah Berlin* (Oxford: Oxford University Press, 1979); A. Gutmann, *Liberal Equality* (Cambridge: Cambridge University Press, 1980); and S.M. McMurrin, *Liberty, Equality, and the Law: Selected Tanner Lectures on Moral Philosophy* (Salt Lake City: Univ. of Utah Press, 1987).

87. To be sure, the interpretivist rejects the distinction between the second and third of these stances, while the noninterpretivist defends it.

88. See D. Hoy, "Interpreting the Law: Hermeneutical and Poststructuralist Perspectives", (1985) 58 *Southern California L. R.* 135; T. Grey, "The Hermeneutics File" (1985), 58 *Southern California L. R.* 221; H-G. Gadamer, *supra* n. 20.

89. The last few paragraphs are to be taken as phenomenological and hermeneutical description. It is not clear to me how, other than through appeal to intuition, any theorist would "prove" these observations.

assumption (a). Judges are indeed constrained, but not by shared rules. They are constrained individually by a particular way of addressing and understanding interpretive questions and they are constrained collectively by the fact that the shared practice embraces a limited range of ways of proceeding. This limitation is mutually understood and recognized.

The idea that there must be a single set of shared rules, or license in the alternative, is dictated by the assumption that practices are like games. This paradigm, which *may*[90] work (as Kuhn suggests it does) for scientific investigation with its emphasis on progress and experimental manipulation of data to confirm or disconfirm hypotheses, works badly and distortingly when applied to deliberative practices, such as constitutional interpretation. But the assumption that license is the only alternative to shared rules runs deep in constitutional theory.

5. Conclusion

Wittgenstein says that philosophy describes our practices but does not change them.[91] Some have argued that the metaphor of games is well adapted to describing our practices, because it points us in the direction of eliciting and investigating the shared rules that characterize practices, rather than changing them. But the metaphor itself is coercive. Our more complex deliberative practices do not fit the simplicity of the metaphor and the attempt to find shared rules becomes, inevitably, a summons to change the practice, to harmonize the several ways of proceeding under a single paradigm. To heed this suggestion is to distort the phenomenon that one seeks to describe. Judges disagree, not only in results but in the ways in which they arrive at those results. It is not within the compass of jurisprudence to change this, nor is it within its power.

90. *Supra* n. 77.
91. *Supra* n. 42.

[6]
Understanding Disagreement, the Root Issue of Jurisprudence[†]

My judgments themselves characterize the way I judge, characterize the nature of judgment.[1]

---

† Professor of Law, University of Connecticut School of Law. I am very grateful to Scott Altman, Ruth Gavison, Mark Miller, Stephen Munzer, Jeremy Paul, Samuel Pillsbury, Margaret Jane Radin, and Michael Shapiro for many insights and valuable suggestions. I owe special thanks to my research assistant, Melinda Westbrook, for the care and intelligence she brought to this project.

[1] LUDWIG WITTGENSTEIN, ON CERTAINTY 22 (G.E.M. Anscombe & G.H. von Wright eds., Denis Paul & G.E.M. Anscombe trans., 1969).

TABLE OF CONTENTS

I. ANTIFOUNDATIONALISM AND CONTEMPORARY JURISPRUDENCE 374
A. *Where We Are* 374
B. *Where We Need to Go* 378
II. LAW AS A DELIBERATIVE PRACTICE 383
A. *Rules, Games, and Judgments* 384
1. The Hardest Question: A Tale of Two Metaphors 384
a. *Centripetal and Centrifugal Reasoning* 385
b. *The Metaphor of Games* 386
c. *Applying the Game Metaphor to Law* 387
2. Judicial Interpretation 389
a. *Consensus Theory* 390
b. *Antifoundationalism* 390
c. *Implications for Theory and Practice* 393
3. Critique 394
B. *Practices and Deliberative Practices* 396
1. Practices in General 396
2. Linguistic Practices 397
3. Deliberative Practices 398
a. *Understanding Disagreement* 398
b. *Agreement and the Bounds of Practice* 399
c. *Discourse and Debate* 401
d. *Persuasion* 402
C. *Judicial Decision as a Deliberative Practice* 403
1. Disagreement Among Judges 405
2. The Bounds of Judicial Disagreement 405
3. The Driving Force of Judicial Persuasion 406
4. The Grounds of Persuasion and Change 409
D. *Immersion in Practice as an Obstacle to Theory* 409
III. LEGAL POSITIVISM AND LAW AS A DELIBERATIVE PRACTICE 412
A. *Positivism and Judging* 412
1. Positivism and the Identification of Law 412
2. Raz's Positivism 413
3. Dworkin's Criticisms 414

B. *The Limitations of Positivism* 414
1. Criteria of Validity 415
2. The Meaning of Legal Justification 416
3. Participants and Theorists 418
4. Dissolving the Dichotomies of Positivism 420
a. *Existing Law and New Law* 420
b. *Law and Gaps* 422
c. *Law as It Is and Law as It Ought to Be* 423
C. *Dworkin's Criticisms and Deliberative Practices* 423
1. The Self-Understanding of Judges 424
a. *The Bases of Disagreement* 425
b. *Understanding Other Judges* 425
c. *The "Best" Interpretation of the Law* 426
2. The Completeness of Law 427
IV. ANTIFOUNDATIONALISM AND PRAGMATISM 428
A. *From Old to New Jurisprudence* 429
B. *The Limits of Critical Theory* 430
1. Myths of Value Pluralism 430
2. Conceptual Frameworks 434
a. *Forms of Conceptual Relativity* 435
b. *Intractable Questions* 436
c. *Abandoning Conceptual Relativity* 438
3. Semantic Relativity 439
C. *Applying the Lessons: Pragmatism as Legal Theory* ... 441
1. Rorty's Pragmatism 443
a. *Rorty on Solidarity and Individuality* 444
b. *Rorty on Theory and Practice* 446
c. *Rorty's Influence* 447
2. Fish and Interpretive Communities 449
a. *Fish and Deliberative Practices* 450
b. *Fish as Pure Theorist* 451
c. *Fish on Interpretive Communities* 452
3. Acceptable Pragmatism and Banal Pragmatism .. 452
CONCLUSION 455

I. ANTIFOUNDATIONALISM AND CONTEMPORARY JURISPRUDENCE

A. *Where We Are*

A pervasive theme of recent legal theory is profound skepticism about the possibility of consensus in social values and goals.[2] Accompanying such skepticism is multifaceted doubt about objectivity, rationality, and the possibility of social progress.[3] Skeptical theorists reject the idea of shared intellectual foundations and therefore are generally called antifoundationalists.[4]

---

[2] This theme, and the various social and legal arguments that elaborate it, are at the heart of critical theory—which embraces critical legal theory, critical feminism, and critical race studies. Mark Kelman, for example, says that from the standpoint of critical legal studies, mainstream (liberal) legal thought is in fact beset "not by 'competing concerns' artfully balanced until a wise equilibrium is reached, but by irreducible, irremediable, irresolvable conflict." MARK KELMAN, A GUIDE TO CRITICAL LEGAL STUDIES 3 (1987). Martha Minow cites the philosophers A.J. Ayer and W.V. Quine for the proposition that "although we can alter the theory we use to frame our perceptions of the world, we cannot see the world unclouded by preconceptions. The impact of the observer's perspective may be crudely oppressive. Yet, we continue to believe in neutrality." Martha Minow, *Foreword: Justice Engendered*, 101 HARV. L. REV. 10, 46 (1987). *See also* Mari J. Matsuda, *Looking to the Bottom: Critical Legal Studies and Reparations* 22 HARV. C.R.-C.L. L. REV. 323 (1987) (commenting on the irreducible distinctiveness of racial points of view); Robin L. West, *The Difference in Women's Hedonic Lives: A Phenomenological Critique of Feminist Legal Theory*, 3 WIS. WOMEN'S L.J. 81 (1987) (discussing the irreducible experiential differences between men and women and the perceptions that follow from them).

[3] Although critical writers generally attack objectivity claims, they frequently take different positions on the notion of social progress. Catharine MacKinnon echoes many other writers when she says that the notion of objectivity is used to mask "such power over reality as comes from methodological hegemony over the means of knowing." CATHARINE A. MACKINNON, TOWARD A FEMINIST THEORY OF THE STATE 107 (1989). On the question of social progress, compare Robert Gordon's observation that the core of traditional liberal thought is the idea that "[t]here is an objective, determined, progressive social evolutionary path" with the confidence of many feminist and critical race theorists that their work brings us closer to a genuine understanding and implementation of equality. Robert W. Gordon, *Critical Legal Histories*, 36 STAN. L. REV. 57, 61 (1984).

[4] Debates between legal foundationalists and antifoundationalists reflect pervasive movements in philosophy. Richard Rorty describes and promotes an antifoundationalist approach to traditional philosophical issues. He describes antifoundationalism as the view that

> the notion of knowledge as accurate representation, made possible by special mental processes, and intelligible through a general theory of representation, needs to be abandoned.
>
> . . . .
>
> [T]he attempt (which has defined traditional philosophy) to explicate 'rationality' and 'objectivity' in terms of conditions of accurate representation is a self-deceptive effort to eternalize the normal discourse of the day . . .

Antifoundationalist arguments have so thoroughly taken hold of the legal imagination that contemporary legal theory seems discontinuous with its quite recent past. This discontinuity has two aspects. First, the new jurisprudence sees the old jurisprudence as naive and superficial, especially in its treatment of value consensus.[5] The aim of the new theorists is not to answer and refute positivism and liberalism, but to subvert them.[6] Second, the new jurisprudence is only tangentially about law and legal reasoning; instead, it is primarily about language, thought, and will, about meaning and truth. Legal implications are treated almost as incidental.[7]

The transition from the old to the new jurisprudence, best exemplified by critical theory, involves three kinds of destabilizing arguments—arguments that in turn defend moral, conceptual, and semantic relativity.[8] The moral argument destabilizes liberalism

---

RICHARD RORTY, PHILOSOPHY AND THE MIRROR OF NATURE 6, 11 (1979).

[5] Many writers go further and characterize liberal assumptions about value consensus as devious and repressive. The dominant groups in society, on this view, universalize their interests and experience and repress the self-expression of groups (e.g. women and minorities) without power. According to Robert Gordon, one can represent law as a legitimating ideology in the view that "[t]he ruling class induces consent and demobilizes opposition by masking its role in widely shared utopian norms and fair procedures, which it then distorts to its own purposes." Gordon, *supra* note 3, at 93. Gordon himself seems to proffer an account wherein these preferences are concealed even from the actors themselves because "[t]he discourse of law—its categories, arguments, reasoning modes, rhetorical tropes, and procedural rituals—fits into a complex of discursive practices that together structure how people perceive." *Id.* at 95.

[6] In the introduction to *Postmodern Jurisprudence*, Douzinas and Warrington observe that

> [t]he orthodox jurisprudence of modernity constructs theories that portray the law as a coherent body of rules and principles. . . . Its predominant strategy is to try and weave the legal texts into a single, seamless veil . . . . In this, postmodern theory could not be more different. It distrusts all attempts to create large-scale, totalising theories in order to explain social phenomena. . . . It tells small-scale, provisional, open stories about our lives and the world. . . . [Therefore,] the bodies of theory brought together here are not staging a confrontation."

COSTAS DOUZINAS ET AL., POSTMODERN JURISPRUDENCE ix-x (1991).

[7] I am not necessarily offering this point as criticism. My examination of antifoundationalist theories in Part IV of this article is itself a discussion of thought and will, meaning and truth—applicable generally to deliberative acts of many kinds.

[8] These are not three distinct and separate arguments. Arguments for conceptual relativity tend to generalize arguments for moral relativity. They put forward a general epistemological position which relativizes both facts and values and which (perhaps) questions or erodes the distinction between facts and values. Arguments for semantic relativity focus not so much on thought and understanding as on

and faith in public values with an assault on the objectivity of rights, encapsulated in the claim that all law is politics.[9] The conceptual argument impeaches ideological neutrality by uncovering multiple narratives and alternative voices that coexist in time and space and offer irreconcilable ways of ordering experience.[10] Finally, the semantic argument undercuts communication with deconstructive arguments that characterize meaning as hearer-determined.[11]

The pedigree of antifoundationalism is endlessly disputable. Any era, suitably interpreted, will yield antecedents.[12] What is distinctive about contemporary theorists is that they address the

---

communication, and they raise questions about constancy of meaning across speaker/hearer, writer/reader dyads.

[9] Mark Tushnet, for example, says that

> interpretivism and neutral principles attempt to complete the world view of liberalism by explaining how individuals may form a society. [H]owever, . . . the only coherent basis for the requisite continuities of history and meaning is found in the communitarian assumptions of conservative social thought. . . . If I am correct, the liberal account of the social world is inevitably incomplete, for it proves unable to provide a constitutional theory of the sort that it demands.

Mark V. Tushnet, *Following the Rules Laid Down: A Critique of Interpretivism and Neutral Principles*, 96 HARV. L. REV. 781, 785 (1983). Roberto Unger explains how the liberal account seeks to use the concept of rights:

> The rights and principles school . . . claims to discern in the leading ideas of the different branches of law, especially when illuminated by a scrupulous, benevolent, and well-prepared professional elite, the signs of an underlying moral order that can then serve as the basis for a system of more or less natural rights.

ROBERTO M. UNGER, THE CRITICAL LEGAL STUDIES MOVEMENT 13 (1986). Duncan Kennedy strikes similar notes when he says, "I will use the term liberalism to describe the mode of mediation or denial that gradually killed off its rivals, before it finally succumbed to the problems it was designed to solve." Duncan Kennedy, *The Structure of Blackstone's Commentaries*, 28 BUFF. L. REV. 209, 216 (1979).

[10] Arguments defending conceptual relativity are frequently defended by feminist theorists and race theorists. For example, in discussing what she calls the "separation thesis," Robin West concludes that legal theory for men is essentially different in its fundamental assumptions than it is for women. Robin West, *Jurisprudence and Gender*, 55 U. CHI. L. REV. 1, 2-3 (1988). Mari Matsuda argues that race affords a theorist a particular conceptual scheme and that racial perspective "cuts across class lines. . . . There is something about color that doesn't wash off as easily as class." Matsuda, *supra* note 2, at 360-61.

[11] Sanford Levinson comments that in light of "ambiguities of interpretation, many legal theorists have substituted for the hermeneutics of objective interpretation what Gerald Graff has termed a 'hermeneutics of power,' where one emphasizes the political and social determinants of reading texts one way as opposed to another." INTERPRETING LAW AND LITERATURE xiii (Sanford Levinson & Steven Mailloux eds., 1988) (quoting Gerald Graff, *Textual Leftism*, 49 PARTISAN REV. 566 (1982)).

[12] Plausible examples include some of the pre-Socratic philosophers, the Sophists, Nicholas of Cusa, Kierkegaard, and Nietzsche.

erosion of foundations on all three fronts: moral, conceptual, and semantic. At least one way of characterizing the elusive and pervasive notion of postmodernism is by reference to these arguments and the attitudes they express.[13]

Some theorists summarize the destabilizing arguments to conclude that any pooling of goals and ideals must be the adventitious result of a "conversation" among persons with irreconcilable ways of thinking.[14] At one level removed from substantive theory (at the level of "How shall we understand what we do?" rather than the level of "What shall we do?"), the emergent theory of truth and meaning is a version of pragmatism.[15] Pragmatists argue that what is true and has meaning achieves that status provisionally; justificatory arguments for one position or another run out.[16]

B. *Where We Need to Go*

The high priests of antifoundationalism draw inspiration from the work of the philosopher Ludwig Wittgenstein,[17] much of it

---

[13] *See, e.g.*, DOUZINAS, *supra* note 6, at 3-51 (arguing that modernist discourses of law contain the unsettling thematics of postmodernity which these texts attempt to deny); *Postmodernism and Law: A Symposium*, 62 U. COLO. L. REV. 439-598 (1991).

[14] According to Rorty:

> [t]o look for commensuration rather than simply continued conversation—to look for a way of making further redescription unnecessary by finding a way of reducing all *possible* descriptions to one—is to attempt escape from humanity. To abandon the notion that philosophy must show all possible discourse naturally converging to a consensus . . . would be to abandon the hope of being anything more than merely human.

RORTY, *supra* note 4, at 376-77.

[15] For Rorty's definition of pragmatism, see *infra* text accompanying notes 207-09. *See also* Symposium, *Renaissance of Pragmatism in American Legal Thought*, 63 S. CAL. L. REV. 1569-1819 (1990) (spelling out the implications of pragmatism for legal theory).

[16] I shall examine how these theoretical moves define a skeptical posture of doubt about the objectivity of shared values, doubt about one's own impartiality, and doubt about both discovering the meaning of texts and imparting meaning to texts. The attitude appropriate to such doubts is modesty about one's goals, understanding, and powers. Doubts and modesty, on this analysis, are equally appropriate for actors (judges, attorneys) and theorists. The forms of destabilization affect practical and theoretical aims equally. And yet this is not the whole story. In both cases, as feminists and other critical theorists are quick to make clear, cutting loose from shared values, impartial rules, and fixed meanings also empowers those who do not share the prevailing values or benefit from the prevailing rules.

[17] For the best recent discussion of Wittgenstein's views on philosophy, see generally ROBERT J. ACKERMAN, WITTGENSTEIN'S CITY (1988). Surprisingly few writers, however, have addressed Wittgenstein's import for legal theory directly. *But see* Stephen Brainerd, *The Groundless Assault: A Wittgensteinian Look at Language,*

filtered through the influential writings of Richard Rorty[18] and Stanley Fish.[19] Rorty explicitly and Fish implicitly play upon Wittgenstein's remarks about the limits of justification and the constructive character of language.[20] In two respects, however, the recent appropriation of Wittgenstein's ideas for legal theory has been deficient.

First, critical theorists have given little attention to the relationship between practice and theory. The relationship, on first impression, seems well captured by the distinction between being inside and being outside a way of thinking and being.[21] Accordingly, the practitioner takes a way of proceeding for granted, and the theorist attends self-consciously and critically to the practition-

---

Structuralism, and Critical Legal Theory, 34 AM. U. L. REV. 1231 (1985) (outlining some of the intellectual moves that have shaped both critical legal theory in general and structuralism in particular); Scott Landers, *Wittgenstein, Realism, and CLS: Undermining Rule Skepticism*, 9 LAW & PHIL. 177 (1990); Symposium, *Legal Theory and Wittgensteinian Thought*, 3 CANADIAN J.L. & JURIS. 3 (1990).

[18] *See supra* notes 4 & 14.

[19] Stanley Fish's most important essays are collected in two volumes. *See* STANLEY FISH, DOING WHAT COMES NATURALLY (1989) [hereinafter FISH, NATURALLY]; STANLEY FISH, IS THERE A TEXT IN THIS CLASS? (1980) [hereinafter FISH, TEXT]. His essays on the connections between literary theory and legal theory appear in the former volume.

[20] Wittgenstein makes the following comments on this subject:

> 189. At some point one has to pass from explanation to mere description.
>
> . . . .
>
> 191. Well, if everything speaks for an hypothesis and nothing against it—is it then certainly true? One may designate it as such.—But does it certainly agree with reality, with the facts?—With this question you are already going round in a circle.
>
> 192. To be sure there is justification; but justification comes to an end.

WITTGENSTEIN, *supra* note 1, at 26-27.

[21] In *The Concept of Law*, H.L.A. Hart uses the notion of the "internal aspect" of rules to distinguish rules from habits:

> By contrast [with a habit], if a social rule is to exist some at least must look upon the behaviour in question as a general standard to be followed by the group as a whole. A social rule has an 'internal' aspect, in addition to the external aspect which it shares with a social habit and which consists in the regular uniform behaviour which an observer could record.

H.L.A. HART, THE CONCEPT OF LAW 55 (1961). *See also* NEIL MACCORMICK, LEGAL REASONING AND LEGAL THEORY 275-92 (1978). My distinction between being inside or outside a practice differs from Hart's in two respects. First, a theorist who is outside the practice in my sense has an "internal" point of view in Hart's sense insofar as she deploys the notion of rules as constraints and guides for action. Second, my sense of being inside a practice goes further than Hart's "internal aspect." I refer to individuals within the practice as having a commitment to a particular interpretive strategy for applying rules and norms in the light of a conception of the purposes they serve.

er's way of proceeding. But Wittgenstein himself had well-founded misgivings about the very possibility of theory. He stressed that *all* persons–theorists and practitioners alike–inhabit ways of proceeding (thinking, acting, taking things for granted) and cannot step outside.[22] The possibility of doing anything, including the possibility of propounding theories, depends on inhabiting a way of speaking and thinking.[23] If this is true, then the relationship between theory and practice may not be an inside/outside relationship but a relationship of two different ways of being inside. To take this position is the beginning, not the end, of wisdom about theory and practice and about its acute implications for legal theory.[24]

The second area of concern is that antifoundationalists fail to appreciate fully the heterogeneous and complex nature of our belief systems. They assume that a single description or phrase (for instance, "value-bound" or "conceptually relative") describes all of one's beliefs collectively. But when we inhabit a way of proceeding (of thinking, acting, taking things for granted), we have different postures toward different beliefs. Our beliefs vary among several dimensions. One is whether they are controversial. Some beliefs, including many based on religious, political, or moral convictions, are inherently controversial and widely disputed; other beliefs, for example beliefs about historical facts, linguistic definitions, physics and biology, are often widely shared and little discussed or controverted.[25]

---

[22] According to Wittgenstein:

> 127. The work of the philosopher consists in assembling reminders for a particular purpose.
>
> 128. If one tried to advance *theses* in philosophy, it would never be possible to question them, because everyone would agree to them.

LUDWIG WITTGENSTEIN, PHILOSOPHICAL INVESTIGATIONS 50 (G.E.M. Anscombe trans., 1953).

> 220. The reasonable man does *not have* certain doubts.
>
> 221. Can I be in doubt at *will*?
>
> 222. I cannot possibly doubt that I was never in the stratosphere. Does that make me know it? Does it make it true?

WITTGENSTEIN, *supra* note 1, at 29.

[23] The position is defended at length by Fish. *See supra* note 19; *cf.* JEAN-FRANÇOIS LYOTARD & JEAN-LOUP THÉBAUD, JUST GAMING 43 (Wlad Godzich trans., 1985) ("[T]here is no outside; there is no place from which one could photograph the whole thing.").

[24] *See infra* text accompanying notes 62-66.

[25] This is obviously an oversimplification. It is more nearly correct to say that within each area–religion, biology, morality, etc.–some matters are settled (for the time being) and others are controversial. Nevertheless, the matters that arouse

A second dimension is centrality to the individual. Some of my beliefs, whether controversial or not, are closely held. I adhere to them, it seems, at the price of my own identity and sanity and use them as tests and justifications for other beliefs. Some of my beliefs, on the other hand, are easily dislodged by counterargument or counterexperience.[26]

Cutting across these two distinctions among beliefs is a structural distinction among the indescribably varied ways in which we use beliefs or facts[27] of one kind to support or justify beliefs of other kinds. Contemporary theorists pay too little attention to the important fact that persons have idiosyncratic and individual ways of sorting knowledge and of reasoning. There is no given ordering among our beliefs such that some are logically basic or foundational.

For example, we all have beliefs about psychology, history, economics, physics; about what is good and bad, possible and impossible, desirable and undesirable, and so on. One person may support normative conclusions with historical, psychological, sociological, economic, or moral arguments, or several kinds of

---

controversy in everyday life characteristically involve moral and political disagreement, while claims about history and science are controversial among those who are specialists and have a vested interest in a research program.

[26] In *On Certainty*, Wittgenstein repeatedly draws this contrast between propositions that are in practice empirically tested and those that are fundamental to one's way of proceeding. Consider the following passages:

> 55. So is the *hypothesis* possible, that all the things around us don't exist? Would that not be like the hypothesis of our having miscalculated in all our calculations?
>
> . . . .
>
> 446. But why *am* I so certain that this is my hand? Doesn't the whole language-game rest on this kind of certainty?
>
> . . . .
>
> 617. Certain events would put me into a position in which I could not go on with the old language-game any further. In which I was torn away from the *sureness* of the game.
>
> Indeed, doesn't it seem obvious that the possibility of a language-game is conditioned by certain facts?
>
> . . . .
>
> 638. "I can't be making a mistake" is an ordinary sentence, which serves to give the certainty-value of a statement. And only in its everyday use is it justified.

WITTGENSTEIN, *supra* note 1, at 9, 58, 82, 84.

[27] For my purposes it is indifferent whether one uses the term "facts" or "beliefs" to refer to those matters a person holds true and is prepared to justify. "Beliefs" is appropriate when one is calling attention to the intentional status of the proposition.

arguments intimately combined. A person may use historical arguments to back economic conclusions (and vice versa), marshall psychological arguments in historical discourse, explain psychological facts with biological ones—or one can forego such reductive moves.[28]

Antifoundationalists generally offer a simple and stream-lined version of relativism. They disparage references to publicly shared values without considering the varied justificatory arguments available to support them. In particular, they dismiss justification by reference to what is publicly shared and universally accepted as masking justification by reference to what is preferred by the individual or the individual's group.[29] In fact, both kinds of justification coexist in deliberative discourse—and a more insightful version of relativism would examine the way in which individuals use both kinds of justification and how they are constrained by what is intelligible and acceptable to fellow discussants.[30]

Similarly, antifoundationalist writers offer a simplistic relativism when they attack the neutrality of conceptual standpoints regardless of the concepts and arguments at issue. All claims, for them, are equally partial, disputable, and controvertible moves in a "conversation."[31] The machinery of antifoundationalism thus homogenizes reasoning in general and legal reasoning in particular, and that homogeneity is expressed in a pragmatic theory of truth.[32]

This characteristic of antifoundationalism is its Achilles' heel,

---

[28] The notion that no domain of knowledge has explanatory priority over others inherently and objectively has become commonplace in contemporary philosophy. The prevailing view is that explanatory patterns are determined by the interests of the inquirer. *See, e.g.*, RICHARD J. BERNSTEIN, BEYOND OBJECTIVISM AND RELATIVISM (1985); JÜRGEN HABERMAS, KNOWLEDGE AND HUMAN INTERESTS 196-97 (Jeremy J. Shapiro trans., 1968); RATIONALITY AND RELATIVISM (Martin Hollis & Stephen Lukes eds., 1982).

[29] A particularly exhaustive attempt to reduce all value justifications to masked preferences is the critique offered by John Hart Ely. *See* JOHN H. ELY, DEMOCRACY AND DISTRUST 43-72 (1980).

[30] This latter and very different kind of relativism is the thesis that I develop and defend in this article.

[31] In this way the framework set up by Rorty seems generally applicable. *See supra* note 14. These matters are discussed at length in Part IV, *infra*.

[32] Another way of expressing this criticism is that simple relativism, which homogenizes all justificatory strategies and which is expressed by some forms of pragmatism, represents the point of view of the pure outsider to deliberative practices. It ignores the complexity of justificatory strategies that are incumbent on any practitioner within a deliberative practice, on someone for whom the distinctions between partiality and neutrality, personal preference and external norm, etc., remain coherent distinctions. These points are discussed in Part II, *infra*.

the key to its limits and mistakes in general and as applied within legal theory. In this article, I analyze those mistakes and propose a more adequate account of the heterogeneity of reasoning and its implications. In my view, understanding agreement and disagreement in legal reasoning requires a careful examination of the relationship between the individual and the group. How are the reasoning strategies of individuals parasitic upon preexisting practices? In what sense are the strategies of individuals unique? How do the variant strategies of individuals produce disagreement as well as the possibility of addressing such disagreement with shared concepts? What allows individuals to transcend their own strategies by using theory to view their practice as a whole? In other words, I shall describe legal reasoning by looking at it as a "deliberative practice."

The main sections of this article examine legal reasoning to show the jurisprudential importance of the two problems I have raised: the inside/outside problem (the relation of practice and theory) and the heterogeneity of justification and belief. Part II explains the idea of a deliberative practice, implicitly relying on Wittgenstein's insights about reasoning, justification, and belief. Part III demonstrates how the understanding of law as a deliberative practice helps to resolve several key issues concerning the merits and defects of a positivist description of law.[33] Part IV discusses the limitations of antifoundationalism and pragmatism by examining the consequences of their relative inattention to the same two problems, the inside/outside dilemma and the heterogeneity of justification. Characterizing law as a deliberative practice sets us on the road to three goals: (1) giving an elastic and convincing description of legal reasoning; (2) building bridges between the old jurisprudence and the new; and (3) examining the foundations of critical theory by questioning the way in which it claims to destabilize value, conceptual coherence, and meaning.

---

[33] One might reasonably object to calling debates over the nature of law and the merits of positivism "old" jurisprudence. Among American writers, discussions of positivism are frequently subsumed under discussions of formalism. *See, e.g.*, THE RULE OF LAW: IDEAL OR IDEOLOGY (Allan C. Hutchinson & Patrick Monahan eds., 1987); Frederick Schauer, *Formalism*, 97 YALE L.J. 509 (1988); Ernest J. Weinrib, *Legal Formalism: On the Immanent Rationality of Law*, 97 YALE L.J. 949 (1988).

II. Law as a Deliberative Practice

The ways in which judges disagree, in method as well as result, have much in common with other kinds of deliberation; indeed, it is not misleading to think of deliberation as a *genus* and judicial deliberation as its *species*. In judicial deliberation, or any kind of deliberation, the relationship of the individual to the group is problematic. In one sense, the individual follows the same rules of reasoning as other members of the group and is therefore intelligible to them. But, in another sense, she has distinct strategies of understanding and decision-making insofar as she has a unique history and unique capacities.[34]

Legal philosophy has tended to ignore or at least skirt the issue of the relationship of the individual to the group (for example, the relation of the judge to the court on which she sits). Philosophers frequently seem to make one of three simplistic assumptions. Some simply assume that all judges follow the same rules, at least to the point at which they exhaust such rules.[35] Others assume that each judge has a personal way of reasoning, distinct and separate from other judges.[36] Still others attribute to judges (and all persons)

---

[34] The pervasive theme of Wittgenstein's reflections on philosophy, understanding, and language is arguably the notion that all understanding and language use depend on pre-existing practices within the community of language-users and fellow-reasoners. Thus, Wittgenstein does not give as much attention to what individualizes one reasoner from another as I shall do in this article. My main point is that the individual does *not* create or initiate *ex nihilo* strategies of understanding and reasoning. Rather, she derives the ingredients from the pre-existing strategies of others and melds and modifies them in her own experience.

[35] This expresses the point of view of most positivists. Neil MacCormick summarizes H.L.A. Hart's position on decision-making as follows:

> Hart does indeed affirm that law essentially comprises rules. He further affirms that a great part of legal business consists in the straightforward and uncontroversial application, observance and enforcement of rules. But he accepts, in partial agreement with the realists, that rules cannot settle everything. Being framed in language, rules are "open-textured" and often vague. . . . So Hart concludes that within the framework of rules whose meaning is clear enough for some purposes, there is and must be a considerable range of discretion left open to judges and other officials.

Neil MacCormick, H.L.A. Hart 26 (1981) (emphasis omitted).

[36] Dworkin summarizes his best understanding of judicial decision-making when he says that

> [l]aw as integrity . . . requires a judge to test his interpretation of any part of the great network of political structures and decisions of his community by asking whether it could form part of a coherent theory justifying the network as a whole.
>
> . . . .

certain distinctive ways of reasoning characteristic of persons of their gender, their social class, or their race.[37] Viewing law as a deliberative practice allows us to relate the strategies of reasoning of judges, and individuals in general, to groups in a more interesting and illuminating way, one that compels us to rethink the nature of legal reasoning.

A. *Rules, Games, and Judgments*

1. The Hardest Question: A Tale of Two Metaphors

I begin by making clear the generality of the philosophical problem of explaining agreement and disagreement and using the idea of a deliberative practice to show that the hardest question, the central question, in philosophy is the coexistence of agreement and disagreement in all discourse.

This question is so familiar and general an expression of philosophical perplexity throughout its history that some may see it as banal. The possibility of philosophical analysis, or any kind of analysis or communication, is grounded on the commonality of what we think and what we say about experience and language. Whether the example of philosophical analysis is Plato on the good, Kant on understanding, or Rawls on justice,[38] philosophical investigation is possible only if it refers to common experiences expressible in a common language.[39]

> [The judge's] answer will depend on his convictions about the two constituent virtues of political morality we have considered: justice and fairness.

RONALD DWORKIN, LAW'S EMPIRE 245, 249 (1986).

[37] Critical legal theorists emphasize this kind of relativity among judges.

> [Judges'] particular backgrounds, socialization, and experiences . . . result in a patterning, a consistency, in the ways they categorize, approach, and resolve social and political conflicts. This is a great source of the law's power: It reinforces, reflects, constitutes, and legitimizes dominant social and power relations without a need for or the appearance of control from outside.

David Kairys, *Introduction*, *in* THE POLITICS OF LAW 1, 5 (David Kairys ed., rev. ed. 1990).

[38] *See* IMMANUEL KANT, THE CRITIQUE OF PURE REASON (F. Max Müller trans., 1966); PLATO, THE REPUBLIC (Raymond Larson trans. & ed. 1979); JOHN RAWLS, A THEORY OF JUSTICE (1971).

[39] For a discussion of the central role of the self-conscious examination of language in the philosophy of the last fifty years, see THE LINGUISTIC TURN (Richard Rorty ed., 1967); IAN HACKING, WHY DOES LANGUAGE MATTER TO PHILOSOPHY? (1975).

At the same time, these matters–the nature of the good, or understanding, or justice–are never settled once and for all. Let's assume this is not because Plato or Rawls is a second-rate thinker but because deep-seated disagreement as well as agreement is characteristic of the understanding of experience. Persons, whether philosophers or not, are bound to disagree about the good or truth or justice as much as they agree. And the framework of agreement gives structure to the process of disagreeing. We argue about the good or justice and give reasons to persuade others to change their minds. Sometimes, perhaps often, persuasion fails and the arguments break down. Sometimes, perhaps often, the arguments barely get off the ground because the disagreements are profound. But sometimes they succeed.[40] Although this all too familiar situation of agreeing and disagreeing is characteristic of all discourse, philosophy represents it in its most self-conscious form. It is *so* familiar that it defies easy analysis.

a. *Centripetal and Centrifugal Reasoning*

One useful metaphor for representing such agreement and disagreement is the distinction between centrifugal and centripetal forces. A centripetal force draws disparate elements to a common center or axis; a centrifugal force scatters elements by driving them away from a common center or axis. The pervasive emphasis of philosophical discourse has been centripetal. Recent philosophy seeks to clarify shared structures of experience and the shared language in which experience is expressed. It draws attention to a common center, clarifies the common conceptual scheme within which disparate experiences and interpretations of experience occur. To the extent that antifoundationalists question the possibility of a common center and assert that shared values, shared concepts, and a common language are illusory, their impact is centrifugal and therefore subversive.[41]

---

[40] Other things being equal, a theory that recognizes and explains the common experience of persuasion is superior to one that denies or ignores the experience.

[41] To say that a theory is subversive is not necessarily criticism (nor is it necessarily praise). The aim of a theory, on my view, is to describe the centrifugal-centripetal mix of forces correctly–or, to speak nonmetaphorically, to describe the causes of and constraints on agreement and disagreement.

b. *The Metaphor of Games*

The centripetal-centrifugal force metaphor is a process metaphor about moving toward or away from agreement. The second metaphor, the metaphor of games, is structural. It concerns the domain of tacit agreement that makes possible a realm of disagreeing discourse, of argument. The metaphor of games, or more specifically that of playing a game by rules, takes us closer to what is puzzling about agreement and disagreement.

Modern thinkers point out that common beliefs about experience and common practice in the use of language provide the context in which we form opinions, engage in discourse, interpret experience, agree and disagree.[42] These common beliefs look like the rules of a game and our individual judgments/arguments seem comparable to the moves of players. Just as touchdowns and home runs are possible only because the shared rules of football and baseball are taken for granted, so too debates about esthetics or politics or morality appear possible only because we have a shared understanding of the range of mutually understandable positions and of the kinds of moves (of reasons) that count as possible justificatory moves in discourse.[43] Moreover, just as with games, our shared participation in such discourse seems to rest on the fact that we have similar physical capacities, emotions, thought patterns, and linguistic capacities.[44]

The impulse to illuminate the acquisition of knowledge and making of judgments by appeal to the idea of games with rules is seductive. For example, Thomas Kuhn's influential attempt to distinguish normal science from scientific revolutions rests on the

---

[42] This kind of observation leads philosophers like Wittgenstein and those influenced by him to speak about pervasive language-games. *See* WITTGENSTEIN, *supra* note 1, at 2-15.

[43] Perhaps the most influential attempt to use the metaphor of games explicitly is in the early articles of John Rawls. *See, e.g.*, John Rawls, *Two Concepts of Rules*, 64 PHIL. REV. 3 (1955). For Hart's use of the game metaphor, see HART, *supra* note 21, at 138-44.

[44] Wittgenstein makes a similar point, focusing not on similarities in physical and psychological endowment but rather on the beliefs that must be shared and taken for granted for linguistic transactions—indeed, for any investigating or questioning or judging—to occur:

> 343. But it isn't that the situation is like this: We just *can't* investigate everything, and for that reason we are forced to rest content with assumption. If I want the door to turn, the hinges must stay put.
>
> 344. My *life* consists in my being content to accept many things.

WITTGENSTEIN, *supra* note 1, at 44.

claim that normal scientific research is pursued by investigators who agree on research procedures, standards of proof, and basic assumptions about what is to be investigated.[45] They are able to carry on moves within the practice of scientific research because they play by the same rules. By contrast, a scientific revolution occurs when the rules themselves need to be changed.

The metaphorical use of the concept of a game quickly gives rise to difficulty. Is there a clear way to distinguish moves from rules? In true games, one has little trouble telling the rules from the individual moves and strategies of players. The rules of chess or baseball are uncontroversial and uncontroverted by players; they are constitutive[46] and define what counts as scoring, as winning and losing, and as a move. The rules are what one must learn to become a participant. On the other hand, in discourse, in discussions of justice for example, the relation between what is assumed and what is controverted and arguable is itself unstable. In fact, the voluminous philosophical literature on justice shows fundamental disagreement about what the constitutive rules are for the "game" of making judgments about justice.

c. *Applying the Game Metaphor to Law*

How can one distinguish the rules for discussing the nature of justice from moves within the game? The fact that debates among judges are intelligible to the participants and all who read opinions implies that in some sense the participants are engaged in a shared practice and therefore are playing by the same rules. But what are the rules for deciding hard cases of law as opposed to moves made by judges in legal argument? Attempting to identify the rules of the

---

[45] *See* THOMAS S. KUHN, THE STRUCTURE OF SCIENTIFIC REVOLUTIONS (2 International Encyclopedia of Unified Science, 2d ed. 1970).

[46] Rawls defines constitutive rules as follows:

> [T]he rules of practices are logically prior to particular cases. This is so because there cannot be a particular case of an action falling under a rule of a practice unless there is the practice. . . .
>
> One may illustrate this point from the game of baseball. Many of the actions one performs in a game of baseball one can do by oneself or with others whether there is the game or not. For example, one can throw a ball, run, or swing a peculiarly shaped piece of wood. But one cannot steal a base, or strike out, or draw a walk, or make an error, or balk. . . . Striking out, stealing a base, balking, etc., are all actions which can only happen in a game . . . . The practice is logically prior to particular cases: unless there is the practice the terms referring to actions specified by it lack a sense.

Rawls, *supra* note 43, at 25.

shared practice is Sisyphean. Such writers as Rawls and Dworkin distinguish formally between concepts and conceptions, implying that those who agree about concepts are playing by the same rules and that disagreements about conceptions are moves within the practice.[47]

This attempt to sort out moves from rules produces four distinct kinds of theoretical responses, based respectively on liberal consensus theory and on the moral, conceptual, and semantic arguments of antifoundationalists. Liberal theorists such as Ronald Dworkin and Owen Fiss try to justify a deep consensus about justice.[48] They seek to settle disagreement by showing that the shared rules of the game, properly understood, yield clear answers to most legal controversies. Antifoundational theorists, by contrast, subvert such efforts by showing that disagreement is well grounded in irreconcilable and partial ways of understanding and describing experience.

This distinction between consensus and antifoundational theorists allows us to bring the two metaphors together. The consensus theorist offers a complex account of the rules of the game in an attempt to show that disagreement is largely a matter of misunderstanding the rules and that there is a conceptual and moral core to our practices that need only be elucidated. Consensus theorists thus exemplify the centripetal process of theorizing. By contrast, antifoundational theorists seek to offer an account that undercuts the possibility of resolving disagreement by shared conceptual and moral understandings. The impulses of the antifoundationalists are centrifugal.[49] This is well illustrated by

---

[47] "[I]t seems natural to think of the concept of justice as distinct from the various conceptions of justice and as being specified by the role which these different sets of principles, these different conceptions, have in common." RAWLS, *supra* note 38, at 5.

"I might say that I meant the family to be guided by the *concept* of fairness, not by any specific *conception* of fairness I might have had in mind. This is a crucial distinction which it is worth pausing to explore." RONALD DWORKIN, TAKING RIGHTS SERIOUSLY 134 (1977).

[48] *See id.*; DWORKIN, *supra* note 36; Owen M. Fiss, *Objectivity and Interpretation*, 34 STAN. L. REV. 739 (1982). Both writers exemplify what I have called the centripetal force of consensus theory.

[49] It is important to note a sense in which the contrast between centrifugal and centripetal tendencies in theorizing oversimplifies the range of views on constitutional interpretation. Both Dworkin and critical theorists such as Duncan Kennedy emphasize the individuality of judging. Neither liberals nor their critics deny that judges reason in ways that reflect personal style, personal history, etc. All, in this sense, have learned some of the lessons of legal realism. But for liberals, the judge

their approaches to constitutional interpretation.

2. Judicial Interpretation

The questions of how and why our efforts at understanding human experience yield agreement and disagreement are especially acute in law. Law involves the deliberate manipulation of some of the most important circumstances of life. Critical theory is surely correct in its claim that law is not just a product of our decisions but is constitutive of consciousness.

Why has judicial decision-making long been the main focus of jurisprudential discussion on the limits and processes of law?[50] First, the received wisdom holds that judges are constrained by law in deciding cases, constrained by legal rather than political, moral, or prudential concerns. The limits of law are, so the theory goes, the limits of what is relevant in decision-making. Second, the traditional account says that hard cases are those in which judges run up against the limits of law, either because the law doesn't speak to these issues or because it speaks in ways that conflict sharply with other reasons for decision. The process of deciding such cases makes evident the relationship of legal and other justifications. Finally, because the Constitution trumps other law and presents the most intractable problems of interpretation, constitutional interpretation fills the spotlight. It does so whether theorists aim to carry out or to debunk this familiar jurisprudential agenda.

Approaches to constitutional interpretation illustrate well the conflict between centripetal and centrifugal theorizing. Consensus theory exemplifies centripetal theorizing while the three distinct moves of antifoundationalists–skepticism about value, conceptual relativity, and stability in meaning–represent centrifugal theorizing.

---

is nonetheless an exemplar of the interests of law and of the community through law, an exemplar that is capable of transcending the partial interests of a subgroup as reflected in a way of thinking that reflects domination of one subgroup by another. Critical writers question the possibility of such transcendence.

[50] Introductory essays by Dworkin and Tushnet illustrate the tendencies of theorists to identify questions of the bounds and nature of law with questions about the role of judges. *See* RONALD DWORKIN, A MATTER OF PRINCIPLE 9-32 (1985); MARK TUSHNET, RED, WHITE, AND BLUE: A CRITICAL ANALYSIS OF CONSTITUTIONAL LAW 1-17 (1988).

a. *Consensus Theory*

The trajectory traced by the relevant recent writings on constitutional interpretation[51] is deceptively simple. The expressed goal of many writers is a criterion for proper decision-making. Such theorists argue that a criterion is needed to constrain judicial license and to validate criticism of judicial reasoning. Accordingly, some argue that a correct understanding of judicial interpretation (of the rules of the practice) requires adherence to the intentions of the founders.[52] Others try to show that interpretation is governed by "disciplining rules" that assure judicial objectivity.[53] Still others describe a method for arriving at the "best interpretation" of tacit principles embodied in our constitutional legacy.[54] The underlying assumption in each case is that the rules of the practice are capable of constraining judicial discretion and thus fostering a neutral, objective, or integrative approach to decision-making.

b. *Antifoundationalism*

Antifoundational skeptics reject this consensus position, arguing that the rhetoric of neutral rules obscures our understanding of a process that is altogether political. Accordingly, these theorists subvert the idea of objective rules by attacking assumptions about shared social values, individual impartiality, and fixed textual

---

[51] By "recent" I refer to the avalanche of writings since 1970 in constitutional theory. This includes, in the first generation of writers, the work of Ronald Dworkin, John Hart Ely, Michael Perry, Paul Brest, Laurence Tribe, Owen Fiss, and Richard Kay. These writers defend particular approaches to decision-making as constraints upon judicial license and as explicating the true meaning of constitutionalism. The range of approaches represented by these writers is wide, from original intent to various kinds of liberalism. In the 1980s, the flowering of critical theory in the work of many writers, including Mark Tushnet, Sanford Levinson, Catharine MacKinnon, Duncan Kennedy, Robert Gordon, Robin West, Joseph Singer, and Roberto Unger, represents a retreat from the claim that judicial decision-making is indeed constrained and that the idea of constitutionalism is rich enough to embrace principles reflecting the shared interests of all.

[52] Raoul Berger is probably the most prolific theorist defending original intent. *See* RAOUL BERGER, GOVERNMENT BY JUDICIARY: THE TRANSFORMATION OF THE FOURTEENTH AMENDMENT (1977). A recent and eloquent defense of original intent theory is Richard S. Kay, *Adherence to the Original Intentions in Constitutional Adjudication*, 82 NW. U. L. REV. 226 (1988).

[53] *See* Fiss, *supra* note 48, at 744-50.

[54] *See* DWORKIN, *supra* note 36, at 225-75. For a succinct statement of Dworkin's position, see Ronald A. Dworkin, *"Natural" Law Revisited*, 34 U. FLA. L. REV. 165, 166-73 (1982) [hereinafter Dworkin, *Natural*].

meaning.

While all of these antifoundational arguments have centrifugal impact, their scope and implications vary. The moral argument of these critics tracks what many see as common sense: the view that judges have and follow political agendas. The spectrum of political agendas embraces on the political left egalitarian and redistributive processes and goals, and on the right laissez-faire and libertarian ones. A particular judge may have a complex agenda, taking left-leaning positions on some issues and right-leaning ones on others.[55] She may even be torn by conflicting approaches to a particular issue. The spectrum of political agendas is often described in terms of competing conceptions of liberalism, from a welfare state model with a broadly redistributive agenda to a laissez-faire model of minimal state intervention.

The conceptual argument maintains that partiality is unavoidable not only in social values but also in conceptual capacities. Thus, it impeaches the basis of liberalism, the idea of government as a neutral and non-interfering arbiter among persons with different schemes of preference. The argument says that non-interference in preference formation is an illusion because persons do not form preferences independently of the institutional and educative context that makes the existence of preferences and choice possible.[56] Moreover, any such context embodies relationships of power and assumptions about value that shape the conceptual categories and language in which preferences are understood, expressed, and acted upon.

Accordingly, the conceptual argument continues, a communitarian description of the role of government and law must replace liberal assumptions. Communitarian theorists make disparate claims. One is that we must recreate a vanished or hypothesized time of shared social values, a time of consensus about the rules of the practice. A second claim is that one must seek to transcend the conceptual partiality induced by the social and institutional context that defines one's personal history.[57] In embracing deconstructive

[55] In contrast to this man-on-the-street description of judges as creatures of politics, Duncan Kennedy offers an attempt to characterize judging "from the inside." *See* Duncan Kennedy, *Freedom and Constraint in Adjudication: A Critical Phenomenology*, 36 J. LEGAL EDUC. 518 (1986).

[56] *See* MACKINNON, *supra* note 3, at 121-25; Gordon, *supra* note 3, at 102-13; West, *supra* note 2, at 81-90.

[57] Not all critical theorists who maintain the conceptual relativism argument end up advocating communitarianism. Nonetheless, the theme is widely supported and

semantic or linguistic arguments, recent constitutional theory offers a third kind of antifoundational (or centrifugal) gesture in addition to the moral arguments against any possible consensus of social values within liberalism, and to the conceptual arguments against liberalism itself as neutrality. This third attack questions whether texts themselves—in expressing rules, goals, and values—have determinate meaning.[58] If constancy of meaning across different hearers/interpreters is an illusion, then any shared understanding of rules is adventitious and unreliable.

The three antifoundational arguments erode the foundations of the metaphor of games. The moral attack on a liberal consensus theory maintains that the shared rules by which judges judge do not produce common answers to hard questions. The rules are at best rules of language and meaning by which judges recognize one another's justifications. The conceptual attack on liberalism as neutrality maintains that different subcommunities play by different rules with differing commitments, and that shared rules of language and meaning mask rather than bridge diversity. Finally, the semantic attack on language and determinate meaning concludes that reliance on *any* determinate rules is itself an illusion. Thus at each level the metaphor of a game as a practice with shared rules erodes further, eventually to the vanishing point.

---

discussed by critical legal theorists and feminists. *See* TUSHNET, *supra* note 50; Symposium, *The Republican Civic Tradition*, 97 YALE L.J. 1493, 1493-1723 (1988); Joan C. Williams, *Deconstructing Gender*, 87 MICH. L. REV. 797, 836-43 (1989);.

[58] Richard Kay summarizes this view in stating that

> [some] critics emphasize that variability of meaning is a necessary consequence of the multiplicity of readers. Every act of interpretation is a shared enterprise between the text (and its author) and the reader. The consequences of that enterprise depend not only on what the text contains but on the outlook, expectations, and preconceptions of the reader. Interpretation must, therefore, vary from reader to reader, from era to era or from group to group.

Kay, *supra* note 52, at 237-38 (footnote omitted). *See also* FISH, TEXT, *supra* note 19, at 1-17 (tracing Fish's theoretical shift from the view that the text provides meaning and constrains interpretation to the theory that the text is a product of interpretation); *id.* at 97-111 (arguing that "literature" is not a formal set of criteria but rather is "made" by a community of readers). Writers align themselves on a spectrum according to their views about the degree of constraint imposed by the text, the reader's community, etc., as opposed to the degree of freedom and indeterminateness in reading. Gadamer and Fish both discuss the constraining impact of interpretive communities. *See* HANS-GEORG GADAMER, TRUTH AND METHOD 267-72 (1975). For a critique of "nihilistic" versions of this relativist thesis, see Dennis M. Patterson, *Interpretation in Law—Toward a Reconstruction of the Current Debate*, 29 VILL. L. REV. 671, 680-82 (1984).

c. *Implications for Theory and Practice*

Consensus (centripetal) theorists who claim to find determinate constraints on judges by identifying original intent or evolving shared values take the point of view of enlightened participants of the practice and highlight the insider's understanding of the rules. As a result, they meld recommendations for the resolution of hard cases with theoretical analysis and commend particular justificatory schemes and outcomes to judges.[59] By contrast, antifoundational (skeptical, centrifugal, deconstructive) theorists tend to take the perspective of outsiders to the practices they criticize.[60] For example, they attempt to explain why the idea of a consensus is illusory.

Accordingly, moral skeptics, who question the availability of shared values, conclude that the rules of the practice (like those of many true games) insure that players will use competing strategies and have irreconcilable aims.[61] Skeptics who stress the partiality of any conceptual framework speak from the point of view of outsiders and assert a conceptual gulf between the points of view of theorist and participant: the participant, as insider, is trapped within a perspective and constitutes reality from that perspective while the theorist, as outsider, characterizes all participant-perspectives as equally partial, and in this sense claims to transcend them. An even greater gulf exists between the linguistic skeptic, who claims that texts and utterances in general have no determinate meaning, and the participant, whose activity presumes that words communicate and justify decisions.[62]

The difficulties that any theory has in coming to terms with the relationship of participant and theorist reflect the complex, Janus-

---

[59] Dworkin, for example, argues that implicit in his theoretical analysis are ways of resolving hard questions about abortion, free speech, affirmative action, and civil disobedience. *See* DWORKIN, *supra* note 50, at 104-16 (civil disobedience), 293-331 (affirmative action), 335-97 (censorship, pornography, and freedom of the press); DWORKIN, *supra* notes 47, at 123-30 (abortion), 206-22 (civil disobedience), 223-39 (reverse discrimination).

[60] This stance is complicated by the fact that antifoundationalists paradoxically argue that there "is no outside." This is an instance of the skeptical paradox so well described by Strawson. *See infra* note 68.

[61] The extent to which this is true in a given community at a given time will vary with the issue and with the range of positions on the issue. There generally will be harmony on *some* issues.

[62] The extent of the gulf depends, of course, on the relative degree of constraint the theorist is willing to concede to continuity of meaning over time, to stability of meaning within a community, etc. *See supra* note 58 and accompanying text.

like role of judges as appliers of rules and interpreters/creators of rules. If judging is like a game, what role—that of rule-maker, umpire, or player—is performed by the judge? In true games, the distinction between participant and non-participant follows immediately from the rules. Theoretical discourse about the rules themselves, rather than about moves that apply the rules, is the activity of outsiders and not of participants. The fact that judges, who are obviously participants, engage in discourse about the rules *and* in applying the rules complicates the distinction between participant and theorist and underscores how problematic the metaphor of games is in this context.[63]

3. Critique

Each theoretical position on judicial interpretation is open to the criticism that it is counterintuitive. Do consensus theorists imagine that an analysis of the constraints on judging can make hard cases easy and displace disagreements that have survived as long as courts have existed? Such assurance has been and remains a jurisprudential sitting duck.[64] On the other hand, the moral skeptic's tendency to sort out conflicting positions along a familiar political spectrum[65] seems to belie the complexity and diversity of judicial reasoning. The conceptual skeptic's implication that each judge is cocooned within a conceptual scheme, one that presumes unquestioningly a particular allocation of power, entails despair ab

[63] *See supra* text accompanying note 46; *cf. supra* note 21 and text accompanying notes 21-24 (discussing the implications of adopting so-called internal or external points of view).

[64] For an acute critique of Dworkin's theory, see David C. Hoy, *Dworkin's Constructive Optimism v. Deconstructive Legal Nihilism*, 6 LAW & PHIL. 321 (1987). *See also* Larry Alexander, *Striking Back at The Empire: A Brief Survey of Problems in Dworkin's Theory of Law*, 6 LAW & PHIL. 419 (1987); Stanley Fish, *Still Wrong After All These Years*, 6 LAW & PHIL. 401 (1987).

[65] Kennedy claims that "there are two opposed rhetorical modes for dealing with substantive issues, . . . individualism and altruism." Duncan Kennedy, *Form and Substance in Private Law Adjudication*, 89 HARV. L. REV. 1685, 1685 (1976). Kennedy's description of the two modes fits some conceptions of the political spectrum defined by "right" and "left." In this sense, classic liberalism is individualistic and right-wing, whereas modern liberalism is collectivistic. My argument implicitly challenges Kennedy's claim that this particular political dyad, or pair of alternatives, is conceptually primitive. I claim that in addition to the metaphor of government as neutral mediator and the metaphor of government as incorporator and nurturer of value, other metaphors drawn from physics, psychology, history, etc., are equally available and primitive. The range of available metaphors seems in principle unlimited.

initio toward the efforts of judges to reflect upon and effectively to transcend such limits. Finally, judges and all who use language presume in their actions that the linguistic skeptic is misguided and that meaning is communicable.

Each of these theories can be criticized for assuming that what can be said of some instances of judicial reasoning can be said for all. Some consensus theorists assume that if judges are constrained by history (original intent) in some cases, then history is equally relevant in all.[66] Others argue that if there is a consensus of value, then cases in general are to be resolved by appeal to it.[67] If judges are ever affected by conceptual bias, by non-neutrality, then they are generally affected in this way. If language is indeterminate, if communication is imperfect, it is generally imperfect. All four of these presuppositions homogenize judicial reasoning. All for that reason seem counterintuitive.[68]

My critique is sketchy and incomplete. It is intended not to dismiss consensus and skeptical theories, but to situate them by reference to their characterization of agreement and disagreement. Consensus theory maintains that disagreement is in principle eradicable. Skeptical theories hold that disagreement is deep and enduring.[69] All of the theories reach these conclusions by taking

---

[66] *See* BERGER, *supra* note 52, at 363-72 (arguing that original intent should always be used as an interpretive guide).

[67] *See, e.g.*, DWORKIN, *supra* note 36; DWORKIN, *supra* note 47; Fiss, *supra* note 48 (discussing the notion of an "interpretive community" as central to his argument on the possibility of objective interpretation).

[68] Theorists often take a characteristic of *some* instances of reasoning and treat it as a characteristic of all reasoning. Everyone can easily summon up instances of values that are relative (variable across individuals), of concepts that reflect bias, of indeterminate language, or of cases in which adherence to historical intent is defensible. But universalizing these observations is not plausible. Not all values are relative in the same way; some values reflect variable preferences while others reflect universal needs. To call the latter "relative" is to remove the term from ordinary usage, and thus not to speak unequivocally. Similarly, the policies of Amnesty International do not reflect bias in the way that, for example, the policies of the State of Mississippi in 1961 did. To say that all policies reflect the biases of the empowered is, again, to give specialized meaning to "bias" and to use it equivocally. Some uses of language give rise to perceptions of ambiguity and to puzzlement; others do not. To say that both are "indeterminate" is to use the term equivocally, employing its ordinary usage in the first instance but not in the second. *Cf.* P.F. STRAWSON, INDIVIDUALS: AN ESSAY IN DESCRIPTIVE METAPHYSICS 106 (1959) ("So with many skeptical problems: their statement involves the pretended acceptance of a conceptual scheme and at the same time the silent repudiation of one of the conditions of its existence. That is why they are, in the terms in which they are stated, insoluble.")

[69] This view is also commonplace among political scientists. The special

shortcuts, by assuming that certain generalizations about legal justification hold universally. Before devising a more complete critique of these theories, I shall offer an account of judicial agreement and disagreement that explains them in terms of the heterogeneity of justificatory strategies.

B. *Practices and Deliberative Practices*

To understand how consensus theorists and skeptics alike overlook essential features of legal reasoning and buy theoretical clarity at the cost of misdescription, we need to look at the heterogeneous character of legal justification and the scope of justificatory patterns that judges use to explain judgments. Doing so requires us to examine the more general idea of a practice and the narrower idea of a deliberative practice before applying the concept of a deliberative practice to judicial reasoning.

1. Practices in General

The concept of a practice is among the most useful (and controversial) tools of twentieth-century philosophy.[70] An intuitive look at practices may begin with such nonlinguistic activities as driving or swimming. In each case, persons acquire skills or ways of proceeding that become habitual and unreflective. When we call such skills "second nature," we mean that, though they are socially and culturally grounded, such ways of proceeding become as much a part of us as our genetic endowment.[71]

---

contribution of critical theory is to give this assumption a conceptual or epistemological character—in reaction to the common disregard of questions of epistemological relativism in debates between positivists and naturalists. So long as the main concern of theory was the nature of law and so long as that issue was not reduced to the nature of resources for judging, epistemology was not of immediate concern. Once judges took center stage, epistemological questions could no longer be avoided.

[70] The conception of philosophy as the examination of practices, preeminently linguistic practices, has come under sustained attack. For one of the earliest sets of critical articles, see CLARITY IS NOT ENOUGH: ESSAYS IN CRITICISM OF LINGUISTIC PHILOSOPHY (H.D. Lewis ed., 1963); *cf.* ESSAYS ON MORAL REALISM (Geoffrey Sayre-McCord ed., 1988) (providing a moral realist view at odds with the practice conception, treating it as a form of conventionalism); REDRAWING THE LINES: ANALYTIC PHILOSOPHY, DECONSTRUCTION, AND LITERARY THEORY (Reed W. Dasenbrock ed., 1989) (examining the implications of the practice conception in reference to contemporary theories).

[71] One might distinguish swimming from driving by arguing that acts involving survival and locomotion in water are, to some extent, natural and spontaneous—although they are not universal and although particular strokes must be learned. Driving, on the other hand, is wholly an adaptation to technology and in no sense is

A habitual repertoire has distinctive features and distinctive ways of perceiving, feeling, and acting. A good driver makes judgments about road conditions and the disposition of other drivers, apprehends dangers, and acts accordingly. What she does unreflectingly can, however, be made conscious.[72] Ordinarily, doing so is neither necessary nor appropriate.

A characterization of what is involved in having such a skill, in being a good driver, is at once descriptive and normative. The characteristics of a driver (in general) are distinguished only in degree from the characteristics of a good driver. To be able to identify driving is also to be able to tell good driving. Both thresholds are inherently vague. No clear and simple criterion distinguishes those who cannot drive from those who do so very badly.[73] Similarly, not everyone will agree on the marks of very good driving. But the range of understandable disagreement is low.

2. Linguistic Practices

Some of our practices are primarily communicative (as driving obviously is not). And some of our communicative practices, by far the most important ones, are linguistic. Wittgenstein attends to such aspects of language as color-descriptions and expressions of pain. Just as driving is a skill that individuals acquire because a public practice, a shared activity, already exists, so too perceptions of color and distinctions among kinds of pain manifest the acquired skills of those who have been initiated into certain practices.[74] Persons identify colors and pains to the extent that a place exists for

---

the repertoire of the behavior natural or spontaneous. Psychologists might regard all these observations as trivially true. Among some philosophers before Wittgenstein, such as Locke and Hume, the notion that the capacity to recognize objects and name them was natural and spontaneous, rather than part of a socially learned repertoire, was a basic tenet of epistemology. *See* 1 DAVID HUME, A TREATISE OF HUMAN NATURE 1-25 (1890, orig. 1739); 2 JOHN LOCKE, AN ESSAY CONCERNING HUMAN UNDERSTANDING 3-164 (Alexander C. Fraser ed., 1959) (1690). For Wittgenstein's criticisms of the natural and spontaneous capacity theory, see WITTGENSTEIN, *supra* note 22, at 2-10.

[72] Perhaps unconscious repertoires of behavior cannot be made completely conscious. Consider the way one conveys attitude by facial expression, intonation, etc. Self-scrutiny can discover some dimensions of the repertoire but probably not all.

[73] *See* THOMAS MORAWETZ, THE PHILOSOPHY OF LAW 11-16 (1980) (noting as an illustrative example the conceptual difficulties in defining a knife).

[74] *See* WITTGENSTEIN, *supra* note 22, at 88-93, 95-104; *see also* LUDWIG WITTGENSTEIN, REMARKS ON COLOUR (G.E.M. Anscombe ed., Linda L. McAlister & Margarete Schättle trans., 1977).

the recognition of color and the expression of pain in the relevant practices of a culture.[75]

3. Deliberative Practices

These considerations about practices in general and about simple linguistic practices in particular have implications for more complex practices involving deliberation. A deliberative practice consists of discourse directed toward forming and defending judgments. Examples of deliberative practices are esthetic debate, moral reasoning, discussions about history, and judicial decision-making. The subject may be whether an object is beautiful, or whether an action is right, or whether an event is a turning point in history, or whether a plaintiff has a right to a favorable judgment.

All such debates have certain features in common. All involve widely shared activities and/or institutions in civilized societies. All involve abstract questions that have preoccupied persons throughout history and seem intractable.

a. *Understanding Disagreement*

All practices allow the possibility, indeed the inevitability, of idiosyncracy within shared ways of proceeding. Even though persons share a sense of what driving is, each driver has a personal style. Similarly, each of us has a distinctive way of using color language: I may tend not to discriminate among various shades of red; one friend may sharply distinguish scarlet and crimson; another friend may use these two terms in a distinctively different way.[76]

In deliberative activities, this diversity within shared mutually understood ways of proceeding is especially significant. No two persons have the same history or have the same dispositions. Some are more credulous than others, more perceptive, more doubting, more impulsive; some are better versed in history, some in physics,

---

[75] Some philosophers have seen this suggestion as revolutionary and counter-intuitive. The philosophical assumption of most empiricists has been that the domain of private experience is fully configured and that the public arena of language is merely a set of conventions and labels attached to the distinct elements of private experience. But Wittgenstein challenges this assumption. He asks us to reflect on what it could be like to experience a color for which a place was not already prepared in the experiential realm shared with others.

[76] Ordinarily, the shared practice offers all of us means for discovering and sorting out our divergent ways of proceeding in those relatively rare cases in which it matters to do so. To that extent, variation exists and is discoverable within a shared context.

some in psychology; and some are generally ignorant. Much more importantly, each has a characteristic way of reasoning that represents an interpretive orientation to the world, a way of making sense of the phenomena of experience by giving order to the many domains of knowledge and opinion in which she or he participates.

Consider the diversity of reasons given to justify and explain esthetic judgments. One person may offer psychological grounds for finding something beautiful. Another may refer to inherent properties of the object itself. Yet another may look to the ways in which the object expresses the intentions of the artist and to the quality of those intentions. A fourth may appeal to the social and political function of the object in assessing esthetic worth.[77]

Other deliberative practices can be broken down in a similar manner. One historian will use the influence of ideas as the *explanans* that unlocks historical change; another will look to economic motives and events; still another will stress the charismatic influence of leaders.[78] In moral discourse, one theorist will see altruistic utilitarianism as offering the most coherent account of moral judgment; another will see psychologistic or hedonistic utilitarianism as basic; a third will argue that moral reasoning is essentially deontological.[79]

b. *Agreement and the Bounds of Practice*

It is as important to see what draws participants in deliberative practices together as to see what separates them. Even when they disagree, participants recognize and understand each others' argumentative strategies. They share a sense of what reasons are relevant to the common discourse. Discussing beauty, they may

---

[77] For a recent collection of articles on various esthetic theories, including cognitivism, representationalism and expressionism, see MODERNISM, CRITICISM, REALISM (Charles Harrison & Fred Orton eds., 1984).

[78] *See* PATRICK GARDINER, THE NATURE OF HISTORICAL EXPLANATION 65-112 (1952) (examining historians' method of explaining events); *see generally* SIDNEY HOOK, THE HERO IN HISTORY (1943) (arguing that historical events are primarily the product of extraordinary individuals).

[79] For recent and thought-provoking discussions of metaethical questions, see THOMAS NAGEL, THE VIEW FROM NOWHERE 164-88 (1986) (analyzing reasons for departing from the general goal of objective ethical criteria); BERNARD WILLIAMS, ETHICS AND THE LIMITS OF PHILOSOPHY 30-93 (1985) (evaluating the contribution of philosophy to coherence in ethical reasoning); *see also* C.D. BROAD, FIVE TYPES OF ETHICAL THEORY (1934) (explaining and criticizing the ethical theories of Spinoza, Butler, Hume, Kant, and Sidgwick); ALASDAIR MACINTYRE, WHOSE JUSTICE? WHICH RATIONALITY? (1988) (arguing for the possibility of cross-cultural rationality in ethics).

consider symmetry and asymmetry, balance and imbalance, representational aspects of the object, context, or purpose. They will not consider relevant whether the artist had a short life, whether her name began with a vowel, or whether the object or performance is privately financed. These observations may seem obvious, but only because they are so familiar, only because they are "second nature." Each participant can generally anticipate the moves that others will make.[80] The practice consists in the recognition of a family of reasoning strategies that allow for a spectrum of judgments.

Thus, it is not the case that anything counts. Just as in driving or in identifying colors, the publicly shared understanding of what moves are comprehensible ways of proceeding circumscribes the practice and makes it possible. To try to imagine a practice in which any act by someone sitting in a driver's seat counts as driving or a practice in which any use of a color word is meaningful is to imagine the impossible.

In deliberative practices, each participant will to some extent take account of the reasons offered by others by trying to accomodate them within her own favored strategy.[81] The utilitarian will generally have considered and, to her satisfaction, explained away

---

[80] It seems to me this is what Wittgenstein had in mind when he said:

> 80. The *truth* of my statements is the test of my *understanding* of these statements.
>
> 81. That is to say: if I make certain false statements, it becomes uncertain whether I understand them.
>
> . . . .
>
> 83. The *truth* of certain empirical propositions belongs to our frame of reference.
>
> . . . .
>
> 149. My judgments themselves characterize the way I judge, characterize the nature of judgment.

WITTGENSTEIN, *supra* note 1, at 12e, 22e. Wittgenstein's insight seems to be that any practice allows certain justificatory moves and not others, and that such other moves are necessarily unintelligible and mark those who make them as nonparticipants, mark their comments as nonsense. This is true of all language-games, true of all discourse: every language-game is comprised of generally understood rules of relevance. Intelligibility of any kind of discourse depends on shared conceptions of relevance and irrelevance. Those who offer irrelevant evidence, justification, etc., are speaking nonsense as far as the shared practice goes.

[81] This is not to say that one participant may not simply be dismissive of others. But the justifications offered by that participant are defective or incomplete unless she can take account of others' reasons either by showing why her way of deciding is superior or by modifying her way of deciding to accommodate and assimilate what she finds valuable in the alternatives.

non-utilitarian strategies and will have a favored account of their appeal; the non-utilitarian will approach the utilitarian in the same way. The person who gives psychological explanations for economic phenomena will have ways of accounting for and rejecting the opposite approach, and vice versa. Judges who find an evolving consensus of values can explain why others find a different consensus or none at all, and can argue why the others are wrong. Thus, an essential part of each participant's way of proceeding will be a strategy for incorporating or dismissing the favored strategies of others. And each in turn will recognize and anticipate such moves as part of the ongoing practice.

Equally essential to each participant's way of proceeding is the recognition of her strategy's limitations. First, she will continually encounter–and expect to encounter–new alternatives, new strategies and new ways of thinking that she has not yet considered. Second, she will appreciate that her strategy does not offer a "transcendental" argument which subsumes the strategies of others but one which is instead on a par with theirs: for each move she makes to answer or accommodate others, these others can in principle make a similar move. The expectation is of perpetual dialogue, not final solutions.

c. *Discourse and Debate*

The diverse strategies that make up a deliberative practice compete because there is no natural order of precedence among categories of facts, among categories of reasons and justifications. Categorical reduction can occur in many directions. For example, some theorists explain political and economic phenomena by reducing them to psychological patterns. Other theorists argue that social experience is not reducible to individual psychological categories and that economic phenomena are based on idealized models and not psychology. The claim that all phenomena are explainable through the hard sciences of physics and chemistry is now widely rejected along with the supposed superiority of microscopic to macroscopic explanations.[82] Reductionism in aesthetics does not fare better. Appeals to the inherent features of a work of art are neither more nor less basic a mode of justification

---

[82] PETER WINCH, THE IDEA OF A SOCIAL SCIENCE: AND ITS RELATION TO PHILOSOPHY 8-9 (1958) (arguing that scientific methods are not capable of answering the philosophical question of "what is real?").

(in esthetic reasoning) than appeals to the creator's intentions or to the work's gestalt.[83]

It is therefore up to the individual to choose among available competing forms of explanation and to favor or reject reductionist arguments. Convictions about relations among categories of knowledge run deep. Try to shake the conviction of one who holds that morality can "ultimately" be explained by chemical events in the brain, or the conviction of someone who rejects this. Try to dispel the reductionist approach of someone who favors a psychological account of, say, the attractions of fascism—or try to instill such an approach in someone who thinks it is simplistic and banal.[84] In defending one's own judgment in a particular case, one is also defending one's style of judgment, one's way of ordering the data of experience to give some kinds precedence. The attempt to convince others is not only an attempt to make them agree with one's own conclusions but also an attempt to bring them around to one's style of judgment.[85]

d. *Persuasion*

The persuasive attempts of each participant are not, as one might think, doomed. To say that each participant has a particular way of proceeding in reasoning is not to say that she is condemned to repeat the same moves forever. Individual participants differ not only in judgments and in ways of reaching those judgments, but also in their susceptibility to persuasion, and to considering and adopting other points of view and other strategies. The practice itself, as a collection of strategies mutually recognized by participants, evolves. Over time some strategies gain currency while others go into temporary or permanent remission. Particular styles of moral reasoning, of thinking about history, or of judging what the appropriate role for government gain currency and then fade.[86]

---

[83] *See supra* text accompanying note 77.

[84] A good example is the controversy that followed publication of HANNAH ARENDT, EICHMANN IN JERUSALEM: A REPORT ON THE BANALITY OF EVIL (1963). *See Hannah Arendt*, Major Twentieth Century Writers, Aug. 1991, *available in* LEXIS, Nexis Library, Allbio File (noting that Arendt's "subtle arguments provoked highly emotional responses" among critics).

[85] The impulse toward harmonizing or reconciling one's way of proceeding with others' may be overridden by practical concerns. A judge will sometimes be content for others to concur with her in result even if the result is reached on different grounds.

[86] For example, emotive approaches to morality, "great man" theories of historical

C. *Judicial Decision as a Deliberative Practice*

The general description of deliberative practices highlights the heterogeneity of the various strategies of reasoning that constitute such practices. Deliberative practices encompass two kinds of heterogeneity.

First there is heterogeneity within an individual's way of proceeding. A given person will solve different problems in different ways—with evidence drawn from whatever realms of experience seem appropriate. A judge may draw on moral arguments in some cases, historical or economic arguments in others.[87] Some judgments will reflect one's deepest convictions, while others will reflect less fundamental beliefs.

Second, there is heterogeneity among those making judgments. Each judgment-maker has her own idiosyncratic ways of ordering experience within the mutually recognized bounds of what is intelligible in the deliberative practice.

Legal theorists have not adequately taken into account the complex nature of judicial decision-making. This is true of consensus theorists as well as antifoundational skeptics. The latter's references to value schemes and conceptual systems oversimplify and exaggerate the sources and nature of disagreement by closeting them into discrete value systems or conceptual frameworks.[88]

Thus, theorists do not look deeply enough into the sources and kinds of disagreement among judges. Certainly, theorists deal with the brute fact that judges reach different results. Theorists also take into account that judges who vote the same way may disagree in

---

influence, mechanistic explanations of behavior, and civil libertarian theories of government all move on and off center stage. These theories may become prevailing modes of thinking, reasoning, and justifying or they may be widely rejected.

[87] To do so is not to be inconsistent. Such a judge may be fairly accused of inconsistency only if she commits herself to inconsistent propositions or if she chooses modes of justification arbitrarily, with no principled manner of selection. Only a theoretical commitment to homogeneity would lead one to expect judges to decide every case on historical grounds (original intent) or on economic grounds. Such theoretical commitments can be defended. *See* RICHARD A. POSNER, ECONOMIC ANALYSIS OF LAW 15-23 (2d ed. 1977) (defending economic efficiency as the ultimate criterion); Kay, *supra* note 52, at 236-92 (defending deference to historical intent as inherent in constitutionalism). Such theoretical commitments to homogeneity, however, are notoriously vulnerable to counterarguments.

[88] *See* Kennedy, *supra* note 65, at 1685; West, *supra* note 2, at 81-90 (arguing that the "male legal culture" frames its justificatory arguments in response to men's hedonic lives and that a different and alternative conceptual framework is offered through an understanding of women's hedonic lives).

their justificatory reasoning. One judge may argue that stopping drivers at random to check for intoxication implicates the fourth amendment, but is justified by exigency and is a minimal infringement.[89] Another judge reaching the same decision may argue that stopping drivers at random does not implicate the fourth amendment at all.

Theorists characteristically ignore the fact that judges disagree in a third and much more interesting way: in their ways of structuring information—counting some kinds of propositions as evidence for other propositions and resting their arguments on one kind of proposition rather than another because the former is conclusive in their particular way of understanding experience. A judge may cite social conditions as ultimate reasons for a decision, for example the fact that one class of individuals is systematically disadvantaged.[90] Another judge may claim that psychological effects on individuals are of primary importance.[91] A third judge may cite economic facts as ultimate, for example the fact that the more-or-less efficient market distribution of goods or benefits in society will be compromised or curtailed.[92] Yet another will look

---

[89] *See, e.g.*, Stark v. Perpich, 590 F. Supp. 1057 (D. Minn. 1984) (holding that stopping vehicles at a roadside drunk driving survey constitutes a seizure under the Fourth Amendment, but that such seizures may still be permissible under certain circumstances); Garrett v. Goodwin, 569 F. Supp. 106 (E.D. Ark. 1982) (same, but also dismissing Fourteenth Amendment considerations); Little v. State, 479 A.2d 903 (Md. 1984) (same).

[90] *See, e.g.*, Bowers v. Hardwick, 478 U.S. 186, 219 (1986) (Stevens, J., dissenting) (stating that a state's justification for selective application of a statute must be supported by a "neutral interest" and not just a mere dislike for the disfavored group); Yick Wo v. Hopkins, 118 U.S. 356, 373-74 (1886) (holding that the result of systematic denial of permission to Chinese people to carry on businesses demonstrated a violation of the Equal Protection Clause of the Fourteenth Amendment).

[91] *See, e.g.*, *Bowers*, 478 U.S. at 205 (Blackmun, J., dissenting) (claiming that "individuals define themselves in a significant way through their intimate sexual relationships with others" and for the Government to dictate the norms of sexual conduct would have severe psychological implications for the individual citizen); Brown v. Board of Education, 347 U.S. 483, 494 (1954) ("To separate [schoolchildren] from others of similar age and qualifications solely because of their race generates a feeling of inferiority as to their status in the community that may affect their hearts and minds in a way very unlikely ever to be undone.").

[92] *See, e.g.*, POSNER, *supra* note 87, at 525 (stating that "although there are pecuniary gains to trade between blacks and whites . . . by increasing the contact between members of the two races such trade imposes nonpecuniary, but real, costs on those members of either race who dislike association with members of the other race"). Wrongful birth cases also illustrate judges' differing strategies in finding moral or economic modes of justification relevant and decisive. *See, e.g.*, Ochs v. Borrelli, 445 A.2d 883, 885 (Conn. 1982) (focusing on the economic injury caused by physician's negligence); Cockrum v. Baumgartner, 425 N.E.2d 968 (Ill. App. Ct. 1981)

to political effects, assessing the likelihood that participation in government and the enjoyment of the benefits of democracy will be diminished.[93] Still another may look to the values or principles deliberately implanted by the founders of the Constitution and will take as ultimate the importance of adherence to those principles.[94]

1. Disagreement Among Judges

One may address the complexity of a deliberative practice by taking note of the different, mutually recognized justificatory strategies that it embraces, different ways of ordering categories of knowledge or of using modes of explanation. One can also describe this complexity as wholly individualized, since each individual judge will have personal ways of juxtaposing and relating justifications drawn from her beliefs. Her strategies of reasoning will necessarily differ, at least in some ways, from those of each of her colleagues. No two judges will write exactly the same judicial opinions. Each will have different starting and finishing points for argument, different ways of deciding what is the *explanans* and what is the *explanandum*.[95]

2. The Bounds of Judicial Disagreement

Why and how does debate among judges persist in the face of this structural bias against agreement and harmony? One must remember what binds judges into a shared practice as well as what is personal and idiosyncratic.

First, any judge understands and anticipates that other judges

---

(in the case of an unwanted birth, finding that "the [emotional] rewards of parenthood should not be allowed in mitigation of rearing costs [damages]"), *rev'd* 447 N.E.2d 385 (Ill. 1983); Berman v. Allan, 404 A.2d 8, 14-15 (N.J. 1979) (apparently weighing moral and economic considerations against each other).

93 These concerns may be seen as central in a wide array of opinions. John Hart Ely has argued at length for their centrality. *See* ELY, *supra* note 29, at 135-99.

94 *See* cases and examples cited approvingly by Berger and Kay, *supra* note 52.

95 An important implication of my analysis is that there is no sharp or clean distinction between facts and values. The justificatory arguments of individuals include both facts and values, as well as intricate logical relationships among factual and value-based beliefs. For example, certain "factual" convictions about how persons are motivated, how they are affected by adversity, and how power relationships are perceived and perpetuated will (in conjunction with other premises and other beliefs) lead to certain "value" conclusions about what is fair and unfair in the regulation of such persons' lives. Convictions about fairness or justice or mercy—all of them "values"—may serve as premises or as conclusions of justificatory arguments. The same multiple roles are assumed by "facts."

will have different patterns or styles of reasoning. More importantly, she understands that only certain patterns are intelligible as being within the practice. Thus a judge who decides cases in favor of the taller party, by reference to astrological projections, or by deferring to the ambassador of Lichtenstein would be intelligible in the sense that one could anticipate her responses but not intelligible as a participant in the practice of judicial decision-making.[96]

The practice involves a family of ways of structuring and ordering relevant evidence for decision-making. Each judge recognizes that other judges reason in certain ways, recognizes how they reason, and can give some account of why they reason as they do. The practice is bounded not by a single shared style of reasoning but by familiar, if unspecifiable, criteria for the kinds of reasoning that count. In the absence of such criteria, the practice would fall apart. Yet the criteria are malleable, and the line between included and excluded ways of thinking and of justifying decisions is not sharp.[97]

3. The Driving Force of Judicial Persuasion

The mutual recognition of permissible styles of justification does not sufficiently explain the persistence of deliberation among judges. When persons recognize that others have different ways of arriving at truth, that others favor economic or psychological or moral arguments, they continue to deliberate. Why do they persist?

---

[96] *See supra* note 81 and accompanying text.

[97] Obviously such criteria evolve; what counts as acceptable, recognizable style or content changes over time. References to natural, inalienable rights "under God" may have been an acceptable mode of justification in the early nineteenth century. The use of natural law in contemporary opinions is more covert and wears the guise of fundamental rights explained in terms of familiar social facts and substantive due process. *See, e.g.*, Moore v. City of East Cleveland, 431 U.S. 494, 503-04 (1977) (stating that constitutional protection of the sanctity of the family is not confined to an arbitrary boundary drawn at the limits of the nuclear family, and that limits on substantive due process should be drawn from basic societal values); Roe v. Wade, 410 U.S. 113, 152-53 (1973) (concluding that the right to privacy existing "under the Constitution" encompasses a woman's decision to terminate her pregnancy); Griswold v. Connecticut, 381 U.S. 479, 486 (1965) (concluding that the institution of marriage confers upon individuals a right of privacy "older than the Bill of Rights"). Evolving notions of what is expected and understood as the appropriate content of justification are even more clearly marked. Efficiency of distribution of resources has come to be treated as a covert but ultimately political value by some judges, *see* POSNER, *supra* note 87, at 415 (stating that "when judges are the makers of the substantive law the rules of law will tend to be consistent with the dictates of efficiency"), a mode of justification unknown and unanticipatable a generation or more ago.

What kinds of success do they hope for?

The answer seems to lie in the *stake* that participants have in their ways of thinking, in their ways of proceeding within the practice. The participants themselves see what they are doing not simply as optional verbal gestures but as manifestations of the process of understanding the world—understanding why events occur, what purposes they serve, and what goals are worth serving. This is true in judicial debate as in all other cognitive and deliberative activity.

One judge, for example, may see economic events and economic motives as the operative levers of human and social action. For the world to be intelligible to her, she will not only describe events in accord with this commitment but will also try to persuade others to see the world in this way. The fact that others do not see the world this way is for her a recalcitrant experience, not just one of several recognized options. At the same time, she recognizes that a different judge will describe things and justify opinions differently, and she will feel committed to move others to understand and adopt her explanatory strategies, her ways of making sense of the world. But she recognizes that there are no agreed-upon or neutral standards of justification, no meta-game wherein she can justify once and for all her way of thinking.[98]

Each individual will hold certain convictions as basic and unshakable, as criteria for weighing the importance of other reasons and justifications. One judge or commentator will see a system that perpetuates any kind of racial discrimination as prima facie unacceptable.[99] Another, believing that freedom to pursue economic goals is essential to any system of liberty and autonomy and that certain groups have been denied this freedom, may view discrimination as justified in some cases.[100] Yet another may see

---

[98] This point is controversial. Any theorist who claims that a particular method or mode of justification—such as original intent—is analytically the only correct method and is implied by the idea of constitutionalism, and any theorist who similarly claims to have identified a value to which all other values are reducible, e.g. economic efficiency, will reject this conclusion. My suggestion is that no method exists to validate such competing claims of correctness.

[99] *See, e.g.*, City of Richmond v. J.A. Croson Co., 488 U.S. 469, 520 (1989) (Scalia, J., concurring) ("I do not agree . . . with [the Court's dicta] suggesting that, despite the Fourteenth Amendment, state and local governments may in some circumstances discriminate on the basis of race in order (in a broad sense) 'to ameliorate the effects of past discrimination.'").

[100] *See, e.g.*, *id.* at 529 (Marshall, J., dissenting) (stating that "the Richmond City Council *has* supported its determination that minorities have been wrongly excluded

the essence of constitutionalism in preserving the limited role of the federal government as envisaged in the Federalist papers and the debates among founders.[101] For a fourth, a perception of our society as involving and perpetuating an invidious social structure may determine what results can and cannot be justified.[102]

It is hard to overestimate the interest any person has in her way of making sense of experience, solving hard questions, and making judgments. One clings to modes or styles of thinking more tenaciously and profoundly than one does to particular opinions.[103] It is more vital to one's continuing identity to believe, for example, that psychological or sociological data are the tools by which issues are resolved than to cling, come what may, to any particular judgment that such data yield.[104] Thus, debates within deliberative practices are perpetuated by the need to assert both solutions to hard and disputed questions *and* particular ways of arriving at such solutions. The attempt to persuade others to "see" the world in the same way as one sees it oneself is parasitic upon

---

from local construction contracting. . . . These are precisely the types of statistical and testimonial evidence which, until today, this Court had credited in cases approving of race-conscious measures designed to remedy past discrimination.").

[101] *See, e.g.*, PAUL BREST & SANFORD LEVINSON, PROCESSES OF CONSTITUTIONAL DECISIONMAKING 422 (2d ed.1983) ("After examining the debates in the Thirty-ninth Congress, [Raoul Berger] concludes that the adopters of the Fourteenth Amendment merely intended to ensure the constitutionality of the Civil Rights Act of 1866 and that *Brown* and almost all other Supreme Court decisions under the Fourteenth Amendment are incorrect." (citing BERGER, *supra* note 52, at 10)).

[102] *See* Brown v. Board of Education, 347 U.S. 483 (1954)

[103] Wittgenstein focuses attention on the importance to the individual of certain ways of reasoning:

> 559. You must bear in mind that the language-game is so to say something unpredictable. I mean: it is not based on grounds. It is not reasonable (or unreasonable).
> It is there–like our life.
> . . . .
> 608. Is it wrong for me to be guided in my actions by the propositions of physics? Am I to say I have no good ground for doing so? Isn't precisely this what we call a 'good ground'?
> 609. Supposing we met people who did not regard that as a telling reason. Now, how do we imagine this? Instead of the physicist, they consult an oracle. (And for that reason we consider them primitive.) Is it wrong for them to consult an oracle and be guided by it?–If we call this 'wrong' aren't we using our language-game as a base from which to *combat* theirs?
> . . . .
> 616. Why, would it be *unthinkable* that I should stay in the saddle however much the facts bucked?

WITTGENSTEIN, *supra* note 1, at 73, 80-81.

[104] *See id.*

the habit of giving structure to one's own experience, of deploying one's strategies of thinking.

4. The Grounds of Persuasion and Change

These strategies are recursive in the sense that they include the possibility, virtually the certainty, of self-modification through understanding and continually reconsidering the strategies of others. This prospect of evolving exists both for the individual and for the shared practice as a whole. What seems false or unacceptable to a person at one time may come to be a central truth by which other claims are judged.[105] For the deliberative practice as a whole, some precepts and justificatory patterns that seem revolutionary at one time may be widely regarded as common sense a generation later. The role of privacy and autonomy in interpreting constitutional rights is just one such example.[106]

D. *Immersion in Practice as an Obstacle to Theory*

The question of whether judges are playing by the same or different rules when they disagree and offer incommensurable justifications is therefore oversimplified and nonsensical. On the one hand, judges recognize and are influenced by each other's moves. They share standards of relevance and recognize each other's ways of reasoning as variant forms within a shared practice. On the other hand, they go about thinking and reasoning in different ways. They have a stake in their own ways of thinking simply because these *are* their ways of thinking and making sense of experience.

They are participants in the same deliberative practice and yet they participate differently. The game metaphor fails because it is not illuminating to view these characteristic ways of ordering experience as a matter of following rules. Rules, even when they

---

[105] Wittgenstein (writing in 1948-50) speaks of the inconceivability of any person getting to the moon or of any person not having two parents. *Id.* at 36, 37.

[106] *See, e.g.*, Roe v. Wade, 410 U.S. 113, 152-53 (1973) (tracing development of the Court's concept of a right to privacy); Griswold v. Connecticut, 381 U.S. 479, 484 (1965) (discussing the growth of privacy "penumbras" around specific guarantees in the Bill of Rights). Consider also the example of the pattern of analysis and justification inspired by footnote four in United States v. Carolene Products Co., 304 U.S. 144, 152 n.4 (1938), which raised the question of "whether prejudice against discrete and insular minorities may be a special condition" in applying the general prohibitions of the Fourteenth Amendment. *See, e.g.*, ELY, supra note 29, at 148-70.

are second nature, can be made completely the objects of consciousness and, hypothetically, the objects of choice. One can imagine alternative rules for playing baseball or for describing colors and say to oneself, "These are the rules that I choose."[107] But a way of thinking and experiencing is not a set of rules. It is an evolving way of thinking, a way of proceeding in which one has a stake and from which one can abstract oneself only provisionally, only tentatively.[108]

The sense in which judicial reasoning is a shared practice is captured by the way in which it has aspects of practices in general. The first aspect is the public character of practices. A mode of thinking, feeling, and speaking must already be generally shared within the culture before it can be appropriated by the individual. It must be present to be learned. Whatever diversity exists in possible ways of thinking and feeling is a publicly shared and mutually acknowledged diversity.[109]

The second aspect is individuality. Since each person has an individual history, her ways of feeling, thinking and expressing herself will reflect that personal history.[110] She will create her personal variation on shared themes. Even judges who share a commitment to, for example, originalism or social equality as methodological constraints in decision-making, will carry out such reasoning in distinctively personal ways.

The third aspect is immediacy. A deliberative practice is not simply a way of using language or a method of moving from evidence to conclusions. It is a way of being in touch with reality, a way of giving shape and order to experience.[111] To say it is

---

[107] Unless one generates a community of fellow-users of the new rules, the rules are useless for communication or other forms of action. *See* WITTGENSTEIN, *supra* note 22, at 75-95 (discussing the difficulties of conceiving of a private language).

[108] *See* FISH, NATURALLY, *supra* note 19, at 436-67 (discussing various processes of self-critical thinking).

[109] Nonetheless, creativity and innovation are possible insofar as each person puts received elements together in unique and unforeseeable ways, ways that may come to resonate within the community. Creativity is possible and explicable within legal doctrine just as it is within the so-called creative arts.

[110] *See* STRAWSON, *supra* note 68, at 41 (stating that "[t]he principles of individuation of [private] experiences essentially turn on the identities of the persons to whose histories they belong").

[111] In other words, the classic philosophical confrontation between coherence and correspondence theories of linguistic meaning and truth is, for my purposes, accommodated by observing that coherence accounts make sense insofar as there is no realm of objects other than the objects of experience and language, and that those objects are experienced as given (and in that sense as real).

immediate is not to say that it is unchangeable. Becoming self-conscious of one's distinctive way of ordering reality may be a precondition of such change.[112] Thus, a judge may surely understand herself as an originalist, for example, or as believing that certain social goals "make more sense" than all others.[113] And she may question that distinctive way of ordering beliefs and change her ways of thinking. At the same time, she cannot abstract herself altogether into a position of indifference or into a sense that her way of thinking is, in the end, arbitrary.[114]

The immediacy of our practices of reasoning has an important implication. Inevitably, we deliberate not about how we see things but about how things are. Since we are within a frame, we lose sight of it as a frame. But we cannot forget it altogether, aware as we are that other persons have other frames. This means that any philosophical reflection about reasoning sensitizes us to a kind of tension between the certainty that attaches to what is most familiar, to the ways of thinking that are second nature, and to the sense that such certainty is ungrounded. Others with a different stake in reality–with other moral, religious, scientific certainties–and with different ways of thinking may be fellow conversants in our practices.

Any adequate theory of legal reasoning must address the consequences of viewing judicial reasoning as a deliberative practice. It must take account of both the heterogeneity of justification *and* the idiosyncratic character of individual strategies of justification. Even more importantly, it must take account of the tension between the role of practitioner and theorist–a tension not reducible to roles, to removing one hat and putting on another. Because engaging in a deliberative practice involves having convictions about reality and explanation, the practitioner asking theoretical questions can never bootstrap herself out of the tension and into a posture of neutrality or indifference about those convictions. A theorist who pretends she can disables herself from describing law adequately.[115]

Failure to understand judicial reasoning as a deliberative

---

[112] *See* FISH, NATURALLY, *supra* note 19, at 141-60 (discussing change within "interpretive communities").

[113] This description emphasizes that values are experienced as given, or incumbent on one, rather than as chosen.

[114] *See supra* text accompanying note 98; *see generally* HUME, *supra* note 71, at 181-218 (discussing the interplay between passion and will).

[115] *See infra* Part IV.

practice colors the contribution of both older jurisprudence, characterized by debates about legal positivism, and newer jurisprudence, characterized by the skeptical claims of antifoundationalists. Thus, the idea of judging as a deliberative practice can bridge the preoccupations of old and new jurisprudence.

III. LEGAL POSITIVISM AND LAW AS A DELIBERATIVE PRACTICE

A. *Positivism and Judging*

Some of the main claims of legal positivism are incompatible with seeing law as a deliberative practice. However, a critique of positivism from this standpoint yields modifications that turn positivism into a stronger, more compelling theory of law. In order to assess this new strength it is necessary to identify the salient aspects of positivism.

1. Positivism and the Identification of Law

The still-evolving debate between positivists[116] and their critics has centered on how judges identify law.[117] The question of what law is and how it is to be identified is also a question about the limits of law. When does law run out? When does a judge exhaust her resources for identifying law and move beyond those limits?[118]

---

[116] Legal positivism, like all philosophical "isms," refers to a family of views and positions. H.L.A. Hart and Joseph Raz are the most influential recent legal positivists. Commenting on "the elusive meaning of 'positivism'," Raz describes its controversies with nonpositivists as a function of the identification of law, the moral value of law, and the meaning of key terms within legal discourse. JOSEPH RAZ, THE AUTHORITY OF LAW 37 (1979).

Note in this context that "the identification of law" can have several meanings since ordinary citizens, judges, and attorneys all need to identify law and do so in different ways.

[117] The background assumption of these debates seems to be that judges are at the fulcrum of decision-making and of debate within the legal system and have as their job the identification of law even when that job is most difficult. Citizens can decline to make judgments in hard cases and attorneys can prepare briefs on both sides of a question, but judges must choose and justify their choices.

The fact that both positivists (for instance, Hart and Raz) and their critics (such as Dworkin) explain the identification of law by observing the behavior and discourse of appellate judges can be explained in a different way. Judges have been recognized in the history of jurisprudence as having the most controversial role of various legal actors. Legislators uncontroversially have the task of creating law. Attorneys and citizens have the burden of obeying the law and working within it. But judges are variously seen as applying the law and/or creating it.

[118] At its inception, legal positivism was not explicitly a theory about the identification of law by judges so much as a theory about the nature of law *tout court*.

Whatever their differences, positivists address the problem of identifying law by emphasizing the importance of distinguishing "law as it is" from "law as it ought to be."[119] Their basic intuition is that the process of identifying the law is separate conceptually from the process of projecting aspirations for what the law might become and the goals it might serve. The first process uses formal criteria to identify the events of law creation. The second process uses moral reasoning, prudential reasoning, and other kinds of normative argument to consider ways in which the law might change in the future.

2. Raz's Positivism

Joseph Raz preserves this distinction when he identifies the "sources thesis" as the essence of legal positivism.[120] To say that one identifies law by resort to formal criteria is to say that one identifies law by ascertaining whether particular law-creating events occurred. One looks, therefore, to social facts. Justificatory arguments play no part in the identification process because law, duly created, stands as law regardless of any justificatory arguments offered in its favor or in criticism.[121]

Early positivists tied law to power, suggesting that the legal order is established when rules are imposed by those who have stable (political) power over those who lack such power. John Austin, for example, represents law as commands backed by sanctions. The capacity to enforce sanctions and to make the threat of sanctions effective depends on power. One aspect of a legal order, according to this account, is that the rules express the wishes of the commander. *See* JOHN AUSTIN, THE PROVINCE OF JURISPRUDENCE DETERMINED ETC. 9-33 (Isaiah Berlin et al. eds., 1954) (1832). Such wishes may be indefinitely variable in their content. They may or may not coincide with the interest of the governed. They may in fact harm the governed in serious and unjustifiable ways.

H.L.A. Hart's positivistic account of law does not depend on particular assumptions about the relative power of individuals. *See* HART, *supra* note 21, at 1-25, 49-76. Austin's account, based on power assumptions, can not explain how law could bind all individuals, authorities as well as citizens, or how law could exist in a system in which power rested ultimately with the population at large, e.g. the electorate. Hart offers an institutional theory of law whereby a legal system exists whenever stable institutions promulgate rules that establish order in the society at large. The rules are of two kinds, primary rules that order the lives of all citizens and secondary rules that instruct and empower authorities in making, interpreting, and executing the rules. *See id.* at 77-96.

[119] H.L.A. Hart, *Positivism and the Separation of Law and Morals*, 71 HARV. L. REV. 593, 594 (1958); *see* RAZ, *supra* note 116, at 37-45.

[120] *See id.* at 47.

[121] It does not necessarily follow that one may ignore morality in identifying the law. Morality may be relevant insofar as it is embodied in social facts that are criterial. A criterion for law might be that a rule becomes law only as a result of a

This positivist account of law has the important corollary that the law has gaps.[122] Whenever (according to relevant social facts) a rule does not exist for a particular situation, the law is undetermined.[123] Determining the gaps may be difficult and controversial, and one may come to feel that the social facts do not, in this sense, speak for themselves.

3. Dworkin's Criticisms

Critics of positivism such as Ronald Dworkin challenge the positivist's claim that identifying the law is a matter of looking at social facts and not a matter of producing justificatory arguments.[124] Dworkin suggests that judges go through a different and more complex process of deliberation when they try to identify the law, one in which social facts and justificatory arguments are inextricably bound.[125] In rejecting positivism, Dworkin argues that justificatory arguments play an essential role in the process of identifying law.[126] Dworkin's critique anticipates some of the insights of law as a deliberative practice, while falling short, as we shall see, in other respects.

B. *The Limitations of Positivism*

Viewing law as a deliberative practice shows how problematic the central claims of positivism are. It requires us to extend and modify the positivist understanding of the identification of law. We must look critically at the positivist's claims about the criteria of validity (the sources thesis), the nature and role of justificatory

---

popular referendum, and the referendum might ask voters for approval or disapproval on moral grounds. In this example the positivist's claim stands. The judge—or other player—who is trying to identify the law appeals to social fact and has no occasion to offer justificatory arguments of her own. *See id.* at 38-39 (explaining that the "social facts by which we identify the law" may "endow [the law] with moral merit," but the law itself does not "of necessity conform to . . . moral values").

[122] *See id.* at 73 (stating that "the source thesis makes [gaps] unavoidable since it makes law dependent on human action with its attendant indeterminacies").

[123] *See id.* at 70.

[124] Dworkin puts to one side whether, from the standpoint of the citizen, identifying and citing the requirements of law are indeed (as Raz maintains) a matter of social fact, as they appear to be. For example, determining the taxability of one's capital gains involves consulting rules that have a particular pedigree, rules that came into effect through the actions of authorized individuals. Being able to point to the "social fact" that these actions occurred is sufficient to identify the law.

[125] *See* DWORKIN, *supra* note 36, at 238-66; DWORKIN, *supra* note 47, at 81-130.

[126] *See infra* part III.C.1.

arguments in law, the appropriate role of theorists and participants (the game metaphor), and the existence of legal gaps.

1. Criteria of Validity

Notwithstanding the positivist suggestion that clear criteria (social facts) identify valid legal rules, the practice of judicial decision-making exists because rules of law are continually and characteristically in dispute. Judges who disagree offer significantly different conceptions of the rules. In considering hard cases, appellate judges necessarily ask whether fellow judges see the law as they do, take differences of opinion and result seriously, and argue about whether and how the law has changed. For positivists, a second-order set of game-like rules applies to judges' deliberations. These rules direct the judge to use certain sources of law.[127] Having identified the law, the judge may decide that the case falls in the gaps of the law[128] and may, in a discretionary way, use considerations outside the law to make new law.[129]

Critics such as Dworkin offer a different picture of judging. They imply that a judge's understanding and use of such game-like rules is necessarily colored ab initio by preconceptions about the interests at issue in the particular case, their weight and importance, and the relation of the case to other situations and contexts. Each judge makes decisions about relevance in the light of a justificatory

---

[127] Hart explains:

> The simplest form of remedy for the uncertainty of the regime of primary rules is the introduction of what we shall call a 'rule of recognition'. This will specify some feature or features possession of which by a suggested rule is taken as a conclusive affirmative indication that it is a rule of the group to be supported by the social pressure it exerts.

HART, *supra* note 21, at 92 (emphasis omitted).

[128] Raz argues:

> Questions of intention and meaning may have no answer. . . . Where the facts which are legal reasons are indeterminate, through vagueness, open texture, or some other factors, certain legal statements are neither true nor false . . . . It is worth noting that this kind of legal gap is not the law's peculiarity. They are totally dependent on and derive from gaps in statements of an ordinary and not a particularly legal kind such as statements about intentions and language. It is the indeterminacy of ordinary everyday facts which generates legal gaps.

RAZ, *supra* note 116, at 72-73 (footnote omitted).

[129] *See* HART, *supra* note 21, at 132 (stating that the "open texture of law means that there are, indeed, areas of conduct where much must be left to be developed by courts or officials striking a balance, in the light of circumstances, between competing interests which vary in weight from case to case").

argument identifying the interests that matter.[130]

Dworkin's view of judging is compatible with seeing judicial decisionmaking as a deliberative practice. Without a framework derived from her own way of interpreting experience and giving value, the judge cannot know where to begin. The process of identifying the law cannot be reduced to rules because it cannot be separated from the judge's distinctive way of conceiving justificatory arguments and using them to work toward a decision. What the judge sees as determinate and indeterminate in the law is colored by her understanding of the justificatory arguments that the law encompasses.[131]

Disagreement among judges therefore extends both to the criteria by which they treat the available body of precedent (decisions and arguments) and to their conception of the goals and interests at issue. Although they may agree on the importance of order and fairness, hard problems are not solved at this level of generality. If they were, judges would not disagree with each other.

The argument against shared second-order rules for judging is that the standards of decision-making are inherently disputable. Judges lack shared bases for determining how the ingredients of decision yielded up by the sources of law are to be weighed and fitted together. As a result, justificatory arguments are needed at every stage to support these controversial determinations. No judge sees herself, as some positivist descriptions suggest, as engaged in a bifurcated task of first applying the first-order rules when possible and then looking to resources outside the rules when application of the first-order rules is not possible. At any level but the most abstract, judges may disagree about the point of their activity and the goals to be achieved.

2. The Meaning of Legal Justification

Do positivists misdescribe the kinds of justification found in judicial reasoning? Their account of law implies that there are three kinds of justificatory moves in legal discourse. One kind is a demonstration that a particular rule is a first-order rule of the system performed by displaying the rule's pedigree.[132] The

---

[130] *See* DWORKIN, *supra* note 36, at 238-66; DWORKIN, *supra* note 47, at 81-130.

[131] Of course, none of this is fixed. The judge's confrontation with the arguments of others or with new circumstances for applying the law—new cases—may lead her to reconceive aspects of her understanding of the law and look at a point of relevant law in a new way.

[132] This notion of justification follows directly from the positivist account of legal

second kind is an account of why (or why not) a case falls within the scope of the relevant first-order rule.[133] If the case falls outside, a third kind of justification is appropriate: an argument for the extension of the law in terms of the purpose that is thus achieved.[134]

Positivists see these three kinds of justifications as offering an exhaustive analysis of justification as it arises in different aspects of the process of decision-making. In the actual use of justificatory strategies by judges, however, justification cannot be analyzed in this way. Questions about the scope of relevant law and about the purposes to be achieved by particular results are typically not distinguishable in judicial opinions.[135] Identifying the law itself necessarily involves justificatory arguments.

Such a melding of the question of identifying the law with the question of justifying particular results is not an aberration from the ordinary context of decision-making; it *is* the ordinary context. Participating in a deliberative practice, a judge has a stake in a

---

validity. *See* HART, *supra* note 21, at 97-107.

[133] This notion of justification falls within the positivist conception of open texture. *See id.* at 124-32 (explaining that rules will at some point prove indeterminate, possessing what is called an open texture).

[134] The role of consequentialist arguments and other kinds of "second-order" justifications are discussed at length by writers in the positivist tradition. *See, e.g.*, MACCORMICK, *supra* note 21, at 100-51.

[135] In *Bowers v. Hardwick*, Justice White, speaking for the Court, wrote:

> [W]e think it evident that none of the rights announced in [such cases as *Pierce*, *Skinner*, *Griswold*, and *Roe*] bears any resemblance to the claimed constitutional right of homosexuals to engage in acts of sodomy that is asserted in this case. . . . [A]ny claim that these cases nevertheless stand for the proposition that any kind of private sexual conduct between consenting adults is constitutionally insulated from state proscription is unsupportable.

Bowers v. Hardwick, 478 U.S. 186, 190-91 (1986) (citations omitted). Was White identifying the law, that is the scope of the right of privacy, or was he justifying a limitation upon it by finding a conceptual difference, embedded in how he and some others view human experience, between some private acts and others? Clearly he was doing both, and the distinction between the two—identification and justification—is idle.

In *Rochin v. California*, the Court held it to be a violation of due process for officers to compel evidence from a defendant by forcing him to yield up the contents of his stomach. The Court said, "This is conduct that shocks the conscience. . . . [These] are methods too close to the rack and the screw to permit of constitutional differentiation." Rochin v. California, 342 U.S. 165, 172 (1952) (Frankfurter, J.). Did this constitute identification of the scope of the law, or did it offer a justification by explicit reference to moral limits and moral similarities? Clearly it did both. The point is perfectly general: in virtually any opinion, the processes of identifying the law and of offering up justifications for a decision are inseparable.

particular way of interpreting experience and therefore in a particular way of putting together the elements of a legal system. Judges mutually understand the various styles and assumptions encompassed within their shared deliberative practice, and such understanding is crucial to the ongoing practice, but it does not generally or necessarily move them toward convergence.

3. Participants and Theorists

Positivists ascribe different roles to participants (judges) and theorists (observers). Participants make justificatory moves in the course of making decisions while theorists analyze the formal structure of rule-governed activities.[136] This means that positivists separate the analytic and the normative aspects of legal theory.[137] What law is and what law ought to be are separate issues. The job of the judge is bifurcated between justifying decisions within the scope of existing law (the first and second kinds of justification) and justifying new or gap-filling law by extralegal considerations (the third kind of justification). The theorist's job is bifurcated between describing the practice of legal reasoning and criticizing its substance.

---

[136] This distinction is implicit in the positivist's separation of law as it is and law as it ought to be. H.L.A. Hart explains:

> [I]t is . . . important to distinguish as belonging to the philosophy of law certain groups of questions which remain to be answered even when a high degree of competence or mastery of particular legal systems [by] . . . empirical and dogmatic studies . . . has been gained. Three such groups may be distinguished: problems of definition and analysis, problems of legal reasoning, and problems of the criticism of law.

H.L.A. HART, ESSAYS IN JURISPRUDENCE AND PHILOSOPHY 88-89 (1983).

For critics of positivism, problems of definition and analysis are not altogether separable from problems of the criticism of law. "It is his neglect to analyze the demands of a morality of order that leads [Hart] throughout his essay to treat law as a datum projecting itself into human experience and not as an object of human striving." Lon L. Fuller, *Positivism and Fidelity to Law–A Reply to Professor Hart*, 71 HARV. L. REV. 630, 646 (1958). The point of stressing the diversity of justificatory strategies in deliberative practices is that each judge conceives of law as "an object of human striving" in a different way, that such commitments affect theorists as well as judges, and that a full account of the definition and analysis of law will betray the theorist's own commitments.

[137] *See* HART, *supra* note 136, at 88-89. In *The Concept of Law*, Hart separates his consideration of analytic questions (chapters one through seven) from his consideration of questions of the criticism of law (chapters eight and nine). *See* HART, *supra* note 21. *Compare* RAZ, *supra* note 116 (discussing analytical questions) *and* JOSEPH RAZ, THE CONCEPT OF A LEGAL SYSTEM (1970) (analyzing legal systems) *with* JOSEPH RAZ, THE MORALITY OF FREEDOM (1986) (discussing moral criticism of law). Both Hart and Raz see these questions as falling into separable domains of jurisprudential inquiry.

To see judicial decision-making as a deliberative practice is to see that such clear lines of demarcation are illusory. Just as a judge will necessarily make justificatory arguments in the course of identifying the law and will have a particular stake in a way of ordering the results, a theorist will look at the institutions of law in terms of the justificatory arguments that are relevant to its existence.[138] The positivist is correct that part of the theoretical task is to understand what law is by identifying law with a particular institutional structure. Making sense of that institutional structure, however, requires a choice among various explanatory data—political, social, economic, psychological, and so on. The choice that a particular theorist makes will represent that theorist's own way of making sense of experience. A theorist will also have to address a range of questions about the functional, dysfunctional, or nonfunctional character of legal decisions and official acts. In so doing, she will have to confront the availability or absence of particular justificatory arguments for what the legal system does.

Thus the tasks of judge and theorist, while hardly the same, are isomorphic in a way to which the game-based metaphor of insider/outsider cannot do justice. It is unsatisfactory to imply, as positivism does, that a judge (insider) applies rules and on occasion creates new law while a theorist (outsider) describes the institutional structure generated by such rules. Both the judge and the theorist are participants in deliberative practices. They deliberate for different ends: the judge deliberates to decide cases, while the theorist deliberates to arrive at an adequate characterization of law. But when both judges and theorists disagree with their peers, their disagreements turn on differences with their peers in the way experience is understood, differences in preferred explanatory strategies. Thus, both judges and theorists have a stake in a personal way of understanding the place of law in the social order because each judge and each theorist is *necessarily* a partisan of some particular and controversial way of arriving at knowledge and certainty.

---

[138] Thus, one theorist may identify the institutions of law with order and discipline, another with the realization of justice, and yet another with the coordination of wants and aspirations. Moreover, the theorist's elaboration of the demands of order or justice or want-satisfaction will depend in turn on that theorist's way of understanding human psychology, history, politics, morality, etc.

4. Dissolving the Dichotomies of Positivism

The main pillars of positivism are undermined by these three criticisms of positivist approaches to identifying the law, to the nature of justification, and to the relation of theory and practice. The claim that law can be identified by recourse to formal sources without the use of justificatory arguments fails. From the standpoint of law as a deliberative practice, every attempt to link disparate elements—statutes, case holdings, constitutional clauses—is a way of understanding and creating order. The shared practice is defined by the collection of permissible and mutually recognizable ways of creating order. Each participant's way of creating order is in part idiosyncratic and each is called upon to justify her way of doing so at every stage.

a. *Existing Law and New Law*

Positivism's conceptual distinction between cases in which a judge applies law at its core and cases in which a judge must reach outside the law to make new law[139] is problematic. In practice, the claim that a judge is making new law is generally reserved as a criticism for some results with which one disagrees. Judges themselves do not use this bifurcation to describe their own decisions, but rather characterize all their own decisions as interpreting and extending existing law. At the same time, they often accuse those with whom they disagree of making new law and therefore of being self-evidently in error.[140]

The implication is *not* that judges always deploy "old law" but that the distinction between old and new law, and the dilemmas it spawns, must be dissolved. Each judge identifies law and legal reasoning with certain analytic strategies and moral/social/political principles, and her decisions use those strategies and principles to address new issues. The decisions are old insofar as the judge does

---

[139] *See* HART, *supra* note 21, at 124-32 (describing legal rules' open texture). *See also supra* note 132.

[140] Even *Roe v. Wade*, a case that seems to many commentators a clear instance of judicial lawmaking, is presented as an application of existing law. "This right of privacy, whether it be founded in the Fourteenth Amendment's concept of personal liberty . . . as we feel it is, or . . . in the Ninth Amendment . . . is broad enough to encompass a woman's decision whether or not to terminate her pregnancy." Roe v. Wade, 410 U.S. 113, 153 (1973) (Blackmun, J.). And dissenters predictably see and accuse the majority of making new law: "I have difficulty in concluding . . . that the right of 'privacy' is involved in this case." *Id.* at 172 (Rehnquist, J., dissenting).

not reinvent strategies and principles with each case, and new insofar as particular issues have not been met before.

Seeing law as a deliberative practice explains why "new law" is an epithet of criticism. Each individual judge, as we have seen, has a favored account of the methods and goals of the enterprise; accordingly, one will try to reconstruct the social order that seemed to be set in place by the founders, another will look to a consensus about goals and rights within the political and cultural community as it has evolved, and so on. Moreover, a particular judge will necessarily have to vary her methods to meet the demands of different kinds of cases. In a consistent and principled way, she may decide some cases by reference to economic considerations, others by reference to historical intent, and still others by looking at fairness, freedom, and other moral values.[141]

Every judge will therefore find some cases that require the use of resources that are not generally seen by others as part of the law. Some judges will use controversial resources more readily than others.[142] What seems to one judge a decision within agreed upon bounds of the law will seem to another a creative extension of the law.

The alternatives confronted by positivists and their critics are therefore a misleading way of posing the issue. Positivists suppose that one can sort cases into applications of pre-existing ("old") law and instances of law creation. Their critics, like Dworkin, argue that all cases are applications of pre-existing law.[143] Both claims fail.

---

[141] For example, she may use economic criteria in antitrust cases, copyright and trademark cases; she may be guided by historical considerations in deciding cases about the balance of powers among the three branches of government; and she may refer to fairness and freedom in deciding cases under the First, Fourth, and Fifth Amendments. She will be able to explain why she finds economic criteria relevant to one sort of case, historical concerns to another, and fairness and freedom to others. Moreover, what distinguishes her justificatory strategies is not only how she categorizes various cases but also the particular economic, historical, and moral convictions that she regards as true and relevant.

[142] Justice William Douglas was, throughout his career, seen, praised, and pilloried for being an innovator of this kind. *See generally* VERN COUNTRYMAN, THE JUDICIAL RECORD OF JUSTICE WILLIAM O. DOUGLAS (1974) (discussing Justice Douglas's career on the United States Supreme Court).

[143] *See* DWORKIN, *supra* note 50, at 119-45. Dworkin states that

> [t]he question . . . of whether there are no-right-answer cases in a particular jurisdiction, [that is, cases in which existing law does not anticipate a right answer]—and whether such cases are rare or numerous—is not an ordinary empirical question. I believe that such cases, if they exist at all, must be extremely rare in the United States and Great Britain. . . .
>
> The argument that I am wrong must . . . be a philosophical argument.

The process for arriving at and justifying decisions does not warrant either description, nor does it afford a perspective from which either description can be made.

Rather than applying existing law or making new law, judges draw on their individual strategies within the mutually familiar dimensions of the practice to solve a problem and create intellectual order. Some cases will be similar to existing precedents and give rise to little surprise or controversy. Other cases will seem more creative and disputable. The latter may continue to be described by theorists as "making" law rather than "applying" it, but such a dichotomy will rightly be treated as naive and oversimple by judges themselves.

b. *Law and Gaps*

The same oversimplification is involved in the question of whether law has gaps, a question which also dissolves under scrutiny. On one hand, some cases involve significantly new questions and give rise to controversy. On the other, the range of strategies of decision available within the deliberative practice are almost always predictable, as is the range of the solutions they would yield. Of course, particular results in close binary cases[144] cannot be anticipated. But the family of relevant arguments for each side of the binary question can and will be anticipated.

c. *Law as It Is and Law as It Ought to Be*

A third positivist claim is that theorists must keep in mind a clear distinction between what law is and what it ought to be. In particular, positivists maintain that justificatory arguments are used in determining what law ought to be but not in determining what it is.

If justificatory arguments in fact play an essential part in both

---

> It must challenge my assumption that in a complex and comprehensive legal system it is antecedently unlikely that two theories will differ sufficiently to demand difficult answers in some case and yet provide equally good fit with the relevant legal materials.

Id. at 144-45.

[144] All cases are binary, of course, insofar as the claim of the plaintiff may either be upheld or denied. My suggestion is that the "gappiness" of a given case dissolves into the answers to such questions as: What decision is consistent with the justificatory argument (within the law) that I (as judge) find most compelling and relevant? How similar is this case to existing precedents? How much diversity can

processes, then the distinction does not hold. Moreover, the distinction between settled law and new law is itself problematic. What one judge considers new law another judge will consider an application of established principles. It is thus simplistic to try to sort decisions into categories of those that reiterate settled law and those that announce what the law ought to be.

The distinction between what the law is and what it ought to be can, however, be translated into two functional distinctions. First, any judge would concede that some cases require creative extension of the law. Judges know that at some point what is generally regarded as settled law runs out. What does not run out is the capacity of each point of view within the practice to generate strategies to address unsettled questions. The distinction between what the law is and what it is becoming, according to the judge's way of viewing the law's justificatory strategies, remains real.

Second, every judge must recognize cases in which constraints of law require a result different from what she would choose had she been free to adjudicate on a clean slate. In that sense as well, therefore, what law is is one thing, what it ought to be is another.[145]

C. *Dworkin's Criticisms and Deliberative Practices*

Ronald Dworkin's response to legal positivism dovetails in some respects with the view of law as a deliberative practice. He claims that justificatory arguments are part of the process of identifying the law, that the law does not have gaps, and that no sharp distinction can be drawn between law as it is and law as it ought to be.[146] His account is, however, deficient in significant ways.

I expect among my colleagues (both in decision and justificatory strategy) in deciding this case? How much controversy will any decision of this case generate?

[145] Throughout this article, I assume that judges use justificatory strategies that they themselves find compelling and that reflect their own stake in a way of thinking, in a way of making sense of experience. I assume, in other words, that judges judge in good faith. For a general discussion of this assumption, see STEVEN J. BURTON, JUDGING IN GOOD FAITH (1992).

[146] *See* DWORKIN, *supra* note 36, at 225-75; DWORKIN, *supra* note 47, at 81-149.

1. The Self-Understanding of Judges

The judge as participant in a deliberative practice is in tension between (1) having a stake in both a particular result and a particular way of defending that result and (2) being aware that the practice embraces other justificatory strategies, some of which yield contrary results.[147] The judge's attitude toward her persuasive powers is also bifurcated. She aspires in the short term to bring other judges around to her way of reasoning and to address the larger audience that reads and criticizes judicial opinions. At the same time, she is aware that she has no transcendental argument for the superiority of her way of proceeding or for a neutral standard by which ways of thinking are to be measured or ranked. She knows that in the long run the diversity of views and strategies that is characteristic of the practice will almost certainly persist.

Dworkin seems sanguine about resolving these tensions. By his account, a judge sees it as her task to offer the most comprehensive and defensible account of the rules and principles of the evolving legal system.[148] The values and rights reflected in her account yield a complete legal system insofar as they anticipate a single "best" resolution of all hard cases.[149] Even if a judge cannot convince her colleagues to adopt the same reconstruction of the legal system, she will remain convinced that all other strategies which yield different results are inferior. This conviction will be an essential part of her position. What is wrong with this characterization?

a. *The Bases of Disagreement*

Dworkin's account distorts the main obstacle to agreement by misconceiving the character of judges' disagreement. The problem is not only that judges accord different weight to different principles, as Dworkin claims, but that they have different ways of

---

[147] Of course, other judges may arrive at the same decision by different means.

[148] *See* Dworkin, NATURAL, *supra* note 54, at 169-73. Dworkin analogizes the interpretation of law to the interpretation of novels:

> We [must distinguish] two dimensions of a successful interpretation. An interpretation must "fit" the data it interprets, in order not to show the novel as sloppy or incoherent, and it must also show that data in its best light, as serving as well as can be some proper ambition of novels.

Id. at 170.

[149] *See* DWORKIN, *supra* note 50, at 143-45 (arguing that rarely, if ever, do judges believe that there is no correct answer).

ordering categories of evidence. Thus, one judge will give argumentative finality to social and moral arguments of a utilitarian character. Yet this judge can also recognize that the deliberative practice includes some judges who justify results by appeal to the structure of original intentions embodied in the Constitution and statutes and still others who argue by appeal to economic efficiency.

It is one thing to have a stake in a particular way of understanding evidence and constructing arguments. It is another thing to have a stake in a particular social agenda with its attendant values and goals. For Dworkin, judges differ essentially in the second way: they reconstruct in different ways the evolved system of social values that comprises the constitutional system.[150] Each judge is in a position to see his reconstruction as superior and as broad enough to encompass the entire practice. Each judge clearly has a vested interest in maintaining this perception.

b. *Understanding Other Judges*

The picture of law as a deliberative practice, however, tells a different story. If judges also differ in the ways in which they understand evidence and construct arguments, and if they are aware of these differences, then they see their peers as not merely telling inferior stories but as telling characteristically different kinds of stories—political stories, economic stories, psychological stories, and historical stories. This awareness may cause them to hesitate before ranking such differences as superior or inferior and may lead them to a better understanding of why others resist accepting their stories.[151]

For Dworkin, all judges are in one sense playing by the same rules or strategies since they are deploying the two dimensions of legal analysis: fit and justifiability.[152] Judges in a deliberative practice, however, play by different rules and have different modes of arguing, reasoning, and thinking, a fact they understand, anticipate, and respect. This acknowledgement creates a tension between their stakes in their individual strategies and in the

---

[150] *See* DWORKIN, *supra* note 36, at 257-58 (concluding that when a judge is faced with a hard case he is forced "to develop his conception of law and his political morality together in a mutually supporting way.").

[151] I am not arguing, however, that this recognition will undercut or diminish one's own stake in one's way of proceeding, one's justificatory and analytical strategies.

[152] *See supra* note 150.

multiform practice itself. The first stake is a stake the judge has by virtue of his position as a participant and a decision-maker. The second stake reflects the judge's awareness of the nature of the practice and his participation in it. The voice of the judge simultaneously expresses both stakes.[153]

c. *The "Best" Interpretation of the Law*

Dworkin says that the task of the judge is to produce the "best" interpretation of the law.[154] What becomes of that claim when law is seen as a deliberative practice? A judge is most likely to defend her interpretation as the best to those who share at least some elements of his own strategy. Two judges similarly disposed to reconstruct original intent may still join issue with divergent views of original intent. On the other hand, two judges with different strategies may have to acknowledge the absence of any measure between them. Certainly each judge will continue to think of his own strategy and judgment as "best" in some sense. But the claim will be enlightened by awareness of this dual challenge, in terms of result and in strategy of thinking.

This distinction between Dworkin's position and mine is not a distinction between objective and subjective conceptions of what is "best." Any judicial opinion is an objective judgment insofar as it is a claim made from the perspective of a particular way of ordering evidence and justified by arguments marshalled from that perspective. All judicial opinions share these traits, and in this sense all arguments are therefore objective.[155] Decisions are not any less objective because they involve strategies of justification that are to some extent individualized.

---

[153] The coexistence of these two stakes should not be reduced simply to the degree of modesty of the judge or the degree of respect she has for her colleagues. It is a conceptual matter that the two stakes coexist, regardless of whether the judge is actively thinking about them or not; it is not an empirical matter dependent on the judge's attitude or personality.

[154] *See* DWORKIN, *supra* note 36, at 239 (comparing judicial decisionmaking to literary story writing).

[155] Both Dworkin and Fish tend to equate the requirement of objectivity with transcendental justification, which is itself impossible to achieve. *See* DWORKIN, *supra* note 36, at 85-86; FISH, NATURALLY, *supra* note 19, at 87-88, 436-37. Dworkin identifies the call for objectivity with the call for a definitive argument refuting external skepticism. DWORKIN, *supra* note 36, at 85-86 (stating that the "only skepticism worth anything is skepticism of the internal kind").

2. The Completeness of Law

Dworkin takes a strong stand on the completeness of law. Along with some other proponents of legal naturalism, he shares the assumption that the principles and values of the legal system anticipate decisions for all cases. Therefore, no decision involves making new law. As reconstructed by each judge, the values and ideals embodied in the law color and shape each new hard case so that it is a reading of what is already implicit.

From the standpoint of law as a deliberative practice, this claim must be sharply qualified. One may agree with Dworkin that every hard case summons up an array of interests and values that have surfaced in other cases and on which any judge has probably taken a stand. Only in this sense is a place in the legal system already prepared for any new judicial decision.

The claim that the decision in every hard case is already part of the law and that judges never create new law is nonetheless counterintuitive. However, the positivists' claim that judges sometimes make new law is also counterintuitive, and both claims rest on oversimplification. Every judge sees some cases as requiring her to extend legal arguments in ways they have not been extended before.[156] At the same time, she does not think of herself as sometimes applying preexisting law and sometimes making new law. Rather, she sees her responses to some cases as creative and innovative, and she expects them to be surprising and controversial. The static metaphor of inside/outside yields to the dynamic metaphor of growth and extended reach.

The idea of closure and completeness is inapposite to the extent that judges are aware that legal reasoning involves not just one strategy of reasoning. Every decision is likely to invoke coexisting yet competing strategies, with each strategy yielding its own innovations and each capable of providing for growth and development of the law in a different way.[157] Again, the claim that the law

---

[156] *See supra* text accompanying notes 139-45.

[157] Again, one could cite examples endlessly. In DeShaney v. Winnebago County Dep't of Social Servs., 489 U.S. 189 (1988), the Court refused to hold a state agency liable when the agency, having intervened in a child abuse situation, failed to take reasonable measures to protect the victim. Speaking for the majority, Chief Justice Rehnquist relied on the framers' intent in interpreting due process to exclude claims against the state when harm resulted from purely private action. *See id.* at 196-97 (stating that the purpose of the Due Process clause "was to protect the people from the State, not to ensure that the State protected them from each other"). In dissent, Justice Brennan examined the evolving duty of the state to protect individuals in

anticipates particular results will seem vastly oversimplified to any judge who understands the law as a collection of different strategies and a perpetual contest among them.

IV. ANTIFOUNDATIONALISM AND PRAGMATISM

Viewing law as a deliberative practice allows us to transform the "old" jurisprudence by reinterpreting the claims of positivists and liberal/naturalist critics. This approach does so largely by questioning the scope and possibility of consensus and by emphasizing that the practice is made up of conflicting and irreconcilable points of view or strategies of decision. This way of summarizing the critique seems to assimilate the description of law as a deliberative practice with critical theory or antifoundationalism—the "new" jurisprudence. That would be wrong. Just as it faults the old jurisprudence for misconstruing agreement, that is, for misdescribing the limits of law and the role of justification, the view of law as a deliberative practice finds in critical theory a defective picture of the scope and nature of disagreement.[158]

A. *From Old to New Jurisprudence*

Antifoundationalists reject what Robert Gordon calls "evolutionary functionalism,"[159] a general conception of law as evolving to realize social values by meeting human needs.[160] Evolutionary

---

whose behalf it has begun to act. *See id.* at 207 (Brennan, J., dissenting) (recognizing "that 'the State's knowledge of [an] individual's predicament [and] its expressions of intent to help him' can amount to a 'limitation on his freedom to act on his own behalf.'") (alteration in original) (citation omitted). Justice Blackmun stressed the general role of the state in preventing harm. *See id.* at 213 (Blackmun, J., dissenting) (calling for a "sympathetic" ruling). It is easy to imagine a more general use of the framers' intent criterion to limit claims against the state and overturn existing precedents in which, for example, public officials acting in what is arguably a private capacity have been held liable. On the other hand, expansive use of the notion of the state's obligation to prevent harm by private persons could lead to new kinds of tort claims against the state, and new obligations for state agencies. Another approach to this issue could be grounded on economic efficiency, specifically on an analysis of which party is best situated to prevent harm in such cases at least cost to the parties and to society.

[158] Obviously, one might argue that the difference between my theory and critical legal theory, or for that matter between my theory and Dworkin's theory, is a matter of nuance and emphasis rather than a difference in kind. That determination, in turn, depends on whether one is impressed more by what the theories have in common or by what differentiates them. Such a determination rests in the hands of the reader.

[159] Gordon, *supra* note 3, at 68.

[160] Positivists and antifoundationalists both attack what I have called consensus

functionalism comes in two guises. For consensus theorists, the law incorporates principles that represent such social values, principles that constantly require interpretation and extension. For positivists, law is a neutral tool that can either be used to realize social values or to subvert them.[161]

Antifoundational skeptics do not simply reserve normative questions about needs and social values; they subvert them. Positivists take no position on the truth of propositions linking law, need, and social values in practice; they commend the conceptual distinctiveness of law as it is and law as it ought to be without regard to whether law embodies social values founded on human needs. Antifoundationalists, however, do take a position on these propositions: they tend to regard the rhetoric of needs and shared values as camouflage for the use of power to create order and to give the veneer of justification without the substance. Like

---

theory, represented in contemporary debates most conspicuously by liberalism. Consensus theory maintains that law embodies shared social values and that the judge's job is to ferret out, interpret, and apply them. If this were all that consensus theory held, then positivists would have no cause for rejecting the view that identifying the law may involve recourse to shared values. Consensus theorists also maintain, however, that the process of identifying the law involves justificatory arguments for particular values—arguments showing both that the values are shared and that they explicate what is good. Consensus theory thus bridges what law is and what it ought to be and takes on a task that is simultaneously descriptive and normative. In this way consensus theory stands directly against a major tenet of positivism.

Liberals modify consensus theory by distinguishing public values, in particular freedom and equality, from personal values. The liberal argument is that by realizing public values, a legal system can remain neutral vis-a-vis personal values. The point is sometimes made more strongly: some liberal theorists claim that the public values of liberalism entail neutrality affecting private preferences. *See, e.g.*, H.L.A. HART, LAW, LIBERTY, AND MORALITY 20 (1963) (noting that legal coercion of positive social morality "calls for justification as something *prima facie* objectionable, to be tolerated only for the sake of some countervailing good"); RAWLS, *supra* note 38, at 207-08 (noting that "from the perspective of the original position, there is no way of ascertaining the relative strength of various doctrines").

[161] *See* Hart, *supra* note 119, at 615-21 (noting the problems posed by the historical example of Nazi Germany for positivist conceptions of law).

Defining law as order effected and sustained through authority, positivism holds that the substance of law, and *a fortiori* any question of whether law serves human needs, is irrelevant to the identity of law. From the point of view of positivism, all three essential claims of consensus theory—that there are universal human needs, that such needs are the ground of social value, and that law expresses and realizes these values—are irrelevant to identifying law. The point of identifying and citing something as law is, in Raz's sophisticated version of positivism, a way of preempting justificatory moves and thus putting such normative claims about law in their separate, distinct, and important place. *See supra* text accompanying notes 124-26.

positivists, they stress order and power; unlike positivists, they give the terms a critical import and tell a normative story.[162]

The new jurisprudence has two aspects: the skeptical and destabilizing arguments of the critical theory espoused by antifoundationalists, and the attempt to resolve these arguments in the social and philosophical theory of pragmatism. Each deserves independent examination.

B. *The Limits of Critical Theory*

1. Myths of Value Pluralism

Critical theory invites the use of the philosophical technique of dissolving questions by undermining their foundations.[163] This technique is exemplified by our discussion of the positivist's question of whether and when judges properly step outside the law when deciding hard cases.[164] No simple answer is satisfactory, and our analysis of the deliberative role of judges explains why this is so.[165]

The same kind of technique applies when the question is

---

[162] Kelman states:

> "Progressivism" may be undercut by the view that legal change simply reflects the dominance of whichever pernicious elite has grabbed a greater degree of control, the view that "modernization" is predominantly gloomy, destroys communal bonds, decent work, faith, and family, and/or that development has generally moved us from a society of independent, civic-minded, and public-spirited citizens to a bunch of atomistic profit grabbers.

KELMAN, *supra* note 2, at 243. Similarly, Kathleen Lahey comments that

> [o]ne of the greatest accomplishments of feminist legal scholarship has been to identify the ideological content of masculist legal theory, of legal reasoning, and indeed, of reasoning itself. To point out that this ideological content actually affects the real and lived lives of women is merely to demonstrate that ideas become real through ideology and that reality affects ideology. . . .
>
> . . . [W]omen who involve themselves with power processes live within the shadow of ideologies that are compatible with the acquisition and exercise of power. Thus it would not be surprising to find that women who are involved in power processes are themselves influenced by the very forces that they think they are combatting.

Kathleen A. Lahey, *Reasonable Women and the Law*, *in* AT THE BOUNDARIES OF LAW 3, 3-4 (Martha A. Fineman & Nancy S. Thomadsen eds., 1991).

[163] *See* WITTGENSTEIN, *supra* note 22, at 51 (stating that "the clarity that we are aiming at is indeed *complete* clarity. But this simply means that the philosophical problems should *completely* disappear.")

[164] *See supra* part III.

[165] *See supra* text accompanying notes 127-45.

whether or not different judges adhere to reconcilable value systems. Naturalist critics of positivism, notably Fiss and Dworkin, struggle to show that reconciliation of value systems is manifest, especially in the light of the liberal's distinction between public values and private values.[166] Naturalists also claim to demonstrate that the public values fleshed out in the constitutional system of rights offer answers to hard legal questions. Answers thus are forthcoming so long as the Constitution is interpreted through the liberal principle that the legal system exists to provide equal concern and respect for all individuals[167] and to position all persons equally in the struggle to achieve personal values.[168] The liberal consensus theorist tries to have both harmony and diversity. Skeptical critics argue that one precludes the other. The price of harmony is coercion; the cost of diversity is strife.

In contemporary jurisprudence, critical legal theorists have the distinction of making this point both descriptively and normatively, and they combine description with normative conclusions in an innovative way. The descriptive element alone is long familiar: philosophers throughout history have claimed that persons have differing value convictions and that value systems are therefore irreconcilable.[169] Even some of the most prominent liberal theorists, including John Ely,[170] acquiesce in this notion.

In contrast, critical legal theorists such as Kennedy,[171] Tushnet,[172] and Gordon,[173] give the claim a normative spin. Recall that consensus theorists refer to fundamental needs and interests,

---

[166] *See supra* note 48. Note that critics of positivism who argue that law and moral argument are indissolubly linked tend to be labeled (sometimes by themselves) "naturalists," although the link to natural law theory is attenuated at best. Natural law theory, properly so-called, stresses universal rules of social organization, while writers such as Dworkin and Fiss discuss the links between the legal and moral rules and beliefs of a particular society or community.

[167] *See* DWORKIN, *supra* note 47, at 180-83.

[168] *See* RAWLS, *supra* note 38, at 90-94.

[169] *See* THOMAS HOBBES, LEVIATHAN 63 (Michael Oakeshott ed., Oxford 1946) (1651).

[170] *See* ELY, *supra* note 29.

[171] *See* Kennedy, *supra* note 9, at 213-17 (discussing the legitimizing nature of legal thinking and categorical schemes).

[172] *See* TUSHNET, *supra* note 50, at 313 (concluding that proponents of the possibility of constitutional theory advocate the imposition of the values of a particular elite).

[173] *See* Gordon, *supra* note 3, at 100-09 (summarizing varieties of critical legal historiography and describing the relationship between constitutive legal rules and the Hobbesian state of war).

such as the need for concern and respect. To reject the idea of fundamental needs and interests and describe the realm of value as one of competing political agendas is, for critical theorists, to conclude that law is used to make one or another political agenda dominant. This turns law into a manifestation of a "legitimating ideology,"[174] a story about value that is one of many possible stories, no one of which has priority. Law is thus inherently subject to criticism for claiming legitimacy that it lacks.

Consensus theorists answer the "one value system or many" question by reconciling diversity within one system; skeptics claim there are many. But the question itself rests on a distinction between fact and value, a distinction with a long history in philosophy and in what passes for common sense.[175] The theory is that since descriptive discourse and evaluative discourse (fact and value) are separate, any general agreement about facts (of science, history, geography, etc.) has no implications for agreement or disagreement about value. Whether there is one value system or many is independently determinable.

To the extent that the "one value system or many" question rests on the fact and value distinction, it should be dissolved rather than answered. To understand deliberative practices is to see that what we call facts and values are interconnected and inseparable in justificatory structures. The justification of what is generally called a value claim, such as the infringement of a plaintiff's right to privacy or of his civil right against discrimination, is a legal argument consisting of facts of various kinds—historical, psychological, sociological, and so on. The judge, in offering a justificatory argument, assumes that there is a logical relationship between the facts and the conclusion. Justification would otherwise be impossible.[176]

The question of whether judges (or persons generally) have reconcilable or irreconcilable value systems dissolves into the question of whether persons have different but reconcilable

---

[174] *Id.* at 93.

[175] *See supra* notes 90-95 and accompanying text (discussing the relationship between fact and value).

[176] Thus, one judge may derive from the fact that the intent of the founders was to limit the scope of governmental intervention the evaluative conclusion that the claimant has no legal right to have privacy claims vindicated. Another judge may derive from the fact that a given allocation of burdens would be economically inefficient the evaluative conclusion that the claimant must bear the burden of a particular economic arrangement.

justificatory patterns, reconcilable ways of pooling their beliefs about human nature, society, and the world, and of drawing conclusions from those beliefs. Differences over capital punishment, affirmative action, the rights of criminal defendants, and abortion are not simply the products of different systems of value, unrelated to fact. They are the functions of differing understandings of human nature, human history, human malleability, original sin, and so on, endlessly. Whether we call some of these beliefs values and some facts is nominal and arbitrary. What matters is that we see them as competing ways of orienting oneself to experience.

Understanding of law as a deliberative practice suggests that participants will generally recognize agreement of three kinds. They will agree on broad generalities about need and social value. They will agree on formal procedures for debate and decision. And they will agree in the mutual recognition of relevant arguments. Through these understandings, participants will know the dimensions of the debate. But none of this agreement assures consensus, not because participants subscribe to different value systems but because they have different histories and therefore different strategies for knowing, reasoning, and justifying. The vital stake that each participant has in ways of thinking will tend to perpetuate such debate, but the fact that their ways of thinking incorporate active consideration and evaluation of others' ways of thinking moves them toward change and accommodation. The most legal theory can tell us is that all debate is carried out in tension between these tendencies. The normative lesson, such as it is, is to maximize empathic consideration of alternative ways of thinking.[177]

2. Conceptual Frameworks

Some critical legal theorists are fully aware that the irreconcilable differences they claim to find are not between value systems as such but between ways of thinking that link fact and value. They regard such ways of thinking as discrete conceptual frameworks or conceptual schemes. Feminist theorists in particular appreciate the relationship between fact and value and argue that gender bias infects ways of describing the world.[178] They are not alone, as

---

[177] To the extent that one kind of value transcends all other kinds, arguably the value of openness and empathy toward the ways of thinking (justificatory strategies) of others is such a value. This claim echoes John Stuart Mill's commendation of a marketplace of ideas. *See* JOHN STUART MILL, ON LIBERTY 18-21 (David Spitz ed., W.W. Norton & Co. 1975) (1859).

[178] *See, e.g.*, MARTHA MINOW, MAKING ALL THE DIFFERENCE 219 (1990) (arguing

Robert Gordon remarks, in "historiciz[ing] consciousness."[179] Their point is simple and in many respects compatible with an understanding of deliberative practices.

For critical theory, the historical dimension is just one of many ways in which conceptual frameworks are said to be relativized. Different groups of persons are characterized by different ways of thinking and feeling, understanding and experiencing. The divisions among groups are both diachronic and synchronic. Kuhn's insight into conceptual revolutions tends to emphasize change over time, resulting in the replacement of one conceptual system by another.[180] Theorists also try to show that different conceptual systems coexist, most obviously in different societies, but also within a given society.[181]

a. *Forms of Conceptual Relativity*

In emphasizing conceptual relativity, critical legal theory distinguishes between the ways of thinking of the empowered and the powerless, between individualists and communitarians, and between the morally self-concerned and altruists. They claim that these fissures run deep, "all the way down" in legal thinking. All law, in this view, is politics.[182]

---

that "relational insights [of feminist theory] show a mutual dependence between 'normal' and 'abnormal' people, and between male norms and women who do not fit them. . . . The act of judgment depends on and simultaneously forges a relationship. What qualities that relationship should attain becomes the most important question of law, informed by feminist theory."); Caroline Whitbeck, *A Different Reality: Feminist Ontology*, *in* ANN GARRY & MARILYN PEARSALL, WOMEN, KNOWLEDGE, AND REALITY 51, 51 (1989) (stating that "[feminist] ontology has at its core a conception of the self-other *relation* that is significantly different from the self-other *opposition* that underlines so much of so-called 'western thought'. Dualistic ontologies based on the opposition of self and other generate two related views of the person and of ethics: the patriarchal view and that of individualism.").

179 Gordon, *supra* note 3, at 98.

180 *See* Kuhn, *supra* note 45, at 144-59.

181 *See* CLIFFORD GEERTZ, LOCAL KNOWLEDGE 215-19 (1983) (arguing that localizing forces of time, place, and narrative must be seen as both constructing knowledge and regulating behavior).

182 According to Duncan Kennedy:

> The fundamental contradiction—that relations with others are both necessary to and incompatible with our freedom—is not only intense. It is also pervasive. First, it is an aspect of our experience of every form of social life. . . . Second, within law, as law is commonly defined, it is not only an aspect, but the very *essence* of every problem. There simply are no legal issues that do not involve directly the problem of the legitimate content of collective coercion, since there is by definition no legal problem until

Similarly, most influential feminists argue that women represent an underexpressed or unexpressed "different voice" not only on moral, social, and political issues, but also on such issues as human nature, history, and psychology.[183] Every field of scholarly activity has been touched by the notion that a feminist perspective is distinctive and relatively unheard. Radical feminists add an important gloss, asserting that the search for this distinctive voice is tainted by the fact that women have always lived in circumstances of domination and alienation. For these scholars, the essential problem is that women cannot know what their voice would say unless and until they are free.[184] Theorists such as Catharine MacKinnon stress the need to create rather than to find women's conceptual systems. She and others admit and address the paradoxical implications of this claim for their own work.[185]

The burgeoning field of critical race and ethnic studies shares this picture of conceptual relativity and fragmentation. Writers such as Richard Delgado and Mari Matsuda broadcast the need for underrepresented voices of Hispanics, African Americans, native Americans, and Asian-Americans to be heard.[186] Others question the authenticity of voices that are the products of domination.

A constant theme of these many forms of critical theory is the

---

someone has at least imagined that he might invoke the force of the state. Kennedy, *supra* note 9, at 213. In a similar vein, Unger states that

> [t]he implication of our attack upon formalism is to undermine the attempt to rescue doctrine through these several stratagems. It is to demonstrate that a doctrinal practice that puts its hope in the contrast of legal reasoning to ideology, philosophy, and political prophecy ends up as a collection of makeshift apologies.

UNGER, *supra* note 9, at 11.

[183] *See, e.g.*, West, *supra* note 2, at 84-85 (suggesting that women's gender-specific, different experience may lack historic and linguistic reality in a male-dominated culture). For the pioneering work on "different voice" theory, see CAROL GILLIGAN, IN A DIFFERENT VOICE (1982).

[184] *See* CATHARINE A. MACKINNON, FEMINISM UNMODIFIED 32-45 (1987).

[185] Catharine A. MacKinnon, *Feminism, Marxism, Method, and the State: An Agenda for Theory*, 7 SIGNS 515, 542-43 (1982) (noting that "[w]omen's bondage, degradation, damage, complicity, and inferiority . . . will operate as barriers to consciousness rather than as a means of access to what women need to become conscious of in order to change").

[186] *See* Matsuda, *supra* note 2, at 358-62 (noting that the "normative intuitions of those on the bottom are often different from the intuitions of those on top"); *see also* Richard Delgado, *The Ethereal Scholar: Does Critical Legal Studies Have What Minorities Want?*, 22 HARV. C.R.-C.L. L. REV. 301, 303-07 (1987) (arguing that critical legal theory analysis does not take account of minority experience, fails to confront racism, and may increase vulnerability of minorities).

relationship of fact and value. Underrepresented groups, it is said repeatedly, not only have different political agendas, but also have different ways of thinking, different ways of assembling the facts of history, anthropology, sociology, psychology, and economics, and different ways of deploying them as justificatory arguments. This concern for the multiplicity of justificatory strategies in all their complexity parallels the lessons derived from attention to deliberative practices.

E. *Intractable Questions*

Nonetheless, viewing law as a deliberative practice underscores the limits and ambiguities of conceptual relativity as expressed in feminism, critical legal studies, and race/ethnic theory. Is a conceptual system monolithic, so that the elements of a system belong to it uniquely? What is a basis for distinguishing one conceptual system from another? Is it possible for those with different conceptual systems to communicate? How? Can a conceptual system change? How? What determines whether an individual has or projects one conceptual system or another?[187]

These questions are basic, difficult, and long familiar. They antedate the recent forays of critical legal theorists,[188] and the implications of failing to answer them seem severe. For example, do the conceptual systems of men and women, white and black persons, privileged and powerless persons differ altogether? If so, how is communication possible? If not, what are the differences and how profound and tenacious are they? If the legal system is wholly the creation and expression of the conceptual system of the powerful (of men, of white persons), what theoretical explanation can be given for the possibility of change? How is a person's conceptual system determined—merely by gender, or by race, or by social class? Is one presumed to have a particular voice merely because of one's gender or race? If not, what follows?

The fact that these questions seem intractable is a clue to the fact that, however much they betray important issues, they too are pseudo-questions, questions to be dissolved rather than answered.

---

[187] *See* DONALD DAVIDSON, *On the Very Idea of a Conceptual Scheme*, *in* INQUIRIES INTO TRUTH AND INTERPRETATION 182, 182-84 (1984).

[188] *See generally* the various essays collected in the following volumes: ACTION AND INTERPRETATION (Christopher Hookway & Philip Pettit eds., 1978); OBJECTIVITY AND CULTURAL DIVERGENCE (S.C. Brown ed., 1984); RATIONALITY AND RELATIVISM, *supra* note 28.

When we discuss deliberative practices, the necessary focus of attention is the individual, with her personal ways of assimilating experiences, making judgments, and offering justifications. Given the heterogeneous character of justification, it should be clear that the individual has many kinds of belief. Some are universal, others idiosyncratic; some are controversial, others not; some are essential to her modes of thinking, while others are ones she would easily abandon.[189] All aspects of the individual's thinking are a function of her personal history and capacities. She may believe, for example, in the free market, in individual responsibility, in personal corrigibility, and in limited government. These beliefs will be rooted in her personal "take" on history, economics, psychology, and so on.

The facts that she is a woman, black, and relatively privileged in terms of wealth and education–if such is indeed the case–will be important in determining some of her beliefs, but largely irrelevant to other beliefs. Her personal history may create unique perspectives on some issues that often distinguish women's or blacks' points of view.[190] None of this can be known apart from her individual history and no pigeon-holing of her in terms of ethnic group or gender will tell us what ways of thinking she has or "should have."[191] Moreover, we underestimate the individual if we disregard her capacity to recognize, anticipate, and respond to the alternative ways of thinking of others–her capacity to see herself as a participant in a diverse and complex deliberative practice.

c. *Abandoning Conceptual Relativity*

These objections play havoc with talk about conceptual systems. The examination of deliberative practices explains how dialogue and change occur, but it implies that it is nonsense to try to distinguish one monolithic conceptual system from another, to say that one ethnic group or gender group has an integrated and distinguishable way of thinking, or to make insoluble the problem of bridging

---

[189] *See supra* text accompanying notes 25-28.

[190] *See* RALPH ELLISON, SHADOW AND ACT xix-xxiii (1972) (asserting the importance of black authors honestly and accurately depicting their attitudes and values as they exist, and not as others have conceived these attitudes and values for them.)

[191] This point was illustrated during the Senate hearings that led to the confirmation of Clarence Thomas to the United States Supreme Court. Aspects of the confirmation process evinced race-based expectations of various parties.

conceptual schemes.[192]

Attending to deliberative practices accomplishes these tasks in two ways. It focuses attention on the heterogeneity of belief and justification as opposed to the homogenizing language of conceptual systems. Thus, it shows that each aspect of an individual's way of thinking aligns her with some individuals and separates her from others. Each aspect—each set of beliefs and mode of justification—places one in a different community of like thinkers. In addition, attending to deliberative practices raises doubts about transcending practices in such a way that one can refer to them as self-contained, transcendable wholes, conceptual systems.

This does not mean that radicals should be less radical. It does mean, however, that radicals should frame their arguments by drawing justifications from within a shared deliberative practice. They misrepresent their aims and means when they insist on replacing conceptual schemes rather than challenging individual beliefs and justificatory strategies within the practice of judging.

3. Semantic Relativity

To summarize, the first subversive move of antifoundationalists is to assert that value relativity is irreducible. We saw that what is correct about this assertion is best captured by talking instead about the relativity of justificatory patterns or strategies—because value claims are underpinned by reasons, and one's reasons are determined by one's factual beliefs.[193] The second subversive move links facts and values in asserting conceptual relativity. The insights achieved by this move are betrayed by the unsupported implication that one can distinguish discrete conceptual schemes and by the pseudo-dilemmas to which this implication gives rise.

A third and final subversive move is influenced by hermeneutic theory and inspired by writers on linguistic deconstruction.[194] It

---

[192] None of these observations is meant to prejudge when persons with different ways of thinking are or are not able to understand each other or when they will indeed reason at cross-purposes. They merely imply that the difference is to be sought in individual patterns of belief, reasoning, and justification rather than in gender- or race-based conceptual frameworks.

[193] *See supra* notes 189-91 and accompanying text.

[194] For provocative and influential writings on this topic, *see generally* JONATHAN D. CULLER, ON DECONSTRUCTION: THEORY AND CRITICISM AFTER STRUCTURALISM 7-12 (1982) (providing an overview of the writings on critical theory in the 1970s); JACQUES DERRIDA, WRITING AND DIFFERENCE xiv (Alan Bass trans., 1978) (1967) (setting forth a deconstructive account of reading texts); JEAN-FRANÇOIS LYOTARD,

is an attack on the claim, implicit in positivistic theories of law and formalist theories of language, that words have determinate meaning.[195] Although there are many sophisticated variations of hermeneutic and deconstructive procedures, they share the idea that the meaning of a text (utterance) is at least partly indeterminate and that therefore meaning varies from one reader to another.

Hermeneutics proceeds from a compelling main insight that one's way of understanding, whether the object be a text or other experience, is irreducibly affected by one's history.[196] One can become self-conscious of these determinants, and thus alter one's ways of thinking, but one cannot cancel out the personal and idiosyncratic character of thinking.[197] One application of the hermeneutic insight is that one can never think as the Founders did, even if one empathetically and perceptively takes account of historical change over two centuries and tries exhaustively to dispel naive assumptions about the Founders.[198]

The main hermeneutic argument can be used in two ways. One

THE POSTMODERN CONDITION: A REPORT ON KNOWLEDGE 3 (Geoff Bennington & Brian Massumi trans., 1984) (1979) (offering a deconstructive analysis of the criteria for knowledge).

[195] H.L.A. Hart reflects at length on the "open texture" of law which makes it impossible for judges to carry out a purely deductive or "mechanical" mode of decision-making. *See* HART, *supra* note 21, at 124-32. Thus, Hart distinguishes between the core and the penumbra of a rule, the latter being the area of application wherein judges may use discretion. This distinction does not go far enough because it suggests that although every rule has a core and a penumbra, the character of the core and the scope of the penumbra are matters fixed by language. This is not necessarily so. Judges and others may disagree about the core. A more satisfactory metaphor for the common or shared element of rules (or words) that make them generally intelligible is Wittgenstein's metaphor of family resemblances, whereby what one speaker regards as core-and-penumbra has some elements in common with what a second speaker regards as the relevant core-and-penumbra, etc. *See* WITTGENSTEIN, *supra* note 22, at 32.

[196] *See generally* HANS-GEORG GADAMER, PHILOSOPHICAL HERMENEUTICS 8-9 (David E. Linge trans. & ed., 1977) (arguing that "there can be no doubt that the great horizon of the past, out of which our culture and our present live, influences us in everything we want, hope for, or fear in the future"); ROY J. HOWARD, THREE FACES OF HERMENEUTICS 16-17 (1982) (noting how hermeneutics differs from Kantian conceptions of reality); HERMENEUTICS: QUESTIONS AND PROSPECTS 4 (Gary Shapiro & Alan Sica eds., 1984) (introducing a collection of essays on hermeneutics, and describing hermeneutics as "a type of philosophical activity or praxis, the effort to understand what is distant in time and culture . . . or obscured by ideology or false consciousness.").

[197] *See* David C. Hoy, *Interpreting the Law: Hermeneutical and Poststructuralist Perspectives*, 58 S. CAL. L. REV. 135, 146-47 (1985) (suggesting that judges' viewpoints are necessarily conditioned by history and individual experience).

[198] *See id.* at 150-52, 154-55.

way is atomistic and skeptical and stresses the provisional character of discourse. It asks whether we can ever trust that meaning is communicated. At its logical extreme, this approach counterintuitively denies the possibility of communication and any kind of shared belief altogether.[199]

The second approach is more moderate and is favored by traditional hermeneutic theorists. David Hoy, for example, finds in Hans-Georg Gadamer the following view:

> [T]he context itself conditions the reader's grasp of the text, not the other way around. Furthermore, the context is historical in that it changes over time with changes in the conditions influencing various readings. This insistence on historical variation in interpretation is not in the least subjectivistic or voluntaristic. On the contrary, the position entails that the reader is not completely free to decide the meaning of the text. The text is already determinate enough, for instance, to narrow the range of possible contexts.[200]

This more compelling and persuasive hermeneutic approach addresses not the impossibility of communication but its difficulties and constraints. It emphasizes equally what draws us together and what is idiosyncratic in strategies of understanding. This is, of course, a way of concerning oneself with the structure of deliberative practices. In contrast to Tushnet and Gadamer, one who looks to deliberative practices emphasizes both diachronic and synchronic variations in ways of understanding experience. Historical change is only one of the determinants of our variant ways of understand-

---

[199] For example:

> [I]deology seems to function best when no one believes in it; more than that, belief, and even belief in the ideology's own principles and assumptions, appears as its greatest enemy. Utopia is not the triumph of (rational) belief but, on the contrary, the total interdiction of belief. Wittingly or unwittingly, the great modern philosophies of suspicion and derealization have brought their modest contributions in that direction . . . ."

Matei Calinescu, *From the One to the Many*, *in* ZEITGEIST IN BABEL 156, 172 (Ingeborg Hoesterey ed., 1991).

[200] Hoy, *supra* note 197, at 138. Mark Tushnet contrasts the same two approaches when he says,

> [a] fanatic adherent of the hermeneutic method might deny that we can ever understand the past because the world of the past is not the world within which we have developed ways of understanding how others act. That, however, goes too far. We can gain an interpretive understanding of the past by working from commonalities . . . both immanent in our history and constructed by us as we reflect on what our history is.

TUSHNET, *supra* note 50, at 44.

ing experience. We are different not only from our ancestors, but also from each other. And yet our differences must be understood as variations on shared themes: what makes our practices shared is the extent to which we can transcend individual strategies, apprehending and appreciating the alternatives encompassed by the shared practice.

C. *Applying the Lessons: Pragmatism as Legal Theory*

What do we gain by thinking of law as a deliberative practice? Is the notion merely a description of law and legal reasoning? Is it theory? If it is theory, does this label imply that it facilitates substantive work, for example judicial decision-making and the evaluation of judicial decisions?

Implicit in the description of law as a deliberative practice is neither hope nor despair. By "hope" I mean something quite specific: the aspiration to make hard cases easy (or easier) by showing that one approach to decision-making is fundamentally correct. Consensus theory is an expression of this kind of hope.[201] Hope in this sense, a malady of philosophers, differs from run-of-the-mill hope, the hope that one's resolution of a hard case will convince others. The first kind is the hope of reconceiving an array of approaches by making a foundational theoretical advance; the second is the hope of applying one's own approach in a persuasive way.

By "despair" I mean a solipsistic conviction that conceptual diversity is unbridgeable in principle. Such despair differs from the despair that one's own answers and strategies of argument will prove unpersuasive in particular cases and also from the despairing realization that human deliberation will always be diverse in approach and result. Deliberative practices involve bridgeable diversity.

The philosophical kinds of hope and despair that must be rejected are based on distorted pictures of actual deliberation. Wittgenstein says that philosophy "leaves everything as it is."[202] This comment is notoriously open to many interpretations.[203]

---

[201] *See* Thomas C. Grey, *Holmes and Legal Pragmatism*, 41 STAN. L. REV. 787, 799 (1989) (contrasting the traditional Western philosophical goal of establishing a foundation of knowledge on basic indubitable beliefs with the pragmatist's claim that knowledge is dependent on context).

[202] WITTGENSTEIN, *supra* note 22, at 49.

[203] *See* ACKERMAN, *supra* note 17, at 205 (stating that "Wittgenstein wants to keep

One plausible interpretation is that theoretical speculation explains our deliberative practices and, in doing so, dissolves misconceptions about practices but does not change them. Speculating about judicial decision-making does not make hard cases easy, but neither does it make them impossible by showing that what appears to be a debate among reasoning strategies is really a confrontation of hermetically-sealed conceptual systems. My description of deliberative practices follows this sense of Wittgenstein's dictum.

The suggestion that law is a deliberative practice is similar in some ways to recent accounts offered by so-called "legal pragmatists."[204] Certainly the goals of the two accounts seem similar, as Thomas Grey implies in his contribution to a recent symposium on legal pragmatism:

> [I]n its very modesty, pragmatism always threatens to usher itself from the philosophical scene. . . . The pragmatist says that theory is no more than commentary on practice, based on premises drawn from that practice itself or from other practices. This account of theorizing sounds question-begging to the standard theorist; its self-imposed practical test (theorize to improve practice) invites responsive insistence on some independent (i.e. "genuinely theoretical") criteria by which "improvement" can be identified.[205]

While law as a deliberative practice disappoints the same "theoretical" aspirations, it serves to "improve practice" only indirectly, if at all. It affects practice through self-awareness, through fostering the

---

the differences, the jagged edges, and accept what is obviously fragmentary, contextual, and incomplete"); S. STEPHEN HILMY, THE LATER WITTGENSTEIN 205-06 (1987) (stating that Wittgenstein regards philosophy as only descriptive); ANTHONY KENNY, THE LEGACY OF WITTGENSTEIN 45 (1984) (stating that "Wittgenstein insists that philosophy is only philosophical problems. The survey which you make does not give you the kind of totally new understanding, a surplus understanding, it merely removes the philosophical problems.").

204 Posner argues that

> [a]lthough pragmatic jurisprudence embraces a richer set of ideas than can be found in *The Nature of the Judicial Process* or "The Path of Law," one can hardly say that there has been much progress, and perhaps in the nature of pragmatism there cannot be. . . . [Pragmatism] signals an attitude, an orientation, at times a change in direction. It clears the underbrush; it does not plant the forest.

Richard A. Posner, *What Has Pragmatism to Offer Law?*, 63 S. CAL. L. REV. 1653, 1670 (1990).

205 Thomas Grey, *Hear the Other Side: Wallace Stevens and Pragmatist Legal Theory*, 63 S. CAL. L. REV. 1569, 1591 (1990). Grey goes on to say that theories offering such independent criteria "are not to be had." *Id.* In this conclusion, he agrees with those who view law as a deliberative practice.

self-consciousness examination of one's assumptions and methods.

How does legal pragmatism compare with the account of law that we have been investigating? Legal pragmatists, as we shall see, arrive at their conclusions by a different route, by appropriating rather than distinguishing the skeptical arguments of critical theory. As the label suggests, they draw links to pragmatic philosophers of almost a century ago.[206]

1. Rorty's Pragmatism

If the revival of pragmatism could be attributed to one philosopher, it would be Richard Rorty. Admitting that the term is "vague, ambiguous, and overworked," he insists nevertheless that pragmatism "names the chief glory of our country's intellectual tradition."[207] For Rorty, pragmatism's greatest importance lies in showing that "there are no constraints on inquiry save conversational ones—no wholesale constraints derived from the nature of the objects, or of the mind, or of language, but only those retail constraints provided by the remarks of our fellow-inquirers."[208] Furthermore, "[t]he pragmatist tells us that it is useless to hope that objects will constrain us to believe the truth about them, if only they are approached with an unclouded mental eye, or a rigorous method, or a perspicuous language."[209] Translated into the language of deliberative practices, this means that consensus theory must fail to make hard cases easy because neither the nature of justice nor human need, nor moral insight, nor linguistic purism can reduce the diversity of interpretive strategies for approaching hard cases or determine which strategies are right and which wrong. That question needs to be dissolved, not answered. No transcendental method, but only our awareness of the range of strategies intelligible within our deliberative practices, can constrain our reasoning.

---

[206] For recent writings on jurisprudence and neo-pragmatism, see *id.*; Steven D. Smith, *The Pursuit of Pragmatism*, 100 YALE L.J. 409 (1990); Peter D. Swan, *Critical Legal Theory and the Politics of Pragmatism*, 12 DALHOUSIE L.J. 349 (1989); Symposium, *The Renaissance of Pragmatism in American Legal Thought*, 63 S. CAL. L. REV. 1569 (1990).

[207] RICHARD RORTY, CONSEQUENCES OF PRAGMATISM 160 (1982).

[208] *Id.* at 165.

[209] *Id.*

a. *Rorty on Solidarity and Individuality*

The overriding purpose of Rorty's many essays on pragmatism is to refute foundationalism. He views the search for foundations, for a transcendental method, as the prevailing aim and conception of philosophy. There is, however, a more troubling positive side to his analysis: a description of how we are situated as reasoners and what our deliberative practices are like.

What does Rorty mean when he says that the only "constraints on inquiry" are "provided by the remarks of our fellow-inquirers"? Does one who participates in inquiry have no other constraints? For a participant in a deliberative practice, each new question and each new judgment must be fitted into the web of beliefs that one already holds, in which some beliefs are deeply held as criterial and others held more tentatively. One is constrained, as we have seen, by one's stake in a particular way of judging. In the face of sufficiently recalcitrant experience, including the persuasive arguments and accounts of others, many beliefs may be reordered; one's stake may change. Nonetheless, for each of us the diverging strategies of fellow-inquirers are not options equivalent to our own strategies, but challenges to be met and if possible refuted. Thus, Rorty's depiction of the individual's relation to other participants and to the individual's strategies needs examination.

Elsewhere, Rorty states:

> There are two principal ways in which reflective human beings try, by placing their lives in a larger context, to give sense to those lives. The first is by telling the story of their contribution to a community. . . . The second way is to describe themselves as standing in immediate relation to a nonhuman reality. . . . [S]tories of the former kind exemplify the desire for solidarity, and . . . stories of the latter kind exemplify the desire for objectivity. . . .
>
> The tradition in Western culture which centers around the notion of the search for Truth . . . is the clearest example of the attempt to find a sense in one's existence by turning away from solidarity to objectivity. The idea of Truth as something to be pursued for its own sake, not because it will be good for oneself, or for one's real or imaginary community, is the central theme of this tradition.[210]

Rorty identifies this move from solidarity to objectivity as the

---

[210] RICHARD RORTY, OBJECTIVITY, RELATIVISM, AND TRUTH 21 (1991).

mistaken move of philosophy. He sees this philosophical gesture as a kind of blindness, blindness to the limits of deliberative practices.[211]

The problem with Rorty's preference for solidarity over objectivity is that it is relevant solely at the level of theory and not at the level of the participant. The sense of "standing in immediate relation to a nonhuman reality" is itself immediate. How could experience be otherwise? The impulse to apply strategies of understanding to find out how things are in "nonhuman reality"—what is behind the tree, what is the sum of these numbers, what is the geography of Antarctica—arises spontaneously as an end in itself.[212] Our stake is expressed in the strategies we employ to answer these questions and in regarding them as yielding truth, as putting us in touch with how things are. Even if truth is not the guarantor of what these strategies yield, as Rorty is correct in asserting, it is the product of what the strategies yield.

b. *Rorty on Theory and Practice*

Taken as descriptive of experience, Rorty's account is paradoxical because it represents participation from the outside rather than the inside. From the standpoint of an outsider/theorist, the practice is indeed, as Rorty says, limited only by the collection of available strategies;[213] truth and reality are whatever those strategies yield.[214] But to say this is to lose sight of the point of view of the insider. And ultimately, all of us experience ourselves as insiders for whom objectivity, or rational deployment of strategies for arriving at what we regard as truth, matters.

Rorty, in other words, speaks from an impossible position, that of the pure outsider who is not a participant in practices and

---

211 *See id.* at 24.

212 The givenness of experience is a central issue for epistemology. *See* ARTHUR C. DANTO, ANALYTICAL PHILOSOPHY OF KNOWLEDGE 141-42 (1968) (stating that even "if we are in fact products of our experience, this fact is irrelevant to the externality of experience as an epistemological relationship"); D. HAMLYN, THE THEORY OF KNOWLEDGE (1970).

213 *See supra* text accompanying note 208.

214 When presented this way, Rorty's argument has most of the earmarks of what Dworkin describes as "external skepticism." Dworkin describes external skepticism as "a metaphysical theory, not an interpretive or moral position. . . . [The] theory is rather a second-level theory about the philosophical standing or classification of [substantive] claims. . . . [Such] skepticism is external because disengaged: it claims to leave the actual conduct of interpretation untouched by its conclusions." DWORKIN, *supra* note 36, at 79-80.

Rorty's recommendations about using the notions of truth and objectivity are made from that perspective. The position is an archetypical kind of skepticism that has always had proponents.[215] Given this perspective, how can one characterize Rorty's own analysis? Is it true and objective as a description of the limits of language? Or is it, on the other hand, simply an expression of solidarity with a linguistic and conceptual community? Rorty aspires to the first characterization and not the second.[216] From the point of view of insiders to the practice shared with Rorty, these claims aim to state what is true and to do so objectively.

Another difficulty in Rorty's position echoes the main themes of this essay. Why does Rorty refer so often to "communities" and so rarely to individuals? Why is solidarity with a community the concept that supplants or corrects the aspiration to objectivity? The clue again lies in Rorty's adoption of the point of view of the outsider. What is essential to individual (insider) self-awareness is what I have called a stake in a particular way of organizing experience, particular strategies of understanding. Each person's strategies are the unique product of a unique history and unique capacities. Because recalcitrant experience is always possible, one's identification with the shared community in which one has learned these strategies is always in principle subject to rupture.

Individuality in this sense gets short shrift from Rorty. Identifying himself as one of the "partisans of solidarity,"[217] he says that "[i]nsofar as a person is seeking solidarity, she does not ask about the relation between the practices of the chosen community and something outside that community."[218] Awareness and self-questioning about the diverse strategies of a deliberative practice are the essence of individuality and are antithetical to solidarity.[219]

---

[215] *See, e.g.*, STRAWSON, *supra* note 68, at 106 (stating that one cannot ascribe "states of consciousness to oneself, or at all, unless the ascriber already knows how to ascribe at least some states of consciousness to others . . . . [W]e must accept [this conclusion] in order to explain the existence of the conceptual scheme in terms of which the sceptical problem is stated.").

[216] *See* RORTY, *supra* note 4, at 315-94.

[217] RORTY, *supra* note 210, at 33.

[218] *Id.* at 21.

[219] Rorty is keenly sensitive to the idea that choice is a condition of solidarity and that privacy matters.

> [T]he important questions will be about what sort of human being you want to become. . . . [T]his question will divide into two subquestions. The first is: with what communities should you identify, of which should you think of yourself as a member? The second is . . . what should I do with my loneness?

Rorty insufficiently distinguishes two roles of community, and therefore two senses of solidarity. One sense refers to each person's debt to her history. In this sense, "community" identifies the context of learning, of becoming a participant in practices. Solidarity with that community is never entirely chosen and is likely to be ruptured over time as one shapes one's ways of thinking around the recalcitrant experiences of life. The other sense of solidarity is one's chosen identification with those who are like-minded. Shared values, backgrounds, and ways of organizing thought ground such voluntary associations, which are always subject to revision; opting out is always a possibility. Solidarity in this sense is never perfect unless it subverts what is individual and unique. Individuality appears in the transition from community in the first sense to community in the second.

c. *Rorty's Influence*

Some critical theorists identify the justificatory and conceptual strategies of individuals with those of discrete communities. Many of them assume, as we have seen, that value "systems" or conceptual "systems" stably define such communities. A failure to address the relation of individual to community allows them to assume that race, class, and gender define separate domains and that individuals simply express and represent the shared experience and understanding of such domains/communities.[220]

Martha Minow and Elizabeth Spelman, for example, assert that for Rorty language "reflects particular human cultures" and describe him as recommending that "it [is] better to speak within particular communities about contingent practices."[221] Joseph Singer draws from Rorty the insight that "[a]ll objectivity means is agreement among people. . . . [O]bjective principles are principles . . . people accept."[222] The outsider standpoint that these writers borrow

---

Id. at 13

[220] *See supra* text accompanying notes 182-92.

[221] Martha Minow & Elizabeth V. Spelman, *In Context*, 63 S. CAL. L. REV. 1597, 1611 (1990).

[222] Joseph Singer, *The Players and the Cards: Nihilism and Legal Theory*, 94 YALE L.J. 1, 35 (1984).

Compare this to the view that objectivity means adherence to a principled and consistent way of forming judgments, one that is as free as possible of accidental emotional bias. All of us have, among our strategies of understanding, ways of checking for consistency and bias as well as relevant modes of self-questioning. Application of these checks and balances sometimes compels us to arrive at different

from Rorty collapses the individual's modes of judgment into those of the group.

More recently Singer has faced the dilemma that this reductive move sets up: the paradox of understanding how the individual, whose resources are reduced to those of the group, can possibly differentiate herself from the group and employ a way of judging that opposes it. Singer accuses Rorty of conservatism, of "deferring to the immanent values of 'our' culture," and urges the "need to understand how our ways of describing the world [illegible] reinforce the power of dominant groups . . . [and the need to understand] the ways in which our categories . . . reinforce illegitimate power relationships."[223] Both the view that Singer criticizes in Rorty and the view that he commends assume that one must choose between conceptual schemes attributable to groups, either the schemes of the dominant class or of the dominated class. Thus, Singer identifies the individual's possibilities with the experience of the group. He also assumes that reasons for judgment are homogeneously classifiable as reasons that reinforce power or that undermine it.

Rorty is therefore seen as discussing value systems or conceptual schemes that are group or class-based. Arguing against an objectively privileged method of understanding, he disparages truth and objectivity by assuming the standpoint of an outsider to any particular practice. He invites the conclusions that the insider's aspiration for truth and objectivity is an illusion and that the individual simply represents the group: discourse is simply a "conversation" among exemplars of discrete conceptually-separated groups. Group-based conceptual schemes subvert the distinctiveness of the individual's unique strategies of understanding and the perspective that the individual as insider deploys toward truth.

By contrast, attention to deliberative practices stresses that each individual's strategies are unique and that shared recognition of strategies is essential to the existence of a practice. It also shows that theorists who talk about truth and objectivity must attend to the ways in which participants in practices understand truth and objectivity. Rorty's remarks on truth and objectivity reflect an attempt to transcend particular strategies. But we remain participants, unable to ascend with Rorty to the ethereal realms and to

---

judgments and use different principles than those with whom we deliberate.

[223] Joseph Singer, *Should Lawyers Care About Philosophy?*, 1989 DUKE L.J. 1752, 1769.

absorb the chaste linguistic admonitions of pure theory.[224]

2. Fish and Interpretive Communities

The critic Stanley Fish is, if anything, even more acute and persuasive than Rorty in showing the mistakes of foundationalism in the context of describing deliberative activities. Challenging the suggestion of consensus theory that "'disciplining rules' . . . will constrain readers or interpreters and mitigate (if not neutralize) the inherent ambiguity of texts," and that the rules will "tell you what to do and prevent you from simply doing whatever you like," Fish argues that rules cannot have this kind of independence as constraints because they do not "declare their own significance to any observer, no matter what his perspective."[225] For each interpreter the rules have an idiosyncratic place within her own interpretive strategies. Given the stake each person has in such strategies, "one cannot," according to Fish, "be meaningfully urged to become more flexible or generous in one's thinking . . . . [A]lthough flexibility and openness may well be the pattern human cognitive performance traces out, it cannot be a program a human performer might self-consciously enact."[226] Clarifying this, Fish explains that he is not saying "that beliefs (and therefore consciousness) cannot change, only that change will not be from a state of undoubted belief to a state in which the grip of belief has been relaxed, but from one state of not-at-the-moment-seen-around belief to another."[227]

a. *Fish and Deliberative Practices*

These descriptions resonate particularly well with the idea of being situated in a deliberative practice. For example, Fish persuasively criticizes Catharine MacKinnon in saying that she "is not, despite her own pronouncements, exhorting us to a new way of knowing, but to know different things than we currently know

---

[224] It may seem ironic to criticize Rorty on these grounds, since he himself insists that all discourse is part of a conversation among participants in a practice and that pure theory is an illusion. However, my argument is that he is inconsistent in holding that ordinary language is the only language we have, while at the same time taking a skeptical and revisionary stance toward the concepts of truth and objectivity. He denies that his position is skeptical or revisionary. *See generally* RORTY, *supra* note 4.

[225] FISH, NATURALLY, *supra* note 19, at 121.

[226] *Id.* at 16.

[227] *Id.* at 18.

(about rape, pornography, etc.) in the same (and only) way we know anything, by having been convinced of it."[228] In this view, it is sensible to interpret feminist theorists not as urging us to reject and replace conceptual schemes but as commending new ways of putting together familiar and unfamiliar experiences by using mutually intelligible strategies of understanding.

Similarly, Fish contends that, although he is not concerned with "deny[ing] the distinction between continuing and inventing, . . . as in the case of explaining versus changing, the distinction is interpretive, and . . . because it is interpretive, one cannot determine whether a particular piece of behavior is one or the other by checking it against the text."[229] In other words, from the standpoint of her own interpretive strategies, each judge will see herself as continuing a course of judgment faithful to existing law and will see others as inventing new law. "[I]nsofar as the distinction is a mechanism for distinguishing between two forms of judicial activity . . . it won't work because there is no *independent* way of determining whether or not a particular judge is acting in one way [or] the other."[230] Fish seems to say that such distinctions make sense for the insider but not the outsider.

b. *Fish as Pure Theorist*

Often, however, Fish himself takes the standpoint of outsider and seems to declare the distinctions meaningless altogether. "The distinction between a 'found' history and an 'invented' one is finally nothing more than a distinction between a persuasive interpretation and one that has failed to convince."[231] This echoes Rorty's pragmatic claim that successful persuasion is the only measure of truth.

But for the insider, predictions of persuasive success cannot be a criterion for truth. For a participant in a deliberative practice, for instance the judge deciding a case, there is all the difference between the argument that flows from his commitments, his strategies of understanding, and an alternative argument he can imagine constructing, or inventing. The distinction has little if anything to do with its anticipated persuasive power.

---

[228] *Id.* at 21.

[229] *Id.* at 109.

[230] *Id.* at 109-10.

[231] Stanley Fish, *Working on the Chain Gang: Interpretation in Law and Literature*, 60 TEX. L. REV. 551, 559 (1982).

Fish also speaks as an outsider when he says that "[i]n searching for a way to protect against arbitrary readings (judicial and literary), Dworkin is searching for something he already has and could not be without. He conducts his search by projecting as dangers and fears possibilities that could never be realized."[232] What does Fish mean by saying that arbitrary readings are not possible? Insider/participants have criteria for what they call arbitrary readings. They reject some readings (and some justificatory arguments) as arbitrary when they are poorly grounded even in the proponent's own reasoning strategies. On the other hand, for the theorist as outsider, there is indeed no transcendental criterion for arbitrariness when she, as theorist, compares one justificatory strategy with another. But to say that all readings are equally arbitrary (or non-arbitrary) is doubly misleading, both because there can be no standard for determining equal (or unequal) arbitrariness and because each of us is in fact an insider, disposed to reason in a particular way and to deploy internal criteria of arbitrariness. None of us is in a position to occupy the pure outsider's seat.[233]

c. *Fish on Interpretive Communities*

In using Fish's writings, theorists tend to assimilate the perspective of the individual into the conceptual categories of the group.[234] Fish's own statement of the notion of an interpretive community, one of his main themes, is ambiguous. He says that

> [i]nterpretive communities are made up of those who share interpretive strategies not for reading but for writing texts . . . . [S]ince the thoughts an individual can think and the mental operations he can perform have their source in some or other interpretive community, he is as much a product of that community (acting as an extension of it) as the meanings it enables him to produce.[235]

---

[232] *Id.* at 562.

[233] Therefore, I regard Fish's comments on the concept of arbitrariness as revisionary from a skeptical standpoint, just as Rorty's comments about truth and objectivity turn out to be revisionary. Both, in spite of themselves, commit the skeptical maneuver analyzed and criticized by Strawson. *See* STRAWSON, *supra* note 68, at 103-10.

[234] Douzinas's recent critical study of postmodern jurisprudence claims that for Fish "every community of interpreters, lawyers and judges, for example, develops its unique sense of professional competence, etiquette and good sense, with its own tacit and explicit conventions." DOUZINAS, *supra* note 6, at 138.

[235] FISH, TEXT, *supra* note 19, at 14. David Luban's discussion of ambiguity in Fish's account of interpretive communities raises the issue of whether

The terms "share," "source," and "product" are all ambiguous. Do persons share strategies only when their strategies are the same or whenever they have overlapping and mutually intelligible strategies? Does Fish mean in referring to sources and products that individuals are limited by and reducible to the strategies they share with all members of the community, or is he saying merely that the origins of interpretive strategies are in the community and that its resources are their endowment and history? The latter reading sheds light on the situation of the individual in a deliberative practice. The former reading ignores individuality and lends itself to caricature, the picture of discrete and isolatable conceptual systems which is at the heart of some critical writings.

3. Acceptable Pragmatism and Banal Pragmatism

Legal (neo-)pragmatism has an individualist face which takes account of the differences of individuals within practices and a collectivist face which ignores such diversity. Theorists such as Rorty and Fish slip from the individualist to the collectivist position. The collectivist position rests on the idea of a homogeneous interpretive community, on unreflective solidarity with like-minded persons.

The elements of the collectivist position are simplifications of reality, traps for critical theorists. Accordingly, on the collectivist view, the individual is merely a manifestation of the community, identifiable by its shared value system or shared conceptual framework. Disagreement is nothing more or less than a conversation among members of different interpretive communities. Truth is nothing more than a label for the interpretive strategy that happens to persuade and prevail in the conversation.

These collectivist theses are congenial to writers who assume that the powerful and the powerless, the genders, and the several races define discrete conceptual systems at war with one another, and that nothing more can be said for judgments than that they reflect one system or another. I have considered at length what is wrong with the collectivist picture: it disregards the idiosyncratic strategies of individuals, the stake each has in her strategies, the implications of that stake for the use of terms like "truth" and

---

Fish extends his strictures to institutions/communities in which "members disagree over interpretive strategies." *See* David Luban, Fish v. Fish *or, Some Realism About Idealism*, 7 CARDOZO L. REV. 693, 694 (1986).

"objectivity," and the way in which the use of these terms illuminates the tension between having a stake and being aware that one's practices are not grounded in transcendental foundations (criteria outside the practice itself). All of these dimensions of deliberative practices are part of the individualist story, lost in the collectivist story.

The individualist story is reflected in some recent writings by jurisprudential neo-pragmatists. Thomas Grey describes "the pragmatists' first thesis [as the view] that knowledge is essentially contextual, situated in habit and practice. . . ."[236] This thesis implies "a kind of perspectivism. Because new beliefs emerge out of a complex of already existing beliefs that can never be made fully conscious and explicit, all useful beliefs may not ultimately prove commensurable with each other."[237] Applied to law, pragmatism claims that law "is constituted of practices–contextual, situated, rooted in custom and shared expectations," and that law is "instrumental, a means for achieving socially desired ends."[238]

For individuals bound in a shared deliberative practice, the deployment of shared *and* individual strategies of interpretation serves ends which are themselves the subject of debate and disagreement. Accordingly, Grey comments that "pragmatism mediates between positivistic and instrumentalist conceptions of law on the one hand and, on the other, idealist legal theories that identify law with the aspiration to justice, and see legal ideas as partly constitutive of social reality."[239] Pragmatism, therefore, reflects the individual decision-maker's commitment to a particular stake in justice as well as her awareness of deliberation as an instrumental practice serving controversial ends.

Grey also takes note of "pragmatism's peculiar rhetorical disadvantages vis-á-vis other theories. . . . For pragmatists, any theory is only a set of reflections on some existing practice, generated out of and attached to that practice, recognizing its contingency and cultural particularity."[240] Rorty similarly dwells

---

[236] Grey, *supra* note 201, at 799. The idea of knowledge and judgments as relativistic, contingent, and historically based existed long before the arrival of contemporary pragmatism; indeed, this concept played a central role in some major strains of nineteenth-century and earlier social thought. *See id.* at 801-03.

[237] *Id.* at 804.

[238] *Id.* at 805.

[239] THOMAS C. GREY, THE WALLACE STEVENS CASE: LAW AND THE PRACTICE OF POETRY 68-69 (1991).

[240] *Id.* at 105.

on "the banality of pragmatism" as a theory that largely "clears the underbrush and leaves it to others to plant the forest."[241] The underbrush in this case is the foundational background of legal formalism, representing the aspiration to make hard cases easy by finding uncontroversial and acontextual modes of decision.[242]

Some limits of pragmatism, seen as contextualism and instrumentalism, are brought out by Margaret Jane Radin when she asks, "How can the pragmatist find a standpoint from which to argue that a system is coherent but bad, if pragmatism defines truth and good as coherence? Inattention to this problem is what makes pragmatism seem complacent, when it does."[243] Viewing the individual's strategies as contextual and seeing the community as a context with instrumental criteria for truth can be criticized as vague and banal. It does not explain how the individual distinguishes himself from the group, how disagreement within the group is possible, and how it is resolved. Even when pragmatism does not take its collectivist posture and identify the individual with the group, it still does not give an account of the relationship between the two. It does not wade deeply enough into the structure of deliberative practices.

CONCLUSION

Legal philosophers have generally spotlighted one act in the complex drama of law and one question in a seamless web of issues. The act is deliberation and decision-making by judges and the question is how the nature of law manifests itself in judicial deliberation. This preoccupation is shared by legal theorists who share little else.

The metaphors and assumptions of legal theorists have characteristically oversimplified judicial agreement and disagreement. Some theorists see judges as joint players of a game with identifiable rules, rules that define which moves are allowed and what resources

---

[241] Richard Rorty, *The Banality of Pragmatism and The Poetry of Justice*, 63 S. CAL. L. REV. 1811, 1813, 1815 (1990) (discussing Posner's characterization of pragmatic jurisprudence).

[242] In that respect, pragmatism repeats the well-digested lessons of legal realism, translated into lessons about language and understanding. *Cf. id.* at 1813 (stating that "new pragmatists talk about language instead of experience or mind or consciousness . . . .").

[243] Margaret Radin, *The Pragmatist and the Feminist*, 63 S. CAL. L. REV. 1699, 1710 (1990). *See also* Frank Michelman, *Private/Personal but Not Split: Radin Versus Rorty*, 63 S. CAL. L. REV. 1783 (1990) (comparing Rorty's pragmatic view of a public-private split with Radin's rejection of such a dichotomy).

can be used. But the game metaphor cannibalizes itself, in part because the rules themselves are the subject of decision-making. An even more misleading variant of the shared-rules model describes judges as joint elaborators of a shared consensus about goals and values.

On the other hand, it is equally misleading to ignore the ties that bind judges into a shared practice. Some theorists, drawn to a subtext of conflict for the sake of domination and of irreconcilable conceptual schemes, flirt with solipsism of the individual or of the group. They ignore that the individual judge is more than a locus of idiosyncratic value or idiosyncratic techniques of understanding, representative only of himself or his group. He is also a participant in a shared practice with other judges, a deliberative practice in which arguments are mutually understood and anticipated and in which mutual influence can and does occur.

Seeing legal reasoning as a deliberative practice focuses attention on two aspects of judging and its implications for law. The first aspect is the complexity of each individual judge's ways of understanding, of making and justifying decisions, and of determining what is and is not legally relevant to a particular case. The arguments that she uses with justificatory force will be configured in a way that reflects her unique way of understanding experience, her knowledge–and her way of understanding the point of law and laws. Her uniqueness is not simply a matter of ethics and politics but a way of situating ethics and politics in a general scheme of understanding.

The second aspect is that, if she is reflective, she will appreciate that other judges have their own ways of understanding experience and accordingly make different kinds of justificatory moves. Her recognition of this, and her familiarity with the conceptual styles of others, constitute her awareness of the joint deliberative practice. This awareness is characterized by the tension between the unavoidable and all-pervasive stake she has in her modes of understanding and her understanding that she is just one of many equally situated participants, that her ways of proceeding have no special sanction. To divorce this last insight from the simultaneous awareness of her stake and to imagine a position outside any particular way of understanding is to divorce theory from practice.

Thinking of law as a deliberative practice allows us to reconceive the fluidity and the boundedness of law. The concept of law refers to several things. First, the law for each judge, and for each observer, consists of decisions and justificatory arguments that that judge regards as appropriate given her ways of reasoning and her sense of law's purposes. Second, the law may include the collection of decisions and justificatory strategies that are *mutually* regarded as legally relevant. Finally, the law *may* be said to refer to decisions apart from the justificatory arguments supporting them.

This third account of law requires it to be possible to identify decisions, identify the law, apart from underlying justificatory arguments. I have argued that this is not possible. The first and second account, however, are alternative ways of saying that law is as fixed and as fluid as the justificatory strategies that are mutually recognized as relevant.

If Wittgenstein is right, and if philosophy "leaves everything as it is," then describing law as a deliberative practice can be neither conservative nor radical. The law itself, the deliberative practice that is law, will be conservative if the society is homogeneous or successfully repressive, if new voices and ways of thinking remain unrepresented. The law will be radical if society is heterogeneous and new ways of justifying and conceiving aims are continually given legal expression. The law will, furthermore, be liberal in Mill's sense whenever it is open to new ways of thinking, whenever judges recognize that their ways of reasoning and justifying, i.e. their stake, do not necessarily have hegemony.

[7]
Law as Experience: The Internal Aspect of Law*

TABLE OF CONTENTS

I. HART AND THE INTERNAL ASPECT: LAW, LANGUAGE, AND PRACTICE 27
A. HISTORICAL PERSPECTIVE 27
B. DISTINGUISHING NATURAL AND SOCIAL SCIENCES 28
C. THE CONCEPT OF A SOCIAL PRACTICE: LAW AND LANGUAGE 31
D. HART ON THE INTERNAL ASPECT OF LAW: FOUR VARIATIONS 33
E. LAW AND LANGUAGE: SOME DIFFERENCES 37
II. THEORY AND PRACTICE: HERMENEUTICS AND SUBTRACTION 40
A. EXTERNALITY AND THE ANTHROPOLOGICAL PERSPECTIVE 40
B. HERMENEUTICS: AGREEMENT AND DISAGREEMENT 43
C. THEORY AND PRACTICE RECONSIDERED 46
D. THE HUBRIS OF THEORISTS 48
E. THE EXTERNAL POINT OF VIEW REDESCRIBED 52
III. BURSTING THE THEORIST'S BUBBLE: RECENT JURISPRUDENCE 54
A. THE FISH/DWORKIN DEBATE 54
B. CRITICAL LEGAL STUDIES 59
C. SCHLAG ON THEORY 63
IV. CONCLUSION 66

I. HART AND THE INTERNAL ASPECT: LAW, LANGUAGE, AND PRACTICE

A. HISTORICAL PERSPECTIVE

H.L.A. Hart is no longer our contemporary. His landmark book, *The Concept of Law*, nearly forty years old, is on its way to becoming a historical text.[1] What does it mean for a work of phi-

---

* Tapping Reeve Professor of Law and Ethics, University of Connecticut School of Law. A.B., Harvard College; J.D., M. Phil., Ph.D., Yale University. I wish to thank my research assistants, David Culmer and James Scrimgeour, for their helpful assistance.

1. H.L.A. HART, THE CONCEPT OF LAW (2d ed. 1994).

losophy to lose contemporaneity? One answer is that it becomes problematic in a special way. Hart, like any philosopher, addresses primarily his contemporaries. Reading him here and now we must take account of the ways in which our assumptions, our questions, and our methods differ, often subtly, from theirs and his.

Our choice is a dilemma. If we ignore the differences attributable to the passage of time and test him as we would our own contemporaries, we risk being unfair. We may fault him for lacking clairvoyance, for not anticipating criticisms and sophistications of the last forty years. On the other hand, if we forgive or ignore such failings in light of historicity, in indulgent deference to age, we risk making him irrelevant to our present concerns.

Hart's discussion of what he calls "the internal aspect of rules" is at once one of the most important and controversial passages in *The Concept of Law*.[2] Here Hart foreshadows what has more recently become the pulse of methodological debate in legal theory (and more generally social/cultural theory), but he does so with understandable ambiguity and some naivete. Hermeneutical self-consciousness about the task of distinguishing internal and external aspects of social and cultural practices has become a characteristic preoccupation in the late twentieth century. Those who examine social practices from a scholarly distance and with the mantle of academic objectivity are typically also participants in such practices. The practices of language and law are obvious examples. Those who study languages also speak them; those who are jurisprudential theorists are also subject to law and have opinions about legal issues. A central question of hermeneutics is how the task of the theorist is affected by her role as practitioner.[3]

Hart's analysis anticipates these concerns, even as it understandably leaves much to be sorted out by later theorists. It remains a convenient and important point of origin for an inexhaustible topic.

B. Distinguishing Natural and Social Sciences

It is useful to situate Hart's discussion of the internal aspect historically and consider how it resonated with the interests of his peers. It is easy to underestimate how much the philosophical context has changed.

One of the widely discussed methodological questions at mid-century was the distinction between the natural and social sciences.[4] Some differ-

---

2. *Id.* at 88-91.

3. Throughout this Article, I shall use the term "practitioner" to refer to all persons who are "inside" a practice. Thus all language users are practitioners vis-à-vis the language they share. Persons may be practitioners with regard to law as a social practice even if they are not lawyers or judges, even if their participation in the practice merely amounts to compliance with the law and attention to its mandates.

4. *See, e.g*, Theodor W. Adorno et al., The Positivist Dispute in German Sociology (Glyn Adey & David Frisby trans., 1976); Richard J. Bernstein, The Restructuring of Social and Political Theory (1976); The Philosophy of Social Explanation (Alan Ryan ed., 1973); Readings in the Philosophy of the Social Sci-

ences were said to be obvious. The natural sciences seek and deal with universal laws. Chemistry and physics are paradigmatic. Falling objects obey universal laws of acceleration, light travels at a predictable speed, and all molecules of sodium chloride have the same structure and behave in the same way. Natural science flourishes through experimental testing, which involves controlled events that are inherently repeatable.[5] Its laws are insensitive to the passage of time. The laws of falling bodies and of reflection of light are assumed to be the same in ancient times as now.

The social sciences, it was argued,[6] have none of these characteristics. Consider the example of psychology. Psychological explanation cannot be expected to yield universal laws. Both prediction and retrospective explanation are individualistic and irreducibly idiosyncratic. We cannot produce universal laws about how abused or spoiled children develop specific pathologies or about how adults come to be sociopathic.[7] We can, at most, describe patterns of experience, ways of growing up that predispose one to be happy, rebellious, insecure, or extroverted. But each person is unique.

Similarly, economics, sociology, and anthropology describe patterns of behavior but do not aspire to universality.[8] Economics must make assumptions about rationality, risk-taking propensities, and other determinants of behavior that vary unpredictably from individual to individual. Sociology may find patterns in phenomena such as suburbanization, cultural homogenization, and class divisions, but each instance is predictably and inevitably unique. Moreover, such phenomena do not lend themselves to experimental testing. Relevant variables cannot be controlled but vary over time and context. Schizophrenia and urban renewal may occur in both first-century Rome and twentieth-century New York, but a significant difference in context makes it sensible to compare such examples as analogous phenomena and not as instances of a universal law.

The analytic and descriptive effort to distinguish natural from social sciences was vulnerable to attack from two sides. On one hand, the very idea of natural sciences as a paradigm of objective knowledge came under attack. Over the last forty years, it has become commonplace to see universal laws of the natural sciences as cultural manifestations. We arrive at a particular way of describing the natural world and characterizing the objects within it because we ask certain questions, have certain criteria for what counts as knowledge, and hold fast to certain methodological

ENCES (May Brodbeck ed., 1968); PETER WINCH, THE IDEA OF A SOCIAL SCIENCE AND ITS RELATION TO PHILOSOPHY (1958).

5. *See, e.g.*, ERNEST NAGEL, THE STRUCTURE OF SCIENCE: PROBLEMS IN THE LOGIC OF SCIENTIFIC EXPLANATION 1-105 (1961).

6. *See generally* sources cited *supra* note 4.

7. *See* ROBERT COLES, THE MIND'S FATE: WAYS OF SEEING PSYCHIATRY AND PSYCHOANALYSIS (1961) (discussing the senses in which psychology meets the criteria of a natural science). *See generally* HENDRIK MARINUS RUITENBEEK, PSYCHOANALYSIS AND SOCIAL SCIENCE (1962).

8. *See* READINGS IN THE PHILOSOPHY OF THE SOCIAL SCIENCES, *supra* note 4, at 457-667.

principles.[9] Our questions, criteria, and principles are not universal; different cultures have different ways of deciding how the world operates. Thus, while we need not abandon the claim that the discoveries of natural sciences are, in a meaningful sense, universal, the claim must be qualified. They are universal *given the perspectives and understandings of our culture*.[10]

On the other hand, the similarities between the social sciences and the natural sciences seem to have been *under*estimated by those who sought to distinguish them. Over the last forty years, the very term "social sciences" has lost its descriptive coherence. Each of the [illegible] [illegible], [illegible]logy, psychology, and anthropology—has turned into a heterogeneous collection of disciplines. In each case the collection includes some pursuits that mimic and incorporate the language and methods of natural science and others that are more discursive, quasi-humanistic, and inherently context-bound.

Psychologists, for example, have seen their discipline subdivide. Some psychologists are essentially physiologists or biochemists, and the practice of some psychologists is primarily psychopharmacology. Their theory and practice fit comfortably within the natural sciences. Other social and clinical psychologists make no pretense to such rigor; their methods are closer to those of the reconstructive biographer and historian.

The same divisions are apparent in economics. Microeconomic hypotheses and techniques typically involve mathematical modeling of phenomena and relationships as well as ahistorical hypotheses. Macroeconomists, on the other hand, often pursue historical, sociological, and political narratives; in many instances, mathematical rigor and universal generalization are either peripheral or irrelevant.[11]

The upshot is that we no longer seek criteria to distinguish natural from social sciences because the data and assumptions on which that inquiry rested are historical artifacts that have failed the test of time. Hart's own inquiry into the internal aspect of rules was part of that context. And yet his insight, his proposed description of the distinctive character of the study of social practices, was a subtle and suggestive anticipation of modern hermeneutical theory.

9. *See* Criticism and the Growth of Knowledge (Imre Lakatos & Alan Musgrave eds., 1970); Thomas S. Kuhn, The Structure of Scientific Revolutions (1962).

10. What does it mean to say that a law of physics or chemistry is universal? One interpretation is to say that it must be accepted by any observer in any culture. A different interpretation is to say that it applies to all relevant objects (all falling objects, all molecules of sodium and chloride) as they are seen within our own realm of discourse, our own culture. The latter interpretation preserves the notion of universality along with an understanding of the fact that we cannot speak for observers in other realms of discourse. We can speak about them but not for them.

11. This needs to be qualified. Historical studies of economic behavior often use sophisticated mathematical tools. Any attempt to distinguish microeconomists from macroeconomists will be rough and general. Nonetheless, microeconomists do generally pursue conceptual analysis and mimic natural science insofar as they seek invariant laws of economic behavior. Macroeconomists characteristically seek to describe and understand unique economic circumstances and contexts.

On Hart's account, social phenomena involve the behavior of self-conscious beings. To do justice to these phenomena, to understand them, it is necessary to make reference to the ways in which the actors understand their own practices.[12] Thus, while an ornithologist may describe swallows without assuming their point of view or a chemist may analyze isotopes without putting herself in their place, one who seeks to understand a social practice must take account of what the practitioners think and feel.

Once one puts aside other and more problematic ways of distinguishing natural from social sciences, the fact remains that the latter deals with self-conscious and self-interpretive behavior. The subjects of study are participants in social practices. They have been inducted into these practices through social and cultural conventions, and they themselves have some kind of understanding of their behavior and roles. Moreover, the social scientist herself is likely to be a participant in such practices and to be familiar with the relevant thoughts and attitudes from the inside.

C. The Concept of a Social Practice: Law and Language

The concept of a social practice is most closely identified with the later work of Wittgenstein, for whom language was a paradigmatic practice in the following ways.[13] The fact that we understand the speech of others and participate in discourse implies that the practice is shared. The fact that certain utterances seem to be nonsense and others, by general consensus, violate grammar, syntax, semantics, or common sense implies that language is subject to shared rules. The fact that we disagree about linguistic matters on occasion—for example, about the status of neologisms and the acceptability of slang—implies that we are not perfectly congruent in our understanding of the use and rules of our shared language.[14]

Language, for Wittgenstein, is not simply a clear example of social practice. It merits special examination because what we say is normally a measure of what we believe and know, individually and collectively. Wittgenstein shows how problematic philosophical analysis can be when it is not grounded in what people ordinarily say and do.[15] For example,

12. *See* Hart, *supra* note 1, at 89-91.

13. *See generally* Ludwig Wittgenstein, Philosophical Investigations (G.E.M. Anscombe trans., 1953). This was the only work in the later part of his career that Wittgenstein prepared for publication. His *nachlass* is voluminous and widely influential.

14. *See generally* Thomas Morawetz, *Understanding Disagreement, the Root Issue of Jurisprudence: Applying Wittgenstein to Positivism, Critical Theory, and Judging*, 141 U. Pa. L. Rev. 371 (1992).

15. Wittgenstein famously uses the metaphor of the fly and the fly-bottle to allude to the plight of philosophy. *See* Wittgenstein, *supra* note 13, pt. I, ¶ 309 ("What is your aim in philosophy?—To sh[o]w the fly the way out of the fly-bottle."). The point is that we fly unencumbered when we engage in ordinary discourse. We use terms ("good," "know," "certain") unproblematically and with easy familiarity with criteria for meaningful use. Conceptual analysis, however, may trap us into unnatural ways of using terms in posing skeptical and other conundrums (Do we really know we are awake? Do we have objective criteria for goodness?) and may thus make us uncertain in finding our way about in discourse. For Wittgenstein, this situation is analogous to the fly being trapped in a fly-bottle and bumping its head against artificial barriers.

discussions of the nature of knowledge must be informed by an inquiry into the everyday use of notions such as certainty and justification.[16] Under what circumstances do persons regard knowledge as *certain*, adhering to knowledge claims in the face of counterevidence and using them as a measure of the correctness of such counterevidence? Under what circumstances do persons regard claims-to-know as standing in need of further justification, and what kinds of justification are treated as appropriate or sufficient?

The answers to such questions are not merely about language. They clarify not only the linguistic rules for using the word "know" but the boundaries and complexity (that is, the nature) of knowledge. It is not clear whether there is any work left for a general epistemological inquiry into the nature of knowledge once the internal aspect of the language-games involving "know" are fully explored and described.[17] The same can be said about other philosophical inquiries as well: the nature of value and goodness, the nature of being, the meaning of life, and so on.[18]

When Hart suggests that an adequate account of the concept of law must embrace the internal aspect, it is clear that he has in mind an analogy between law and language. His example is the distinction between habitual behavior that occurs with regularity and rule-governed behavior (stopping at red lights).[19] Our capacity to distinguish between the two kinds of phenomena requires access and attention to the internal aspect. Analogous to this is the distinction between regularly emitted inarticulate sounds and speech. One's ability to distinguish between these kinds of utterances presupposes the *internal* understanding that the latter are intentional and governed by shared rules of communication.

The analogy between rules of law and language is especially evident when Hart refers to uncertainty in the law, saying that rules characteristically have a core (in which their meaning and application is certain) and a penumbra (in which both meaning and application are uncertain and potentially controversial).[20] His example bridges law and language. He

---

Note that the term "philosophy" can be used in two ways. Although philosophy (in the sense Wittgenstein is criticizing) is in the business of generating these conundrums, these bumps, philosophy (in the way he commends and practices it) exposes the snares, the artificial obstacles, for what they are. It is, therefore, a form of conceptual therapy.

16. Directing our attention to ordinary discourse, to what he calls "language-games," Wittgenstein would decline to dignify such an investigation as a discussion of the nature of knowledge. To do so would be misleadingly essentialist and therefore an invitation into the fly-bottle. *See* THOMAS MORAWETZ, WITTGENSTEIN AND KNOWLEDGE: THE IMPORTANCE OF *On Certainty* (1978).

17. *See supra* note 15. In other words, "philosophy" in the criticized sense is fully displaced by philosophy as conceptual and linguistic therapy.

18. All of these essentialist inquiries are variants of the fly-bottle trap. *See supra* note 15.

19. *See* HART, *supra* note 1, at 89-90.

20. Hart makes this distinction most clearly in *Positivism and the Separation of Law and Morals*:

> A legal rule forbids you to take a vehicle into the public park. . . . If we are to communicate with each other at all, and if, as in the most elementary form of law, we are to express our intentions that a certain type of behavior be regu-

says that a prohibition on bringing "vehicles into the park" is uncertain to the extent that the scope of "vehicles" has "open texture."[21] Does the term include toy cars, bicycles, or ambulances? The clear implication of Hart's analysis is that because the rules of law are framed in language, whatever uncertainty inheres in legal rules is due to the uncertainty of meaning that characterizes words-in-context.[22]

D. Hart on the Internal Aspect of Law: Four Variations

Hart offers two different ways of conceiving the distinction between the internal and external aspect of rules. On one hand, he says that

> [w]hen a social group has certain rules of conduct, . . . it is possible to be concerned with the rules, either merely as an observer who does not himself accept them, or as a member of the group which accepts and uses them as guides to conduct. We may call these respectively the 'external' and the 'internal points of view.'[23]

An external observer "may, without accepting the rules himself, assert that the group accepts the rules, and thus may from outside refer to the way in which *they* are concerned with them from the internal point of view."[24]

On the other hand, Hart conceives of a different observer "who does not even refer in this way to the internal point of view of the group."[25] "[C]ontent merely to record the regularities of observable behaviour," such an observer will offer a "description of their life [that] cannot be in terms of rules at all, and so not in the terms of the rule-dependent notions of obligation or duty."[26] Understandably, Hart refers to this as the "extreme external point of view."[27]

> lated by rules, then the general words we use—like "vehicle" in the case I consider—must have some standard instance in which no doubts are felt about its application. There must be a core of settled meaning, but there will be, as well, a penumbra of debatable cases in which words are neither obviously applicable nor obviously ruled out. These cases will each have some features in common with the standard case; they will lack others or be accompanied by features not present in the standard case. . . . Fact situations do not await us neatly labeled, creased, and folded, nor is their legal classification written on them to be simply read off by the judge.

H.L.A. Hart, *Positivism and the Separation of Law and Morals*, 71 Harv. L. Rev. 593, 607 (1958); *see also* Hart, *supra* note 1, at 124-36.

21. Hart, *supra* note 1, at 127-28.

22. Hart's discussion of the "vehicles in the park" example has different nuances in The Concept of Law and in *Positivism and the Separation of Law and Morals*. In the former, the emphasis of the discussion is on the relevance of policy considerations in resolving uncertain applications of the rule. *See generally* Hart, *supra* note 1. In the latter, however, the focus is not on how uncertainty may be resolved, but on the linguistic nature of the uncertainty, the relationship between the open texture of rules, and the penumbral character of terms. *See generally* Hart, *supra* note 20.

23. Hart, *supra* note 1, at 89.

24. *Id.*

25. *Id.*

26. *Id.*

27. *Id.*

The distinction between the two external points of view is straightforward. The first is exemplified by cross-cultural analyses. Consider a French scholar of the American legal system. She is entirely at home with the concept of legal rules and obligations and has the internal point of view toward the French system. She assumes that Americans have a comparable set of attitudes toward their own system and use the rules to guide their own behavior, observe others, and so on.

The second point of view, altogether different, is that of the natural scientist who makes no assumption that observed behavior instantiates a learned and ongoing practice. Her stance mirrors that of an entomologist toward a colony of ants or a geologist toward tectonic plates. She observes and notes regularities of behavior. The internal consciousness and understanding of the observed subjects plays no role in her interpretation or her account. The distinction between the two external points of view is easily transposed to the practice of language: the first point of view is that of the speaker of one language to the discourse of those who speak a different language; the second point of view is that of the observer for whom language is indistinguishable from inarticulate sounds. A scream may, functionally, serve the same role as words of warning.[28]

Having identified these two senses in which one may speak of an external point of view, that of the cross-culturalist and the natural scientist, Hart muddies his account. He says that "[t]he external point of view may very nearly reproduce the way in which the rules [of law] function in the lives of . . . those who reject its rules and are only concerned with them when and because they judge that unpleasant consequences are likely to follow violation."[29] And further,

> the external point of view, which limits itself to the observable regularities of behaviour, cannot reproduce . . . the way in which the rules function as rules in the lives of those who normally are the majority of society[,] . . . the officials, lawyers, or private persons who use them . . . as guides to the conduct of social life. . . . For them the violation of a rule is not merely a basis for the prediction that a hostile reaction will follow but a *reason* for hostility.[30]

We can interpret this new characterization of the external point of view as the contrast between the outlaw and the citizen. Hart seems to be saying that the external point of view is that of the outlaw,[31] but not the

28. The reactive behavior of the person warned is accessible even to the extreme external observer. But the distinction between rule-governed uses of language and emotive non-verbal (but intentional) sounds is not.

29. Hart, *supra* note 1, at 90.

30. *Id.*

31. I am using this term in the sense in which Holmes referred to the "bad man" in explaining his theory of legal positivism:

> You can see very plainly that a bad man has as much reason as a good one for wishing to avoid an encounter with the public force, and therefore you can see the practical importance of the distinction between morality and law. A man who cares nothing for an ethical rule which is believed and practised by his neighbors is likely nevertheless to care a good deal to avoid being made to pay money, and will want to keep out of jail if he can.

citizen. In proposing this, he introduces a new sense of the external standpoint. Neither of the first two senses can explain the difference between the outlaw and the citizen.

According to the first sense of externality (the external observer as cross-cultural), both the outlaw and the citizen are internal. Both have learned and incorporated the rules of their legal system. Both understand that they are likely to incur sanctions and criticism for violating the rules and that the rules are intended to be used as guides. The foreign observer, noting the conduct of outlaw and citizen, is external to their system; notwithstanding the difference in their *attitude*, the outlaw and the citizen are both internal.

Similarly, according to the second sense of externality, that of the natural scientist, both the outlaw and citizen are again internal since they are observed rather than observers. It is surely wrong for Hart to analogize outlaws to natural scientists as behaviorists (externalists in the second sense) in saying that outlaws "are only concerned with [rules] when and because they judge that unpleasant consequences are likely to follow violation."[32] Outlaws, like all other members of the social practice, are aware of rules as standing prohibitions and act in light of that awareness. Their attitudes toward such rules and consequent behavior may differ from those of other members, but it is a mistake to suggest that they are not aware of rules at all and merely observe inductively that certain conduct produces certain kinds of pain.[33]

How, then, can we characterize this *third* kind of externality? Hart's own explanation is ambiguous. The distinction between putative outlaws and "the majority of society . . . the officials, lawyers, or private persons who use [rules of law] . . . as guides to the conduct of social life"[34] can be understood in two ways. One way is by reference to acceptance and moral attitude. On this understanding, one is internal if one thinks that the rules of law, by and large, are justified and deserve support. One accedes to the purposes that the law seems to embody. On this account, one is external if one disfavors the law in general, sees it as lacking moral justification, and would ideally replace it with a significantly different system.

Note, incidentally, that lawyers and judges can readily be external in this sense. They may go through the motions of using, applying, and interpreting the law—emulating the moves of its supporters—and covertly harbor anarchistic or revolutionary attitudes. Indeed, they may become more adept and creative at mimicking the moves of insiders than the in-

Oliver Wendell Holmes, Jr., *The Path of the Law*, 10 HARV. L. REV. 457, 459 (1897).

32. HART, *supra* note 1, at 90.

33. Even outlaws are aware that punishment has an expressive function and reflects community values. Most contemporary writers agree that punishment has both utilitarian and retributive aspects. *See* JOEL FEINBERG, DOING AND DESERVING: ESSAYS IN THE THEORY OF RESPONSIBILITY 95-118 (1970); H.L.A. HART, PUNISHMENT AND RESPONSIBILITY: ESSAYS IN THE PHILOSOPHY OF LAW 234 (1968).

34. HART, *supra* note 1, at 90.

siders themselves.[35]

A different understanding of the contrast between the "majority of society" and those who do not guide their conduct through law is conceptual. While both citizens and the latter persons understand that they are subject to rules, only the latter take the rules piecemeal as standing orders or commands. Laws, whether obeyed or not, are seen as lacking formal or substantive validity. For the citizen as insider, however, the rules of law form a coherent order. There are formal processes by which rules become valid laws, and there are procedures that judges, lawyers, and ordinary citizens can and do follow to determine the pedigree of such laws.[36] Thus the insider, but not the outsider, sees the law as an ordered system. In this sense, the judge or lawyer *cannot* be external to the law. The nature of her occupation *entails* that she will recognize the law as an ordered system.[37] Non-officials (ordinary citizens) may or may not have that degree of sophistication vis-à-vis the rules of law; they may or may not in this sense be internal rather than external.

Note that the two variations of the internal/external distinction we have just considered, our two understandings of what Hart means by saying that some persons do and others do not use the law as a guide to conduct, apply to law as a social practice, but *not* to language. (Recall that the first two versions of that distinction—the externality of the cross-cultural observer and the externality of the natural scientist—referred equally well to external observers of law-related behavior and of language use.) The social practice of language does not, for the most part, allow room for variant attitudes of moral adherence and moral dissent. One cannot *morally* be an outlaw with regard to language. One may, perhaps, insist on using offensive language, may use neologisms excessively and puzzlingly, or may even opt to become mute and forego language, but none of these alternatives quite captures the sense of being a linguistic outlaw. The person who uses offensive language is following rules, not breaking them, insofar as we have rules for the effective use of such words as communicative tools. The addict of neologisms may break rules, but the only sanction she incurs is a failure to communicate. And the volitional mute merely drops out of the practice.

Similarly, there is no room in language for the opportunity, as an insider, to see rules cohere into an ordered system of valid rules.[38] Language is by nature less orderly than law. There are no language courts

35. Hart suggests that in a healthy and viable legal system this attitude will prevail only among a minority of citizens. If a majority loses faith in this way, the system is jeopardized. *See* HART, *supra* note 1, at 117-23 ("The Pathology of a Legal System").

36. Hart refers to these rules and procedures collectively as "the rule of recognition." The concept of a rule of recognition plays a central role in his version of legal positivism. *See id.* at 100-10.

37. This point should be evident to anyone who knows about the formal role of legal texts. The nature of legal research, involving attention to relevant statutes, legal precedents, and so on, pervasively reflects this recognition.

38. In other words, there is no rule of recognition and no formal criterion of validity for language.

charged with instructing us how to use language, and there is no legislature charged with setting down the rules of correct usage. Dictionaries and manuals of usage tend to chase fashions in language rather than dictate it.[39] In this sense, the insider in the practice of language is likely to appreciate its incoherence, its openness to change, and the inevitability of misunderstanding.

We have now identified *four* senses of the distinction between an internal and external point of view: (1) the externality of the cross-cultural observer, (2) the externality of the natural scientist, (3) the externality of the outlaw, and (4) the externality of the participant who fails to apprehend the coherence and systemic nature of law. Hart explicitly addresses the first two senses. And, it seems, he stumbles upon the third and fourth senses without making clear (perhaps without seeing) that they *are* altogether different from the first two senses and without distinguishing them from each other. One explanation is that he was seduced by the model of language as a social practice and failed to see the ways in which the social practice of law is distinctively different.

E. Law and Language: Some Differences

We can identify at least three ways in which language is a misleading model for law. First, the point of language is, for the most part, taken for granted. It is a banal truism to say that language makes possible and facilitates communication. Of course, it arguably does other things as well, such as facilitating and channeling creativity, cultivating individuality and a unique style, making self-consciousness possible, and so on.[40] But all are secondary effects of its use for communication.

The point of law, by contrast, is inherently controversial. It seems natural to say that law, at a minimum, exists to secure order and predictability in social lives.[41] Even this modest proposal merits scrutiny. Is order the overriding purpose of law? A system of rules that achieves order through radical regimentation, curtailment of civil liberties, and even enslavement of the underlying citizenry forfeits its claim to be called a *legal* system in the eyes of many observers and theorists.[42] Indeed, according to various accounts, the nature of a legal system is to embrace not only

39. It is arguable that law, as well as language, has customary and formal aspects. Legal positivists, such as Hart and Joseph Raz, take for granted the centrality of formal criteria for law. Natural law theorists, on the other hand, typically deny that law is identified exclusively through formal criteria and tend to find law in such resources as custom, tradition, and human nature. *See generally* Natural Law Theory: Contemporary Essays (Robert P. George ed., 1992).

40. The role of language in facilitating or making possible self-awareness is a controversial matter among philosophers, psychologists, and anthropologists. *See generally* Jerome Bruner, Acts of Meaning (1990); Rodney Needham, Belief, Language, and Experience (1972); Selected Writings in Language, Culture and Personality (David G. Mandelbaum ed., 1949).

41. *See* Hart, *supra* note 1, at 185-93.

42. This view is often identified with some forms of natural law theory. *See, e.g.*, Lon L. Fuller, The Morality of Law (1964).

order, but some kinds of disorder, the kinds of disorder (or non-order) that are compatible with individual self-expression, creativity, and political innovation.[43] If so modest and minimal a characterization of the point of law stirs debate, more ambitious proposals are likely to be even more controversial.

Second, law, unlike language, is an inherently normative social practice. Stephen Perry defines a social practice as normative if "it is a social institution that also systematically gives rise (or at least is perceived to give rise) to reasons for action."[44] Thus, a proper response to "Why should I do *x*"? is "because it is right," "because it is good," "because you promised," or "because it is the law." The finality and nature of such reasons are subject to debate.[45] One may argue that another has identified the relevant moral or legal norm incorrectly or that what another has correctly identified as a promise or as the law should be overridden in a particular case.[46] In addition, explanations of *why* promises or the law give reasons may themselves be controversial. One may say that promises should be kept to prevent the pain of disappointment, that the institution of promise-keeping is a civilizing influence and merits support, and so on.[47] And the same controversies attend law. One theorist may argue that law gives reasons for action because the practice can be justified along rule-utilitarian lines, another may argue that it secures order and order is inherently desirable, and yet another may argue that it permits altruism and individuality to coexist.[48] All these disagreements, however, are not about *whether* law is normative, but about *the way* in which it is normative.

Are the rules of language also normative? We use rules of syntax, semantics, and context to guide our conduct and in self- and mutual criticism just as we use rules of morality or law. We claim to have standards for correct usage, and we can single out some utterances as violations. In

43. Critical legal theorists, such as Duncan Kennedy, describe individualism, autonomy, and freedom from constraint as belonging to competing sets of *desiderata* in legal decision making. *See* Duncan Kennedy, *The Structure of Blackstone's Commentaries*, 28 BUFF. L. REV. 205, 212 (1979).

44. Stephen R. Perry, *Interpretation and Methodology in Legal Theory*, *in* LAW AND INTERPRETATION: ESSAYS IN LEGAL PHILOSOPHY 97 (Andrei Marmor ed., 1995).

45. *See* JOSEPH RAZ, THE AUTHORITY OF LAW: ESSAYS ON LAW AND MORALITY 51-52 (1979).

46. In other words, identification of valid law, even from a positivistic standpoint, may well involve controversy. Application of relevant formal procedures is hardly mechanical. The judgment that a particular rule is relevant to a case can be questioned, and there may be disagreement over the claim that a rule incorporates a particular exception or other (tacit or not).

47. One may claim that the question of what policies or principles underlie a rule is separable from the question of what the rule is. The first question may be said to involve moral and prudential arguments while the second involves mere application of formal procedures. This distinction, which lies at the core of many versions of legal positivism, is vulnerable to the objection that any rule, however identified by formal methods, is subject to interpretation, and interpretation in turn involves debatable normative premises.

48. These jurisprudential accounts can roughly be identified, respectively, with the work of David Lyons, Joseph Raz, and Duncan Kennedy.

this sense of normativity, there are norms whenever there are rules, and every rule-governed practice is normative.

But this sense of normativity is more general than the kind of normativity attributable to law. The rules of language do not give reasons for action, nor do they instruct and inform us how to conduct our lives. They do not confront us with choices for action that we may adopt or reject.[49]

A third characteristic of the social practice of law distinguishes it not only from language, but also from other normative practices such as morality and etiquette. Law has formal and institutional procedures for creating, applying, and interpreting its rules.[50] Moreover, officials participating in these institutions have occasion to explain their actions and decisions. Some of these explanatory accounts and arguments (legislative debates, legislative history, legal briefs) are unofficial and reflect partisan contributions to the process of making and interpreting law. Others (judicial opinions) are official documents. Accordingly, as we have seen, there are two categories of insiders, officials who have designated roles in rule creation and application and all those who are simply subject to the rules. Moreover, consideration not only of the scope and interpretation of particular rules, but also of the collective aims of the social practice, is formalized.[51]

Any satisfactory account of the internal aspect of law must take account of the special characteristics of law as a social practice. Hart's account dates from mid-century, when the general idea of a social practice crystallized as a byproduct of the attempt to describe the distinctive nature of the social sciences. Hart saw that the internal aspect of law requires a special analysis, one that for example allows us to distinguish two kinds of insiders: outlaws and citizens. But his account was limited by the assumption, inherent in the philosophical strategies of his time, that the openness and indeterminacies of law as a social practice were to be explained through the indeterminacies of language.

Underlying the four options that can be teased out of Hart's account for explaining the external point of view vis-à-vis law is the implication

49. In other words, identifying an action as complying with law ("That's the law.") is one kind of justification. It is on a par with other kinds of justifications such as, "that's good," "that will make you happy," and "that would be prudent." Each justification has discursive finality insofar as it is reasonable to assume that persons wish to be law-abiding, moral, happy, and prudent. Only in exceptional cases and contexts would such assumptions be questioned.

50. This point is one of the fundamental tenets of legal positivism and, accordingly, of THE CONCEPT OF LAW. *See generally* HART, *supra* note 1.

51. This point is controversial. According to many positivists, including Hart, there are formal criteria for identifying the rules of a legal system. A system has a rule of recognition. But there is no corresponding formal procedure for identifying the collective aims of the legal system, a matter about which there may be much and persistent controversy. Naturalist legal philosophers such as Ronald Dworkin maintain that what is appropriately called "the law" embraces an evolving consensus about the aims and principles of the system as much as it does particular rules. *See* RONALD DWORKIN, LAW'S EMPIRE (1986) [hereinafter DWORKIN, LAW'S EMPIRE]; RONALD DWORKIN, TAKING RIGHTS SERIOUSLY (1977) [hereinafter DWORKIN, TAKING RIGHTS SERIOUSLY]; *see also supra* note 47.

that the quintessential external point of view is that of the scholar or theorist. If so, the contrast between the internal and the external aspect of rules is the contrast between the point of view of the legal practitioner (or citizen) and the jurisprudential theorist. In refining our understanding of the external point of view, as we will do in part two of this essay, we will also refine our understanding of the parameters and limitations of jurisprudential theory.

II. THEORY AND PRACTICE: HERMENEUTICS AND SUBTRACTION

A. Externality and the Anthropological Perspective

No legal theorist is a person without a country. Scholarly isolation (or distance) is a pose, one artificially and precariously assumed. Every scholar, we can assume, is a citizen of some state, subject to the laws of some legal system or other. Moreover, we can assume she has some attitudes toward the laws of her system and toward the purposes that the laws, individually and collectively, serve.

Jacques Derrida posits that we inhabit the structures that we deconstruct.[52] We are all necessarily insiders to a multitude of social practices. All of us, linguistic theorists included, have a mother tongue. We are familiar with our local norms of morality, etiquette, and law. Indeed, our ability to engage in scholarship, at a distance, presupposes such a history and such a predicament. To suggest that one might try to characterize laws or language without having learned the social practice first-hand and experienced it as second nature is to presuppose the absurd handicap of Hart's natural scientist as an extreme externalist, one who lacks the concept of any internal aspect of rules.

Derrida's statement deserves more scrutiny. Is it merely a reminder of common sense, or is it an admonition or even an expression of wistful regret? The common sense interpretation is simply a reiteration of the obvious, that it is possible to study social practices because we also experience them first-hand. The admonition, amounting to a difference in nuance, is that we must remember that we are not merely observers and cross-cultural scholars, but that we inhabit a particular instantiation of various social practices. This is a warning that scholarship insufficiently

---

52. *See* Jacques Derrida, Of Grammatology 24 (Gayatri Chakrayorty Spivak trans., 1976). Derrida states:

> The movements of deconstruction do not destroy structures from the outside. They are not possible and effective, nor can they take accurate aim, except by inhabiting those structures. Inhabiting them *in a certain way*, because one always inhabits, and all the more when one does not suspect it. Operating necessarily from the inside, borrowing all the strategic and economic resources of subversion from the old structure, . . . the enterprise of deconstruction always in a certain way falls prey to its own work. This is what the person who has begun the same work in another area of the same habitation does not fail to point out with zeal.

Id.; *see also* Thomas C. Grey, *The Hermeneutics File*, 58 S. Cal. L. Rev. 211, 226 (1985).

informed by such awareness is deficient in ways that will be considered below. Finally, the statement seems wistful if it reflects the scholar-as-outsider's aspiration to purity of perspective, to a position that favors no practices over others, a stance of critical neutrality purged of normative commitments. We will consider the implications of that aspiration.

Do anthropologists, who are arguably more self-conscious than other social scientists about the extent to which "we inhabit the structures that we deconstruct," have anything to teach legal theorists? Imagine a cultural anthropologist studying a language, economic system, religious structure, or legal and moral culture not her own. The common sense presumption is that, insofar as she inhabits her own culture, one that has all of these dimensions, she can look for analogous social practices elsewhere and explain them to readers from her own culture using analogy and comparison.[53]

If Derrida's reminder is seen as an admonition in this context, it is triple-edged. The anthropologist must be alert to the dangers of over— and under—assimilation. One mistake is to use one's own social practices as the template for cross-cultural investigation and assume that every observed kind of behavior is assimilable to familiar practices in one's own culture. The opposite mistake is to assume that one must always refrain from using familiar practices to understand alien ones. A third source of error is to regard such questions as closed and to disregard the inherently controversial character of every determination of similarity and difference. The cross-cultural anthropologist inevitably tacks between analogizing the unfamiliar to the familiar and questioning whether these analogies are useful or misleading.[54] Any misgivings about this predicament or any desires for greater neutrality and independence from one's home base are aspirations to the impossible.[55]

Richard Hyland, in his provocative essay, *Babel: a She'ur*,[56] sees the jurisprudential scholar as a kind of cultural anthropologist. He begins with observations about translation. Different languages represent different ways of representing and structuring experience and thought. Hyland notes that English is peculiarly idiomatic, rife with exceptions to rules and especially hard for non-native speakers to learn.[57] At the same time, English is uniquely creative and malleable. Other languages, Latin and German for example, are rigorously logical. Their rules are complex, and the formation of compound terms is a complex but lucid process.[58]

53. For scrutiny of this position from the standpoint of cultural anthropology, see CLIFFORD GEERTZ, LOCAL KNOWLEDGE: FURTHER ESSAYS IN INTERPRETIVE ANTHROPOLOGY 167-234 (1983).

54. John Rawls' general strategy of seeking "reflective equilibrium" in philosophical analysis is a useful notion in this context. JOHN RAWLS, A THEORY OF JUSTICE 48 (1971).

55. *See also infra* text accompanying notes 59-62.

56. Richard Hyland, *Babel: A She'ur*, 11 CARDOZO L. REV. 1585 (1990).

57. *See id.* at 1607.

58. *See id.* at 1604-07.

Hyland's point is that the master of several languages gains variant perspectives upon experience and thus comes to understand that it can be assimilated in different ways. This kind of insight comes as a gain and a loss.[59] It is a gain insofar as it represents a kind of wisdom and sophistication about experience, a capacity to apprehend matters from different points of view. The loss is a kind of alienation, an awareness that the priority one has given to familiar practices is an accident of personal history and has no natural priority in the sense of either being superior or being basic. One becomes a refugee in one's own culture.[60]

Hyland makes the same point about legal systems.[61] Each legal system addresses the need to order society around legal institutions and rules in a unique way. The scholar who becomes familiar with different legal systems comes to understand *both* what it means to inhabit each system *and* that the assumptions and procedures of his familiar and local system have no natural priority. Hyland also claims that the features of a culture's language and its legal system tend to mirror each other.[62]

The anthropological perspective in general, and Hyland's appropriation of it in particular, is a persuasive way of characterizing the distinction between the internal and external points of view. But it is misleading. For one thing, it implies that such social practices as law and language have internal homogeneity. It minimizes or ignores the extent to which disputes about rules and their point are part of the *internal* aspect of the practice. In other words, it understates the self-consciousness of the participants and the extent to which they question and are alienated from *their own* practices. The poet stumbles into the limitations of words and coins new and surprising usages. Judges disagree about the scope and interpretation of laws, about interpretive techniques, *and* about the purposes that laws serve. The Derridian notion that "we inhabit the structures we deconstruct" identifies a tension that exists even when we are not cross-cultural observers, one that arises whenever we scrutinize our own social practices internally.

Just as Hyland underestimates the tension as it surfaces for the monocultural theorist, perhaps he *over*estimates what one gains by assuming a cross-cultural perspective. Familiarity with foreign social practices, linguistic and legal, does not necessarily undercut the priority of one's own familiar practices. That priority may survive in two senses. It necessarily survives in the practical sense that one's own language and one's own legal system are points of origin. One may persist in translating from and into one's own language and other practices. One explains the features of other legal systems as being like or unlike one's own, as serving or disserving familiar functions.[63]

59. *See id.* at 1611-12.
60. *See id.*
61. *See id.* at 1597-1603.
62. *See id.* at 1603-08.
63. Reservations and complications attending this process are discussed *supra* note 52 and accompanying text.

A second sense of priority is that one *may* continue to favor one's own practices. Awareness of other practices raises questions about comparative value, but it does not answer them. The posture of the cross-culturalist is not necessarily one of indifference and neutrality nor one of alienation. Understanding others' social practices makes one's attitude toward one's own practices problematic, but it does not resolve the problem.

The general problem of studying social practices is a problem of hermeneutics. In the following passage, Quentin Skinner identifies the predicament of any theorist, whether she is trying to interpret a text or to deconstruct a social practice.

> [I]t will never in fact be possible simply to study [a social practice] . . . without bringing to bear some of one's own expectations about what [is happening within the practice]. . . . [T]hese models and preconceptions in terms of which we unavoidably organize and adjust our perceptions and thoughts will themselves tend to act as determinants of what we think and perceive. We must classify . . . the unfamiliar in terms of the familiar. The perpetual danger, in our attempts to enlarge our . . . understanding, is thus that our expectations about what someone must be saying or doing will themselves determine that we understand the agent to be doing something which he would not—or even could not—himself have accepted as an account of what he *was* doing.[64]

What Skinner sees as "danger" is what Hyland would see as a fortuitous albeit inevitable result of scholarly theorizing. Skinner assumes that we do an injustice to the internal perspective of a practice, that we misrepresent it, if we describe it in terms that the participant would reject or fail to recognize. Hyland, by contrast and less plausibly, sees this as the singular mark of success. The theoretical perspective transcends and leaves behind the parochial assumptions of the internal participant.

B. Hermeneutics: Agreement and Disagreement

This apparent disagreement between Skinner and Hyland illustrates diversity among hermeneuticists and shows how much is methodologically unclear (or open) in the enterprise of hermeneutics. Before examining the external point of view from a hermeneutical standpoint, consider the base line, the ways in which those who take a hermeneutical approach to social practices agree on several aspects of methodology.

First, they recognize that they themselves are participants in the kinds of practices they study as theorists. They see themselves as necessarily wearing two hats, as practitioner and as theorist.

Second, they also recognize that their role as practitioners makes possible their work as theorists. In other words, one can adequately describe (and theorize about) a social practice only if one takes account of the

64. Quentin Skinner, *Meaning and Understanding in the History of Ideas*, 8 Hist. & Theory 3, 6 (1969) (footnote omitted).

internal aspect, the acts, thoughts, and self-awareness of the participants.[65] While a theorist need not belong to the *particular* practices she describes (a German may engage in political or legal theory relevant to the American system), she must belong to *some* social practice of the same general kind, some political or legal system.

Third, they stress that the theorist's work is inevitably colored by her experiences as participant in a practice. The fact that one has a particular personal and intellectual history, has idiosyncratic expectations, and belongs to a particular culture will affect how one carries out the theoretical enterprise.

[illegible] noted, however, this last concession may be seen in various ways. It is misleading to see it as the inevitability of bias. To ascribe bias is to imply that one understands what it is to lack bias; the idea of universal and inevitable bias collapses into an oxymoron or nonsense. The point may, therefore, be put non-critically as a warning to any theorist who aspires to neutrality or objectivity. She must take pains to clarify what she means by such notions and must remain vigilant about the obstacles to meeting that standard.[66]

If we are to go beyond these three points, we must address ambiguities of the hermeneutical task which are implicit in the distinction between theory and practice, between the external point of view of the theorist and the internal point of view of the practitioner. A useful metaphor haunts such discussion. It comes from Otto Neurath, the Viennese epistemologist and philosopher of science whose main works date from the 1920s and 1930s.[67] He offers the warning that "[w]e are like sailors who must rebuild their ship on the open sea, never able to dismantle it in dry-dock and to reconstruct it there out of the best materials."[68]

The logician, Willard V.O. Quine, draws the following lesson:

> The philosopher's task was well compared by Neurath to that of a mariner who must rebuild his ship on the open sea.
>
> We can improve our conceptual scheme, our philosophy, bit by bit while continuing to depend on it for support; but we cannot detach ourselves from it and compare it objectively with an unconceptualized reality.[69]

---

65. *See supra* notes 12 and 25 and accompanying text.

66. In other words, conceding the hermeneuticist's points about investigative and theoretical practices does not entail that we abandon aspirations to objectivity and neutrality. Rather, it requires us to understand the criteria for objectivity and neutrality that are inherent in the practice—the "language-game." In particular, these criteria are likely to mandate habits of self-scrutiny and empathetic attention to alternative positions. Practicing such habits leads to greater objectivity and greater neutrality. In this context, objectivity and neutrality are relative terms, not absolutes.

67. *See, e.g.*, OTTO NEURATH, EMPIRICISM AND SOCIOLOGY (Marie Neurath & Robert S. Cohen eds., 1973); DANILO ZOLO, REFLEXIVE EPISTEMOLOGY: THE PHILOSOPHICAL LEGACY OF OTTO NEURATH (David McKie trans., 1989).

68. Otto Neurath, *Protocol Sentences*, *in* LOGICAL POSITIVISM 199, 201 (A.J. Ayer ed. & George Schick trans., 1959).

69. WILLARD VAN ORMAN QUINE, FROM A LOGICAL POINT OF VIEW: LOGICO-PHILOSOPHICAL ESSAYS 79 (2d ed. 1961).

The metaphor is peculiarly fecund. On one level, it describes the work of natural scientists, historians, indeed all who are in the business of knowledge. Each, through training and on-going participation, is part of a community that shares certain assumptions about what questions are to be asked, what counts as research and evidence, what is in dispute, and what is to be taken for granted. In subtle and not-so-subtle ways this structure is constantly changing; the enterprise of writing history, for example, is not what it was twenty or fifty years ago.[70] But, for the vessel to stay afloat, the change must be piecemeal, and the vessel, over its course, must remain nominally the same enterprise however many changes have accumulated. Thucydides and Gordon Wood are both historians.

On a second level, the metaphor is particularly illuminating with regard not to scholarly enterprises but to social practices. Languages and legal systems suffer constant evolution and repair like Neurath's boat. The process is both self-conscious and a response to a felt need. The process looks backward and forward at the same time.[71] The structures of language and law are inherently conservative; existing rules and conventions constitute the enterprise and keep it from capsizing. This stability makes it possible to write a dictionary, a manual of grammar, or a legal code, and each, however reformative it may be, reflects pre-existing ways of proceeding. But stability is also an illusion. The rules are necessarily in constant flux. Circumstances make necessary neologisms, and breaches of grammar become accepted. New legislation passes, and new situations force lawyers and courts to reinterpret existing laws, setting new precedents.

On a third level, the metaphor identifies the predicament of the *theorist* of social practices. As theorist, she seems to aspire to get off the boat. Her "external" point of view appears, on first impression, to be that of an observer of the boat who transcends it, who occupies a balloon or bubble that floats above the boat and is not subject to its vicissitudes. She records the changes and repairs and takes note of the basic structure, but

70. Examining Neurath's metaphor one may ask whether Kuhn's distinction between normal science and paradigm shifts applies outside the context of natural science to investigations such as history. Perhaps the distinction is not as sharp and uncontroversial as Kuhn suggests. It is consistent with Neurath's metaphor that methodological shifts may be more or less radical, more or less discontinuous. In the face of such shifts, the enterprise may be in some recognizable way *the same* while its methods and preoccupations are indelibly altered. *See generally* KUHN, *supra* note 9.

71. Wittgenstein felicitously compares languages with old cities surrounded by newer suburbs. The old sections have become accumulations of idiosyncratic patterns; streets are narrow and curve unpredictably, numbers on buildings may not run sequentially, and structures have been rebuilt many times in different ways. Only an old inhabitant is likely to know her way about, and only through experience rather than by following rules. In the suburbs roads are straight, buildings are in orderly rows, and anyone can follow a simple map.

It is easy to transpose the metaphor to language. Some words and idioms have a long and tortured etymology; others are neologisms, and the rules of usage may be straightforward. Neurath's boat fits these situations well. Parts of the boat have been rebuilt many times with criss-crossing rough-hewn planks, and other sections have been cleanly and simply crafted from scratch. *See* WITTGENSTEIN, *supra* note 13, at pt. I, ¶ 18.

is not a party to these activities. But her independence is unstable and illusory. Her balloon is tethered to the boat. Her attempts to distinguish the essential structure of the boat from adventitious repairs and changes are necessarily provisional. She cannot tell what will need to be changed over time, and her understanding of the boat's history, purpose, and essence are but one interpretation among many. In that respect, she is no more or less equipped to handle the so-called theoretical enterprise than the sailors on the boat themselves. She may have the advantage, from her precarious perch above the boat, of glimpsing or scrutinizing other boats in similar predicaments, but just what difference does that make?

C. Theory and Practice Reconsidered

The third application of Neurath's metaphor returns us to our main concern, the difference between theory and practice and the question of how the difference is captured in the distinction between an external and an internal point of view. How do the occupants of the balloon and the boat differ? We have seen that Hart offers several ways of characterizing an external standpoint. Two of these ways are of limited help in illuminating the distinction between theory and practice. Let us reconsider why that is before looking at more helpful characterizations.

If the quintessential participant is a lawyer, legislator, or judge, someone charged with affecting, making, or interpreting the law, then one is external if one has no such institutional role. But this simply leaves us with ordinary citizens. They are external, as we have seen, in the sense that they are not professionally expected to reflect on law or understand its institutional structure, although they *may* do so. But they are internal in the sense of being subject to the law, responsible for their actions under the law. Although the theorist, *qua* theorist, does not have an institutional role, one needs additional criteria to distinguish the theorist from the citizen.

A second way of being external is to see the law as lacking justification. This is the outlaw attitude, Holmes' "bad man" posture, or what Hart identifies as a sense of being obliged, rather than having an obligation.[72] Outlaws, like other citizens, are subject to the law and held responsible—and, in this sense, are internal to it. And theorists, while they may abstain from taking sides on controversial moral issues within the law, do not thereby become outlaws.[73]

Even if the non-official and the outlaw are, in a plausible sense, outsiders rather than insiders of the legal system, they do not have the external

72. *See* Hart, *supra* note 1, at 82-86.

73. Even if we concede to Hart that most persons typically do not have the outlaw posture, we may also observe that there are likely to be some persons who have an "outlaw" attitude to the system as a whole and many persons who have an outlaw posture toward *some* laws, e.g. taxes. Moreover, it is debatable whether a system in which the outlaw attitude is widespread is, *pro tanto*, less of a legal system or an uncharacteristic legal system.

point of view of the theorist. The theorist's posture has three distinctive characteristics that we have not yet considered.

One characteristic is dissociation. Those who are internal to a legal system are associated with it in two senses: the rules of the system apply to them (they are held responsible accordingly), and they have views on what the law should be as well as what it is (whether or not they are empowered to change and interpret the law in accord with such views). Theorists are external in both senses. First, their job as theorists is ostensibly unaffected by whether or not the laws apply to them. Second, their particular views about disputed normative questions within their legal system should not affect their construction of theory. They may well refer to the fact that insiders have such disputes, that some persons are empowered to take official roles vis-a-vis such disputes, and even that the centrality of such disputes is a necessary and pervasive feature of a legal system. But, as theorists, they do not enter into the disputes themselves.[74]

A second characteristic is that theorists are expected to be generalists insofar as they address sets of social practices and offer characterizations that are equally relevant to all members of the set. The theorist of language tells us about languages; the theorist of law claims to analyze legal systems in general. The description and analysis is, in this sense, external to any particular practice.

Can one say that a theorist seeks to identify the *essence* of language or legal system rather than what is *accidental* to a particular language or legal system? This distinction presumes that social practices do in fact have essences. Wittgenstein warns us against this kind of presumption, suggesting that the practices we call languages may at most have "family resemblances," features that they tend to share and that help explain why a common term is used to assimilate them.[75]

At best, the notion of an essence is an ideal and a potentially misleading one. Both the assumption that we have a satisfactory theory only when we have isolated the essence of law and that we can distinguish uncontroversially between essential and accidental features may be untenable assumptions setting unrealizable goals.[76] As such they misdescribe the external point of view of the theorist.

A third characteristic is reflection and self-scrutiny. Theorists, being philosophers, reflect on assumptions that participants use unreflec-

74. Accordingly, positivists distinguish sharply between analytical legal theory and normative legal doctrine. The first involves the analysis of the nature of legal rules, legal validity, institutional structure, and so on, but not normative questions such as what rights should be part of the system and how those rights are to be understood. Critical theorists, like positivists, characteristically distinguish between questions about the nature of law (e.g. as legitimating ideology) and the particular merits, demerits, and uses of normative responses to legal issues. On the other hand, natural law theorists often address these issues in ways that bridge analytical and normative questions. *See generally* DWORKIN, TAKING RIGHTS SERIOUSLY, *supra* note 51.

75. WITTGENSTEIN, *supra* note 13, pt. I, ¶ 67.

76. *See infra* text accompanying note 84.

tively.[77] A language user may be proficient in using the idioms of English without being able to identify the rules of idiomatic use. She may leave it to theorists to explain when and how languages change, how languages come to reflect class distinctions, and so on. A judge may have no need to be self-conscious about the ways in which he and his peers use similar interpretive tools, are constrained by moral norms, share or fail to share an understanding of the point of legal institutions, reflect unidentified biases under the camouflage of objective decision-making, and so on. The claim is not that insiders/practitioners (judges, lawyers) are generally or necessarily blind to these dimensions, but rather that participation is compatible with remaining blind and that levels of awareness will vary. The philosopher's job as theorist is to shed light and make explicit what may have otherwise remained implicit.

D. The Hubris of Theorists

These characteristics of the work of theorists—dissociation, generalization, and self-consciousness—are easily misunderstood. They are distillations or refinements of conceptual moves that insiders may also make. The sophisticated judge, attorney, or citizen will generally monitor her opinions in all these ways.

The characteristics of theory are often misunderstood as giving theorists a privileged position. Theory is seen as defining a superior practice, the terms of which expose the systemic mistakes and impostures of the practice under scrutiny. We will examine the strategies and implications of this understanding of the external point of view of theorists.

In general, this is precisely the kind of move that Wittgenstein identifies and criticizes, the kind that gives flies in fly-bottles their headbumps and headaches.[78] Simple examples are the epistemologist who claims that all wakefulness is *really* a form of dreaming or that all objects *really* exist only as long as they are being observed and the moral theorist who says that all altruistic action is *really* a form of selfishness or that all attempts to find meaning in life are doomed because life *really* is meaningless. What is deceptive and fraudulent about these "insights" is that they appropriate distinctions that have a home within a familiar language-game and a way of thinking (dreaming/wakefulness, dependent/independent existence, altruism/selfishness, meaningfulness/meaninglessness) and suspend the normal criteria of usage without introducing coherent alternatives. They produce nonsense masquerading as insight.[79]

---

77. *See generally* Arthur C. Danto, What Philosophy Is: A Guide to the Elements (1968); The Linguistic Turn: Recent Essays in Philosophical Method (Richard Rorty ed., 1967).

78. *See supra* note 15.

79. This process is well described by P.F. Strawson in his discussion of philosophical skepticism:

> This gives us a more profound characterization of the sceptic's [sic] position. He pretends to accept a conceptual scheme, but at the same time quietly rejects one of the conditions of its employment. Thus his doubts are unreal.

In legal theory, this occurs when dissociation is confused with neutrality. A theorist may claim that to be disengaged from normative debates is to see that all positions are equally favored or disfavored, that no arguments are better than others. The idea that one argument may be superior and thus trump another is a position for insiders, but from a "theoretical standpoint" it is simply a delusion.

Such a theorist may also claim the high ground of neutrality in *comparing* legal systems. The idea that one system may be more sophisticated or more just is seen as a determination open to a member of one system looking at other systems comparatively, but not open to the theorist who eschews an insider's perspective.

It follows that theorists are often seduced by the idea of dissociation into seeing all participants in a social practice as systematically blinkered and deluded. Insofar as insiders participate in controversies and use notions such as fairness, justice, correctness, and rights, they fail to recognize that all such arguments are systematically devalued by bias and partisanship, by commitments and dispositions hidden from disputants themselves.

This point may be expressed in terms of subjectivity and objectivity. The insider is accused of dressing subjective judgments in objective terms, while the theorist sees through this imposture. Only the theorist, in her rejection of all arguments as infected by subjectivity, has a tenable claim to be objective.

These misguided theoretical moves come about through misunderstanding of the process of dissociation and involve inattention to the ways in which the external (theoretical) point of view is parasitic on the internal aspect, the ways in which the balloon is tethered to the boat. The external stance of dissociation, correctly understood, involves a kind of subtraction or refraining. If every theorist is, first and foremost, a practitioner and if it is only her internal experience of the practice that informs and makes possible her activity as theorist, then dissociation is a matter of refraining from making judgments that are controversial and unsettled within the practice. Judge A and Judge B take conflicting positions on the disposition of a case; attorneys C and D file briefs on opposite sides of a case; legislators E and F take opposed positions on proposed legislation. In each case, it is part of the theorist's job *as theorist* to describe the forms of disagreement, to consider why various positions of partisans are mutually understood and embraced as moves within the social practice, to

---

> not simply because they are logically irresoluble doubts, but because they amount to the rejection of the whole conceptual scheme within which alone such doubts make sense. So, naturally enough, the alternative to doubt which he offers us is the suggestion that we do not really, or should not really, have the conceptual scheme that we do have; that we do not really, or should not really, mean what we think we mean, what we do mean. But this alternative is absurd. For the whole process of reasoning only starts because the scheme is as it is; and we cannot change it even if we would.

P.F. STRAWSON, INDIVIDUALS: AN ESSAY IN DESCRIPTIVE METAPHYSICS 35 (1959).

show how it is that agreement and disagreement coexist within the bounded practice and the theorist suspends or subtracts her hypothetical contribution as partisan.

It is important that insiders as participants are not foreclosed from sharing the theorist's insights. A well-informed and sophisticated judge, lawyer, or legislator can easily anticipate the arguments, assumptions, and strategies of those who disagree with him, can see "where they are coming from," and can describe such structures of thought and discourse in the way a theorist might.

Misunderstanding comes when the theorist claims to substitute a different position or attitude toward the internal arguments from that of the participants and claims that her substitution takes precedence. Thus, the theorist's neutrality seems to imply that, insofar as disagreement exists and is an inherent part of the practice, conflicting postures are in fact to be taken as equally meritorious, equally limited. But the theorist's dissociation affords no basis for such a judgment. Internal participants have argumentative strategies that are part of the practice and can be produced to support their positions. Theorists have no such grounds at all, and certainly no superior grounds, to assess that internal positions are of equal, unequal, or any particular degree of merit or persuasiveness. Their theory-construction is not an independent practice which yields conclusions that can decide internal disagreements.

The idea that the theoretical standpoint defines an independent and superior linguistic practice fosters a misunderstanding and misapplication of familiar truisms about social practices in general and law in particular. Among these truisms are the claims that the positions of judges, lawyers, and legislators are "politics all the way down,"[80] that all processes of justification come to an end in presuppositions that are assumed, and that insiders underestimate subliminal biases that inhere in their personal history and cultural background. None of these claims are obviously wrong, and each is instructive in its way, but it is important to see how each can be misconstrued.

What does it mean to say that legal reasoning is "politics all the way down"? In a sense, law and politics are bound together. Participants in legal practices differ in their value preferences and their styles of argument and justification. Their arguments involve a mix of empirical observations, moral premises, prudential considerations and strategies, and idiosyncratic background influences. The arguments, and the language games to which they belong, have a complex structure. Sometimes an empirical argument is a trump; a finding that a government program does not produce the benefits intended may doom the program. Sometimes there will be conflicting moral premises, but one competing premise may, by general agreement, occupy the higher humanitarian ground and proponents of other positions may wither in its face. Sometimes a position

80. Duncan Kennedy, *Freedom and Constraint in Adjudication: A Critical Phenomenology*, 36 J. LEGAL EDUC. 518 (1986).

will obviously be imprudent, and again by general agreement it will recede and disappear. And sometimes, issues will be resolved through the competition of incompatible political agendas and through a counting of votes and allegiances. But the last of these strategies of resolution often occurs when the others have failed, when the processes of rational debate have been exhausted and proven futile.

To suggest that judicial and legislative decisionmaking is politics all the way down is to imply that rational debate is always a mirage: that no empirical findings are ever trumps, that no moral positions ever emerge as superior by general consensus, and that there are no general criteria of prudence. From the fact that *some* decisions are obviously political by default, one cannot conclude that, to the theorist's eye, all of them indifferently have this character.

What are we to make of the fact that all processes of justification come to an end, that all arguments depend on some moral and cultural premises that appear to their adherents to need no justification, premises that are *logically susceptible* to being challenged? This does not show that adherence to such premises is a delusion. Rather, all social practices involving normative argument and decision-making necessarily involve such premises, and taking note of that fact does not degrade the practice. All insiders see their premises, the bases and origins of their claims, imperfectly. And the influence of their own background, training, ways of thinking, cultural experience, and so on, is never fully transparent to them. But that does not mean that they are deluded or unreasonable, merely that self-awareness is an inexhaustible and Sisyphean obligation for persons in their roles, and the theorist's job is to outline the parameters of that obligation.

The theorist, as we have seen, is an insider to some legal system, participant in such a practice either as official or citizen, before and while he is a theorist. Being an insider is, as we have seen, a precondition for doing theory. In Derrida's terms, inhabiting the structure is a precondition for deconstructing it and, in Neurath's terms, occupying the boat and participating in its reconstruction is a prerequisite for hovering in a bubble above the boat and observing the process. As insider, the theorist is privy to all issues at all levels of abstraction that are matters of contention within the practice and to the relevant strategies of argument, but more importantly he also has a position on these matters, favoring one side or another and using one or another kind of argument.

When he takes the "external point of view" as theorist, he may disengage or dissociate himself from these debates. But he does not thereby join a different or transcendent practice that affords him a different way of looking at these debates. In particular, nothing warrants his commending a posture of neutrality, whereby conflicting positions are in equipoise, or an attitude of indifference. And there is no vantage point from which he can argue that the participants are systematically unjustified or mistaken in holding the positions and making the arguments that they in fact make. The claim that a particular argument is unjustified and that the person making it is mistaken is always available, but it is an internal move within the practice, one that rests on evidence the relevance of which is established by the rules of the practice.

E. The External Point of View Redescribed

An understanding of the links between jurisprudential theory and the internal aspect of legal practices has two very different kinds of application. First, it makes clear the perspective of a theoretical point of view on the normative questions, arguments and decisions that constitute moves within the practice. I addressed this issue in the last two sections.

Second, an understanding of links between theory and the internal aspect clarifies the job of theory. When theorists claim to consider the structure and point of the practice as a whole, to what extent are their views parasitic upon their experience and dispositions as insiders?

We have seen that every theorist begins by generalizing from a home base. She seeks to identify structures and procedures that are common to her own and other comparable practices and make sense of them by identifying the *point* of the practice in general. Her question becomes not "Why does my culture have a legal system"? but "Why do cultures in general have legal systems"? What point do they serve?

The answers to these questions, however, will themselves be matters of contention, not only among those theorists who compare legal systems, but also within the theorists' own legal system. In that sense, the situation of Anglo-American jurisprudential theorists is illustrative. H.L.A. Hart's sophisticated version of positivism emphasizes the separation of law and morals and internal attitude. For him, the distinctive features of a legal system include, first, an institutional structure by which legal rules can be identified and implemented independently of moral considerations and, second, a normal attitude of acceptance on the part of those subject to the law.[81] Acceptance occurs when the laws give rise to a sense and a language of obligation and citizens act accordingly.

Oliver Wendell Holmes, Jr., defends a different kind of positivism, one that resonates with the work of John Austin.[82] Finality and the independence of law from morals are central features. In this model, law is a set of directions and prohibitions that may or may not be "accepted" in Hart's sense. Order may simply be imposed and security achieved by making certain forms of behavior non-optional and sanctioned.

A third model, consistent with Ronald Dworkin's work, de-emphasizes finality and concerns itself with the intersection of law and morals.[83] It describes law as a system of rules and moral principles that works itself

81. *See* HART, *supra* note 1, at 79-99.

82. *See* Hart, *supra* note 20, at 593-94.

83. *See generally* RONALD DWORKIN, FREEDOM'S LAW: THE MORAL READING OF THE AMERICAN CONSTITUTION (1996) [hereinafter DWORKIN, FREEDOM'S LAW]; RONALD DWORKIN, A MATTER OF PRINCIPLE (1985) [hereinafter DWORKIN, A MATTER OF PRINCI-

pure over time through a process of evolution, interpretation, and refinement. Law, in this view, implements shared social goals and moral convictions.

Proponents of these models and others defend their generality and claim to have identified the underlying presuppositions of the enterprise, the point of law. At the same time, proponents of each model anticipate theoretical controversy and know how models can be faulted. A positivist disposed to agree with Hart may concede (to Dworkin) that moral principles play a large role in deliberative processes (judicial and legislative) *and* (to Holmes) that some legal subjects, sometimes many of them, have the outlaw mentality. One who defends a version of Holmes' "bad man" theory is likely to concede (to Hart) that citizens often agree with the law and identify with it as a parameter for moral action and criticism.

These sketches of possible theoretical orientations reflect different points of view that typically coexist not only among theorists but within a legal system—the point of view of the ordinary citizen, that of the outlaw, and that of the official or decision-maker empowered to interpret, create, and transform the law. But role and point of view are not strictly matched. The ordinary citizen may understand and play out the role of armchair legislator or judge, and he may favor that account as most illuminating. The judge or legislator, in turn, may understand and even harbor the outlaw attitude. Various opinions about the point of law and its distinctive characteristics will coexist not only within any legal system that embraces different kinds of roles and players, but (more importantly) within the attitudes and understanding of each player. Each can see, however darkly, through the others' eyes.

When theorists spell out the structure and point of law, generality is purchased at a high price. The external point of view as theorist does not in fact afford insights that are denied to insiders, participants in legal practices. To the contrary, theoretical insights are merely partial internal perspectives, writ large and universalized.[84] The debates that naturally occur within any legal practice, struggles not only over laws and cases but implicitly over the point of the practice as a whole, simply have their reflection in the debates of general theorists.

The special self-awareness of the theorist is therefore not an attitude distinctive of the external point of view at all. Every insider can and may benefit from having the same kind of self-awareness. Such awareness of law as a social practice by an insider has three dimensions. First, the in-

PLE]; DWORKIN, LAW'S EMPIRE, *supra* note 51; DWORKIN, TAKING RIGHTS SERIOUSLY, *supra* note 51.

84. Accordingly, every insider in the practice will be sensitive to such considerations as the importance of finality, the relevance of moral arguments, the need for law to be "accepted," the role of sanctions, and so on. Theorists choose among these aspects of the legal practice, giving one or another aspect analytical precedence. Compelling jurisprudential arguments are constructed in this way, but the resulting jurisprudential disagreements among theorists merely mirror the internal debates of insiders. And they are similarly unlikely to be resolved. *See supra* note 44.

sider cannot only take positions on substantive questions (disposition of cases, legislation) and give reasons that others will see as reasons, but she can also anticipate and construct the positions and arguments of those other insiders who may disagree with her. Second, she can take positions on more general questions of the point and structure of the legal system, and she can recognize that different insiders can conceive the point and structure differently. To some extent, she can understand how these different "theoretical" conceptions adumbrate various internal roles, that of judge, lawyer, legislator, citizen, outlaw, and so on. Third, she can extrapolate from these "theoretical" conceptions about her own legal system to an understanding of other legal systems and offer not so much a general theory of law as a general account of the coexistence of conflicting positions on the nature of law.

Awareness in all of these dimensions involves tension between the conviction that one is prepared to defend answers to questions at each of these levels *and* the conviction that one can see through the eyes of other insiders whose answers and modes of defense are different from one's own. The sophisticated insider inhabits this tension and constantly refines her views and modes of argument in light of it. It is a misconception, therefore, to identify the internal and the external aspects of law respectively with the two sides of this tension. The insider embraces both sides. The external point of view, by default, is parasitic on the internal standpoint because it is an attenuated form of the tension, the internal understanding of the practice with the observer's internal commitments provisionally subtracted or put aside.

III. BURSTING THE THEORIST'S BUBBLE: RECENT JURISPRUDENCE

Many contemporary writers of jurisprudence see the relationship between the internal and external point of view imperfectly. They fail to see that a theorist of law remains tethered to Neurath's boat, remains an inhabitant of the structures he deconstructs. Various recent theoretical accounts of law can be seen as ignoring or denying this truism. In this part, I will look at the way in which the disposition to do so devalues their claims.

A. The Fish/Dworkin Debate

Ronald Dworkin's jurisprudential writings[85] have been widely influential over the last twenty-five years. As a self-styled naturalist critic of

85. *See generally* Ronald Dworkin, Freedom's Law, *supra* note 83; Ronald Dworkin, Law's Empire, *supra* note 51; Dworkin, A Matter of Principle, *supra* note 83; Dworkin, Taking Rights Seriously, *supra* note 51.

positivism[86] and an articulate defender of liberalism,[87] Dworkin has often drawn fire. Stanley Fish, a literary theorist much concerned with hermeneutics and with the internal and external standpoints of interpreters of texts, has been one of Dworkin's more persistent critics.[88] Their debates illuminate the interplay of insight and confusion about internal and theoretical points of view.

Dworkin offers a characterization of law as a social practice. His theory is preoccupied with the centrality of the judicial function. It stresses the dynamic, open-ended character of law by scrutinizing the role of judges as interpreters of law. Dworkin is particularly concerned with the resources that judges are expected to use, the ways in which they use them, and the nature of their results:

> I shall argue that legal practice is an exercise in interpretation not only when lawyers interpret particular documents or statutes but generally. . . . Judges develop a particular approach to legal interpretation by forming and refining a political theory sensitive to those issues on which interpretation in particular cases will depend; and they call this their legal philosophy. It will include both structural features, elaborating the general requirement that an interpretation must fit doctrinal history, and substantive claims about social goals and principles of justice. Any judge's opinion about the best interpretation will therefore be a consequence of beliefs other judges need not share.[89]

Dworkin concludes that

> judges should decide hard cases by interpreting the political structure of their community in the following, perhaps special way: by trying to find the best *justification* they can find, in principles of political morality, for the structure as a whole, from the most profound constitutional rules and arrangements to the details of . . . private law.[90]

In this way, what Dworkin calls the "adjudicative principle" instructs that the total set of laws be seen as morally coherent.[91] It is this that he calls the ultimate legal and judicial mandate of "integrity."[92]

Dworkin's account of law thus addresses the question of the determinateness of law, and it does so in a way that claims to be more sophisticated than any positivistic account. For positivists, law is determinate to the extent that there are formal criteria for legal rules.[93] A legal system is defined in terms of the availability of such criteria. The question of formal identification of law is treated separately from the question of law's

86. *See generally* Ronald A. Dworkin, *"Natural" Law Revisited*, 34 U. FLA. L. REV. 165 (1982).

87. *See* DWORKIN, A MATTER OF PRINCIPLE, *supra* note 83, at 181-233. *See generally* DWORKIN, FREEDOM'S LAW, *supra* note 83.

88. *See* STANLEY FISH, DOING WHAT COMES NATURALLY: CHANGE, RHETORIC, AND THE PRACTICE OF THEORY IN LITERARY AND LEGAL STUDIES 87-119, 356-71 (1989).

89. DWORKIN, A MATTER OF PRINCIPLE, *supra* note 83, at 146, 161-62.

90. Dworkin, *supra* note 86, at 165.

91. DWORKIN, LAW'S EMPIRE, *supra* note 51, at 176.

92. *Id.*

93. *See supra* note 36.

normativity, the question of the distinctive attitude of those who are inside a legal practice.[94]

For Dworkin, determinateness and normativity come together. In his theory, law is not determinate in the positivistic sense that judges and citizens who disagree about the principles and point of their legal system will nonetheless agree about how to identify its rules. Rather, it is determinate to the extent that all who take a role in interpreting the law will be doubly constrained, first, by the general ideal of a process of interpretation defined by integrity and, second, by the more particular avenues of moral justification that are made relevant within the shared social practice. Thus, the principles that constitute law's normativity at the same time make it determinate. In doing so, they allow us to make sense of the claim that there are better and worse ways of interpreting the law, right and wrong answers to legal questions.

Stanley Fish has repeatedly argued that Dworkin's account is incoherent, that (following Dworkin's premises) one cannot make sense of the idea of better or worse ways of interpreting the law or of right or wrong judicial answers.[95] He points out that such normative conclusions presuppose that one can distinguish between the judge's apprehension of the facts of the case and the relevant rule(s), the judge's use of certain principles to decide the case, and the ways in which an observer of the process may assess the choice of principles and may see other principles and a different resolution as preferable. For Fish, these are not separate processes; to apprehend the facts and relevant rules is *already* to see them in the light of a moral commitment to the principles that define the point of law.

> [T]o have a belief (or an interpretation) is to believe it, to believe it is to think that it is correct, and to think it correct is to prefer it to someone else's belief. In short, everything that Dworkin would secure in the name of the "right-wrong" picture—a ground for assuming "that interpretations may be sound or unsound, better or worse, more or less accurate"—already is secured by the fact that the interpreter is embedded in a structure of beliefs of which his judgments are an extension. The entire project of explaining how "ordinary interpreters think" as they do—think that they are right and others are wrong and that what they believe is true—is unnecessary because they could not possibly think anything else.[96]

The distinction between explaining a text and changing it can no more be maintained than the others of which it is a version (finding vs. inventing, continuing vs. striking out in a new direction, interpreting vs.

94. In other words, Hart treats as separate issues the distinctive existence of use of a rule of recognition for valid legal rules and the distinctive attitude (acceptance, the non-outlaw attitude) of those subject to a legal system. His discussion of the internal point of view is ambiguous, but only one of four possible interpretations of it links the internal point of view to awareness and use of a rule of recognition. *See supra* notes 35-37 and accompanying text.

95. *See generally* FISH, *supra* note 88.

96. *Id.* at 115-16 (footnote omitted).

creating). To explain a work is to point out something about it that had not been attributed to it before and therefore to change it by challenging other explanations that were once changes in their turn. Explaining and changing cannot be opposed activities . . . because they are the same activities.[97]

The debate between Dworkin and Fish defies easy summary and brief analysis. Each arguably makes compelling arguments about the relation between theory and practice while mistaking significant aspects of it. According to Fish, Dworkin seems to imply that understanding and mastery of the interpretative process give the theorist a purchase on rightness that may not be available to the judge or insider (except in an idealized role). If Fish's characterization is correct, Dworkin, as we shall see, is surely mistaken. Fish, in turn, argues that many distinctions made by insiders (judges, practitioners) and appropriated by outsiders (theorists) are meaningless, but he arrives at that conclusion only through a misdescription of the internal aspect of practices, only by flattening and homogenizing them.

Once we are clear about the dependence of theory on practice, the dependence of the external upon the internal aspect of law, it is easy to see that Dworkin and Fish are arguing at cross-purposes. Fish is surely correct that Dworkin *would be* in error in suggesting that legal questions present themselves as "brute issues" to judges, with interpretations *subsequently* to be laid on them. Every judge sees every problematic question as problematic in the light of an evolving social practice; the question is framed for her initially by a shared understanding of evolving legal doctrine and legal controversy, by the interpretive options that are part of the social practice of legal interpretation, by more general aspects of culture, and by the idiosyncracies of understanding traceable to her personal history.

Moreover, the only perspective from which it makes sense to speak of resolutions of these issues being better or worse, right or wrong, is the perspective of an insider. The judge herself recognizes various strategies of solution offered up by the practice. The process of thinking them through *is* the process of seeing and preparing arguments why some resolutions are better, others worse. Anyone who takes issue with her, whether as an official or merely an observer, will necessarily do so by using another available strategy within the practice. Rightness and wrongness are notions that these disputants deploy to characterize their arguments.

This does not mean that it is impossible for a judge to be creative, but it means that creativity is to be understood internally. The practice *itself* embraces criteria for evaluating radical variations on existing strategies and judging them to be creative, misguided, or both. Attributions of creativity are often retrospective. A judge looking back on earlier decisions

97. *Id.* at 98.

that affected the course of law, that reshaped the available ways of thinking about specific legal issues or legal decision-making in general, will call some creative. A historian or theorist who makes that judgment will do so, if at all, in the same way that a later-generation insider does.

It would be a mistake for Dworkin or any theorist to see the constrained, or rather contextual, character of legal judgment and interpretation as implying that internal strategies converge over time, that the legal system "works itself pure." There is no independent external point of view from which the strategies of reasoning within the practice can be evaluated as better or worse, right or wrong, or intelligent. The moral parameters that make possible such judgments, controversial or not within the practice, are all artifacts *of* the practice.

Even the term "constraint" to describe the contextual character of legal judgment is potentially misleading. Judges themselves are constrained in the sense that the practice defines and determines the strategies they have available, their options in framing and resolving the interpretive task at hand. It determines what is imaginable to them as a real option. It is *not* a constraint in the sense of being a conscious barrier or prohibition that is part of their deliberations, an awareness of forbidden but imaginable options.

Fish is helpful in pointing out that cases present themselves to judges already interpreted, as artifacts of the social practice shaped by the interpretive framework of the culture and by the idiosyncratic conceptual habits of the judge. But he is mistaken when he implies that because the case is already contextualized, there is no further work for the judge to do, no process that one can refer to as done well or badly. The case presents itself not with a solution but as a problem. The judge's familiarity with the practice and with the job of interpretation is such that she envisions different ways of addressing and resolving the case, all of them understandable and largely anticipatable[98] as part of the shared practice.

The practice itself, however, is complex enough so that different approaches will be seen and labeled, *by herself and others within the practice*, as variously sound and unsound resolutions, as evolutionary or revolutionary, as instances of developing law incrementally or as radical reinventions of it. Thus, the conceptual moves of insiders, an important aspect of the internal point of view of the practice, embrace self-criticism and mutual evaluation. The distinctions between finding and invention, explaining and changing, interpreting and creating—which Fish criticizes as meaningless—have a home within that point of view.

98. This raises the complex issue of creativity and change within ongoing practices that involve disagreement and decision-making. The parameters of the practice are more or less fixed to the extent that any judge, for example, understands the range of responses and arguments that are appropriate to a particular case. But the mutually understood parameters of the practice are not frozen. A judge may deploy arguments in a way that surprises colleagues and turns out to "have legs," to influence other judges in their strategies. A judge has room for creativity, and thus the practice evolves over time.

And there is no other point of view. It is simply a fallacy for a theorist like Fish to assume that the external point of view is a vehicle for moving from the observation that all judges belong to and work with social practices (or, in Fish's terms, "interpretive communities") to the observation that all moves within the practice are indifferently interpretive, inventive, or creative, and that none are better or worse. Judgments about rightness and wrongness, strength, weakness, and creativity of arguments have their only home as they are deployed within the practice by insiders who distinguish and mutually criticize each other's moves.

B. Critical Legal Studies

Recent as it is, the movement called "critical legal studies"[99] is as much a historical artifact as Hart's positivism. Its energies and insights have been diffused through the work of current theorists who have struck out in various directions.[100] I shall consider some distinctions between theory and practice that seem implicit in the critical point of view.

Duncan Kennedy's early articles put forward arguments that have achieved a substantial afterlife in legal pedagogy and discourse, even as they have been disclaimed by their author.[101] Accordingly, "there are two opposed rhetorical modes for dealing with substantive issues [in American private law], . . . individualism and altruism."[102] Any issue can be treated in either rhetorical mode, and "the choice of form is seldom purely instrumental or tactical."[103] Thus, it is a quixotic quest to seek the "best" resolution of a legal issue. The most that can be said is that any resolution is political in the narrow sense, reflecting *not* the collective political will of the culture but the partisan political aims of one of two equally available approaches. "At [a] deeper level, [this shows that] we are divided, among ourselves and also within ours[e]lves, between irreconcilable visions of humanity and society. . . ."[104] Kennedy labels this a "fundamental contradiction."[105]

Proponents of this approach tend to describe it as making clear from the external point of the theorist what is obscured from the practitioner. But this is an illusion. The internal point of view, as we saw in Part II of this Article, is more complex and nuanced than Kennedy implies. It is

99. *See, e.g.*, ANDREW ALTMAN, CRITICAL LEGAL STUDIES: A LIBERAL CRITIQUE (1990); CRITICAL LEGAL STUDIES (James Boyle ed., 1992); MARK KELMAN, A GUIDE TO CRITICAL LEGAL STUDIES (1987); THE POLITICS OF LAW: A PROGRESSIVE CRITIQUE (David Kairys ed., 1982); Symposium, *Critical Legal Studies*, 36 STAN. L. REV. (1984).

100. Among the movements that owe a significant debt to the methodology of critical legal studies are communitarianism, legal feminism, race studies, legal hermeneutics, and legal postmodernism.

101. *See* DUNCAN KENNEDY, A CRITIQUE OF ADJUDICATION (FIN DE SIÈCLE) 55 (1997).

102. Duncan Kennedy, *Form and Substance in Private Law Adjudication*, 89 HARV. L. REV. 1685, 1685 (1976).

103. *Id.* at 1710.

104. *Id.* at 1685.

105. Kennedy, *supra* note 43, at 211.

not simply the captive of a particular political approach, delusionally seen as neutral and correct. Rather the practitioner in principle is capable of appreciating the availability of competing solutions, the possibility of bias, and the certainty of the contextualism of any hermeneutical task, but understands as well that the relevance and defensibility of decisional strategies must and can be assessed case by case. Even if we concede what is questionable, namely that most competing approaches to most legal issues can be characterized as individualistic or altruistic, the internal point of view includes the sense that on some issues one or another approach can be supported with better arguments concerning such matters as justice, social interest, and economic welfare. The fact that competing approaches are available does not entail that, from an "external" or any perspective, they compete equally, that one side always has as much and no more to be said for it than the other.

The pretense that the external point of view yields this kind of illumination distinguishes critical studies even when Kennedy's bipolarity thesis is left behind. In a seminal early article, Robert Gordon critically examines the assumption that "[l]egal systems should be described and explained in terms of their functional responsiveness to social needs[,] . . . [the working hypothesis that [t]he legal system adapts to changing social needs."[106] He suggests that this is a "legitimating ideology,"[107] one that conceals from those inside a legal system the fact that the connections between law and society are radically indeterminate.

> It will . . . help us to relativize our understanding of the past's relation to the present if we see that our conventional views of that relation are mediated by familiar narrative story-lines, that are so deeply entrenched in our consciousness that we are often unaware of their rule over our conception of reality. These story-lines, like other mentalities, have a history filled with ideological purposes, and there always exist . . . competing stories that impress the same historical experience with radically divergent meanings.[108]

Three different ideas coexist in Gordon's analysis. Two are well supported. It is surely correct that the task of historian, the retrospective analyst, differs from that of the practitioner. The historian appropriately second-guesses practitioners, seeing influences and patterns that may be invisible to those *in media res*.

It is also surely correct that every practitioner needs to remind herself at every turn to assess issues through the eyes of others, to weigh the kinds of arguments that she can well anticipate will be offered by those who differ with her. She has the twin obligations of justifying her position against those who think otherwise and understanding their positions. Inevitably this requires her to make the grounds, motives, and personal his-

106. Robert W. Gordon, *Critical Legal Histories*, 36 STAN. L. REV. 57, 63-64 (1984).

107. *Id.* at 93.

108. *Id.* at 101-02.

tory governing her approach as transparent to herself as possible, to ask herself what role legitimating ideologies play in her thinking.

But all of this does not warrant a third idea, one that is not necessarily Gordon's but that may all too easily be inferred from his comments. It is that the theorist for whom the contingent history of the practice is clearly evident and who can identify "legitimating ideologies" is thereby justified in criticizing all decisions, all uses of decisional strategies by insiders, as equally blinkered by unacknowledged ideologies and delusions of objectivity. Piecemeal self-scrutiny of the kind illuminated by theorists is an inherent part of the insider's role, and it does not leave the insider/judge bereft of the capacity to choose one resolution over another.[109]

Some critical theorists want to have it both ways. They want to criticize insiders as systematically blind to determinants of their decisions and, at the same time, to defend an agenda for substantive decisions. This can sometimes be seen in the work of critical feminist theorists as well as critical race theorists. Catharine MacKinnon, for example, argues that laws and decisions that aspire to neutrality, fairness, and justice are typically biased against women.[110] The point is not that male dominance affects how some, even many, aspects of law are seen; rather it is that the legal system for all insiders is pervaded by male dominance. "Its point of view is the standard for point-of-viewlessness, its particularity the meaning of universality."[111] Male and female insiders are equally tainted, men insofar as they are blinded by the legitimating ideologies that institutionalize their engendered preferences, women insofar as they have been brainwashed by that very system. Only an external point of view affords awareness of the system's biases and partiality.

MacKinnon, to her credit, recognizes the paradox. "The practice of a politics of all women in the face of its theoretical impossibility in traditional terms is creating a new process of theorizing. . . . Its project is to uncover and claim as valid the experience of women, the major content of which is the devalidation of women's experience."[112]

This rhetoric, however powerful and reductive, rests on the same misleading premises as critical theory. The external point of view offers *no* resources that are *in principle* unavailable to an insider. There may be compelling advantages in self-delusion in many cases, but an insider contemporaneous to MacKinnon can uncover and use the same insights about male dominance that feminist theorists put forward. Indeed, the insights are available to the theorist only to the extent that they are also

109. By contrast, to see all decisional strategies as determined by unacknowledged biases and predilections is to undermine the possibility of rational, self-conscious decision making. It is paradoxical for a theorist to take this position and also advocate an agenda for rational and autonomous reformers.

110. *See generally* CATHARINE A. MACKINNON, FEMINISM UNMODIFIED: DISCOURSES ON LIFE AND LAW (1987); CATHERINE A. MACKINNON, TOWARD A FEMINIST THEORY OF THE STATE (1989) [hereinafter MACKINNON, THEORY OF STATE].

111. MACKINNON, THEORY OF STATE, *supra* note 110, at 116-17.

112. *Id.* at 116.

available to an insider in the context of addressing particular legal issues.[113] There are feminist theorists only insofar as there can also be feminist legislators and judges. The theorist may have less of a vested interest in self-delusion, but whether that is so depends not on her situation as insider or outsider but on the particular issue at hand. In the end, there is no paradox. The feminist agenda, like the agenda of reformers concerned with racial attitudes, is a possible internal agenda for judges, legislators, and citizens. Feminist proposals are not revelations available only outside social practices, revelations that implement a distinctive critical theoretical method. One is likely to believe that only if one ignores the relevant complex moves within the social practice of legal reasoning and decision-making.

Duncan Kennedy, in his most recent and most ambitious book, *A Critique of Adjudication (fin de siècle)*,[114] wrestles once again with the relationship between theorist and practitioner. He defines the book's methodology, which he labels "[m]odernism/postmodernism (mpm)," as "a project with the goal of achieving transcendent aesthetic/emotional/intellectual experiences at the margins of or in the interstices of a disrupted rational grid."[115]

> [Moreover, m]pm is a critique of the characteristic forms of rightness of [our legal] culture and aims at liberation from inner and outer experiences of constraint by reason, in the name, not of justice and a new system, but of the dialectic of system and antisystem, mediated by [arguments that] . . . are supposed to put in question the claims of rightness and, at the same time, induce a set of emotions—irony, despair, ecstasy, and so on—that are crushed or blocked when we experience the text or representation as "right."[116]

Kennedy offers a more accessible account of this process, less imbued with the mystique of postmodernism, when he says the following:

> We don't get to the point of psychologizing American judges until we have decided that, at least for the moment, there's no sense in continuing our investigation of their views on the merits, because those views are wrong and, indeed, there is no sense in further dialogue with them on their own terms, because, for the moment, it is more

113. It follows that some of the ways in which liberal feminism and radical feminism are differentiated are illusory and self-serving. Liberal feminism is typically grounded in practice. Liberal feminists identify issues in which the equal rights of women have been ignored, distorted, or violated. They use rhetorical strategies that are available within the practice, and they reinterpret equality, respect, and other relevant notions.

The radical theorist who seems to believe that all strategies within the legal practice and even the available rhetoric, the language of practice, is irremediably tainted presents us with a self-refuting paradox. We not only recognize her language as part of the practice, as an available if creative strategy, but we can also readily imagine it in the voice of an insider, a judge or legislator. If no judge or legislator in fact takes these positions, the reason is likely to be political rather than conceptual. The radical feminist insider may, perhaps, have trouble being appointed or elected, but her approach to legal issues is not one that insiders *in principle* cannot voice.

114. KENNEDY, *supra* note 101.

115. *Id.* at 7.

116. *Id.* at 340-41.

interesting to figure out why they say what they say, on the assumption that it's wrong, than to investigate further whether it is wrong.[117]

And yet he also backpeddles when he observes that "the mere adoption of the psychologizing posture doesn't close off the possibility that there is no misrepresentation, that the view we're about to psychologize is correct."[118] Conceding that "I don't claim to have shown that it is impossible to exclude the ideological," he concludes nonetheless that "for the time being, it seems worthwhile to psychologize."[119]

These brief excerpts display well Kennedy's pervasive and largely unquestioned assumptions about the prerogatives of the theorist. Judges and other insiders are, he presumes, wrong and ideological—wrong *because* they are ideological. They are, according to Kennedy, doubly wrong insofar as they see themselves as nonideological *and* insofar as the claims to objectivity of ideological pieces of legal reasoning are wrong. The critical theorist, on the other hand, has the job of laying bare her pretenses, demonstrating (by psychologizing or by using "postmodern" dialogic techniques) that what *she* calls "rational" is merely ideological.

All of this rhetoric veils a congealed mix of truism, pretension, and plain error. It is true, as we have seen, that every practitioner (and for that matter *every theorist*) does not come naked into the world of theory, but comes clothed with beliefs about why law is worth having, what arguments and solutions to some issues are better than others, and so on. She also comes clothed in awareness that others, participants in the same legal practice, see things differently and that some of her own motives and reasons for holding views may not be transparent to her. If this predicament is labeled "ideological," then we are all always ideological. Wisdom comes, not in seeing "being ideological" as *wrong*, but in understanding the inevitable context, nature, and contestability of rightness claims. Not all insiders appreciate this, of course, but the most sophisticated and self-critical of them do. What is clear is that the external point of view, the pretenses of the postmodernist and the psychologizer, has little to add to the self-reflection of such insiders. It is plain error to label all inside arguments as "wrong" when, by the critical theorist's own argument, there can in principle be nothing one could call "right."

C. Schlag on Theory

The distinctions and arguments of critical theory, represented in their most refined form by Kennedy's writings, have influenced a generation of legal scholars. The idea that the external point of the theorist affords a pinnacle from which to mock the blinkered objectivism of those within the practice is taken for granted by many self-styled postmodernists. For example, Pierre Schlag claims that

117. *Id.* at 198.
118. *Id.*
119. *Id.*

> [for legal thinkers,] values are taken to be self-evidently self-grounding and it is presumed that participants in the legal conversation already take values to be the primary source of authority. . . . Once emancipated from their generative history, values tend to become the ethical equivalent of currency—endlessly recyclable, ready for appropriation by any force, ready to underwrite any end.[120]

From any internal point of view, of course, terms such as justice, freedom, and equality are contested and contestable in many contexts, but they are not, as the critic would have it, simply and equally available to all comers. It is one thing to note the possibility that they *may* be used carelessly or promiscuously. It is something else, and unwarranted from any external perspective, to say that all uses are equally unjustifiable, equally "wrong." Insiders will not take that position because each will have her own favored strategy for achieving justice and furthering other values. Outsiders have no independent grounds for such claims.

According to Schlag, "legal thinkers" fall into error because they "self-identify" with judges.

> [This is a practice] that enables and sustains the fundamental formal ontology of law—the notion that law comes in object-forms such as rules, doctrines, principles, precedents, methods, models, theories, and so on. . . . Judges are supposed to produce decisions that maintain the rule of law, advance efficiency, keep the peace, produce justice, or achieve some such desired normative goal. . . . In short, they are supposed to honor the norms, values, and beliefs that generally hold in the relevant authoritative community. . . . In their self-identification with judges, legal thinkers take on the same orientation.[121]

In other words, legal thinkers are disabled from seeing that values are nothing but "currency . . . ready to underwrite any end" and realizing that rules, doctrines, and so on are nothing but "legitimating ideologies."[122]

One could treat as an empirical question whether judges and theorists, either or both, fit this description. No doubt some do. My argument in this Article is conceptual, not empirical. It considers whether *any* judges or theorists can go beyond the simple-minded formalization of rules, values, or principles to see them as artifacts of the practice and, therefore, as the contestable ingredients of internal debate. If this point of view is available to the "external" theorist, that is because it is also available to the reflective internal practitioner, whether judge, lawyer, or citizen. And neither the theorist nor the practitioner has reason to infer from the character of rules, principles, and values as artifacts and as contestable that they are devalued, that they are currency that can be used with *equal* justification by all comers, or that something less important is at stake in internal debates and disagreements than practitioners suppose.

---

120. Pierre Schlag, Laying Down the Law: Mysticism, Fetishism, and the American Legal Mind 44, 58 (1996).

121. *Id.* at 136.

122. Gordon, *supra* note 106, at 93.

Schlag considers the paradoxical nature of theory. He discusses Fish's notion of interpretive communities to raise questions about the vantage point from which such "theoretical" observations are made.[123] The paradox seems to arise because, on one hand, our categories of thought are determined by our interpretive community, and we are wholly *inside* those categories. On the other hand, we are supposedly able to refer to and think about our interpretive community as one among other possible interpretive communities, and doing so implies that we can position ourselves *outside* our interpretive community. The paradox is, of course, self-referential and impeaches Fish's own position as theorist.

Schlag notes that Fish devises the notion of "relatively autonomous self" to address the paradox.

> The self knows that there is something irreducible about the act of interpretation that simply cannot be . . . captured by anything so systematic, so universal, or univocal as a theory. . . . The self cannot choose its interpretive constructs. It is always already within them. But at the same time (and quite conveniently), very little can be known about these interpretive constructs, so the self need not feel closeted by an overly determined objectivity. The concept of interpretive communities offers the self *a formal closure* against the claims of theory, reason, and history. But at the same time, the concept is *substantively empty*, so that the self can project into "interpretive communities" just about anything it wants. . . . Of course, the relatively autonomous self (as its name indicates) is not entirely stable. Being only *relatively* autonomous, it is constantly called upon to adjudicate the boundaries of its own autonomy. Indeed, it is constantly being seduced or bullied into accepting some insuperable subjectivism or some intolerable objectivism.[124]

Schlag concludes with a series of celebratory self-contradictory conclusions, such as "[t]he relatively autonomous self is a relatively accurate description of the modern self," "[t]he relatively autonomous self is a fiction," and "[t]here is no reason to believe . . . in the relatively autonomous self."[125]

As obfuscation (whether attributable to Schlag alone or conjointly with Fish), this is exemplary. As analysis, the imprisonment metaphor breaks down. To say that we cannot choose our interpretive constructs or choose to belong to another interpretive community is to note the truisms that we cannot live someone else's life or have a different history from our own. This is, to be sure, a kind of limitation, but one that is not quite as limiting as Schlag supposes. Nothing prevents us, using the tools of our conceptual community, from inquiring into the experiences and beliefs of anyone in history and making *the effort* to understand them. Nothing prevents us from addressing the consequences of this effort, the ways in which it partially succeeds, partially fails. And nothing prevents us from

123. *See* SCHLAG, *supra* note 120, at 91-113.
124. *Id.* at 98, 100, 103.
125. *Id.* at 106.

seeing our own conceptual community as one of many or from understanding diversity within and among interpretive communities. We can do all of this from inside. One who thinks we cannot do so underestimates the resources and nature of interpretive communities. In other words, nothing stops us from occupying Neurath's boat and being aware of it *as the kind of boat it is*. It is our nature as participants in our practice to "occupy the practices we deconstruct."[126]

Thus, relative autonomy is not the dilemma. Autonomy makes sense *within* the practice in the sense that we can exercise autonomy by resisting physical, psychological, and conceptual coercion. We engage in self-questioning, entertaining alternative arguments and points of view. That is how we experience autonomy. But it makes no sense to look for autonomy *from* the practice, any more than it makes sense to seek autonomy from life itself. Being internal to this rich practice is a condition of our being, but that being exists as tension. We struggle both with others who see things differently and would bring about what we see as an inimical state of affairs, and with ourselves to the extent that we question our own point of view and try out those of others. But these are ways of exercising autonomy within the practice, not autonomy from it.

IV. CONCLUSION

The philosopher Wittgenstein is sometimes interpreted as placing the role of philosophy in question and in jeopardy and concluding that philosophy can, at best, be a kind of therapy.[127] It cures us of using terms and arguments outside their natural use in linguistic practices, cures us of asking abstractly about the nature of reality, knowledge, or goodness. It directs us instead to attend to what goes on inside social/linguistic practices and how terms like "real," "know," and "good" acquire meaning through use. If philosophy survives at all, its role is to make us self-conscious about the nature of our practices or "language games" (which have as much to do with how we think as what we say).

One can agree with Wittgenstein about philosophy or "theory" and yet find it to be a fairly robust enterprise. The ways in which we are oblivious or unselfconscious about our practices can be considerable and can lead us to make odd and misleading claims. To the extent that moves within the practice *include* reflections about the practice, theory does not stand apart from but is included within it.

I have tried to spell out some of the consequences of seeing the external point of view of legal theory as dependent upon the internal point of view of individuals inside legal practices. The balloon of the theorist is tethered to Neurath's boat. To forget this is to indulge that dangerous arrogance of some theorists, those who devalue the role of internal points of view and do so at their peril.

---

126. *Supra* note 52 and accompanying text.

127. *See, e.g.*, THE INSTITUTION OF PHILOSOPHY: A DISCIPLINE IN CRISIS? (Avner Cohen & Marcelo Dascal eds., 1989).

Part II

Essays on Liberalism

[8]
Persons without History: Liberal Theory and Human Nature

For some time and from many standpoints liberalism has been under seige. It is attacked on both practical and philosophical levels. The last twenty years have seen the partial eclipse of the liberal Democratic agenda and the simultaneous erosion of the political label "liberal" as a term of confident self-regard. Ironically, the same period has seen a revival of political theory in general and of liberal theory in particular.[1] The relationship between liberal practice and theory is complex. Philosophic liberalism cuts across the boundaries of various practical political agendas; similarly, the practice of modern liberal politicians is rooted in various political theories. Certainly liberal theory is not coextensive with the current liberal political agenda.[2]

I shall consider whether liberal theory rests on a conception of experience that is inconsistent with human nature. I am concerned with the implications of the notion that liberal theory requires governmental neutrality with regard

---

[1] For affirmations and reformulations of liberal theory, see B. ACKERMAN, SOCIAL JUSTICE IN THE LIBERAL STATE (1980); R. DWORKIN, TAKING RIGHTS SERIOUSLY (1977) [hereinafter R. DWORKIN, RIGHTS]; R. NOZICK, ANARCHY, STATE AND UTOPIA (1974); J. RAWLS, A THEORY OF JUSTICE (1971); Dworkin, *Liberalism*, in PUBLIC AND PRIVATE MORALITY 113 (S. Hampshire ed. 1978) [hereinafter Dworkin, *Liberalism*]. For a comparison of Dworkin's position to that of Rawls and Nozick, see Dworkin & Magee, *Three Concepts of Liberalism*, NEW REPUBLIC, April 14, 1979, at 41. For critiques of liberalism, see S. HOOK, THE PARADOXES OF FREEDOM (1962); A. MACINTYRE, AFTER VIRTUE (1981); H. MARCUSE, ONE DIMENSIONAL MAN (1961); M. OAKESHOTT, RATIONALISM IN POLITICS (1967); R. WOLFF, THE POVERTY OF LIBERALISM (1968). For one of the more sweeping critiques of liberalism, see R. UNGER, KNOWLEDGE AND POLITICS (1975) (identifying liberalism with the underlying psychological, political, and epistemological strategies of modern philosophy since Descartes). For a narrower analysis that in part parallels the arguments of this article, see Galston, *Defending Liberalism*, 76 AM. POL. SCI. REV. 621 (1982).

[2] I discuss the relationship between liberal theory and practice in Part VI. *See also* Galston, *supra* note 1, at 627.

to conceptions of the good life and conceptions of how persons ought to live their lives. This notion is defended as the heart of liberalism by some of its most thoughtful and rigorous proponents.[3] Likewise, this idea is the primary target of liberalism's most influential critics.[4]

In Parts I and II I explain the relationship between political and moral neutrality. The requirement that government be neutral with regard to conceptions of the good life has two bases. One is the conviction that any institutional preference is illegitimate because it rests on an illegitimate moral judgment. Judgments about the superiority or inferiority of ways of life are, in this view, unjustifiable in principle. The illegitimacy of the moral judgment infects the consequent political judgment. A second basis for the neutrality requirement is that, even if moral judgments about ways of life can be justified, any institutional preference is illegitimate because of the nature of institutional constraint and power. Private moral positions should not, in this view, be translated into institutional policies. In Part I I proffer evidence that liberal theory is based on the first of these arguments. In Part II I evaluate that evidence by drawing more clearly the distinction between the two views.

Part III is a critique of the notion of moral neutrality as the basis for liberalism. The examination unavoidably raises epistemological questions. What do we know about human experience and how do we know it? Are political and other judgments grounded in common sense or in the more formalized learning of the social sciences? In what way is the social and cultural self-understanding of man relevant to the liberal project and to political and moral neutrality? I argue that these questions, however intractable, must be raised if the foundations of liberal theory are to be understood.

In Part IV I return to the alternative bases of liberal theory and political neutrality to consider two special, but flawed, arguments about institutional morality. One argument insists that political neutrality is mandated by equality. A second argument rests on the possibility of institutional abuse. I show that the first argument is incoherent and the second, while coherent, mandates something less than political neutrality.

In Part V I use my examination of liberal theory to illuminate the concept of freedom. I try to clarify the relationship between negative and positive freedom and examine the role that political and moral neutrality plays in this debate. In Part VI I summarize my conclusions about the relationship between liberal theory and practice and the role of institutional neutrality in the liberal political agenda.

---

[3] *See* Dworkin, *Liberalism*, *supra* note 1, at 127; J. Rawls, *supra* note 1, at 446-52.

[4] *See* Galston, *supra* note 1, at 621-22; *see also* "Between Utility and Rights" and "Rawls on Liberty and Its Priority" in H.L.A. Hart, Essays in Jurisprudence and Philosophy 148-247 (1983).

I. Institutional Neutrality and Human Nature

A. *Rawls, Dworkin and Neutrality*

John Rawls and Ronald Dworkin, two of liberalism's most thoughtful and influential contemporary exponents, rely on the notion of institutional neutrality as a basis for liberal theory.[5] Of course, any attempt to identify liberalism with contemporary writers, let alone with just two writers of any period, must run the gauntlet of predictable criticisms. Even the assumption that Rawls and Dworkin share a single theory demands more qualifications than I can set forth.

Rawls and Dworkin do not offer a theory of human nature.[6] They claim to be skeptical of the possibility of finding a determinate theory of human nature;[7] for them liberalism is the political theory that best accomodates such disquietude.[8] Their explicit concern is the moral justification of political and legal constraint.[9] When does constraint constitute just, fair, or respectful treatment? What kinds of constraint are compatible with diversity in pursuits of the good life?[10] Their central moral concern mandates that persons be equally well-positioned in conceiving and carrying out their particular plans of life.[11]

Under this view of institutional neutrality, liberty is a political value with a

---

[5] *See generally* Dworkin, *Why Liberals Should Believe in Equality*, N.Y. Rev. Books, Feb. 3, 1983, at 3 (insisting on moral neutrality only to the degree required by the notion of equality); Dworkin, *What Liberalism Isn't*, N.Y. Rev. Books, Jan. 20, 1983, at 47; Dworkin, *What Is Equality*, 10 Phil. & Pub. Aff. 186 (1981) (discussing distributional equality and theories of equal resources and welfare); J. Rawls, *supra* note 1, at 114.

[6] *See infra* text following note 32, where I distinguish between "thick" and "thin" theories of human nature.

[7] *See infra* Part II.

[8] In Parts II and III I explain and criticize the dependence of the liberal account of neutrality on moral skepticism. In Part V I argue that Dworkin, among others, tries to disassociate liberal neutrality from moral skepticism. Most liberal neutralists do not believe that political activity, as opposed to political abstinence, is necessary for the full realization of human potential. But what are the standards of human potential, and how fully realized must a life be before it can be encompassed by a determinate theory? I shall assume that a theory is determinate if it yields standards for judging whether others are living well or badly. I will leave open the question of whether a certain degree of moral responsiveness is a necessary part of living well.

[9] *See, e.g.*, R. Dworkin, Rights, *supra* note 1, at 272-75; J. Rawls, *supra* note 1, at 202.

[10] I have some reservations about the possible interpretations of the phrase "the good life." I wish it to connote shared intuitions about ways of living, particularly about what constitutes health and sickness, success and failure, and wisdom and folly.

[11] *See* R. Dworkin, *supra* note 1, at 272-78; J. Rawls, *supra* note 1, at 302.

distinctive role; liberty may be limited for its own sake, but for no other reason.[12] For example, when Rawls says that the right is prior to the good,[13] he means that a particular plan of life is morally justifiable if it is constrained by principles of justice under which everyone is equally well-positioned to realize life plans within the context of certain basic liberties. Thus, the first principle of justice is that "each person has an equal right to the most extensive system of basic liberties compatible with a similar system for all."[14] Dworkin's similar intuition is that the dispensation of political and legal rights must flow from government's equal respect and concern for individuals. Such rights must secure a system in which each person is positioned to realize the set of personal preferences that constitutes his or her individual conception of the good life.[15]

B. *A Closer Look at Neutrality*

Three dimensions of these views need further elaboration. First, the distinctive role of liberty in current liberal theory is illuminated by the tension between liberty and other values. Second, the neutralist account of liberalism may be explained as a critical rejection of utilitarianism. And third, the neutralist account implies an untenable view of human nature.

(1) Certainly any treatment of institutional neutrality must address the inevitable clash between the value of liberty and other conflicting values. The perennial balancing questions over conflicting exercises of liberty illustrate this point. For example, conflicts often arise between the freedom to hold and use property and freedom of expression. (Consider, for example, speechmaking or pamphleteering on the grounds of a private university or shopping mall.[16]) In addition, any treatment of liberty must distinguish between unconstrained actions that are morally justifiable and those that are not. This second point is illustrated simply by the very existence of criminal law, which condemns certain unconstrained actions as illegitimate uses of liberty.[17]

---

[12] *See* H.L.A. HART, *supra* note 4, at 232-38; J. RAWLS, *supra* note 1, at 60-65.

[13] J. RAWLS, *supra* note 1, at 446-52 (saying that considerations of right are prior to considerations of the good is a way of saying justice is prior to utility).

[14] *Id.* at 302.

[15] *See* Dworkin, *Liberalism*, *supra* note 1, at 127-28.

[16] *E.g.*, Pruneyard Shopping Center v. Robins, 447 U.S. 74 (1980) (holding that state protected right to petition and leaflet on private shopping mall property does not infringe on property rights under the taking clause of the fifth amendment); Cologne v. Westfarms Associates, 192 Conn. 48, 469 A.2d 1201 (1984) (holding that state constitution permits political advocacy group to distribute leaflets on private shopping mall grounds).

[17] This can be said about civil law as well. The criteria for criminalization are controversial in two ways. Controversies can easily arise over what conduct should be forbidden. In addition, there can be controversy over what it is that makes criminal acts criminal, i.e., what general feature (harm?) they have in common.

A theory of liberty can treat such balancing dilemmas in one of two ways. First, liberty can be regarded as an instrumental value, its significance in a particular act dependent on the significance of the end being pursued by that act. Significant and protectable ends might include security, enlightenment, and, in some instances, pleasure. The second approach, that chosen by Dworkin and Rawls, takes liberty as an independent value, significant even if we do not take into account the significance of other values or ends. Indeed, under their approach, liberty is an independent value precisely *because* we lack knowledge of the significance of other values.

In this second view, justifications for limiting or qualifying liberty must be framed by an appeal to liberty itself.[18] According to Dworkin, rights are not to be understood and justified from an insight of the good life or from any hierarchy of values.[19] Rather, they are justified by equal respect for individual lives and life plans. Such respect demands a procedure that heeds personal preferences (A's conception of living well for himself), but not external preferences (A's conception of how B should live).[20] Thus, equal respect really consists of maximizing the realization of each person's personal preferences to the extent possible without encroaching on others' realization of their life plans.

Rawls embraces a similar conception of liberty. The principle of maximizing liberties[21] has basic and constant priority over all other principles of justice. This means that no increment in other values—general security or welfare, for example—can justify a diminution of equally distributed basic liberties.[22]

Why do Rawls and Dworkin regard liberty this way? Their shared intuition

---

[18] *See, e.g.*, H.L.A. HART, *supra* note 4, at 208-21. I agree with Hart's interpretation of Dworkin. I am uncertain about the relationship between Dworkin's discussion of external and personal preferences and his discussion of policies in legislative decisionmaking. By properly determining and effecting policies, legislators are giving political voice to external preferences.

[19] Dworkin, *Liberalism, supra* note 1, at 128-40.

[20] For a critique of this distinction, see H.L.A. HART, *supra* note 4, at 208-21; *see also* Nickel, *Dworkin on the Nature and Consequences of Rights*, 11 GA. L. REV. 1115, 1125 (1977) (critiquing Dworkin's theory of external preferences); Richards, *Rules, Policies, and Neutral Principles: The Search for Legitimacy in Common Law and Controversial Adjudication*, 11 GA. L. REV. 1069, 1090 (1977) (arguing that the justification of principles, unlike social rules, need not depend on group acceptance).

[21] *See* J. RAWLS, *supra* note 1, at 195-257 (chapter IV); H.L.A. HART, *supra* note 4, at 226-32. Hart's discussion of the distinction between liberty and basic principles is very helpful. *See also* J. RAWLS, *supra* note 1, at 61 (Rawls's initial account of the notion of basic liberties).

[22] *See* J. RAWLS, *supra* note 1, at 195-257 (chapter IV); H.L.A. HART, *supra* note 4, at 226-32. Hart's discussion points out complexities and subtleties in Rawls's argument that I do not consider here.

is that no one way of living deserves special moral preference in the institutional fabric of society. Any such assignment would be arbitrary and in some sense discriminatory.[23] In developing this conception of liberty and neutrality Rawls and Dworkin presuppose that there are two levels of theory. The first level is the attempt to describe the good life, to assign a moral preference to one way of living. For Rawls and Dworkin, no such institutional preference can be justified; all preferences are equally worthy of respect. At the second level of theory is the justifiable preference for a system that maximizes the realization of life plans. Dworkin repeatedly says that the core of liberalism is that "government must be neutral on what might be called the question of the good life."[24] In what follows I question their distinction between these two levels of theory.[25]

(2) The fundamental agreement between Rawls and Dworkin on the special role of liberty helps us locate their account of liberalism on the map of moral and political analyses. In particular it helps us understand their shared rejection of utilitarianism. It is important to appreciate both what links them to utilitarianism and what in it they reject.

Liberal theorists criticize utilitarianism for not taking seriously the individual's own moral importance.[26] The utilitarian's justification of action is the collective common good. The welfare of any particular individual may in principle be overridden for a sufficiently great benefit to the community. In particular, each exercise of liberty or freedom is to be weighed against other constituents of the common good. In utilitarianism, liberty does not have constant priority as it does in Rawls's theory.[27] Similarly, Dworkin's notion of equal respect is intended as a corrective of the utilitarian "mistake."[28] He attempts to explain the moral significance of individual choices and to refer to the requisite conditions for melding conflicting life plans. At this level of criticism, liberalism claims to address utilitarianism's failings.[29]

---

[23] *See supra* text accompanying notes 38-40.

[24] Dworkin, *Liberalism*, *supra* note 1, at 127.

[25] *See infra* Parts II, III and IV.

[26] *See* R. DWORKIN, RIGHTS, *supra* note 1, at 94-100; J. RAWLS, *supra* note 1, at 22-27.

[27] *Compare* J. RAWLS, *supra* note 1, at § 82 (stating that liberty takes priority in ideal circumstances, although urgent material acquisitions can have some priority in nonideal circumstances) *with* J. MILL, ON LIBERTY 125-27 (1891) (arguing that society is justified in enforcing upon each citizen a proportionate share of the labor needed to free society from injury).

[28] R. DWORKIN, RIGHTS, *supra* note 1, at 199 (violations of human dignity, for example, are said to have no place in a utilitarian account).

[29] I am not suggesting that the utilitarian cannot reply effectively to the liberal's criticisms. Utilitarian writers have busied themselves with replies to Rawls and Dworkin and with refinements to utilitarianism. *See generally* R. BRANDT, A THEORY OF THE GOOD AND THE RIGHT 214 (1979) (discussing the interplay between rational choice and utilitarianism); Sen, *Rawls Versus Bentham: An Axiomatic Ex-*

None of this can obscure the shared dimensions of this version of liberal theory and utilitarianism. Both claim to be neutral with regard to differing conceptions of the good life. Both identify living well with the realization of life plans, whatever they may be. And each theory seems to have an arbitrary stopping point. Liberal theory rests with the intuition that if no preference can be justified, government must dispense rights so that all the governed are equally well situated to realize their individual life plans. Utilitarian theory rests with the intuition that if no preference can be justified, governments are required to secure the optimal mix of collective satisfactions.[30] Both intuitions, though not obviously untenable, are decidedly incomplete. What does it mean for the liberal to say that persons should be equally well situated? Should the content of the life plan be taken into account in determining whether a person is situated as well as others? For example, should a life plan that is evidently the product of self-delusion give rise to an inference that the chooser is not well situated and that the government is obliged to alter his circumstances? The liberal theorist would surely resist this kind of intervention, but it is not clear what theoretical adjustments he would have to make to accommodate this reservation. A utilitarian's response to this problem, on the other hand, would be to decide whether intervention would optimize the mix of collective satisfactions or, more simply, whether intervention would make society as a whole better or worse off. This too is an elusive task.

(3) There are several ways of characterizing the distinction between those theorists that are and those that are not neutral with regard to a conception of the good life. Dworkin, for example, identifies these respective poles unpersuasively with liberalism and conservatism.[31] But a theory that is not neutral (one that commends a particular view of the good life) may be radical

---

amination of the Pure Distribution Problem, in READING RAWLS 283 (N. Daniels ed. 1974) (a comparison of the decision rules yielded by the Rawlsian conception of justice and by classical utilitarianism).

[30] For a discussion of utilitarianism as a maximizing theory, see Marshall, *Egalitarianism and the General Happiness*, in THE LIMITS OF UTILITARIANISM 35 (H. Miller & W. Williams eds. 1982); *see also* S. SCHEFFLER, THE REJECTION OF CONSEQUENTIALISM 29 (1982) (arguing for a utilitarian conception of the collective good that provides a standard by which "some human interests can be judged more important than others").

[31] *See* Dworkin, *Liberalism*, *supra* note 1, at 128. Dworkin seems confused about the nature of conservatism. In his discussion of the conservative's attitude toward a market economy, he equates the dispositions of the utilitarian with those of the conservative. The utilitarian would favor a market economy but the conservative might well constrain it. *Id.* at 130. Dworkin undercuts his own position when he suggests that neutral principles can equalize the unequal opportunities available to individuals when seeking to realize their life plans. *Id.* at 132-33. It is unclear why the methods that determine when individuals have unequal opportunities are not the same methods that yield information about personal interests.

or revolutionary rather than conservative. And a conservative theorist may in certain ways espouse neutralism. In purporting to reject conservatism generally, Dworkin rejects only the special strain of conservatism that treats any consensus developed over time as meriting perpetuation *because* it is the received tradition. This particular type of conservative theory is indeed undermined by the insight that traditions can be the repository of prejudice and inhumanity as well as of wisdom.[32]

Another way of characterizing the distinction is as follows. Liberal theorists who offer a theoretical defense of neutrality characteristically rely on what I call a "thin" theory of human nature. Conversely, critics of such theorists can be said to rely on a "thick" theory. A thin theory is committed only to the notion of persons as framers of a conception of the good life, as loci of arbitrary preferences. Both liberals and utilitarians hold such a thin theory. Living well, in this view, means being in a position to choose and to satisfy one's choices. (The liberal distinguishes himself from the utilitarian by drawing different implications from the thin theory for the special place of liberty among values.) A thick theory, on the other hand, requires substantive standards for what it is to live well.

Having now identified some marks of the liberal theorist's concept of human nature and experience, with its emphasis on individuals as choosers of life plans, I shall argue in Part II that this concept governs moral as well as political judgment. The liberal theorists will be seen to offer a form of moral skepticism. In Part III I criticize the concept of human nature and experience underlying this form of moral skepticism.

II. Neutrality and Moral Skepticism

The liberal theory of neutrality may be motivated by either political or moral skepticism, two quite different rationales. Political skepticism questions the trustworthiness of governments and government officials and is not a theory of human nature per se. Political skeptics hold that if governments are allowed to allocate rights favoring a particular way of living, governments will abuse that power. Similarly, if persons are allowed political expression of their opinions about how others should live, they too will abuse that power.[33] Accordingly, we cannot allow political institutions or

---

[32] *See* R. Dworkin, Rights, *supra* note 1, 248-53.

[33] I do not consider whether Dworkin intends his strictures to apply to the decisions of legislators as well as judges and to citizens as well as officials. *See id.* at 89-90. Dworkin implies that judges, but not legislators, act improperly when they employ a conception of society's interest as a whole (such as setting policy rather than deciding on the basis of principle). Yet when Dworkin revises or refines this distinction, and condemns the expression of external preferences, he discusses legislators, citizens, and judges as actors in political roles.

citizens as political actors to favor a particular view of the good life. The possibility of coercion and abuse of those with different views of the good life is too strong.[34] The choice seems to be between limiting official power, on the assumption that officials cannot moderate themselves, and limiting the options of the governed, on the assumption that they might choose badly. The political skeptic opts for the former. In this light, the agenda of so-called political liberals fits liberal theory badly. The minimal role political skeptics allow government is more easily fitted to a conservative agenda.[35]

Whatever its merits, however, political skepticism cannot explain the position of Rawls and Dworkin. Political skepticism is an element of a remedial or non-ideal theory of just government, not an element of an ideal theory. Such skepticism anticipates political failure and tries to prevent it. Rawls's theory, though, is explicitly non-remedial.[36] For Rawls, liberty has constant priority over other values, not for prophylactic reasons, but because of the just circumstances of political association.

Similarly, political skepticism is not what motivates Dworkin. Were he a political skeptic he would be obliged to investigate the line between the use and abuse of relevant knowledge about living well, obliged to distinguish benign from malign external preferences. But he does not do so. To the contrary, Dworkin wants to neutralize all effects of external preferences: all use is abuse.[37]

Thus, the form of liberalism found in Rawls and Dworkin is grounded not on political skepticism but on moral skepticism.[38] Liberals generally deny that the criteria of the good life can ever be known. This is a view with a long pedigree, and I can do no more here than evoke the more familiar elements of the argument. One venerable basis is the so-called "is-ought" dilemma,

---

[34] *See* J. MILL, *supra* note 27, at 29-39. *See also* R. WOLFF, *supra* note 1, at 19-21 (a lucid discussion of the ways in which Mill's position has been used to support both welfare state liberalism and libertarianism).

[35] Certainly the modern welfare state offers up a rich set of questions requiring decision. Society must decide which aspects of human nature engender good citizenship and therefore deserve encouragement.

[36] *See* J. RAWLS, *supra* note 1, at 8-11 (analyzing the concept of social justice, not the ways it can be achieved in ongoing, imperfectly just, societies).

[37] *See* R. DWORKIN, RIGHTS, *supra* note 1, at 234-48; Dworkin, *Liberalism*, *supra* note 1, at 134. Clearly Dworkin accepts this conclusion, which seems inherent in the definition of personal and external preferences.

[38] Dworkin argues that he is not a skeptic: "Liberalism cannot be based on skepticism. Its constructive morality provides that human beings must be treated as equals by their government, not because there is no right and wrong in political morality, but because that is what is right." Dworkin, *Liberalism*, *supra* note 1, at 142. It should be clear that this does not answer the critic's charge that (a) any meaningful understanding of equal treatment must involve judgments about original opportunity, and (b) such judgments involve a determination of others' interests in such a way that preferences (life plans) are not determinative of interests.

which involves the claim that there is an unbridgeable gap between descriptive and normative judgments.[39] No description of the world or of experience can yield conclusions about what persons ought to do, particularly about how they ought to live their lives. To be sure, a moral skeptic concedes that we can investigate what makes people happy, what preferences people tend to have, and what their bodily needs are. But this investigation cannot determine whether persons ought to seek happiness (or how they ought to seek it), whether they ought to satisfy preferences (or which preferences they ought to satisfy), or whether they ought to be mindful of bodily needs.

It follows that man's accumulated knowledge is irrelevant to any conclusion about what persons ought to do to achieve the good life. Is the good life grounded in self-denial or self-indulgence? Perhaps one could decide this if one could uncover a distinctive human function, just as one can conclude that one has a good car in the light of the distinctive function of cars. But persons are not artifacts like cars and, it is said, one cannot claim a distinctive function for human beings.[40]

To summarize, the fundamental maxim of liberal theory as moral skepticism is that autonomy (the realization of individual identity)[41] consists of first, being able to act according to one's values, second, being the author of a life plan, and third, being aware that one is the author of such a plan, that one has this special kind of liberty. What distinguishes moral skepticism at this point is the view that no normative judgments can be made about particular life plans because there is no critical standpoint for evaluating

---

[39] For the traditional source of this argument, see D. Hume, *Treatise of Human Nature*, in 2 THE PHILOSOPHICAL WORKS 245-46 (T. Green & T. Grose eds. 1964). *See also* MacIntyre, *Hume on "is" and "ought"*, in THE IS-OUGHT QUESTION 36, 37 (W. Hudson ed. 1969) ("The standard interpretation [argues that] . . . Hume [is] asserting . . . that no set of non-moral premises can entail a moral conclusion."). Twentieth-century ethicists generally accepting Hume's argument include R. HARE, LANGUAGE OF MORALS 29, 44 (1952); P. NOWELL-SMITH, ETHICS 36-38 (1954); and A. PRIOR, LOGIC AND THE BASIS OF ETHICS 32-33 (1949).

[40] Attempts to theorize about the function of individuals (and the good life) are likely to find methodological support in Aristotle. *See* R. SULLIVAN, MORALITY AND THE GOOD LIFE: A COMMENTARY ON ARISTOTLE'S NICOMACHEAN ETHICS 28-33 (1977) (explaining Aristotle's analysis of the components of human action). But Aristotle is not the major naturalist targeted by Hume and others who employ the "is-ought" argument.

[41] Some of the assumptions in the Humean tradition of British empiricism parallel those of twentieth-century European existentialism. For example, in J. SARTRE, NAUSEA (1949) and A. CAMUS, THE STRANGER (1942), the overarching preoccupation is with radical freedom, the freedom to create through one's own choices whatever moral universe there can be. In addition, one of Kant's major themes is the individual's liberation from a personal history and submission to freely chosen rules and principles. Kant is of course a major influence on Rawls. *See generally* I. KANT, CRITIQUE OF PRACTICAL REASON 45 (C. Beck trans. 1956).

them. Values exist within life plans, but life plans as a whole cannot be ranked or judged by appeal to them. The implementation of external value preferences, views about how others should live, are seen as usurpations of personal autonomy.

The moral skepticism implicit in Rawls and Dworkin, which is at the heart of modern liberalism, stands in stark contrast to a long tradition of liberal thought. John Stuart Mill, the paradigmatic traditional liberal theorist, was essentially a political skeptic.[42] For him, critical standpoints for making moral judgments did exist. But Mill believed that the resulting models of the good life should not be embodied in the rules of political association.[43] Such rules, justified as being for the good of others, may be attacked as paternalistic.

III. A Critique of Moral Neutrality and Moral Skepticism

A. *Knowledge About Values*

Rawls and Dworkin do not claim to be moral skeptics. My suggestion that they are moral skeptics despite themselves is based on what is missing from their work as much as on what is there. For a non-skeptic, it is possible to know the criteria for living well and successfully. Obtaining such knowledge undercuts moral neutrality by undermining the notion that all life plans are equally worthy of respect and that equal respect of persons entails equal regard for their capacities as autonomous and self-conscious choosers of life plans. I shall consider how an argument for such knowledge can be made and what its (superable) obstacles are.

More than a quarter of a century ago, H.L.A. Hart, following David Hume,[44] referred to the minimal content of natural law, those few universal features of social experience that could be expected to shape the basic content of virtually all legal systems.[45] Predictably, social experience universally recognizes and responds to such needs as food, shelter, and security.[46] Hart's list was hardly an advance over the list Hume compiled 200

---

[42] The interpretation of Mill on this matter is controversial. Chapter Two of On Liberty, *supra* note 27, is largely given over to a description of the ways in which governments have abused their power over individuals and a warning that they are generally likely to do so. In Chapter Four, on the other hand, Mill implies that individuals are typically the best judges of their own interest. But throughout the entire discussion he never takes the position of a moral skeptic.

[43] *See* J. Mill, *supra* note 27, at 125-33.

[44] D. Hume, *supra* note 39, at § 2.

[45] *See* H.L.A. Hart, The Concept of Law 189-95 (1961). Hart appears to consider it a virtue of his account that the minimal content of natural law rests on a truism about human nature. It is difficult to see why more sophisticated and controversial claims about human nature (drawn from psychology, anthropology, etc.) might not also be candidates for foundational theories.

[46] *Id.*

years earlier. It selected only timeless, uncontroversial, and self-evident features of experience. Yet if these features would have been as evident to an observer at the dawn of history as they are to a contemporary, one might ask whether there are other such features that have been uncovered through the cumulative activity of human imagination. Why are the efforts to understand human nature by philosophers, artists, and others irrelevant? Though the liberal as moral skeptic is committed to perceiving such resources as meager and even nonexistent, an observer without skeptical bias might think them inexhaustible.

Two points undermine the skepticism that buttresses a commitment to neutrality. First, Hart's modest argument bridges the abyss between descriptive and normative discourse. Hart's point is not just that legal systems happen to respond to certain human needs and that some of those needs happen to be widespread. Hart says it is a "natural necessity" that the law serves these needs.[47] For Hart, this truth about the law is contingent merely on the plausible notion of "human beings and the world they live in retaining the salient characteristics which they [now] have."[48]

Secondly, *any* political program, even one predicated explicitly on neutrality, is in fact a normative constraint on the function of legal systems. To be sure, a program based on Hart's minimum content for legal systems does not in itself subvert neutrality. The features Hart picks out are not in themselves incompatible with a scheme that is basically neutral among life plans. However, the full political agenda that espouses neutrality must fail by its own standards to the extent that it misconceives the normative character of governing in general. Thus, there is inevitably a reservoir of shared knowledge about human nature and successful living. Equally inevitably, those who govern will have to draw on that reservoir.

Our cultural products survive, when they do, presumably because they both reflect and generate widely shared satisfactions and understandings. Novels, plays, movies, and other art forms not only express what we are but shape and alter our self-understanding. This process has been described as a hermeneutic circle.[49] Philosophical skepticism notwithstanding, there is no shortage of analyses that try to make explicit what is implicit in a given culture. It is probably a truism to say that social and political culture reflects and molds self-understanding. Our fundamental decisions—what we choose

---

[47] *Id.* at 195.

[48] *Id.*

[49] A traditional hermeneutic circle describes how the whole and the part, in the process of learning, are related in a circular way: in order to understand the whole it is necessary to know the parts, and in order to teach the parts it is necessary to know the whole. *See* D. Hoy, The Critical Circle: Literature, History, and Philosophical Hermeneutics vii, 166-68 (1978); *see also* H. Gadamer, Truth and Method 11 (1975) (expanding the role of the circle to describe man's self-understanding).

to criminalize, how we choose to house, feed, medicate, and educate, for example—are all arenas of substantial consensus as well as arenas of controversy.[50]

B. *Naturalism and Relativism*

What does this tell us? What does the attempt to understand human nature over time and in the face of diversity yield? It is easy to identify the Scylla and Charybdis of this task. On one hand, a unified image of the fully realized good life can be drawn from cultural representations of health and pathology, and from theories of psychology, sociology, and pedagogy. On the other hand, this image is arguably shattered by the simultaneous flourishing of mystical religious fundamentalism and earthbound Western humanism. The list of contrasting views of the good life is almost endless. The attempt to describe human nature, to be a naturalist, seems to falter in the face of relativism. And the relativist is, of course, the liberal theorist as moral skeptic.

The naturalist has several replies to relativism. The first is to argue that Western culture represents a powerful consensus. If one can trace a continuing thread in the dialogue over the nature of the good life from Aristotle through Freud and Kant, from Milton to Tolstoy and Bellow, from Michelangelo to Picasso, then perhaps the view of human nature arising from this "discussion" is to be taken more seriously than others. A second reply is that the naturalist is not trying to give an account of human nature valid for all times and places, but one valid for those times and places where categories of judgment involve arguments for and against liberalism. They are necessarily part of the so-called Western humanist tradition. Third, the theory of human nature that the naturalist is willing to defend may be expressed in subjective rather than objective characteristics and therefore may more convincingly be said to be universal. It may use notions like self-control, satisfaction, and self-knowledge, virtues like honesty and kindness. Such notions of success and failure in living are arguably transcultural.

I shall not take these three possible bases for naturalism any further, although I think each has merit. I want instead to consider a fourth reply, namely, that naturalism and relativism are not truly alternative positions at all. This view is that naturalism is a position that is the spontaneous expression of one's cultural and personal history. Each individual's personal history recapitulates to some extent the culture's history, the rediscovery of the cultural, social, and personal assumptions which give rise to standards of

---

[50] At times agreement seems to predominate; one can rest assured of a general dismissal of radical dissenters. At other times the range of possible alternatives seems very wide and there can be much disagreement. *See generally* J. FINNIS, NATURAL LAW AND NATURAL RIGHTS (1980) (discussing the nature of value consensus).

judgment. Such standards are expressed as knowledge about when others are acting in their own interest or against it, when they are flourishing or suffering. Relativism, on the other hand, is an unnatural position because it mandates standardlessness and commends agnosticism toward any knowledge of human flourishing, of success and failure.

It is easy to misunderstand this point. I am not giving a reason for embracing naturalism and rejecting relativism. My point is more complicated because it is dialectical. Though we live within a particular culture, we are compelled to be, at the same time, distanced from it. While holding and employing values, we simultaneously question them and know how limitedly we can defend them. We question the unknown or partially known reasons for our beliefs. This is to say that the values of self-examination and self-criticism have special roles in our culture. They are, from the naturalist point of view, ingredients necessary for living what many regard as a rational and successful way of life. But they tend to undercut their own ground by making it inevitable that we see the allure of relativism as a challenge to any confident assertion of particular values as "natural."

C. *Liberalism Reconceived*

It is time to return to the critique of liberalism. Given that standards of judging are spontaneous and inevitable, we must be able to make two distinctions. The first is between knowledge about well-being and mere preferences. It is one thing for me to prefer the company of A; it is quite another to know that I am better off with A. It is one thing to prefer that others live in a certain way; it is another to know that they are better off if they live that way. The liberal theorists who share Dworkin's framework must assume that the distinction is empty and that there are only preferences. (This is simply a restatement of moral skepticism and the need for value neutrality.) A second, closely related distinction is between preferences and interests. What one prefers is not necessarily in one's interest.[51] One's preferences about how others should live are not the same as a judgment about what is in their interest. While I do not deny that these distinctions are full of snares, I suggest only that the categories are intelligible and useful.

To make these distinctions is to claim that the perspective from which one uses such standards of judgment cannot be abandoned. The liberal theorist *qua* moral skeptic would have us move to a position of neutrality about the interests of others and the merits of life plans, but we cannot do so. This observation has distinctive implications from three points of view.

For one thing, the idea of personal freedom or liberty must be rethought. Liberty is not the liberty to determine, from a blank tablet, what one shall be and do and what values one shall have. It is rather the liberty to frame and

---

[51] *See* Schwartz, *Human Welfare: What It Is Not*, in THE LIMITS OF UTILITARIANISM 195 (H. Miller & W. Williams eds. 1982).

carry out choices within the history and values that one discovers and reappropriates.[52]

For the observer, neutrality is not available. This is not to say that the observer inevitably has a conception of the good life, of a particular mix of values and activities that mark the flourishing of human nature.[53] It is to say that he will inevitably be using and struggling with standards for judging, and will be trying to distinguish interests shared by mankind from interests that are personal and idiosyncratic. This will lead him to do what is incompatible with neutrality, to try to judge how well others know their own interests, and how close they are to satisfying them. Ideally, such judging will be done with discretion and care, and with respect for the freedom to experiment and err. Neutrality in action, expressed by the refusal to intervene except in exceptional circumstances, is not the same as neutrality in judgment; the latter is a mirage.

Finally, the point of view of the political or legal decisionmaker is a special instance of the point of view of the observer. Because of her special power to affect others, the decisionmaker must be especially respectful of idiosyncratic choices. She must also know that political institutions exist in part because wisdom about human affairs or knowledge about interest may not coincide with the popular will. If that is so, she cannot defer equally to all life plans. Moreover, *any* political decision resets the stage and adversely affects *someone's* life plan.

IV. Political Neutrality and Equality

A. *The Argument for Neutrality as Equal Respect*

To this point I have interpreted modern liberal theory as (1) advocating political neutrality, (2) based on moral neutrality regarding ways of living, and (3) mandated by moral skepticism. I also considered the possibility of justifying political neutrality on the basis of political rather than moral skepticism. However, the severance of political neutrality from moral skepticism requires further examination.

In his recent writings Dworkin has explicitly denied that he is a moral skeptic.[54] His arguments are initially appealing. He says he rejects the idea

---

[52] Analogies to the psychoanalytic model of human nature are relevant. *See* G. Klein, Psychoanalytic Theory, An Exploration of Essentials 275-79 (1979) (pointing out that human activity combines mere motor activity with a subjective self-conception).

[53] This is a centuries-old criticism of natural law theories. It would be interesting to trace the historical roots of Dworkin's disclaimers of a theory of the good life and his claims that there is a "right answer" to judicial questions. *See* R. Dworkin, Rights, *supra* note 1, at 279-90 (chapter 13).

[54] *See* Dworkin, *What Liberalism Isn't*, *supra* note 5, at 47.

that neutrality is justified by moral skepticism in favor of the idea that neutrality is based on a commitment to equality. Institutional neutrality is mandated by equality because neutrality is a way of showing respect for persons as equals, and any institutional preference for one way of living over another discriminates invidiously among persons. Since this argument, in one form or another, is one with which most liberals are familiar and to which many are sympathetic, it is important to see whether neutrality based on equality is a camouflaged form of moral skepticism or a genuine alternative to it.

Consider how Dworkin tries to demonstrate that he is not a moral skeptic. He argues that even if liberalism is neutral about ways of living, it need not be neutral about "what would count as a good society":

> Liberals can (and do) believe that politics should aim at a society of people who are happy rather than miserable, who respect rather than condemn one another, and who have an imaginative rather than a conformist approach to the question of what kinds of lives they should lead. Still less does it mean that politics must be neutral among principles of justice.[55]

But can politics aim at these goals and, at the same time, be neutral with regard to ways of living? Consider three responses that might show how this can be so, thus saving Dworkin's view from inconsistency.

First, one might hold that *all* ways of living lead equally well to happiness rather than misery, to mutual respect rather than condemnation. Clearly this is implausible. Obsessive lives with unattainable goals lead to misery rather than happiness; lives grounded in bigotry and self-righteousness are appropriately condemned. The project of respecting all life patterns equally will tend to undermine the "good society."

A second response is that *any* conscientious effort by the government to differentiate among ways of living will cause more unhappiness, more disrespect, and more conformity than a strict policy of maintaining neutrality. This too is hardly persuasive. A sincere and well-grounded policy of fostering open-minded and imaginative living is not certain to backfire. Some such policies will work better than others, but it is hard to see why the principle is misconceived *ab initio*.

Clearly, Dworkin has a third and more subtle response in mind. He is prepared to concede that some policies of fostering open-mindedness and encouraging mutual respect are properly part of a liberal program. Yet, in Dworkin's view, such policies do not breach the requirement of neutrality. It is hard to see how this can be so, although it is easy to see what examples Dworkin would cite to support his thesis. A proper policy of neutrality, by his lights, is one in which no particular religious preference is favored by government, or one in which persons with different kinds of sexual prefer-

---

[55] *Id.*

ence are equally protected by the law.[56] His policy of neutrality is one in which the government does not approve of some cultural activities and proscribe others. In these ways, official neutrality is likely to foster happiness, diversity, and mutual respect.

Dworkin's response is nonetheless weak. It resolves the apparent inconsistency in liberalism only by assuming that all kinds of religious practices, styles of living, and cultural practices are equally conducive to happiness and respect both for practitioners and for society at large. Homosexuals can be as happy (or unhappy) as heterosexuals. Lovers of punk rock can find as much enjoyment in their preferences as lovers of Bach. This may well be the case, but it is a stream of argument that rapidly runs dry when considerations other than potential happiness are at issue. Certainly not all kinds of religious practice and belief are equally conducive to a secular or political context of toleration and mutual respect. Not all styles of familial organization are likely to foster lives of imagination rather than conformity.

Thus, Dworkin's notion of neutrality is doubly vulnerable. First, it confuses respect for persons with blindness toward the perhaps destructive effects of the ways they may choose to live. Although this kind of liberal would like to think that all choices of sexual preference, cultural practice, and religious belief are equally congenial to a regime of mutual respect, it is not obvious that this is correct.[57] Even if it is, there is a second problem. The resolution cannot go as far as the liberal wants it to go, to toleration of the intolerant. It follows that the liberal must choose between neutrality on one hand and a political disposition that aims "at a society of people who are happy rather than miserable, who respect rather than condemn one another,"[58] on the other.

B. *Freeing Choosers and Determining Choices*

Dworkin has available one final argument, an argument which draws in a different way on the claim that political neutrality is based on equality. This

---

[56] *See, e.g.*, R. Dworkin, Rights, *supra* note 1, at 240-48 (discussing Lord Devlin's controversial position on law and morality).

[57] It is important to distinguish several points. First, I am certainly not denying that one may plausibly hold that religion A and religion B, or sexual preference A and sexual preference B, are equally conducive to happiness or successful living. I am merely suggesting that this type of argument is weak because it involves generalizations about heterogenous classes and their unmeasurable features. Second, the liberal's best argument is to concede that the possibility of happiness in these cases is indeterminable, and to argue for the desirability of free choice on that basis. Third, this point does not mean that all information is irrelevant to such choices. One can argue that, in the choice between a life of addiction to drugs and a drug-free life, the advantages of the latter are so clear as to permit government interventions. Cases must be decided on their individual merits; no general rule of neutrality seems to be supported by general intuitions.

[58] Dworkin, *What Liberalism Isn't*, *supra* note 5, at 47.

is to deny that equal respect means equal respect for one's *choices*, and to concede that a liberal cannot respect the choice of religious intolerance or personal bigotry.[59] Rather, equal respect means respect for persons as *choosers*. It involves separating the chooser from the choice, respecting the autonomy of the individual as a chooser but not necessarily respecting what the individual becomes if he chooses to be a bigot, fanatic, or conformist. Accordingly, neutrality and respect mandate policies that free the avenues of choice.

This gets us back to liberal theory's flawed characterization of the relationship between persons and life plans.[60] Dworkin's last point assumes that we can isolate judgments about conditions that prevent one from being a free chooser from judgments about the choices that are actually made. It assumes that government can intervene only to overcome conditions of the first kind. In this view, government can provide subsistence and education because these conditions set the background for choice and involve no breach of neutrality. Government thus does not delimit choice but leaves the individual free to "make" herself at the moment of choice into a homosexual, a zealot, or a devotee of the Rolling Stones.

The difficulty with this argument is that there is no way to distinguish those permissible interventions that raise a person to the plateau of becoming a free chooser from those impermissible interventions that violate neutrality by conditioning and shaping the choice. Of course, some interventions are easy to classify. Requiring early education in communication skills *does* contribute to making one a self-aware chooser. Outlawing homosexual acts *does* limit the range of choices. But most interventions defy classification because the values of open-mindedness, self-control, tolerance, and rational thinking are both preconditions of choice and desired values. Setting the conditions for achieving such virtues involves a clear violation of neutrality. Either we can try to secure the conditions of mutual respect or we can be neutral, but we cannot be both.

Dworkin says that the ideal of neutrality is preserved when "it cannot count, as a justification for any decision about the political . . . structure of our society, that either of us is inherently superior to the other, or that either's idea of a valuable life is superior."[61] But the liberal cannot preserve that ideal. The conclusion that he cannot do so can be expressed in two ways, as we have seen. First, one can say that the liberal must be committed, on pain of contradiction, to regarding as superior that idea of a valuable life that best comports with autonomous choice and mutual respect. Second, and more radically, one can say that the determination of when one is so

---

[59] R. DWORKIN, RIGHTS, *supra* note 1, at 275-78.

[60] *See supra* Parts I and II. I reject the notion of individuals as simple and autonomous choosers of life plans. The process of growth and development is a mixture of interdependent internal and external forces and opportunities.

[61] Dworkin, *What Liberalism Isn't*, *supra* note 5, at 48.

situated that one can frame the "idea of a valuable life" freely is conditioned by determinations about what sorts of lives are superior to others. In either case, the ideal is unattainable.

It follows that political neutrality remains undefended as a tenet of liberal theory. On one hand, it cannot be supported by moral skepticism if moral skepticism is itself indefensible, resting on a false picture of experience and judgment. On the other hand, it cannot be supported by the requirement of equal respect. The creation and maintenance of a political structure in which respect is sustained requires that genuine self-reflection and autonomy be fostered. If respect is taken seriously, government can be neutral only among those choices that are genuine avenues of such self-realization.

C. *Political Skepticism Reconsidered*

Consider again political skepticism.[62] This view concedes that we can choose among ways of living, and that we know which ways are more likely to be successful, happy, and worthy of respect. But the political skeptic holds that governments are likely to botch the job. Neutrality is offered as a prophylactic policy. While political skepticism is a coherent and persuasive argument, it is hard to accept as a general and uniform truth. A government that should not be trusted to endow and favor particular forms of cultural expression might well be trusted to provide the conditions for mental and physical health. While governments can certainly abuse the mandate to secure, for example, conditions of mental and physical health, the likelihood of such abuse cannot be determined as a matter of principle. Some judgments about health needs are more controversial than others. Some interventions are more disruptive than others, and some are more likely to be freely accepted by the beneficiary. Certainly, governments that would intervene bear a heavy moral burden of proof. But that is a far cry from moral skepticism, from saying that we cannot in principle know what conditions are better or worse, or that we must advocate political neutrality because that is how we secure the conditions of mutual respect. It is also a far cry from saying that even the wisest and most benign government will inevitably guess wrong.

V. Negative and Positive Freedom

A. *The Relationship Between Negative and Positive Freedom*

The debate among political theorists about "two concepts of freedom," stirred if not initiated by Isaiah Berlin,[63] provides an opportunity to clarify my critique of the neutrality of liberal theory. First, consider Gerald MacCal-

[62] *See supra* Part II.

[63] Berlin, *Two Concepts of Liberty*, in Four Essays on Liberty 118 (1969).

lum's convincing argument that freedom (or liberty)[64] always posits a triadic set of relations such that A (an actor) is free from B (some constraint) to do C (an act, a range of actions, etc.).[65] Negative and positive freedom, therefore, are not two distinct concepts so much as they are different aspects of the single notion of constraint. The proponent of negative freedom holds that one is free to the extent one is not prevented by law or other governmental intervention from doing what one chooses to do. The proponent of positive freedom maintains that freedom is only enjoyed by the person who, in addition, is free of internal constraint. This implies that she possesses the conditions of self-realization. Charles Taylor lists these conditions as self-awareness, self-understanding, moral discrimination, and self-control.[66]

Negative freedom is not necessarily the absence of rules. It follows from the strict definition of negative freedom that persons have more freedom in a state of nature than in a civil society with, for example, criminal prohibitions. One can kill or steal only in a state of nature. But those who would kill and steal exercise their freedom by undercutting the freedom of their victims. Thus the proponent of negative freedom must choose between anarchy and civil society with its prohibitions on the freedom to prey on others. Choosing the latter maximizes only *significant* exercises of freedom, not indiscriminate or licentious exercises of freedom.

B. *Semantic Issues*

Before exploring the implications of the two concepts let us clarify some semantic issues. Consider first the different nuances of liberty and freedom. Liberty seems to be a political virtue. Liberties are conceded to citizens by the state (in a bill of rights, for example) and safeguarded by the state. Liberty in the state of nature is a self-contradictory notion. Freedom, on the other hand, is more general, and liberty seems to be a special kind of freedom. One can talk about freedom and constraint in the state of nature as well as in civil society. In this section, I have chosen to consider freedom rather than liberty because it is the more comprehensive notion.

A second issue is that the term "freedom" is obviously used in mutually incompatible ways, ways that support both negative and positive theories of freedom. On one hand we say that a person must be free to make mistakes, free to be self-deluded or ignorant. On the other hand, we espouse positive freedom when we say that one is not really free if she lacks relevant information or suffers from self-delusion. We speak of freeing someone from ignorance. Usage, therefore, will not resolve the debate.

---

[64] MacCallum, *Negative and Positive Freedom*, in PHILOSOPHY, POLITICS AND SOCIETY 174 (4th Series, P. Laslett, W. Runciman, & Q. Skinner eds. 1972).

[65] *Id.* at 176.

[66] Taylor, *What's Wrong with Negative Liberty?*, in THE IDEA OF FREEDOM 179 (A. Ryan ed. 1979).

A third point about the use of these concepts is that, contrary to McCallum's suggestion, the debate is not a question of value disguised as a question of fact. He argues that questions about when persons are free and what is to count as an interference with freedom are confused with questions about when persons are best left to act freely and what is a legitimate interference with freedom.[67] He concludes that proponents in the debate can agree on answers to the factual questions and can agree to disagree about the values, about what is best and what is legitimate. This, for MacCallum, is the real underlying debate.

MacCallum is wrong insofar as theorists of negative freedom often claim to make factual points when they deny the existence of inner constraints. They claim to believe that the existence of inner constraints has nothing to do with freedom. They assume that inner constraints are so speculative that any attempt to deal with them is tantamount to imposing (what Dworkin calls) an external preference on another. The response to MacCallum is that it is far from clear that we can distinguish questions of fact from questions of value in this area, and that it may be senseless to try to do so.

This point can be clarified by linking it to moral skepticism since, as we have seen, the strategy of separating fact from value is a cherished strategy of the moral skeptic.[68] Applying this strategy to the problem of negative and positive freedom, the skeptic might conclude with MacCallum that the debate is about values, about the range of the three variables discussed above. The disagreement would be about what interventions are legitimate, and about when persons are best left alone. The moral skeptic concludes that these determinations are expressions of personal preference and that freedom truly exists when we decline to apply our personal preferences to others.

The response to the moral skeptic is that the existence and nature of inner constraints is a factual matter, and only the theorist of positive freedom is willing to consider inner constraints. The skeptic's (and MacCallum's) distinction between questions of fact and questions of value is unhelpful and untenable. In particular, it cannot be used by the proponent of negative freedom to defend his view that all attempts to affect inner constraints are illegitimate applications of preferences.

I addressed this strategy of labeling facts as mere value preferences above when I defended the distinction between knowledge and external preference and between interest and personal preference.[69] Just as we know that it is not in the interest of persons to be enslaved or to be told how they must use their property or their leisure, we know that it is not in their interest to be ignorant, lack self-awareness, or be without self-control. We do not merely *prefer* that they be self-aware. (We may, in fact, prefer that those

[67] MacCallum, *supra* note 64, at 192.

[68] *See supra* text accompanying notes 33-35.

[69] *See supra* text accompanying notes 18-20.

whom we would exploit not be self-aware.) Our justifiable actions affecting others are based on our *knowledge* about their own interests and their well-being, not on our mere external preferences. Sometimes we are more clearly aware of the interests of others than they are themselves.[70] Freedom, as the notion of positive freedom demonstrates, is best realized when the actor's preferences and interests coincide.The proponent of negative freedom, like the liberal theorist who stresses neutrality, claims not to have a theory of human nature. Yet if my analysis is correct, he is committed to one that makes tacit normative judgments about external constraints, a theory that is implausible because it denies that internal constraints can alienate a person's actions from her interests.[71]

C. *Neutrality and Positive Freedom*

I have said nothing yet about neutrality or the particular role of government in the realization of freedom. The liberal neutralist may concede that there are external constraints and still argue that, to maximize freedom, government could abandon neutrality with regard to the external, but not the internal, constraints of the governed. There are three arguments for this position, and each can be refuted.

The first is that each individual's choice is an expression of that person's values, and that no critical standpoint exists for judging these choices except from the critic's own arbitrary preferences. This is the position of the moral skeptic, and I have shown why this is inadequate.[72]

The second argument draws on the notion of equal respect. It says that, whether or not there exists a moral standpoint for criticizing the choices of others, equal respect mandates treating the governed as equally competent choosers once the government has provided a plateau of opportunity. From this plateau choices made are without external constraint.

---

[70] This point can be easily abused. A fuller treatment is given in Taylor, *supra* note 66, at 187-89.

[71] To be sure, we describe the effects of the two kinds of constraint in different ways. When the constraint is external, we tend to say that the person is unable to act on her interest, but also unable to realize her preference. When the constraint is internal, we tend to say she acts on her preference, and that it is adverse to her interest. But there are exceptions even to these conventions of usage. An external constraint that is not physical, but economic or psychological, can affect preferences so that the actor prefers to remain constrained. The exploited employee can come to prefer the system of exploitation to destitution while unemployed. Similarly, an internal constraint may not necessarily work by affecting preferences. Lack of self-control may lead the actor to do neither what is in her interest nor what she prefers. In any case, the most helpful insight in all these examples is the identification of freedom with the capacity to recognize and pursue one's interests. The theorist of positive freedom is better able to represent these several dimensions of freedom.

[72] *See supra* Part III.

For reasons given in Part IV, it is unclear how this notion of respect is to be interpreted and why it should be compelling. One of the undisputed grounds of the argument is that some external conditions, such as compulsory education and mandatory treatment for the severely self-destructive, provide the necessary plateau for unconstrained choice. Yet this concedes my basic point; external conditions *necessarily* reshape one's internal preferences and the characterization of one's available personal choices. If basic interventions in the areas of education and health are justified, where is the line to be drawn? Certainly many other types of well-intentioned interventions, likely to put persons in touch with their own interests, could also be justified as a manifestation of respect. There is no clear distinction between setting the conditions for identifying one's interests and setting the conditions that predetermine which interests will seem most compelling. The internal constraints of self-awareness and self-control are not merely conditions of choice. The attempt to secure them as conditions will also shape the choices that are made. Thus, respect for individuals should not be identified solely with neutrality; rather, it should be identified with the maintenance of conditions that foster self-awareness and self-control, both as conditions of choice *and* as aspects of the very choices that are made.

The third argument is the argument of the political skeptic. In this view the institutions of the state are suited to securing protection from external but not internal constraint. David Cooper, writing on positive and negative freedom, says that the genuinely free man "will think that it is through education, culture, and most of all personal endeavor—rather than through legal and political arrangements—that his freedom will be won."[73] The distinction is useful but in part artificial. Political institutions determine the character of education and culture. The question is not whether, but how, education and culture are affected by political policies. No government, under the guise of respect for neutrality, can disclaim responsibility for how education and cultural opportunities appear to its citizens.

Nonetheless, Cooper's distinction between education and culture on one hand and political arrangements on the other is helpful. We have seen that in dealing with external constraint, political institutions alleviate constraint by constraining. This is not a paradox. Laws constrain persons, either officials or private individuals, from constraining others. Thus, governments are constrained from interfering with free expression. Internal constraints, on the other hand, are not typically removed by political external constraint. External constraints involve two agents, she who would interfere and she who would be the victim of interference. The first is constrained so that the second is free. With internal constraints, there is only one agent, and it seems paradoxical to think that one can be forced to be free. The notion, to be sure, is not incoherent and has clearest application in the compulsory treatment of those who, through temporary derangement, would do violence

[73] Cooper, *The Free Man*, in OF LIBERTY 134 (A. Griffith ed. 1983).

to themselves. It is also arguably appropriate as a characterization of compulsory education. But the notion will not go very far. Self-awareness and self-control are dispositions that must be nurtured, not elicited by command. In this way, Cooper is correct that culture and education, not politics and law, are the appropriate arenas for such nurture.[74]

VI. Theory and Practice

I raised at the outset the question of how closely liberal practice is to be identified with the theory of neutrality. Given the scope of this article, I cannot do this question full justice. I shall look briefly at only two aspects of this question, first, whether liberal practice seems to presuppose the theory of neutrality, and second, whether the theory of neutrality seems to imply liberal practice.

(1) Dworkin lists some of the elements of liberal practice or policy when he says that liberals are generally thought to be "for greater economic equality, for internationalism, for freedom of speech and against censorship, for sharper separation of church and state, for greater procedural protection for accused criminals, for decriminalization of 'morals' offenses . . . and for an aggressive use of the central government power to achieve these goals."[75] Putting aside whether these goals are mutually compatible or whether they are still part of the liberal agenda, the question remains: are they best realized through the principle of governmental neutrality, or are they better seen as the embodiment of a particular recommended kind of life?

It is tempting to try to reconcile the two positions by saying that the program does embody a particular ideal, encouraged by government, and that the ideal is simply freedom of choice. This is ambiguous. The principle of neutrality is captured by this reformulation only if freedom is understood as radical freedom. Each element of the liberal program can then be seen as a way of making it more likely that persons are free to choose their values, to live without determination. But if the idea of radical freedom is a chimera, then the underlying conception of liberal practice seems to be that certain determinants of choice are properly seen as constraints and are to be minimized, while other determinants are to be seen as appropriate cultural preconditions of choice. The liberal thus claims to know that persons are

---

[74] Consider one last possible misunderstanding. The notion of freedom as positive freedom is not the same as the notion of radical or absolute freedom. Radical freedom couples the conclusion that there are internal as well as external constraints with the suggestion that to be truly free is to be free from the influence of others. We have already seen why this romantic notion is a chimera. *See* Taylor, *supra* note 66, at 180-81. Just as we must distinguish our preferences from interests, we must distinguish constraints from historical and personal determinants that have become part of our nature. It is helpful to recall that for the relativist, all life plans are of equal value. Similarly, for the proponent of radical freedom, all determinants are constraints.

[75] Dworkin, *Liberalism*, *supra* note 1, at 113.

best off when they are made aware of a plurality of nonofficial religions, when different kinds of cultural products clamor for their attention, when they are aware of themselves as choosers among such options and strive for self-knowledge and self-control. The liberal not only claims to know this about others; he also claims to know that it is valuable for the individual to know this about herself or himself. If liberals thus try to create institutions that fortify a particular conception of human nature, their theory is badly misrepresented by the ideal of neutrality.

(2) The second question is whether Rawls's and Dworkin's theory of neutrality implies anything like the elements of the liberal agenda. The discussion in Part IV suggests that it does not, and that the theory of neutrality is indeterminate with regard to political agenda.

One way of developing this idea further is to take seriously the concept, dear to the liberal neutralist, of a plateau of choice from which a life plan can be projected. The neutralist has the burden of saying which interventions are justifiable because they raise persons to that plateau, and which are not justifiable because they predetermine the choices that would be made once the plateau is reached. But it is quite arbitrary how a particular intervention is classified. From one point of view freedom of expression and economic redistribution make choice equally available. From another they mean that the loudest or most powerful voices will shape public opinion.

These remarks need three final qualifications. First, the distinction among politicians will not be between those who are for and those who are against freedom of expression or economic redistribution. It will be among those who would support different systems of free expression and redistribution. Second, I emphasize that I am in no way criticizing the liberal agenda or saying that it cannot be justified. My point is only that it must be defended by arguing from a completely articulated theory of human interests and experience on which it rests, not by denying that it rests on such a theory. Third, a resolution of the controversy among differing attitudes toward, for example, free expression, must begin by conceding that any system of free expression enhances awareness of alternative courses of action, *but also* shapes the world in which those courses exist, cutting off other imaginable courses of action and shaping the attitudes of the chooser. This is the truth that the relativist is concerned to convey. It is, as we have seen, a partial truth. The naturalist reminds us that, however self-critically we do so, we also inhabit a set of standards that allows us to judge just what realizations of freedom contribute to the fullest realization of human nature.

[9]
Liberalism and the New Skeptics

The concept of autonomy is the bulwark of liberal theory in politics and law. Accordingly, contemporary debates between liberal and communitarian theorists frequently concern the role, nature, and scope of individual rights implementing autonomy. Joel Feinberg has been as persuasive as anyone in explaining and defending the liberal theory of rights. Notwithstanding his powerful analysis,[2] liberalism and the concept of rights remain controversial among legal and political theorists who reject some of the presuppositions of his approach. The contemporary forms of critical jurisprudence – critical legal studies, feminism, critical race theory, neopragmatism, modern civic republicanism – incorporate skeptical forms of antifoundational arguments. The picture of law and society generated by these antifoundational arguments is, according to critical theory, incompatible with the liberal account of rights.

I begin by summarizing Feinberg's interpretation and defense of a liberal account of rights. In part II, I explain the skeptical version of antifoundationalism and show how it constitutes a strong thread that ties together various forms of critical jurisprudence. Then in part III, I discuss a different version of the antifoundational argument, a version that does not incorporate skepticism. I argue that the skeptical form of antifoundationalism is flawed because it involves a paradox about theory and practice, a paradox that implicates the metaphor of (the scholar-observer) being inside/outside a practice or conceptual scheme. In part IV, I defend the second version of antifoundationalism, purged of its skeptical basis and the accompanying paradox. Finally, in part V, I reassess the liberal account of rights in the light of this revised antifoundational critique and, more generally, relate liberalism to individualism.

I. Liberalism, communitarianism, and rights

The liberal conception of rights rests on a principle of limited government. It presumes that government prevents and mediates conflicts among persons through rules that define and safeguard personal autonomy. Government, according to this principle, may not use law to restrict autonomy to shape and condition persons' preferences. It may not, in other words, tell persons what they may say and do or place conditions on what they say and do, unless such limitations are justified in terms of autonomy. "Autonomy" embraces both liberty and equality: Legal interventions may be justified in terms of autonomy when they protect the liberty of persons *and* when they are consistent with rights of action being distributed in an egalitarian way.

The catechism of legal rights spells out, in part at least, the dimensions of autonomy protected by the state through law. The history of the Supreme Court's interpretation of the Bill of Rights offers up countless examples of the protection of autonomy *and* of its costs. The enforcement of civil rights and liberties characteristically has social costs and is therefore controversial. For example, the exclusionary rule, derived form the Fourth and Fifth Amendment rights of criminal defendants, restricts the use of evidence even when such evidence is indisputably probative and reliable. The protection of First Amendment rights allows the dissemination, largely without regard to content, of newspapers, magazines, television programs, and other media that shape our shared environment. No one would argue that what is offered is for the most part edifying.

Feinberg's characteristically careful and open-minded defense of liberalism responds to such controversies. First, he clarifies the scope and intent of liberal theory. For Feinberg, liberalism is neither a theory about human nature nor a theory about social interaction.[3] In particular, it does not rest on an individualistic claim that "each person is an atom, or island, whose essential character is formed independently of the influences of social groups and who is in principle self-sufficient."[4] Autonomy characterizes neither human essence nor actual social conditions but describes a fundamental norm under which persons, whatever their nature and whatever their mutual dependence, are able to experience respect and exercise choice.

Having addressed the scope of liberalism, Feinberg answers the first of two substantial communitarian challenges. So-called communitarian theorists argue that some account of the common good is an essential ingredient of political justification and that liberal theory is flawed because it precludes any justification of governmental acts by reference to the common good. Feinberg responds that some conceptions of the common good, for example a conception of loyalties based on "mutual respect" and "devotion to the ideal of a national community in which an unrestricted myriad of social groups prosper and flourish,"[5] are in fact *implicit* in liberalism and in the idea of a community of autonomous persons. On the other hand, Feinberg points out, critics who argue that more controversial characterizations of the common good should play a justificatory role tend in fact to demand that legal interventions be justified by the common good *even when* they do not comport with social justice and respect for the rights of persons. In other words, either appeals to the common good are innocuous from the liberal standpoint because they reinforce respect for the rights of autonomous persons or they are to be unacceptable precisely because they fly in the face of such rights.[6] Note that this response does not rule out in principle the common good as an *independent* justification, but it emphasizes the cost of doing so. For the liberal the cost of choosing the common good over justice and rights is always too high.

Feinberg also addresses the second substantial communitarian challenge, that the liberal ignores the value of tradition and the role of law as a repository of traditional values.[7] Again, Feinberg poses two circumstances. Liberals can accommodate traditions when preserving them comports with respect for persons' autonomy, but when tradition is not compatible with such respect for the rights of persons, preserving tradition is too costly.

Feinberg points out that liberals are wary of using tradition as the repository of shared ideals when doing so frustrates pluralism. A society embraces many subcommunities and many traditions. "When each person is a member of many groups, the phenomenon of overlapping membership is greatly magnified. The naturally diverse needs and attitudes of the people will unite some in one context and separate them in another."[8] For liberals, communitarian appeals to tradition often disguise contests between the will of the majority and the non-conforming preferences of individuals. Accordingly, nontraditional choices that neither harm nor offend other discrete individuals in significant ways deserve protection from majority coercion.[9]

Liberalism, in the view that underlies Feinberg's analysis, holds that rights and autonomy are related conceptually and instrumentally. Conceptually, the realm of autonomy is defined by the scope of rights. But the ongoing articulation of rights through legal and political decision making is also the instrument or vehicle by which autonomy is secured. The difference between liberals and communitarians is a difference between two forms or styles of justification. For liberals, the first question regarding any legal intervention is its effect upon relevant rights; rights trump justifications based on appeal to the common good. For communitarians, the scope of rights is limited by *prior* delineation of the common good. Liberals and communitarians thus invert each other's justificatory priorities.[10]

II. Critical theory

A premise of the liberal debate with communitarians is that conflicts between autonomy rights and the common good will be exceptional. In general the common good can be pursued in harmony with the rights of persons. The disagreement between liberals and communitarians focuses on whether rights trump the common good or whether the common good trumps rights in the relatively narrow domain of conflict.

Duncan Kennedy, as a proponent of critical legal studies, questions the possibility of valid and neutral criteria for deciding such questions and offers what may be regarded as an antifoundational critique of liberalism. Both liberalism *and* communitarianism can be seen as foundational theories at least to the extent that they rest on the possibility of justifying policies by appeal to neutral criteria, the possibility of evaluating political arrangements and legal decisions objectively. (In part IV, I discuss antifoundational forms of liberalism.) Kennedy challenges the possibility of having and using such criteria. He argues that "there are two opposed modes for dealing with substantive [legal] issues . . . individualism and altruism. . . . [W]e are divided, among ourselves and also within ourselves, between irreconcilable visions of humanity and society, and between radically different aspirations for our common future."[11] Nonetheless, "the rhetoric of individualism so thoroughly dominates legal discourse at present that it is difficult even to identify a counterethic."[12] Liberalism, with its focus on autonomy and rights as a trump, expresses that individualist ideal.

Altruism, on the other hand, "enjoins us to make sacrifices, to share, and to be merciful. It has its roots in culture, in religion, ethics and art, that are as deep as those of individualism."[13] Altruism underlies the communitarian regard for tradition and the common good. It denies both the "arbitrariness" and the "subjectivity" of values. "Ends are collective and in process of development."[14]

Even though Kennedy stresses that "the 'freedom' of individualism is negative, alienated, and arbitrary" and "has no moral content whatsoever,"[15] he does not defend altruism over individualism. He is concerned instead with the epistemological significance of both modes and of their inevitable clash within our debates. "We cannot 'balance' individualist and altruist values. . . . The only kind of imagery that conveys the process by which we act . . . is that of existential philosophy. We make commitments and pursue them."[16]

Kennedy echoes liberals in rejecting the communitarian assumption that rights must be balanced against the common good. But he does so for altogether different reasons. Liberals hold that rights have priority over interests (or the common good) while Kennedy suggests that decision makers opt "existentially" for some notion of the common good and circumscribe their accounts of rights accordingly. In this sense, Kennedy is sympathetic to communitarians. Nonetheless he distinguishes himself from "altruists" because his references to "existentialist" commitment imply that values used by decision makers are arbitrary and subjective.

Kennedy's tale is essentially one of reciprocal delusion. Liberals are deluded in thinking that individualist values provide a neutral standpoint for decision making, neutral among conflicting conceptions of the common good. Altruists are deluded in thinking that the conceptions of the common good that they deploy are anything but arbitrary or subjective. Liberals and communitarians, for better or worse, simply make commitments with regard to ends and the shared goals of community and implement those commitments.

In light of this analysis, critical theorists such as Kennedy characterize law in terms of power, domination, conceptual relativity, and legitimating ideologies. If law is the arena of conflicting and arbitrary values or value-compromises, and if power is unevenly distributed, then law is bound to embody the choices of those with power. So-called neutral justifications of the legal system through foundational arguments, the kind of arguments that he sees as the core of liberalism, mask systems of domination. The true nature of the system may *also* be masked from the dominators. "The ruling class itself is taken in by legal ideology; it believes that it's acting justly when it acts according to law, that everyone is getting approximately the best possible deal, and that change would make everyone worse off."[17] The prevailing political and social rhetoric becomes a legitimating conceptual and ideological scheme for maintaining "hegemony."

Many feminist theorists and critical race theorists draw on this fund of ideas. Feminists have two characteristic analytic postures. Some argue that the experiential differences between men and women give women a distinctive "voice" and orientation. The conception of rights embodied in individualism, based on separateness and on the distinctiveness of each person, is a so-called masculinist position. Unlike men, women gain access by virtue of their "hedonic" experience to a distinctive way of regarding what is important personally and socially. They may express that view with different concepts.[18] The importance of the concept of rights in liberalism and of a neutral, foundational argument for rights is thus tied to male conceptual demands.

Radical feminists, representing a different feminist position, embrace the paradox that women, having been dominated and subjected to male categories over history, are alienated from their distinctive voice. "Feminism criticizes this male totality without an account of our capacity to do so or to imagine or realize a more whole truth. Feminism affirms women's point of view by revealing, criticizing, and explaining its impossibility."[19] The fissure that entails an antifoundational form of argument is not, as it is for Kennedy, between irreconcilable values or political choices. It is deeper, a division grounded in epistemology and language. Domination has deprived women, on this view, of the tools to express their experience and their dignity.

"Different voice" feminists and radical feminists agree in regarding the liberal language of rights, insofar as it has pretensions of neutrality and objectivity, as a "legitimating ideology" for a male conceptual perspective. According to Robin West, the "total subjective experience of masculinity" entails the fundamental value of autonomy as separateness. Only the male ideal is reflected by the concern that "[t]he individual must be treated by his government (and by others) in a way that respects his equality and his freedom"[20] through the definition and protection of autonomy by a system of rights.

The antifoundational position shared by critical legal theorists like Kennedy and feminist theorists is elaborated by Roberto Unger. He says critically that the role of rights within liberalism, with its claim to be based in an atemporal, nonideological, nongender-based view of autonomy, dissolves into a discredited doctrine asserting "a canonical form of social life and personality that could never be fundamentally remade and reimagined [illegible] [The history of liberalism] consists in the attempt to deflect the critique of objectivism and formalism by accepting some of its points while saving increasingly less of the original view."[21]

Feminism's critique of objective foundations is echoed in critical race theory, which attempts "to identify and emphasize . . . what *distinguishes* the 'voices' of minority men and women from the voices of other persons."[22] Many race theorists reject the so-called homogenization of persons implicit in arguments for autonomy and the implication that the liberal conception of rights of autonomy embodies objective values rather than the preferences of a dominant race.

The antifoundational arguments of critical legal theory, from critical legal studies through feminism and critical race theory, have their philosophical ground in the work of Richard Rorty. His highly influential contemporary version of pragmatism concludes that the assumption and pursuit of "objectivity" is an illusion. He argues that "it is useless to hope that objects will constrain us to believe the truth about them, if only they are approached with an unclouded mental eye, or a rigorous method, or a perspicuous language."[23] The liberal account of autonomy and rights aspires to be objective in this sense, to explain the importance of personal respect and dignity by a rigorous method and with an unclouded eye. It presupposes the possibility of a posture of neutrality with regard to political agendas and personal goals. For Rorty, what is crucially in error is "the tradition in Western culture which centers around the notion of the search for Truth. . . . [This tradition] is the clearest example of the attempt to find a sense in one's existence by turning away from solidarity to objectivity."[24]

Rorty concludes that only solidarity as "the idea of Truth as something to be pursued . . . because it will be good for oneself, or for one's real or imaginary community"[25] adequately justifies political and social ends. The most we can do is to offer competing conceptual schemes and remain mutually engaged in endless "conversations"[26] – the conversations between the genders, between the races, and between the empowered and the powerless.

III. Inside and outside: skepticism

Kennedy's critical attack on objectivity and the liberal account of rights rests on the metaphor of inside/outsideness. Insiders characteristically entertain the illusion of objectivity. Liberals/individualists and altruists suffer reciprocal illusions. Liberals are self-deluded in regarding their account of autonomy as more or less objective and independent of any particular scheme of social preferences or political order. Altruists, who frankly embrace a conception of the common good, are self-deluded in thinking that the scheme is neither arbitrary nor subjective. Kennedy claims to unmask such illusions. In this crucial sense, he posits himself as an outsider to the process of choice and decision making, an outsider describing the inevitable illusions of insiders.

The theme of delusion and an appeal to the inside/outside metaphor run pervasively through feminism and critical race theory. For feminists, the alienation of women from power is said to give a privileged perspective, an outsider's perspective, for seeing that what is thought to be universal is in fact partial, power-based, and gender-based. "Different voice" feminists condemn the assumption of separateness at the root of ideas about autonomy and rights and speak metaphorically about the equally gender-based ideas of connectedness. Radical feminists condemn *any and all* received concepts and terms that emanate from a system of sexual domination because their use perpetuates that system. Using a parallel argument, some minority critics attack the vocabulary of autonomy and individualism as manifesting the "voice" and therefore the preferences of the dominant race. In all these arguments, being "inside" is equated with having delusions about objectivity and about the availability of neutral foundations.

Kennedy exposes the paradox inherent in the inside/outside metaphor when he remarks that our concepts are thoroughly determined by the individualist framework of autonomy, rights and objectivity. When we step outside that framework to criticize it as partial and subjective we have no alternative conceptual scheme. We can speak only negatively and identify delusions and mistakes.

From the standpoint of critical scholars, the separation between insider and outsider is total. Any insider must believe in her preferences as objective in order to justify imposing them on society at large; any outsider must see such a belief in objectivity as misguided. To observe with Rorty that solidarity with like-minded persons must replace belief in objectivity and universality and that discourse (the "search for truth") is no more than a conversation among groups with different preferences and agendas, is necessarily to associate oneself with the outsider's perspective. The outsider's analysis indicts insiders with the charge of objectifying an arbitrary conceptual scheme.

Feminist and race theorists struggle with this paradox. How can one participate in decision making with commitment, if any agenda of rights, any claim of neutrality or objectivity, is tainted with partiality? Their attempt at an end-run consists of displacing substantive theory with biographical narrative. They embrace subjectivity and the notion of conversation. Chastened by outsiders that claims to objectivity in developing a theory of rights and an explication of autonomy are *necessarily* ill-founded, they narrow their account-from-the-inside to that which is personal and relative.

If there is a central flaw in the critical argument, it can be uncovered by questioning the polarity between the perspectives of the insider and the outsider, the polarity between what the insider believes and what the outsider knows to be the case. As long as the theorist can speak as outsider, she can disable the insider from claiming objectivity and, among other things, from aspiring to give a neutral account of autonomy and its associated rights. Thus, she can assault liberalism conceptually and epistemologically. The critical argument succeeds *if* it gives, in turn, a correct account of the insider's use of objectivity claims about autonomy and rights. But *is* the account correct?

The critic's disabling argument has a much longer pedigree than its modern incarnation in legal theory and in the Rortian revival of pragmatism. It replicates traditional skeptical arguments of the form, "You cannot claim *x* unless you can show *y*." In its most banal and familiar guise the argument is that you cannot claim to know that you are awake now unless you can show that you are not now merely dreaming and merely imagining you are awake. You cannot claim that other persons have minds unless you can show what difference it would make in your experience for others to offer all the *external* manifestations of mind but lack subjective cognitive experience.

P. F. Strawson's seminal diagnosis of skepticism is that such skeptical arguments are viciously and fatally self-defeating. "[W]ith many skeptical problems[,] their statement involves the pretended acceptance of a conceptual scheme and at the same time the silent repudiation of one of the conditions of its existence. That is why they are, in the terms in which they are stated, insoluble."[27] Or, in other words, "[skepticism] allows us the alternatives of meaning something different from what we do mean, or of being forever unsure; because the standard for being sure while meaning what we do mean is set self-contradictorily high."[28]

Drawing on this insight one can ask whether critical theorists set the standard for objectivity so high that *in principal* it cannot be met. In particular, how can one ever make the defense that an analysis of autonomy is not gender-relative, race-relative, or determined by the preferences of the class with power? Is it sufficient for the critical theorist to demonstrate subjectivity by showing that the analysis is controversial, that opinions differ? Is it sufficient for the critic to show that a different and internally consistent agenda can be produced?

130

Questions can be raised about the partiality that critical theory associates with an individualist account of autonomy and rights. Is individualism, as Kennedy argues, systematically at odds with altruism because the two notions express irreconcilable conceptual perspectives on human nature and society? Or are individualism/autonomy and altruism reconcilable, with the former a precondition of the latter? Do care, concern, and identification with others not *presuppose* respect for their choices and decisions, for their freedom?

One may question other critical assumptions about autonomy. Is autonomy an expression of the characteristic separateness of male experience; or, on the contrary, is autonomy a condition of women's freedom and self-regard just as it is for men? Such questions are linked by asking whether critical theory's assumptions about partiality rest on the self-defeating skeptical paradox and whether critics have raised the stakes for legitimating talk of objectivity, neutrality, autonomy, and rights so high that they can never be satisfied.

A second philosophical tool for examining critical theory, closely related to Strawson's analysis of skepticism, is Donald Davidson's critique of the idea of a conceptual scheme. Whether or not they use the term explicitly, feminists, critical race theorists, and critical legal theorists often write as if they commend seeing legal discourse as a contest among competing conceptual schemes. On this view, as the domination of the powerless by the empowered is ameliorated, these conceptual schemes move toward engagement in what Rorty terms "conversation."

Davidson says that "[c]onceptual relativism is a heady and exotic doctrine, or would be if we could make good sense of it."[29] He argues that "[t]he dominant metaphor of conceptual relativism, that of differing points of view, seems to betray an underlying paradox. Different points of view make sense, but only if there is a common coordinate system on which to plot them; yet the existence of the common system belies the claim of dramatic incomparability."[30] Critical theorists are on the horns of a dilemma, implicitly presupposing a conceptual scheme that they explicitly reject as untenable.

They may attempt to salvage talk of conceptual schemes by contending that the language of theorists as outsiders provides the common coordinate system by which to plot the different "insider" points of view. But this attempt is open to two serious objections. First, the critical theorist assumes rather than argues that the language of objectivity, autonomy, and rights belongs to particular subjective points of view and not to the common coordinate scheme. Secondly, the kind of empirical challenge that the critical theorist offers to *particular* claims about rights and autonomy, for example that they reinforce power and/or are self-defeating, implies that the *language* of rights and autonomy is inescapably the common scheme for debate. It is the language needed and used by the critical theorist herself to make her points.

These two objections suggest that the implicit use by critical theory of inside/outside metaphors begs serious questions. For one thing, the argument from skepticism puts in question whether critical theory uses the terms, "objectivity," "autonomy," "rights," in a way that conforms to normal use. Davidson's analysis implies that such terms and points of view can and perhaps must be seen as belonging to a bridging vocabulary or array of concepts, one that binds the powerless and the powerful, men and women, minorities and majorities as much as it distinguishes them. One cannot assign concepts and arguments by fiat to the realm of partiality rather than the realm of mutuality.

Some critical theorists themselves anticipate these objections. Unger draws attention to a distinction between what he calls ordinary skepticism and true skepticism. "The only true skepticism about knowledge is the radical one – as irrefutable as it is empty – that denies that controversies over particular truths could ever reveal anything about the world other than the stratagems of our self-deception or that they could even allow us to pursue our practical interests more successfully."[31] Distinguishable from such true skepticism is "ordinary" or "normative" skepticism which "represents an attack upon one form of normative argument by the proponents of another. Behind such attacks we are likely to find disagreements over what personality and society are really like and how we may live in society."[32]

Unger denies that he is a "true skeptic." Thus, unlike Kennedy, West, MacKinnon, and others who concern themselves primarily with strategies of self-deception, he employs a conceptual apparatus for positive normative argument. Unlike most critical theorists, he does not raise the stakes for normative argument about truth beyond the possibility of realization. Rather, he engages liberals and others in intelligible disagreements over the nature of personhood and society.

Rorty's remarks about "outsideness" also convey insight into the problem of changing meaning by speaking from "outside" a conceptual scheme. Rorty concerns himself with outsideness in trying to refute foundationalism. As a pragmatist, he seeks to show (as we have already seen) "that it is useless to hope that objects will constrain us to believe the truth about them, if only they are approached with an unclouded mental eye, or a rigorous method, or a perspicuous language."[33] No method, no language lets us go *outside* our methods and languages to find out how "things really are." That sort of aspiration is a quixotic quest.

In this form, Rorty's critique of foundationalism harmonizes with the Strawsonian critique of skepticism. Both foundationalism and skepticism ratchet up the stakes for objectivity and truth and do so by changing the use of terms. But Rorty's account of the argument is flawed in a way that makes him in fact speak in the voice of an outsider *malgré lui*. If the foundationalist's notions of objectivity and truth carry unacceptable baggage, *so too* does Rorty's claim that all opinions are subjective and that the notion of truth must yield to the notion of solidarity. To make the latter claim is to digest only half of the rejection of foundationalism because it is to deploy the notions of subjectivity and falsity *as the foundationalist would use it.* A fully consistent antifoundationalist account would say, by contrast, that the criteria for using objectivity, subjectivity, truth, and falsity descriptively must be the criteria used by insiders, but insiders who are not hostage to foundationalist assumptions. Thus, Rorty, in commending subjectivity and solidarity, stands foundationalism on its head but continues to use terms as a foundationalist, an outsider, would use them. This instantiates the skeptical paradox by employing untenable criteria for objectivity/subjectivity and truth.

IV. Antifoundationalism without skepticism

I have argued that some critical theorists assume that political and legal disagreements are produced by rival conceptual schemes, each scheme harboring its own illusions about truth and objectivity. This picture generates skeptical paradoxes and embodies incoherent assumptions. It must therefore yield to a more complex picture of agreement and disagreement than one positing rival conceptual schemes. The task is to accommodate the best insights of antifoundationalism without stumbling over this misleading picture and its skeptical implications.

Links between (a) the epistemological alternatives of foundationalism and antifoundationalism and (b) the debate between liberals and communitarians need to be clarified. As portrayed by its critics, liberalism rests on a limited notion of the common good based on respect for persons' autonomy and on a shared conception of the rights ingredient to such autonomy. Such critics of liberalism argue that the notion of the common good is not thin but empty because autonomy is itself an altogether indeterminable value, because the political and legal rights of autonomy cannot be specified without favoring one or another controversial system of ideas and power.

What forms of foundationalism are associated with liberalism? Liberal legal philosophers such as Ronald Dworkin sometimes argue that over time a legal system "works itself pure."[34] Others, for example Owen Fiss, argue that objectivity is secured by the disciplining rules that govern judicial interpretation.[35] This idea of an objective consensus achieved through collective articulation of shared goals and values is an example of what Rorty criticizes as the search for truth with a privileged method and an unclouded eye, the search for foundations.

Even if the foundational version of liberalism must be given up, the project of liberalism can be construed and defended on alternative (antifoundational) grounds. Let's distinguish two antifoundational perspectives. The first, as we have seen, is distinguished by an assault on truth and objectivity as masks for bias and coercion. It is harnessed, as in Rorty's analysis, to a social picture in which society is divided into subcommunities each with a distinctive conceptual scheme and in which law is the legitimating ideology of those with power.

A different kind of antifoundationalism focuses on individuals rather than groups. This approach, like the first, rejects the notion of a privileged method to "truth" (foundations) and affirms a plurality of conceptual strategies, ways of understanding and interpreting experience and ascribing value. But this second kind of antifoundationalism attends to those aspects of consciousness and language that bind an individual, conceptually and experientially, to the rest of society as well as to those aspects that separate and distinguish one person from another.

The second kind of antifoundationalism rests on the following observations. In legal and political debate, as in other kinds of deliberation, persons characteristically understand and anticipate the arguments and responses of others. They share language, not only rules governing reference but also shared communicative techniques of irony, nuance, implication, and so on. They share a sense of what is and what is not relevant to debates. Their disagreements – whether about civil rights, or abortion, or the general scope of liberty or privacy – generally have a predictable shape even when they have an unpredictable resolution. In such debates, disagreement reflects not merely different value orientations. For example, debates about abortion rights or privacy inevitably reflect differences about many kinds of belief – about human nature, about the course of history, about the ideals at the heart of our culture, and about the nature of human suffering. Fact and value are bound inextricably, and each person's mode of understanding reflects her personal history, the evolution of her personal strategies for understanding.

If all this is correct, then in any debate it is an open rather than a closed question whether the conceptual strategies of individuals are bridged or not by shared beliefs regarding respect for persons and basic rights. Neither agreement nor disagreement on such fundamental issues can be presupposed in general. Agreement on these issues depends on the pervasiveness of underlying beliefs about such matters as the efficacy of self-awareness and action, the circumstances of human flourishing, the role of government and law, and the meaning of history. When agreement on these relevant beliefs extends across the disparate groups of society – across groups in and out of power, across the races, across genders – then the ideals of autonomy will also be shared and generally serve as the parameters of debate. In these circumstances liberalism correctly mirrors and articulates a shared heritage of value and shared projections of goals.

If it is possible to harmonize liberalism (holding autonomy and rights provisionally to be bridge concepts) with an antifoundational epistemology in this way, then liberals may claim that their descriptions of social value and legal rights are true and objective in the important but limited sense of being deeply embedded in shared belief systems. Each individual has some beliefs or convictions that are readily overturned by evidence: a belief in the quality of a restaurant may be unseated by one bad meal, and a belief in the life dates of Flaubert may be revised upon inspection of an encyclopedia. She has other beliefs and convictions that are so basic to her interpretive and justificatory strategies that they serve as the measure for other beliefs; religious beliefs, beliefs about human nature (human capacities, vulnerabilities, etc.), and beliefs about politics or economy often have this character. The latter kind of belief, one by which the individual organizes and judges experience, is what that person holds true, what one who is necessarily "inside" her way of understanding means by "truth." When such beliefs have the same deep role for persons generally in the society, their status as truths is widely shared. Liberals can be said to claim that their observations about autonomy and the rights of autonomy are true in this sense.

Similarly, reasoning about rights is objective *not* when it involves a privileged insight into eternal verities but when it follows justificatory patterns that are generally recognized as part of the shared practice. Judges who disagree can nonetheless be said to be objective when they justify their decisions by using understandable beliefs about human nature, the role of government, deference to history, and so on. Judgments not grounded in these ways are appropriately called subjective preferences, arbitrary conclusions even in relation to what their author is presumed to believe.

These accounts of truth and objectivity reflect the way these concepts are understood by "insiders" and yet are compatible with an antifoundational account of reasoning. This account does not imply that insiders are deluded about the truth or objectivity of their claims because it does not describe the claimants as appealing to timeless verities. Moreover, antifoundationalism of this (second) kind does not imply that individuals as insiders are trapped within irreconcilable and discrete conceptual schemes.

The second and preferable kind of antifoundationalism does not generate skeptical paradoxes because it does not involve distorted criteria for truth and objectivity in political and legal discourse. It does not claim to find foundational assumptions at the heart of "insider" reasoning and therefore does not discredit such reasoning from an "outsider's" perspective. Rather, this second kind of antifoundational analysis is committed to a univocal sense of truth and objectivity, terms that characterize judgments made by participants who follow divergent justificatory strategies that are, nonetheless, mutually understood to have a certain epistemological precedence within a shared practice. Given this epistemological basis, liberalism as a theory asserts that autonomy and a particular account of the rights of autonomy are widely and deeply presupposed.

V. Liberalism and critical theory reassessed

We have seen that liberalism may be challenged in two altogether different ways. The first kind of challenge, characteristically offered by conservatives but also by left-oriented communitarians, is framed as an attack on liberal *policy*. Liberalism, from this standpoint, lacks a coherent and well-formed sense of the common good as well as respect for the values implicit in tradition. Because the role of government is to define and pursue the common good and to perpetuate the traditional norms and bonds of the community, liberalism subverts that role insofar as it emphasizes minority rights or individual rights as a trump over government policy.

This first (communitarian) challenge is intuitive and is an appeal to what John Rawls, in defending liberalism, calls "reflective equilibrium." "It is an equilibrium because at last our principles and judgments coincide; and it is reflective since we know to what principles our judgments conform and the premises of their derivation. At the moment everything is in order. But the equilibrium is not necessarily stable."[36] The method of reflective equilibrium is one of testing intuitions about the justice and fairness of particular decisions against more general (tentative) principles which order and explain them. To what extent do various ways of elaborating the notion of autonomy through the articulation of rights fit our intuitions of justice? The method of reflective equilibrium tends to yield agreement on abstract and general principles rather than on more specific ones. The persuasiveness of liberalism over communitarianism depends on acceptance of quite general principles, principles giving priority to rights of autonomy in the face of the claims of tradition and of a richer notion of the common good.

Critical theory's challenge to liberalism is altogether different. We have seen that communitarians agree with liberals that intuitions about justice and fairness are shared and are to be regarded as objective. These intuitions can therefore serve as parameters of discourse in pursuit of reflective equilibrium. But communitarians believe that these intuitions yield communitarian and not liberal principles. Critical theory makes no such methodological concession. Indeed, it condemns appeals to justice and fairness just as it condemns appeals to autonomy and rights as masking preferential agendas with the legitimating rhetoric of neutrality. It condemns, in other words, the idea of a bridging set of concepts that transcends conceptual schemes. On this analysis, liberalism is not bad (or counterintuitive) policy but incoherent epistemology. Competing agendas are all there can be.

My point in parts III and IV was not to defend liberalism in general but rather to identify the flawed and paradoxical character of the critical challenge. Not all writers identified (or self-identified) with critical theory speak of irreconcilably diverse conceptual schemes. My diagnosis of critical theory as flawed by skepticism and its paradoxes applies only to this one form of argument found within critical theory, not to critical theory in general. Critical writers in fact offer both kinds of criticisms of liberalism, that it has counterintuitive policy implications *and* that it is based on an incoherent epistemology. Having considered the second of these criticisms, I turn once more to the first.

In part critical theory confronts liberalism with a series of admonitions rather than counterarguments. One admonition is unexceptionable and is the common denominator of all forms of hermeneutics, the proposition that theoretical discourse reflects the perspective of the theorist. Among other things, this means that the way in which an issue is formulated, the purpose served in addressing the issue, the tools used in addressing it, and the criteria of successful analysis or resolution of the issue are all affected by the personal history of the theorist and the culture to which she belongs. To concede this is not to concede that all theorizing is biased and subjective. It is, however, to concede that one's practical assumptions about neutrality and objectivity must be tested continually in discourse with diverse fellow discussants. Claims of neutrality and objectivity are always provisional and always made relative to the shared tests for bias and partiality within a particular shared deliberative practice.

A second admonition is that debates about liberalism, autonomy, and rights can be general and abstract in a way that conceals genuine disagreement. Liberals who try to show that there is broad and deep agreement about important aspects of autonomy – self-awareness, self-respect, and the capacity to make and implement choices – *may* camouflage disagreement about the political, social, and economic circumstances that make autonomy possible. Disagreement about concrete instances of these rights may and will exist within the context of adherence to a more general framework. The success of an argument for liberalism depends essentially on how well this array of general insights solves concrete problems.

The most destructive charge made by critical theory is that liberals cannot solve problems because agreement even on basic terms and commitments is illusory. I have tried to show why this charge fails insofar as it rests on a skeptical form of antifoundationalism. On the other hand, the challenge of communitarianism to liberalism is that at the most abstract level the ideal of autonomy cannot adequately express and serve the ends of society. On this point, debate must remain open.

This essay is about individualism in two different but complementary senses. First it identifies respect for individuals as a defining characteristic of liberalism. The story that guides liberals is one in which individuals are doubly threatened, by other persons who may harm or offend them and by government. The power of government may not only harm persons but may impose on them a particular version of the common good, the version held by the majority or by those who are otherwise in control. For liberals, government and law function justifiably and well whenever they show sensitivity to these threats and act to minimize them. Critical theorists tend to regard this view of government and law as naive about power and domination – physical and conceptual – in social arrangements. Communitarians, on the other hand, are less concerned with power and domination than liberals *or* critical theorists and argue that government and law must shape and limit individual choices in the light of a larger conception of the common good.

This essay is also individualistic in its methodology. It questions and rejects the implication of critical theorists that individuals merely instantiate groups with which they share conceptual schemes and values, groups that they represent by virtue of race, gender, or a history of powerlessness (or of power). My methodological assumption, which draws on the liberal notion of autonomy, is that individuals have unique justificatory strategies and ways of understanding, and yet are bound to deliberative practices that bridge their several unique perspectives. They recognize each other's ways of thinking as belonging to a shared practice and, while maintaining a stake in their own ways of thinking, recognize that others have a corresponding stake in theirs. A model of deliberative practices that takes account of these features is different from a model in which individuals inhabit discrete and separate conceptual domains. Such a mistaken model can explain neither the bridging concepts through which discourse occurs nor the self-awareness of individuals engaged in such discourse.

Individualism and liberalism are sometimes attacked as tools of cultural and ideological imperialism. To think of them, as I have suggested, as bridging theories rather than as ingredients of a parochial conceptual framework is, it is said, to mask and rationalize the cannibalization of one framework by another. But those who make this kind of critical argument may themselves perpetrate a kind of imperialism and abuse of power. They may rule out the possibility of communication by suggesting that all political discourse is legitimating and none is legitimate.

Notes

1 I wish to acknowledge the care and insight which my research assistants of the University of Connecticut School of Law, Melinda Westbrook and Marcella Hourihane, brought to this project.

2 See, for example, J. Feinberg, *Harmless Wrongdoing* (New York: Oxford University Press, 1988), 81–121.

3 Ibid., 83–6.

4 Ibid., 84.

5 Ibid., 88.

6 Ibid., 87–90.

7 Ibid., 90–8.

8 Ibid., 107.

9 These themes are explored and defended in the first three volumes of Feinberg's

138

The Moral Limits of the Criminal Law, of which *Harmless Wrongdoing* is the last. The others are *Harm to Others* (1984), *Offense to Others* (1985), and *Harm to Self* (1986).

10 Compare, for example, Ronald Dworkin's defense of liberalism in *Taking Rights Seriously* (Cambridge: Harvard University Press, 1977), 82–90, with Michael Sandel's discussion of the self as moral subject in *Liberalism and the Limits of Justice* (Cambridge University Press, 1982), 15–65.

11 D. Kennedy, "Form and Substance in Private Law Adjudication," 89 *Harvard Law Review* 1685 (1976).

12 Ibid., 1717.

13 Ibid.

14 Ibid., 1772.

15 Ibid., 1771.

16 Ibid., 1775.

17 R. Gordon, "Critical Legal Histories," 36 *Stanford Law Review* 57, 94 (1984).

18 This view is associated with the work and influence of Carol Gilligan. See especially *In a Different Voice: Psychological Theory and Women's Development* (Cambridge: Harvard University Press, 1982). Among legal scholars Robin West has drawn heavily and provocatively on Gilligan's work.

19 C. MacKinnon, "Feminism, Marxism, Method and the State," 7 *Signs* (1982): 515, 516.

20 R. West, "Jurisprudence and Gender," 55 *University of Chicago Law Review* 1, 5–6 (1988).

21 R. Unger, *The Critical Legal Studies Movement* (Cambridge: Harvard University Press, 1986) 12.

22 S. Brewer, "Choosing Sides in the *Radical Critiques* Debate," 103 *Harvard Law Review* 1844, 1851 (1990).

23 R. Rorty, *Consequences of Pragmatism* (Minneapolis: University of Minnesota Press, 1982), 165.

24 R. Rorty, *Objectivity, Relativism, and Truth* (Cambridge University Press, 1991), 21.

25 Ibid.

26 See R. Rorty, *Philosophy and the Mirror of Nature* (Princeton University Press, 1979), 389–95.

27 P. F. Strawson, *Individuals: an Essay in Descriptive Metaphysics* (London: Methuen, 1959), 106.

28 Ibid., 34.

29 D. Davidson, "On the Very Idea of a Conceptual Scheme," in *Inquiries into Truth and Interpretation* (Oxford: Clarendon Press, 1984), 183.

30 Ibid., 184.

31 Unger, *Critical Legal Studies Movement*, 96.

32 Ibid.

33 Rorty, *Consequences of Pragmatism*, 165.

34 See R. Dworkin, "'Natural' Law Revisited," 34 *University of Florida Law Review* 165 (1982).

35 See O. Fiss, "Objectivity and Interpretation," 34 *Stanford Law Review* 739 (1982)

36 J. Rawls, *A Theory of Justice* (Cambridge: Harvard University Press, 1971), 20.

Part III

Essays on Criminal Responsibility

[10]
Retributivism and Justice

I. The Justification of Punishment

In two respects legal scholarship mirrors legal pedagogy. First, effective teaching demands description of how things are, explanation of why they are as they are and consideration of how they can be justified. Similarly, scholarship is often designed to explain as well as describe and to explain in such a way as to provoke normative questions about how things should be.

For some legal topics the relevant normative questions are patterned and predictable. The justification of punishment is one such topic. The competing theories are familiar and are the subject of most students' first immersion in the subject. Familiarity may however be a disguise for confusion. This observation brings us to the second shared goal of scholarship and teaching. Both may provoke the student and the reader to look behind the familiar forms of justification and ask whether these familiar forms really make sense.

The simplest theory of the justification of punishment is met in the law student's first brush with criminal law. This theory says that criminal punishment serves four goals: to incapacitate offenders (special deterrence), to give a general disincentive for crime (general deterrence), to rehabilitate, and to achieve retribution.[1] The first three goals are identified as forward-looking in contrast with the problematic fourth. The first three goals are forward-looking in that special deterrence, general deterrence, and rehabilitation describe goals that are part of a picture of a future in which persons collectively are better off. The de-

---

* Professor of Law, University of Connecticut School of Law. A.B. 1963, Harvard; J.D. 1968; M.Phil. 1968; Ph.D 1969, Yale. Professor Morawetz teaches Criminal Law, Criminal Procedure, Jurisprudence, and Legal Profession.

My seven years at the University of Connecticut have been years of transition from scholarship and teaching in pure philosophy to the application of philosophy to law. I am indebted in countless ways to Dean Phillip Blumberg for his support and for easing that transition. This article is an attempt to illustrate as coherently as possible the role of philosophy in contemporary thinking about criminal law.

1. *See, e.g.*, W. LaFave & A. Scott, Criminal Law 21-25 (1972).

terrence of crime and the rehabilitation of offenders help create a future in which overall happiness is maximized and the pursuit of individual goals is facilitated. This form of justification is normally called utilitarian.[2]

Retribution is problematic because it is not forward-looking and therefore seems to certain critics an irrational goal. Some of these critics contend that retribution is revenge, that it reflects the domination of emotion over reason.[3] This argument can be met by saying that reasonable persons have shared standards for determining the just deserts of offenders,[4] and that retribution is really another term for justice. Although this argument may establish the rationality of justice, it does not make it a forward-looking consideration. Justice is the test of the thing that should be done regardless of consequences. It is a rectification demanded by the past rather than a "making better" determined by the future. This apparent opposition between two modes of moral justification is familiar and deep-seated. To the forward-looking theorist, only anticipations of a desirable future can justify punishment. To the theorist who invokes justice (the retributivist), any theory that does not entail just treatment is morally groundless. The very idea of a compromise that embraces all four goals is unacceptable to either side. A middle way is suspect to the extent that these methodological standpoints seem irreconcilable.

One can, of course, try to shrug the problem away. One can move to the level of intuitions about acceptable results in particular cases and embrace a kind of eclecticism in method, a middle way by default.[5] This consists in middle-level generalizations from particular intuitions. For example, if deterrence is most effective when a minor but widespread offense like shoplifting is punished severely, justice may still require that punishments be scaled to what is fair even if deterrence is compromised. But a series of such observations may not yield much of

2. The term "utilitarianism" originated in the work of Jeremy Bentham. The forms of utilitarianism are described superbly well by J.J.C. Smart in Smart, *Utilitarianism*, 8 THE ENCYCLOPEDIA OF PHILOSOPHY 206-12 (1967). In the text accompanying note 54, *infra*, I discuss the relationship between the terms "utilitarian" and "forward-looking" as characterizations of theories.

3. *See* T. HONDERICH, PUNISHMENT: THE SUPPOSED JUSTIFICATIONS 29 (1971). Honderich quotes critically F. STEPHENS, LIBERTY, EQUALITY, FRATERNITY 161 (1873): "[Punishment exists] for the sake of gratifying the feeling of hatred—call it revenge, resentment, or what you will—which the contemplation of such conduct excites in healthily constituted minds."

4. *See* J. KLEINIG, PUNISHMENT AND DESERT 115-29 (1973).

5. *See, e.g.*, B. WILLIAMS, *Conflicts of Values* and *The Truth in Relativism*, in MORAL LUCK 71-82, 132-43 (1981); T. NAGEL, *The Fragmentation of Value*, in MORTAL QUESTIONS 128-41 (1979).

a general theory even if it describes intuitions particularly well. It is the nature of theoretical investigation to view eclecticism with suspicion, to view it as capitulation in the face of difficulty. Eclecticism is the theorist's admission of failure unless the theorist's job is reconceived not as the job of finding a theory but of finding out whether it is possible to find a theory.[6]

The merits of eclecticism are peripheral to my main concerns. My questions will be methodological as well as substantive. They will draw upon a remark made by H.L.A. Hart in a context having nothing to do with the theory of punishment.[7] In his recent criticism of Dworkin, Hart says that "a satisfactory foundation for a theory . . . will [not] be found as long as the search is conducted in the shadow of utilitarianism."[8] Debates about punishment continue to be conducted in this shadow whether they involve its acceptance, its rejection, or the quest for a middle way between utilitarianism and retributivism. My critique of these debates has two parts. I shall first show how theoreticians gravitate to one or the other pole as a consequence of taking the opposition seriously. I shall then question the very idea that there is an irreconcilable opposition between the two polar modes of justification and give reasons for thinking it a myth.

II. Four Theories of Punishment

Four influential theories of punishment are attempts to come to terms with the classical goals of criminal law. Three of the four are trapped on the horns of the methodological dilemma. They take seriously only one of the modes of justification and distort or disregard the other pole of debate.

A. *Quinton: The Logic of Retributivism*

In his important article, *On Punishment,*[9] Anthony Quinton argues that retributivism has been misconceived. In his view, retributivism is reconcilable with forward-looking theories because it is simply making a *logical* point while forward looking theories make an *ethical* point, a point about justification. First, Quinton interprets retributivism as de-

6. *See* T. Nagel, *supra* note 5. Nagel is especially illuminating on this point.

7. H.L.A. Hart, *Between Utility and Rights*, in Essays in Jurisprudence and Philosophy 198-222 (1983).

8. *Id.* at 222.

9. Quinton, *On Punishment*, in The Philosophy of Punishment 55-64 (H.B. Acton ed. 1969).

manding that a person be guilty before he may be punished. He acknowledges that a pure forward-looking theory could dispense with this limitation. The overall economy of deterrence might be such that punishment is most effective when those who are generally *believed* to be guilty are punished (as scapegoats) along with those who are really guilty. For Quinton, any conflict is illusory because the retributivist does not intend his limitation to have ethical force. Quinton states that

> the necessity of not punishing the innocent is not moral but logical. It is not, as some retributivists think, that we *may* not punish the innocent and *ought* only to punish the guilty, but that we *cannot* punish the innocent and *must* only punish the guilty. Of course, the suffering or harm in which punishment consists can be and is inflicted on innocent people but this is not punishment, it is judicial error or terrorism or . . . 'social surgery.' The infliction of suffering on a person is only properly described as punishment if that person is guilty. The retributivist thesis, therefore, is not a moral doctrine, but an account of the meaning of the word 'punishment'.[10]

Quinton's theory, however, fails because it misses the retributivist's point and confuses a description of the conditions of punishment with a justification of punishment. It is correct descriptively to say that guilt is a condition of punishment. The institution or practice of punishing has this as a pervasive and unexceptionable feature. But this is not the retributivist's point. The retributivist claims that to be justified morally, punishment *may* be imposed only on the guilty. He identifies justice with this feature and says that any practice that lacks it *a fortiori* lacks justification.

The same point can be made somewhat differently. Quinton writes as if restricting punishment to the guilty were merely a feature internal to the practice of punishment. This characterization, however, does not answer the utilitarian's challenge that punishment need not be limited to the guilty because the challenge is made from outside the practice and has the form, why this practice and not another? Quinton notwithstanding, the retributivist, like the utilitarian, makes a normative and not a logical point.

Quinton cannot succeed in defusing the retributivist claim or the utilitarian challenge because the retributivist's purpose cannot be to de-

10. *Id.* at 58-59.

scribe a contingent internal feature of the system of punishment. This point can be seen in terms of the link between retribution and justice. If the retributivist merely identified retribution with punishment conditioned on guilt, he could be interpreted as offering a description without normative intent. He could be uncommitted on whether retribution in this sense is desirable. But to describe the connection between punishment and guilt as a requirement of *justice* is to make a normative claim. If the connection is an essential feature of justice, then a system that lacks this feature is unjust. For the retributivist, the aspirations of a justificatory theory framed in nonretributive terms are incoherent. The retributivist, thus, leaves us not with the task of finding a justification other than justice, but with the task of understanding what it could possibly mean to justify a system of punishment while conceding the irrelevance of justice.

Quinton avoids the choice between the two modes of justification only by declining to identify the retributivist claim as one of justice. Once the retributivist claim is so identified, the abyss between the two modes seems unbridgeable. Quinton defends utilitarianism by interpreting retributivism as a noncompetitor.

B. *Rawls: Rule-Utilitarianism*

"Two Concepts of Rules,"[11] John Rawls' early and influential article, directly addresses punishment. It is concerned with utilitarian justification and puts forth an ingenious model called "rule-utilitarianism."[12] Under this model, "one must distinguish between justifying a practice as a system of rules to be applied and enforced, and justifying a particular action which falls under these rules; utilitarian arguments are appropriate with regard to questions about practices, while retributive arguments fit the application of particular rules to particular cases."[13]

Utilitarian justification has this limited role because the system itself is found to work better when actors within the system may consult only the rules and need not make utilitarian judgments. The obvious analogy is to games: the game of baseball serves utilitarian ends, but

11. Rawls, *Two Concepts of Rules*, in CONTEMPORARY UTILITARIANISM 59-98 (M. Bayles ed. 1968).

12. The tenets of rule-utilitarianism were first spelled out by J. O. Urmson in Urmson, *The Interpretation of the Moral Philosophy of J.S. Mill*, in MILL: A COLLECTION OF CRITICAL ESSAYS 179-89 (J. B. Schneewind ed. 1968).

13. Rawls, *supra* note 11, at 62.

only when the players follow the rules without claiming exceptions (take a fourth strike) whenever utility would prescribe the exception in the individual case.[14] Rawls' theory suggests rules of justice are internal rules like the three strike limit. They cannot be waived for reasons of utility in the individual case, but only because the package of rules serves utility effectively *as* a package.[15]

Rawls further explains this theory by comparing the role of judge and legislator.

> [T]he judge and the legislator stand in different positions and look in different directions: one to the past, the other to the future. The justification of what the judge does, *qua* judge, sounds like the retributive view; the justification of what the (ideal) legislator does, *qua* legislator, sounds like the utilitarian view. Thus both views have a point . . . and one's initial confusion disappears once one sees that these views apply to persons holding different offices with different duties, and situated differently with respect to the system of rules that make up the criminal law . . . . One reconciles the two views by the time-honored device of making them apply to different situations.[16]

Rawls, like Quinton, offers two levels of analysis, internal and external. Unlike Quinton, however, he does not confuse this distinction with the distinction between description and normative justification.[17] By distinguishing the internal move of justifying a particular action within a practice (a particular application of a rule) from the external move of justifying the practice itself as a system of rules, Rawls allocates the two modes of justification to different domains. Justice (retribution) becomes a virtue of the application of rules, and forward-looking (utilitarian) considerations justify the choice of rules.

It is important to see why Rawls' theory fails. The theory makes the existence of just treatment a provisional consideration of a fully justified practice. Just treatment is a feature of a system that, *qua* system, is justified by considerations other than justice, and these other

14. I discuss this analogy to games in Morawetz, *The Concept of a Practice*, in PHILOSOPHICAL STUDIES 209-26 (1973) and in T. MORAWETZ, THE PHILOSOPHY OF LAW 46-51 (1980).

15. *See* Rawls, *supra* note 11, at 76-77. *See also* Urmson, *supra* note 12. Urmson's discussion is full and clear.

16. Rawls, *supra* note 11, at 63-65.

17. Rawls' distinction is between two compatible kinds of justification. He concedes the normative force of each kind.

(forward-looking) considerations have conceptual priority. As Rawls realizes by the time he writes *A Theory of Justice*,[18] justice cannot be purely an intrasystemic criterion of normative criticism. If it makes sense to assess an application of a rule as just, it also makes sense to refer to the rule itself as just (in its general application). If there are just rules, there are also just systems of rules. The notion of moral justification is not severable, and the moral standpoints of intrasystemic participant and extrasystemic observer (judge and legislator) are not distinct.[19] Justice makes the same claim on both.

Many theorists offer a different criticism of rule-utilitarianism. They complain that the rule-utilitarian could countenance a general practice of secretly punishing the innocent.[20] According to this claim, Rawls could get counterintuitive results because punishing the innocent violates an intuition that we all accept: the innocent should not be punished. A rule-utilitarian like Rawls may reject the suggestion that he would countenance a system in which the innocent are officially sanctioned and the public is kept in ignorance of this in four ways. As a preliminary matter he might say that such examples are farfetched and unpersuasive and that bad examples make bad theory.[21] He may then attack the example on its facts. He may say there is an ineradicable risk that such a policy would become known and that public confidence and obedience would be dramatically threatened. This reply, however, is pragmatic rather than principled, and seems to concede the objection. Under this defense, the rule-utilitarian would approve of the situation if in theory the risk could be eliminated.

The utilitarian's third and fourth responses are more interesting. The third response is that the weight that must be assigned to harming the innocent—the subjective disappointment, the pain of unfair treatment—is so great that it necessarily outweighs whatever benefits the practice may yield. The suggestion here is that even if the utilitarian adheres to the criteria of evaluation most often associated with utilita-

18. J. RAWLS, A THEORY OF JUSTICE (1971). By this time, Rawls has explicitly rejected utilitarian forms of justification and puts forth an account of justice as a concept to be deployed in criticism from an external standpoint. *Id.* at 22-53.

19. The inapplicability of Rawls' model to justification as it occurs in "open" practices like law (as opposed to "closed" practices like games) is the main subject of my paper, *The Concept of a Practice, supra* note 14.

20. For this and other examples of objections to utilitarianism, see Williams, *A Critique of Utilitarianism*, in J.J.C. SMART & B. WILLIAMS, UTILITARIANISM: FOR AND AGAINST 77-150 (1973).

21. *See* Anscombe, *Modern Moral Philosophy*, in ETHICS 186-210 (J.J. Thomson & G. Dworkin eds. 1968).

rianism and speaks of maximizing happiness or satisfaction,[22] it is open to him to make interpersonal comparisons in various ways. It is open, that is, to say that the disappointment of the punished innocents has such intensity and such qualities that it has overwhelming, decisive weight.[23] The final response is for the utilitarian to adopt nonstandard criteria of evaluation and to speak not of happiness and subjective satisfaction, but of well-being and the common good. He is then in position to conclude that a regime of injustice cannot serve the common good.

The third and fourth responses are opening shots in a theoretical dialogue. The third response, it will be objected, throws justice out the front door only to admit it through the back by saying that special and decisive weight should be assigned by the utilitarian to the sense of justice outraged. The final response merely puts in question what terms of utility determination or forward-looking evaluation are satisfactory.

C. *Hart: A Multiplicity of Values*

Both Quinton and Rawls seek to accommodate the notion of justice within a utilitarian framework. Although Rawls' theory fares better than Quinton's, both undervalue and misrepresent the apparent role of justice in normative reasoning. H.L.A. Hart, in his extensive writings on punishment and criminal responsibility,[24] offers a theory superficially similar to Rawls' but one that is more sensitive to the imperatives of the competing modes of justification.

Hart says that a "morally tolerable" theory of punishment must be "a compromise between distinct and partly conflicting principles."[25] Hart, therefore, distinguishes the "general justifying aim" of punishment—crime minimization through general as well as specific deterrence—from its secondary aim, the distribution of punishment.[26] Justice is relevant to only the second of these problems while deterrence is

22. Utilitarianism, as propounded by Mill and Bentham, speaks of the greatest happiness for the greatest number. In the twentieth century, utilitarians have frequently refined these references to ones about "want satisfaction" and "preference satisfaction." *See, e.g.*, Gauthier, *On the Refutation of Utilitarianism*, in THE LIMITS OF UTILITARIANISM 144-63 (H. Miller & W. Williams eds. 1982).

23. *See* T. MORAWETZ, *supra* note 14, at 101-06.

24. H.L.A. HART, PUNISHMENT AND RESPONSIBILITY (1968), collects Hart's various papers and essays on criminal law.

25. *Id.* at 1.

26. *Id.* at 8-13. Hart is usually careful to be agnostic about whether the general justifying aim of criminal law goes beyond deterrence and crime minimization to include other goals and values.

relevant to both. Thus, in particular cases, the degree of punishment must be determined by a variety of criteria so that it is exemplary, proportionate, and fair all at the same time.

Commentators have found Hart's theory ambiguous. Certain passages make Hart sound much like a rule-utilitarian. He says, for example, that

> [f]airness between different offenders expressed in terms of different punishments is not an end in itself, but a method of pursuing other aims which has indeed a moral claim on our attention; and we should give effect to it where it does not impede the pursuit of the main aims of punishment.[27]

Hart adds that "justice is a method of doing other things, not a substantive end."[28] These passages suggest that deterrence is the end while justice is the means. They also suggest that deterrence is the external justification while justice remains a counter used internally by players of the game. Just treatment is justified only as long as, and to the extent that, it serves the external end.

This Rawlsian reading, however, is not the most plausible reading of Hart, who also argues time and again that the unwillingness to be unjust, for example to punish scapegoats in the interest of forward-looking considerations like deterrence, is based on independent values. This unwillingness "would still remain even if we were certain that in the case of the 'punishment' of one who had not broken the law the fact of his innocence would not get out or would not cause great alarm if it did."[29]

Hart's theory is distinguishable from Rawls' view because it makes use of what Nozick calls "side constraints."[30] Under this view, utilitarian goals cannot be pursued in ways that violate justice, not because rules of justice are provisionally or contingently the best rules for pursuing utility, but because they represent an independent value that limits such pursuit. Hart concludes that "the pursuit of a single social aim . . . has its restrictive qualifier" and that "our main social institutions *always* possess a plurality of features which can only be understood as

27. *Id.* at 172-73.

28. H.L.A. HART, THE MORALITY OF THE CRIMINAL LAW 54 (1964).

29. H.L.A. HART, *supra* note 24, at 77-78.

30. *See* R. NOZICK, ANARCHY STATE AND UTOPIA 28-33 (1974). Nozick observes: "The side-constraint view forbids you to violate . . . moral constraints in the pursuit of your goals." *Id.* at 29.

a compromise between partly discrepant principles."[31] Most simply, this means that the *distinctive* aim of criminal law, the control and minimization of crime, is pursued in the context of other values. Although these values are affected by what we do with criminal law, they are not unique to or distinctive of criminal law.

D. *An Expanded Version of Retribution*

The three theories considered so far all identify one theme with retributivism; punishment must be fair or just, and therefore limited to those who are guilty. This theme is offered as a constraint on the pursuit of forward-looking goals. In other words, under these theories fairness is a necessary condition for punishing, but it is not a sufficient condition. Forward-looking goals must also be served.

A true retributivist, on the other hand, argues that considerations of desert (or justice) are sufficient to justify punishing. Thus, while Hart clearly invokes justice to safeguard the rights of potential subjects of punishment, a true retributivist invokes retributivism to emphasize the right of "society"[32] to punish offenders with a suitable degree of severity. As we have seen, Hart sees guilt as a threshold condition for punishment. For him, the application of punishment must not only be justly deserved (i.e., only the guilty may be punished and only with severity no greater than the seriousness of the offense), but it must also serve the "general justifying aim" of furthering common ends.

In order to evaluate retributivism we must try to separate the principle of retribution from the principle of justice. There is no need to do so if we are considering only the requirement that punishment be limited to the guilty; this may be called either a requirement of retribution or one of justice. But we must consider two additional requirements often identified with the notion of retribution, namely (a) that the state be seen as having a duty to punish the guilty and (b) that intuitions of proportionality set a lower limit as well as an upper limit to the severity of punishment.[33] Although these requirements are implicit in the notion of retribution, they are, as we shall see, not necessarily requirements of justice.

Three aspects of this expanded version of retributivism are imme-

31. H.L.A. HART, PUNISHMENT AND RESPONSIBILITY, *supra* note 24, at 10 (emphasis added).

32. Many political philosophers suggest that rights belong to individuals rather than collectivities. *See generally* A. GEWIRTH, HUMAN RIGHTS 1-19 (1982); R. DWORKIN, TAKING RIGHTS SERIOUSLY 90-94 (1978).

33. *See, e.g.*, T. HONDERICH, *supra* note 3, at 22-23.

diately apparent.

(1) This scheme makes no appeal to forward-looking considerations as justification. It may be said to have benefits from a forward-looking standpoint, but it is not justified in terms of those benefits.

(2) These principles are echoed in statutory schemes of sentencing, in the announced aims of sentencers, and in the expectations of laypersons.[34] It is often said, virtually as a truism, that the guilty should be punished and punished with sentences they deserve.

(3) These principles do not match legal practice, where many norms flout retributive guidelines. Defendants may buy immunity from prosecution by choosing to incriminate their associates. Prosecutions are dropped and convictions overturned when the state violates the statutory or constitutional rights of "guilty" defendants.[35] The first of these practices may be justified only by expediency, but the latter is typical of a large class of practices justified by accepted principle.

The expanded version of retributivism carries a long tail of controversy; it is easy to see why. Although the processes of pleading and trial are designed to separate the guilty from the innocent, other aspects of criminal law show the artificiality and the idealization involved in this separation. Criminal law everywhere recognizes a range of excusing and mitigating conditions, and it recognizes that each condition expresses a heterogeneous mix of situations and dispositions.[36] The awareness that many offenders are at the cusp of excusability should make us wary of claiming that there is a duty to punish the guilty as a discrete and isolable class. The same awareness of heterogeneity should make us see how unclear it is to claim that the punishment should fit the seriousness of the offense. Is seriousness measured by the amount of harm caused, the amount of harm intended, the atrocious character of the offense as opposed to the degree of harm,[37] or the degree of commitment, ambivalence, or remorse of the offender?

These problems are not fatal to the retributivist view. We all in

34. Consider, for example, § 1170 of the CAL. PENAL CODE (1976 amendment) (West Supp. 1984): "The Legislature finds and declares that the purpose of imprisonment for crime is punishment. This purpose is best served by terms proportionate to the seriousness of the offense with provision for uniformity in the sentences of offenders committing the same offense under similar circumstances."

35. The development of this practice under the U.S. Constitution is documented and explained in MODERN CRIMINAL PROCEDURE chs. 5, 10, & 11 (Y. Kamisar, W. LaFave & J. Israel eds., 5th ed. 1980).

36. *See, e.g.*, G. WILLIAMS, CRIMINAL LAW: THE GENERAL PART chs. 8, 10, 11, 17, & 18 (2d ed. 1961).

37. *See* J. KLEINIG, *supra* note 4, at 123-29.

fact rank instances of offensive conduct using the language of comparative seriousness.[38] We sympathize with the duty to punish the guilty as long as we understand it to refer to those who are morally as well as legally guilty. Jeffrie Murphy has argued that both utilitarianism and retributivism are based on evident principle and not merely disputable intuitions or emotions. "That the maximization of social utility is important is no more obviously true than that a man should not unfairly profit from his own criminal wrongdoing. . . ."[39] Murphy goes on to remark that retributivism draws its theoretical underpinnings from that aspect of justice that deals with reciprocity. Kant also identified retribution with reciprocity when he argued that criminal law exists to prevent those who disobey the rules of conduct from gaining an unfair advantage over those who obey.[40]

The Kantian view has not stood unchallenged. We have seen that retributivism and the underlying theory of reciprocity underestimate the mix of offenders. Not all offenders seek to profit from crime, and some who seek to profit do not achieve any gain, even when punishment is left wholly out of account. The notion of reciprocity between the criminal and society or between the criminal and her victim is a metaphor drawn from a relationship that is both simpler and different.[41] Although justice requires reciprocity in the case of an actual compact or within a small group with voluntary and mutual undertakings, it is much less clear what justice requires under the conditions of an actual criminal offense.

In this section I have indicated the gravitational force of the utilitarian and retributive modes of moral justification, and the difficulty of imagining and defending a middle way. Quinton and Rawls exemplify the utilitarian or forward-looking mode while Hart offers an account that gives sound attention to both modes without trying to reconcile them at the theoretical level. Quinton and Rawls give insufficient attention to the *extrasystemic* role of justice. Retributivism, in the form considered here, may be at odds with justice. Although justice is congruent with the weak form of retributivism which merely asserts that only the guilty should be eligible for punishment, it is not obviously congruent

38. *Id.* at 115-29.

39. J. MURPHY, RETRIBUTION, JUSTICE, AND THERAPY 79 (1979) (emphasis deleted).

40. I. KANT, METAPHYSICAL ELEMENTS OF JUSTICE 36-39 (J. Ladd trans. 1965) (translation of METAPHYSISCHE ANFANGSGRUNDE DER RECHTSLEHRE (1797)).

41. The use of such metaphors and of this style of reasoning is criticized persuasively by M.B.E. Smith in Smith, *Is There a Prima Facie Obligation to Obey the Law?*, 82 YALE L.J. 950 (1973).

with a stronger form of retributivism, which asserts that there is a duty to punish the guilty with fitting severity.

III. Toward a New Methodology

The opposition between forward-looking justifications and justice as justification can be bridged not by eclecticism but by reconceiving the terms of a forward-looking theory. Only in this way can reasoning about punishment emerge from "the shadow of utilitarianism," from a context in which familiar forms of utilitarianism are swallowed whole, rejected, or adopted with demarcated constraints.

A forward-looking theory will be incomplete as long as it fails to consider every effect the practice of punishing has on the common good. The effects of criminal adjudication and punishment on the incidence of crime are surely the first effects that come to mind, but there are others. Hart reminds us that the public process of trial and conviction affirms values that bind society.[42] A society in which stable standards of punishment generally reflect and reinforce moral values is one in which persons rest secure in their capacity to act and plan, and in which they experience little discontinuity between public events and private expectations. The notion of the common good is not severable from the notion of a society with these latter characteristics.

The best discussion of the social benefits of punishment is in Joel Feinberg's essays, "Justice and Personal Desert" and "The Expressive Function of Punishment."[43] Feinberg draws attention to what he calls natural responsive attitudes to the actions of others. For example, he notes the congruity—logical as well as emotive—between gratitude and kindness, resentment and intentional injury. Feinberg asserts that there is a natural fit between "one person's actions or qualities and another person's responsive attitudes."[44] These responsive attitudes are the foundations of a shared sense of what treatment persons deserve; they owe nothing to forward-looking goals. But, Feinberg notes, consideration of the common good "give[s] a reason (in addition to natural inclination) for expressing . . . our attitudes and appraisals" in such institutions as criminal adjudication and punishment.[45] Individual responsive attitudes and institutional criteria for decision-making mutually reinforce and condition one another. Feinberg notes that whether

42. H.L.A. Hart, *supra* note 24, at 169-73, 182-85.
43. J. Feinberg, Doing and Deserving 55-94, 95-118 (1970).
44. *Id.* at 82.
45. *Id.* at 83.

or not symbolic public disapproval helps or hinders deterrence and reform, it serves other functions that are inherent in such expression. Among these functions are authoritative disavowal of certain kinds of harmful conduct, vindication of the law as rooted in moral values, and formal absolution of those who are free of blameworthy conduct.[46] It is easy but wrong to think of these functions as means to an end and as needing vindication in the light of some aspect of the common good. The following argument demonstrates why no such vindication is needed.

First, there is an important distinction between resentment and justified disapproval.[47] Unlike resentment, justified disapproval carries with it a claim to be able to justify or demonstrate that the disapproved conduct violates shared norms of mutual respect and dignity. Resentment is a personal responsive attitude toward actions affecting oneself, while disapproval is a responsive attitude backed by reasons and concerned with actions affecting oneself or others. Resentment and justified disapproval are different categories of response—one emotive, one cognitive—but they are responses to the same kind of action.[48] Second, there is a logical relationship between resentment or disapproval on one hand and certain kinds of conduct on the other. What we resent or disapprove of (and what we generally praise or blame) is not typically arbitrary or a matter of idiosyncratic preference. Rather such judgments are appeals to shared standards, to a shared sense of the common good. This is what John Rawls taps when he finds and describes the "sense of justice."[49] Third, any forward-looking characterization of the common good will describe social institutions in which the sense of justice is realized and reinforced, not as a means to some other end but as an indispensable aspect of living well with others. Finally, the requirement that a system of punishment be just (that punishment be allocated to the guilty and that moral blameworthiness play some role in determining the severity of punishment) is an inherent requirement of any characterization of the common good.

If all this is true, one of the recurrent criticisms of forward-looking theories—that such theories fail because a system justified in forward-

46. *Id.* at 101-04.

47. The best treatment of this distinction and of its significance for moral philosophy is P.F. STRAWSON, *Freedom and Resentment*, in FREEDOM AND RESENTMENT AND OTHER ESSAYS 1-25 (1974).

48. *Id.* at 13-16.

49. *See generally* J. RAWLS, *supra* note 18, at 453-512.

looking terms could encompass conviction and punishment of the innocent if it was generally believed that those punished were guilty—misses the mark.[50] This criticism is irrelevant because a forward-looking theory is an attempt to describe a future in which the common good is in fact secured, not one in which persons happen to believe that the common good is secured. The criticism would suggest itself only to someone who thought that there was no difference between reality and belief about reality. The difference, however, could hardly be greater. One would not confuse a situation in which persons wrongly believed that they were safe from crime with one in which potential offenders were really deterred. One should, accordingly, keep distinct a situation in which persons believed they lived in a just society from one in which they were in fact treated justly.

The point here is methodological. To understand it we must distinguish conceptual relationships from contingent ones.[51] For example, the relationship between the common good and security from harm is conceptual, not contingent. It is part of the notion of the common good that persons be safe and secure, and the inquiry into why deterrence is a desirable goal is otiose.[52] The relationship between the common good and just treatment is also conceptual and not contingent. The question why punishment should be limited to the guilty requires no answer. The attempt to refute the criticism on its own terms by showing that systematic injustice would not (as a contingent matter) be balanced by gains from enhanced deterrence, is misconceived *ab initio*. It is misconceived not because the empirical question is close or undecidable, but because the empirical question is not meaningfully raised; gains in added safety are, in principle, not the sorts of things that can justify

---

50. *See supra* notes 20-23 and accompanying text.

51. I am drawing on the familiar and highly problematic distinction between analytic (conceptual) truths and synthetic (contingent, empirical) truths. Very roughly, the distinction is between propositions whose truth is apprehended through one's understanding of the meanings and uses of the terms and to propositions whose truth is determined by inspection of empirical situations. "Ethics is a branch of philosophy" is a proposition of the first kind while "Harold Stassen is the Republican nominee for President" is an example of the second. The distinction has spawned endless debate among philosophers. Among the most influential discussions are W. QUINE, *Two Dogmas of Empiricism*, in FROM A LOGICAL POINT OF VIEW 20-46 (1961) and Grice & Strawson, *In Defense of a Dogma*, 65 PHIL. REV. 141-58 (1956).

52. Of course, one can describe the ways in which persons benefit from safety and security, but those descriptions do not have explanatory value. If the value of safety and freedom from harm is not self-evident, there's little to be said to demonstrate their value. Compare Hart's discussion of the minimal content of natural law in H.L.A. HART, THE CONCEPT OF LAW 189-95 (1961).

systematic injustice.[53]

The familiar opposition between maximizing the collective happiness or satisfaction and satisfying justice is a chimera. Happiness and satisfaction are understandable and realizable not *in vacuo* but in a social context. The kind of happiness or satisfaction realizable in a just context is not comparable or commensurable with happiness or satisfaction realizable in an unjust context. The kind of happiness that is relevant to forward-looking anticipations of the common good is necessarily the former.

The term "forward-looking theory of the common good" is preferable to "utilitarianism" because the latter is tainted. Throughout its tangled history utilitarianism has been associated with the notion that happiness or satisfaction is only contingently or accidentally related to the moral features of a social context. A context in which the greatest happiness is gained by the greatest number may or may not be a just society; its justice remains to be demonstrated.[54] In Hart's most recent work he sees, I think, the vulnerability of traditional utilitarianism. He says that we must move away from debate about "the ways in which utilitarianism has ignored certain values taken to be uncontroversial."[55] At the same time, he calls for "a more radical and detailed consideration of the ways in which rights relate to other values."[56] My remarks are intended to be in the spirit of these observations.

It may be objected that any attempt to integrate justice into a forward-looking theory must fail. He who takes justice seriously is oblivious to consequences and affirms that justice be done even if the heavens fall.[57] This objection fails in two ways. First, appearances notwithstanding, the objection does not set justice in opposition to future consequences, but rather sets in opposition two different sets of consequences, the effects of just treatment and the effects of unjust treatment. In this sense, the objection itself is forward-looking. Secondly, the on-going debate about justice and forward-looking theories is con-

53. The distinction between what is true "as a rule" and what may be true as an exception is crucial here.

54. This position, as we have seen, is held by rule-utilitarians as well as other utilitarians. It is compatible with this position that intuitions of what is just may be clearer than intuitions of what is best in utilitarian terms. If that is true, the measure of just institutions by utilitarian criteria may never be made.

55. H.L.A. HART, *supra* note 52, at 195.

56. *Id.*

57. *Fiat justitia ruat coelum*, proverb attributed to Lucius Calpurnius Piso Caesoninus [d. 43 B.C.], *quoted in* J. BARTLETT, FAMILIAR QUOTATIONS, 133 (15th ed. 1980).

cerned with on-going systems of rules (practices), not particular cases of injustice. The objection would have to be rewritten to refer to just rules, not to justice in a particular case. That said, one who holds the view I have defended may concede that individual cases of injustice may occur and need to be excused; but in principle they must remain exceptions within a system of justice. If the objection is that the heavens would fall were justice done systematically, i.e., were just rules adopted, then it adopts a pessimism to which there is no reasonable response.

It could also be objected that integrating justice into a forward-looking theory absorbs the retributivist's notion that there is a duty to punish the guilty and to do so proportionately. This objection forgets the caveats laid out above. Justice, in my view, speaks uncertainly to such issues. It may counsel us to distinguish among the guilty in the light of circumstances and to weigh ameliorating or aggravating circumstances in deciding when and how to punish. The following propositions illustrate this point.

> (1) A forward-looking theory of the common good will prescribe a system of just rather than unjust treatment.

This, I have argued, is a conceptual matter.

> (2) A just system of punishment will restrict punishment to the guilty.

This too is a conceptual matter and not an empirical question.

> (3)(a) A just system of punishment will always punish the guilty and will punish them with severity proportionate to the seriousness of their offenses.

This proposition is treated as conceptual by retributivists. Compare it with the following.

> (3)(b) In a just system of punishment there are ordinarily good reasons to punish the guilty and to do so with severity proportionate to the seriousness of their offenses.

I have suggested that (3)(b), and not (3)(a), best describes the requirements of justice.[58] It follows from (3)(b) that whether and how an offender should be punished in a particular case is a matter to be decided on the basis of all relevant reasons.

58. It can be argued, I think, that this best fits Hart's position as well.

IV. Questioning the Genealogy of Morals

The paper has one unexplained premise. It is that the most familiar way of characterizing a forward-looking theory, identified over the decades with utilitarianism, is incoherent. To defend my premise would bring us deeply into the epistemology of moral reasoning and is beyond the scope of this paper. Nonetheless, an underlying characterization of forward-looking theories, shared by both most utilitarians[59] and anti-utilitarians,[60] can and must be described, however briefly and roughly. By its terms, individuals are seen as entertaining life plans involving identifiable ends (plans for maximizing happiness or satisfaction) atomistically.[61] The ends reflect personal choices or dispositions, and they may have any content. For the utilitarian, the point of moral reasoning is to ascribe moral justification to the coordination of such plans to maximize collective and cumulative satisfaction. For the anti-utilitarian the point of moral reasoning is to uncover the appropriate constraints on the pursuit of these ends so that each individual is accorded the protection of respectful treatment. These constraints are, at least in part, the constraints of justice. For the anti-utilitarian, moral justification lies in satisfaction of the conditions set by such constraints.

To begin to see the incoherence of the traditional characterization one must challenge the underlying picture of human experience and aspiration. One must sketch an alternative picture, one in which the genealogy of personal awareness of the good lies *ab initio* in social interaction and is describable essentially in interpersonal terms of reciprocity. It would follow that the notion of a personal good is best seen as derived from participation in the common good and that the common good inherently involves, as I have argued, a system of just rather than unjust treatment. A move away from the atomistic epistemological premise is a move away from the utilitarian dialogue, a move (as Hart would have it) out of the shadow of utilitarianism. Its elaboration is a project for another time.

59. *See, e.g.*, J.S. Mill, Utilitarianism (1861); J. Bentham, Principles of Morals and Legislation (1789); R. Brandt, A Theory of the Good and the Right (1979); and D. Lyons, Forms and Limits of Utilitarianism (1965).

60. *See, e.g.*, R. Dworkin, *supra* note 32, at 94-100; J. Rawls, *supra* note 18, at 22-53.

61. In other words, each person is seen as determining what shall count as her/his personal goals and as going about maximizing the satisfaction of these goals. One individual's goals may or may not include the empathetic realization of the goals of others to whom she/he has affective ties.

[11]
Reconstructing the Criminal Defenses: The Significance of Justification

The intersection between morality and law is nowhere more evident than in the criminal defenses. The general notion underlying the criminal defenses is captured by the claim, "Yes, I have committed harm but there are decisive reasons why I should not be held to blame or punished for my action."[1] The harm involved is the kind of harm anticipated by the criminal law (taking life, doing injury,

---

[1] In his comprehensive and illuminating survey of criminal defenses, Paul Robinson sets out five categories of criminal law defenses which he defines as "any set of identifiable conditions or circumstances which may prevent a conviction for an offense." Robinson, *Criminal Law Defenses: A Systematic Analysis*, 82 COLUM. L. REV. 199, 203 (1982)[hereinafter Robinson]. *See also* P. ROBINSON, CRIMINAL LAW DEFENSES (1984)[hereinafter CRIMINAL LAW DEFENSES]. The five catagories are: failure of proof defenses, offense modification defenses, justifications, excuses, and nonexculpatory public policy defenses (such as the statute of limitations). Robinson, *supra* at 203. In line with most discussions of criminal law defenses, I am concerned here only with the third and fourth categories: justifications and excuses. These involve situations in which the elements of the offense are satisfied and the actor claims that there are sufficient grounds for personal exculpation, moral as well as legal. The first two categories on the other hand involve situations in which the elements of the offense are, for various reasons, not established. The last category involves situations in which the grounds of nonprosecution do not amount to moral exculpation. These distinctions notwithstanding, Robinson's caveats concerning overlaps and intersections among these categories should be kept in mind. Robinson, *supra*, at 232-43.

In limiting my discussion to justifications and excuses, I concern myself with problems and suggestions raised by George Fletcher and Kent Greenawalt in articles prepared for a workshop on comparative German and Anglo-American criminal law held in Freiberg, West Germany, July, 1984. *See* Fletcher, *The Right and the Reasonable*, 98

depriving one of property) and the defensive reasons are ones recognized by law. At the same time criminal defenses represent moral judgments. Each category of criminal defense mirrors and amplifies what is arguably a criterion for moral blamelessness[2] and every species of moral exculpation seems to demand legal recognition.[3]

The familiar categories of defenses[4]—self defense, duress, necessity, mistake, privilege,[5] intoxication—are heterogeneous. The situations and sources of human action are varied and complex and there is no a priori reason to think that the bases of moral exculpation sort themselves into simple categories. At the same time, not just the law, but also human understanding, demands categorization, however Procrustean the result. The criminal defenses, with relatively little deformation, seem to sort themselves out into two groups, justifications and excuses. Privilege and self-defense are examples of justifications. The policeman, empowered to place sus-

HARV. L. REV. 949 (1985) and Greenawalt, *The Perplexing Borders of Justification and Excuse*, 84 COLUM. L. REV. 1897 (1984).

2 Some criminal defenses exculpate only in part and are thus the grounds for a finding of diminished responsibility. In accord with the relevant statutes in a particular jurisdiction, negligent conduct or extreme emotional distress may justify a diminution of the charges from murder to manslaughter or manslaughter to negligent homicide (in the case of homicide), from aggravated assault to simple assault, etc. *See* W. LAFAVE & A. SCOTT, SUBSTANTIVE CRIMINAL LAW § 3.7 (1986). Intoxication will often mitigate rather than exculpate. *See id.* at § 4.10.

To simplify, if the discussion I address mainly exculpating rather than mitigating defenses. In doing so I follow Fletcher, *supra* note 1, and Greenawalt, *supra* note 1.

3 This conclusion needs to be qualified in at least two ways. First, in some cases that do not fall under any standard legal defenses, the actor may be morally blameless because her motives are "pure" or admirable. Acts of civil disobedience are punishable notwithstanding the fact that the general public and indeed the judge may admire and sympathize with the actor's motives. The law distinguishes between motive and intent; intent to do harm is usually required as an element of the offense and the moral praiseworthiness of the purpose or motive is ordinarily irrelevant to the question of guilt or innocence. *See* W. LAFAVE & A. SCOTT, CRIMINAL LAW § 3.6 (2d ed. 1986).

Secondly, an exception to the statement in the text is represented by strict liability offenses. In certain instances the legal response is determined by a public policy imposing a special duty of care upon actors, forcing them to assume the risk of liability if any harm results from their action. In such cases, legal liability may exist even when the actor is morally blameless. For an exhaustive discussion of the theory of strict liability, see G. FLETCHER, RETHINKING CRIMINAL LAW 713-36 (1978).

4 The general theory of criminal defenses is discussed *infra* text accompanying notes 22-35.

5 I shall use the term "privilege" to refer to those justifications, sometimes called "authority," which Robinson describes as follows:

> The use of public authority justification is often limited to certain persons whose position or training makes them particularly appropriate protectors of the interest at stake. These interests may be personal or societal; they include law enforcement, child-rearing and education, safety and order on public transportation vehicles or in institutions, life or health . . ., judicial, military, and other public authority generally.

Robinson, *supra* note 1, at 216.

pects under arrest, may use minimal force and thus inflict harm but he does not thereby commit an assault. Rather, he is justified in using minimal force. Analogously, one may use force sufficient to ward off an (impermissible)[6] assault even if the resulting harm is fatal to the attacker.

In his extensive writings on criminal law generally and the criminal defenses in particular, George Fletcher finds it useful to identify a distinctive feature of justifications as allowing us to distinguish cases of causing harm from cases of doing wrong.[7] Justified cases of harming are not wrong and do not stir feelings of blame and retribution; rather, they are socially approved. Social approval, in turn, may be explained by the appeal to shared social interests or shared moral beliefs.[8]

Excused behavior, on the other hand, is not approved. A harmful drunken assault is wrong and morally blameworthy. In allowing involuntary intoxication as a defense, the law does not part company with morality, but rather recognizes a distinction in seriousness and blameworthiness. Deliberate assaults by those who have their wits about them and carry out harmful intentions are more blameworthy than assaults by those who have lost control. Criminal law exists to punish the more serious lapses.[9]

George Fletcher and Paul Robinson[10] have both commended the conceptual clarity that comes from distinguishing sharply between justifications and excuses. Fletcher makes three claims in support of this distinction. First, criminal defenses can usefully be

---

6 An assault is not an offense if, for example, one has the explicit or implicit consent of the victim. CRIMINAL LAW, *supra* note 3, at § 5.11. In other words, for legal purposes, an assault is an unconsented touching.

7 The relationship of wrongdoing and harm is discussed at great length and with much subtlety by Fletcher in RETHINKING CRIMINAL LAW. G. FLETCHER, *supra* note 3, at 454-91, 515-79 (particularly 472-83). The theory that I attribute to Fletcher in this article is a simplified one and is to be gleaned from *The Right and the Reasonable*. *See* Fletcher, *supra* note 1. I have not attempted to discuss the relationship between the fuller discussion in Fletcher's book and the briefer discussion in his article. *See infra* text accompanying notes 45-61.

8 I discuss *infra* part II whether or not a utilitarian account of justifications provides the best understanding of their moral foundations. Fletcher seems to reject a utilitarian account for a retributive one, while Robinson seems sympathetic to utilitarianism. *Compare* Fletcher, *supra* note 1, at 957-61 *with* Robinson, *supra* note 1, at 216-20.

9 This is not to deny, of course, that criminal law sometimes punishes minor lapses under the rubric of misdemeanors. The point rather is that one who is convicted of a serious offense must be said to have had some opportunity to comply with the law and to have foregone that opportunity either through extreme recklessness or malign intent. *See infra* text accompanying note 48.

10 *See supra* note 1. *See especially*, CRIMINAL LAW DEFENSES, *supra* note 1, at 100-01; Robinson, *supra* note 1, at 234-36, 241-43.

sorted out into these two categories. Secondly, these categories illustrate and use an important distinction between two sorts of questions that criminal law must answer in every case of criminal liability: whether there has been wrongdoing and whether the wrong is to be attributed to a particular actor with the consequence of liability.[11] The first question has, according to Fletcher, natural priority over the second. Unless a wrong has been done, there is not a wrong to attribute.[12] Third, Fletcher's most abstract and perhaps most important claim is that such an ordering of questions, one that he finds in the German criminal code, demonstrates the virtues of structured legal thinking. This claim may take two forms. It may take the relatively modest form of stating that an ordered set of abstract questions and categories is indispensable for organizing and understanding a heterogenous body of empirical data, even when there are evident limitations and distortions in so doing. This form of the claim may be close to a truism, but it is also a reminder of what is implicit in investigation. The more ambitious form of the claim is that the categorical framework orders the data without distortion or ambiguity and indeed answers questions about the data that can be answered in no other way.[13]

Fletcher sometimes appears to defend structured thinking in this second way.[14] He seems to hold the view that the categories of

---

[11] An exposition of structured thinking about criminal law in this form is the backbone of RETHINKING CRIMINAL LAW. *See* G. FLETCHER, *supra* note 3, at 454-514. A major theme of Fletcher's book is that

> the German analysis of the distinction between wrongdoing and attribution goes far beyond the questions of insanity and infancy . . . . The primary focus of German theory in this century has been the attempt to elaborate a structure of liability for criminal acts by determining which issues are properly classified in one category or the other.

G. FLETCHER, *supra* note 3, at 456. Fletcher is in sympathy with this attempt and his assumption that the categories are hard-edged is one of the main topics critically examined *infra*.

[12] This notion seems to have all the earmarks of a truism. *But see infra* text accompanying notes 94-95.

[13] There is more to this Procrustean problem than meets the eye. It is one thing to say that descriptive categories can be misleading because they involve unwarranted simplification or distortion. But legal categories are created with the *purpose* of simplifying the relevant data and making some factors relevant to the disposition of a problem and others irrelevant. The problem at hand is not, however, that of organizing chaotic and irrepressible nature into the categories of justification and excuse, but of observing how well and easily the various and familiar criminal defenses fit within the legal categories of justification and excuse.

[14] Having identified structured thinking with the German legal culture and flat thinking (in terms of reasonableness) with the American legal culture, Fletcher repeatedly cites the clarificatory advantages of structured thinking.

> The divergence of common law thinking from continental thinking on putative self-defense derives from a matrix of inter-related assumptions. . . . At the foundation

justification and excuse are exhaustive and divide the defenses without residue or ambiguity. Secondly, he claims that difficult questions about borderline examples can be answered satisfactorily by an application of the structure.[15] Kent Greenawalt has challenged this view by offering counterexamples to Fletcher's arguments and by questioning the usefulness of this application of structured thinking. Greenawalt argues that a fully systematic working out of the distinction between justifications and excuses is misguided in principle because the boundary between the concepts is inevitably unclear and because the distinction is undermined by "disagreements about substantive morality."[16]

This article will reexamine the boundary between justifications and excuses in order to assess Fletcher's structure of analysis in particular and the role of structured thinking in this area in general. Part I sorts out criminal defenses into three, rather than two, categories: justified acts *tout court*, excused acts *tout court*, and "justified wrongs." One theme of Part I is that the concept of a justified wrong is useful as a category of classification and is necessary to reconcile ordinary usage of the notion of justification with its legal usage. Part II applies this analysis to two closely related problems. It reviews some familiar difficulties of classifying and understanding the necessity defense and explains these difficulties by reference to uncertainty in the concept of wrongdoing.

Part III considers the relationship between justified wrongs and excused behavior in the context of trying to understand and classify the defense of duress. It concludes that our difficulties in understanding duress are reflections of deeper difficulties in understanding the psychology of control and responsibility. In this context the

> of these assumptions lies the cement of reasonableness, a concept that enables Americans to blur distinctions between objective and subjective, self-defense and putative self-defense, justification and excuse.

Fletcher, *supra* note 1, at 979-80. Presumably blurring is not a good thing, especially since the several listed distinctions are said to be useful and to have hard edges. Yet Fletcher also protests that he is not being critical of "flat" thinking or thinking in which there is no "natural order" of questions: wrongdoing first and attribution second. *See* Fletcher, *supra* note 1, at 953.

15 Perceptive discussions that illustrate Fletcher's sensitivity to unresolved and unresolvable issues can be found in RETHINKING CRIMINAL LAW where he considers difficult applications of the defenses of necessity and duress. *See* G. FLETCHER, *supra* note 3, at 817-35, 855-64. Robinson's own diagnosis of problematic cases appears in *Criminal Law Defenses*. *See* Robinson, *supra* note 1, at 232-43.

16 *See* Greenawalt, *supra* note 1, at 1904-05. One of my arguments is that the difficulties inherent in understanding justifications and excuses have much less to do with moral disagreement than Greenawalt supposes and the kinds of disagreements he relies on are more or less irrelevant. In other words, the conceptual disagreements would persist even if there were perfect agreement on moral norms.

defense of reasonable mistake[17] is compared with duress for the purpose of seeing both defenses as plausible examples of different kinds of justified wrong. Part IV examines the familiar problems that flow from the rights and obligations of third parties in the face of justified and excused actions. Part V is about the implications of this analysis for the claim that justifications refer to general characteristics of the *act* and excuses refer to idiosyncratic characteristics of the *actor*.[18] Finally, Part VI draws matters together with observations on the use and abuse of structured thinking in analyzing the criminal defenses.

I. Justifications, Excuses, and Justified Wrongs

It would be idle to discuss whether the distinction between justifications and excuses is moribund in Anglo-American law and legal scholarship.[19] For many theorists, the distinction remains an important tool for pedagogy and investigation in the theory of criminal law.[20] It is one thing, however, to attend to the distinction, and it is another to treat the distinction as hard-edged. Fletcher sees it as a tool for resolving uncertain examples and clarifying hard cases. Among other things, this article argues that it is unhelpful to see the current debate simply as one between those who view the distinction as a sharp one (Fletcher and Robinson) and those who view it as inevitably unclear (Greenawalt).[21] The choice is not between a crystalline ordering and no ordering at all.

[17] In referring to the defense of "reasonable mistake," I have in mind the Model Penal Code formulation of the defense according to which a reasonable mistake (of law or fact) exculpates if the act the actor thought he was carrying out, in the circumstances as he thought them to be, was a lawful act at the time of the action. For a discussion of the problematic distinction between mistakes of law and mistakes of fact, see Model Penal Code, § 2.04 (1) (Proposed Official Draft 1962) and accompanying comments.

[18] *See, e.g.*, Robinson, *supra* note 1, at 229. "In determining whether conduct is justified, the focus is on the act, not the actor. An excuse represents a legal conclusion that the conduct is wrong, undesirable, but that criminal liability is inappropriate because some characteristic of the actor vitiates society's desire to punish him." Robinson, *supra* note 1, at 229. *See also* Fletcher, *supra* note 1. "Claims of justification direct our attention to the propriety of the act in the abstract; claims of excuse, to the blameworthiness of the actor in the concrete situation." Fletcher, *supra* note 1, at 955. We shall see in Part V that the act/actor distinction is substantially misleading.

[19] *See* Fletcher, *supra* note 1, at 953-57.

[20] *See, e.g.*, W. LaFave & A. Scott, Handbook on Criminal Law 356-413 (1972). *See also* Eser, *Justification and Excuse*, 24 Am. J. Comp. L. 621 (1976).

[21] A distinction between two terms can be interestingly complex if each term has, for example, several overlapping criteria of use and the criteria for the two terms overlap. Identifying the criteria and illustrating the overlap can itself be a clarifying analysis. Vague references to "fuzzy" terms are simply a way of turning one's back on this job. *See* Greenawalt, *supra* note 1, at 6. For some methodological constraints, see L. Wittgenstein, Philosophical Investigations, Part I, § 1-34 (1953).

Fletcher's ordering is simple, intuitively appealing, and may be assessed as follows.[22] The basic distinction in this ordering is between two questions: Has the actor committed a wrong? Is the actor to be punished for his/her wrong action? Two conditions must be satisfied in a given situation before *either* of these questions is reached. First, the accused must in fact be the person who committed the acts in question, and second, the acts must have caused harm. The refined first question, is thus, Is the harmful act committed by this actor a wrong? The second question, in turn, must also be qualified. Even if the actor has committed a wrong, the second question may not be reached if the court does not have jurisdiction over the defendant, for example if he/she is an infant. The second question presupposes jurisdiction.[23]

The prima facie usefulness of the distinction between wrongdoing and attribution in explaining justification and excuses is clear. For example, justified acts, privileged acts of law enforcement or acts of self-defense, are harmful but not wrong. Any viable social policy would be likely to endorse the use of effective force by those employed to enforce the law and the right to defend oneself against imminent harm.

If it is clear that this result fits our moral intuitions, it is less clear what moral theory best explains the result. On the one hand, a utilitarian explanation seems satisfactory since it can be argued that society as a whole is best off, in the long and short-run, if law enforcement and self-defense are approved and encouraged.[24] Utilita-

---

[22] This ordering, as Fletcher correctly observes, is characteristic of the criminal codes of continental legal systems, but perhaps Fletcher underestimates the extent to which it also pervades common law. *See* Fletcher, *supra* note 1, at 954-57, 962-64. *See also* sources cited *supra* note 20. The MODEL PENAL CODE draws a similar sharp distinction between excuses and justifications, treating the former under "General Principles of Liability" and the latter under "General Principles of Justification." *See* MODEL PENAL CODE §§ 2, 3.

[23] As Robinson points out in explaining his fifth category of criminal law defenses, nonexculpatory public policy defenses, there are many ways in which a culpable defendant can escape the jurisdiction of the court. Having mentioned the statute of limitations and constitutional protection derived from the fourth, fifth and sixth amendments, Robinson refers to "diplomatic immunity, judicial, legislative, and executive immunities, immunity after compelled testimony or pursuant to a plea bargain or other agreement, and incompetency. . . . Such nonexculpatory public policy concerns are at work whenever a dismissal is based on factors other than the innocence of the defendant." Robinson, *supra* note 1, at 231.

[24] The nature and scope of utilitarian ethical theories have been matters of controversy for well over a hundred years. I am using the term in a way that has become generally favored among writers on ethical theory and that escapes some of the criticisms that classical formulations invited. Accordingly, an act or general practice is morally justified according to utilitarianism if it tends overall to benefit, rather than harm, those who are affected by it, if those affected by it are better off than they would be if the

rianism also seems to account for the distinction between justifications and excuses. While justifications are just the sort of acts that contribute to well-being overall, excused acts do not contribute to well-being. The harmful acts of someone acting under a mental disability are not to be encouraged. There is no resulting benefit that outweighs the harm.

A utilitarian criterion for the defenses has limitations, however. Even if it yields a prima facie intelligible distinction between justification and excuses, it does not tell us why *both* justification and excuses are defenses but only why justifications are defenses. The utilitarian may respond that justifications and excuses are defenses for different reasons: justified acts contribute to well-being overall, while excuses should be defenses because harming the actor will neither undo the harm she has caused nor deter her from taking further harmful action since her original harmful act was not in her control. This response, however, is flawed.[25] Punishing those who lack control may well contribute to well-being by (a) giving an incentive to those who can affect their actions to keep them out of trouble, (b) restraining and incapacitating them so that they are not in a position to cause harm and (c) giving persons in marginal situations, like duress,[26] an additional reason to resist the pressure to act harmfully.

Utilitarianism is not only inadequate to explain excuses, but to explain justifications as well. A utilitarian endorsement of self-defense must presuppose that the harm done by a self-defender is less than the harm threatened to him. This assumption is unjustified when the response involves force approximately equal to the threatened force. The utilitarian may reply that justification does not depend on the results in the particular case, but on the results overall when self-defense is encouraged. This reply depends on the uncertain assumption that potential victims are less likely to get hurt, or are likely to get hurt less, if they resist than if they yield. Moreover, as the details of the utilitarian response are spelled out,

act or general practice did not occur. This account says nothing about the components and characteristics of benefit and harm, but rather assumes that there is some social consensus about these matters. For a discussion of utilitarianism, consequentialism, and "welfarism," see D. LYONS, THE FORMS AND LIMITS OF UTILITARIANISM (1965); H. MILLER & W. WILLIAMS, THE LIMITS OF UTILITARIANISM (1982); T. MORAWETZ, THE PHILOSOPHY OF LAW (1980); A. SEN & B. WILLIAMS, UTILITARIANISM AND BEYOND (1982).

25 For a discussion of this point, see H. HART, PUNISHMENT AND RESPONSIBILITY 19 (1968); Fletcher, *Excuse: Theory*, ENCYCLOPEDIA OF CRIME AND JUSTICE 727 (1983).

26 Part III *infra* examines at some length the proper classification and understanding of duress. Robinson raises the question of whether it is an excuse or a justification in Robinson, *supra* note 1, at 240.

they seem less and less relevant *in principle*. The right of self-defense seems to demand some vindication regardless of the consequences of self-defensive actions.

One suspects, therefore, that not only utilitarianism but some account of justice or retribution is implicated in the notion of wrongdoing that underlies the criminal defenses.[27] On this view, certain kinds of purposeful action show disrespect for the integrity and rights of other persons and thus merit punishment, whatever the utilitarian consequences. Privileged acts and acts of self-defense do not fall into this category. The person who provokes harm loses his claim to respect or invulnerability to the extent that he himself commits a wrong. Wrongdoing in this sense is thus a necessary, if not a sufficient, condition for punishment.[28]

Any account of the criminal defenses will therefore have to invoke both utilitarian assumptions and intuitions of justice and retribution. If Fletcher is correct, an account of justification depends on using these resources to analyze the distinction between harm and wrong and to show that justified conduct is harmful and not wrong. Excused conduct, on his account, is both harmful and wrong, but nonetheless the results are not "attributable" to the actor and therefore punishment is not appropriate. To explain this, Fletcher distinguishes between willful or purposeful choice and attenuated or diminished self-control because of exigent circumstances.[29] For hu-

---

27 Fletcher's discussion of retribution as the relevant ordering principle for the proper understanding of the structure of justifications and excuses is presented in Fletcher, *supra* note 1, at 961. A much fuller and significantly different analysis of the foundations of wrongdoing appears in G. FLETCHER, *supra* note 3, at 454-91, 552-69. *See also supra* note 7. Although I argue that the concept of wrongdoing is both ambiguous and overdetermined, see *infra* text accompanying notes 45-55, my provisional adoption of a roughly utilitarian account of wrongdoing does not reflect a disagreement with Fletcher's point that, in the final analysis, our sentiments about wrongdoing also roughly track our sentiments about justice and punishment. This conclusion, however, leads me to disagree with Fletcher's point that determinations of wrongdoing and attribution are separate tasks since I argue that both are rooted in our sentiments about what is just.

28 The notion that sentiments of justice and retribution are a threshold for punishing, but that some additional justification is required once the threshold conditions are met, is explained in H. HART, *supra* note 25, chapter 9; T. MORAWETZ, *supra* note 24, at 219-21; and Morawetz, *Retributivism and Justice*, 16 CONN. L. REV. 803 (1984).

29 *See* Fletcher, *supra* note 1, at 961-62. Throughout Fletcher's discussion, the salient feature of excuses is the attenuation of control through some disability. Robinson seems to understand excuses in exactly the same way:

> Each of the excused defenses has the following internal structure: a *disability* causing an *excusing condition*. The *disability* is the abnormal condition of the actor at the time of the offense. We say, for example, that the actor is suffering from insanity, intoxication, subnormality, or immaturity. The disability is a real condition with a variety of observable manifestations apart from the conduct constituting the offense.

Robinson, *supra* note 1, at 221 (emphasis in the original). If this is indeed the mark of an

manitarian or compassionate reasons,[30] certain kinds of wrongful behavior may be excused because the actor did not and could not be expected to exercise choice and control. The reasons may be internal or external: temporary derangement because of intoxication or illness, or external pressure from threats or coercion. Intoxication, insanity, and duress are recognized as excuses or as bases of diminished responsibility.[31] Wrongdoing is present, but justice does not mandate punishment.[32] Thus, Fletcher invokes justice and retribution as relevant to the second question, the question of attribution.

Two important consequences flow from explaining justification in terms of the absence of wrongdoing and explaining excuses in terms of the justice of attribution and punishment. Suppose that Al sees Bo struggling with Cal, wrongly imagines that Bo has assaulted Cal, and goes to Cal's aid. If Bo is in fact a policeman effecting an arrest or a victim resisting Cal's original attack, Al's misconceived intervention is excusable but not justifiable. Since Bo's action is not a wrong, forcible interference with it is a wrong, albeit an excusable one. On the other hand, if Bo is in fact the aggressor (whether excusable or not), Al's intervention is justifiable.[33] (Just as Cal is privileged to defend himself, Al is privileged to go to his assistance.) In general, then, according to this model,[34] interference with justifiable behavior can only be excused, not justified, while interference with excusable behavior can be justified.

The second consequence of distinguishing justifications from excuses in this way is that one separates judgments about acts from

excuse, then mistake and duress are surely not excusing conditions, as I argue in Parts I and III. An exigent circumstance is not the same thing as a disability; if it were, self-defense would be an excuse. Throughout his article, Robinson is uncharacteristically vague in defining mistake, hampered as he is by a counterintuitive linkage between mistake and disability. Robinson, *supra* note 1, *passim*.

30 The terms are Fletcher's. *See supra* note 29.

31 Three points are significant: (1) Intoxication is an excuse only if it is "involuntary intoxication," i.e., if the actor was not reckless in becoming intoxicated, reckless in the sense of being able to anticipate in his misconduct. (2) In many cases of reckless conduct, intoxication may tend to mitigate rather than excuse the actor. (3) I discuss in part III *infra* whether duress is properly conceived of as an excuse. *See also supra* note 29.

32 Fletcher's reference to compassion raises the question of whether justice or mercy is the guiding moral principle behind excuses. *See* Fletcher, *supra* note 30. Can justice and mercy be distinguished in these situations?

33 As Robinson properly reminds us, the defensive responses that are properly classifiable as justifications include defense of others and defense of property, as well as self-defense. *See* Robinson, *supra* note 1, at 215.

34 *See* Fletcher, *supra* note 1, at 964-71; Robinson, *supra* note 1, at 273, 278. Greenawalt's misgivings regarding the clarity of the distinction between justifications and excuses are, as I point out *infra* in Part IV, well grounded. *See* Greenawalt, *supra* note 1, at 1918-27.

judgments about the blameworthiness of actors. In determining that an act is justified and therefore not wrong, one need not refer to idiosyncratic characteristics of the actor. In excusing a wrong, on the other hand, one must take into account these idiosyncratic characterstics.[35] One finds, for example, exigent circumstances to show how and why self-control in the particular case was diminished or absent.

This analysis of justifications and excuses has the virtue of clarity, but faces the following problems. First, many familiar defenses do not fit comfortably into this framework. Not all cases of excusable wrongdoing are cases of diminished control or derangement of purpose. The most obvious example is reasonable mistake.[36] For instance, if Dee puts white powder from the sugar bowl into Eldon's cocoa and has every reason to think that it is sugar, but in fact it is poison, Dee's defense is mistake of fact,[37] as every first-year law student knows. But is this a justification or an excuse? Dee will say that her belief that the substance was sugar was justified since she had good reasons for thinking so and no reason to think otherwise. Because she had good reasons for believing what she did, she also had good reasons for acting as she did. She will say, correctly, that no one would have suspected that the "sugar" was poison.

Another example illustrates the same point. Flo, a police officer walking in a deserted alley sees looming before her the silhouette of an armed man. She turns and shoots the child with a toy gun who produced the looming shadow. Assume there is no negligence in her actions. She will claim mistake and say, again correctly, that she had good and sufficient reasons for her actions, and therefore that she was justified in doing what she did.

Cases of reasonable mistake and putative self-defense are usually counted as cases of excused misconduct. Unlike privileged acts

---

35 *See supra* note 18.

36 *See supra* note 17. In chapter nine of RETHINKING CRIMINAL LAW, Fletcher offers a compendious inventory of the various kinds of mistakes that can affect our perception of the actor's culpability. He goes on to discuss several theories about the relevance of mistakes to culpability. Obviously I cannot do justice to this analysis. I restrict my examples to mistakes of fact falling within the categories of mistakes about the elements of the definition and mistakes related to justificatory claims. Fletcher's list and examples appear in G. FLETCHER, *supra* note 3, at 684-85.

37 The use within criminal law of the term "mistake" seems to some extent to be at odds with ordinary usage. In criminal law we refer to a relevant false belief as a mistake whether or not there was any possibility of the actor arriving at a true belief instead of the false belief. In ordinary discourse we say that someone made a mistake only if it was possible for him not to have made a mistake. Thus, in law "mistake" does not necessarily carry the connotation of fault, while in ordinary discourse it does. I am indebted to Arthur Hessel for pointing this out to me.

of law enforcement and acts of genuine self-defense these actions are not encouraged by society. They are to be seen as regrettable accidents; no one is made better off by them and a utilitarian would have no trouble condemning them (but not necessarily punishing them).[38] At the same time they do not have the salient characteristic of excused conduct.[39] The actor is in control, is acting purposefully and on the basis of good reasons. There is no suggestion of inner or outer coercion or derangement.

Ordinary linguistic usage seems to support the notion that this behavior is justified rather than excused. In this respect, Greenawalt seems correct when he argues that acting on good reasons is the essence of *justified* action.[40] However, the structure of justified action on the basis of good reasons is distinguishable from the structure of such legal justifications as privilege and simple self-defense. In the former cases, the actor has good and sufficient reasons for action but they are incomplete reasons from the point of view of hindsight or omniscience. One must distinguish what the actor could have been expected to know and do from what the actor may come to know after the fact or what the omniscient observer would know. It is important that one does *not* say an actor is justified if he has any reasons whatever for acting;[41] only good reasons in the senses required by law will do. This is captured by the requirement that the mistake be reasonable.

---

[38] *See supra* note 24. A utilitarian would not punish if the result would merely be the accumulation of harm with no offsetting benefits.

[39] Here I am adopting Fletcher's and Robinson's account of the distinguishing marks of excuses. *See supra* note 29.

[40] *See* Greenawalt, *supra* note 1, at 1903.

> "Justified" is most definitely not a special legal term. In discussions of ethics, justified action is morally proper action. "Justification" is also used in relation to the reasons one puts forward for one's choices; an action is "justified" in this sense when one has defended it with sound arguments. . . . In epistemology, reference is made to "justified" belief, belief about facts that is well-founded. What joins these various senses is the idea that to be justified is to have sound, good reasons for what one does or believes.

See id. This seems to be quite correct, and it reflects the distinction made by philosophers (and based on observations of usage) between justified belief and true belief. A justified belief can be false; it is justified if there are good reasons for holding it. Fletcher seems to reject this analysis of justification throughout his article, but this is especially evident when he says that putative self-defense (grounded on a well-founded but erroneous belief that one is threatened) can be an excuse but not a justification. *See* Fletcher, *supra* note 1.

[41] Throughout his discussion of putative self-defense Fletcher clearly regards it as irrelevant whether the actor had *good* reasons for acting as he did or whether he simply had reasons for doing so. Fletcher, *supra* note 1, at 973-77. Presumably he would regard the distinction as relevant to the question of the availability of excuse, but it is hard to see how that argument could be made, given the linkage between excuses and disabilities.

It will be said that this extended account of justified conduct confuses the notion that the mistaken actor is justified with the claim that the actor thinks and believes erroneously that she is justified but is in fact, from the point of view of law, only excused. The difficulty with this objection is that the actor does not really "believe she is justified." What she believes is that the substance is sugar, and that Eldon wants sugar in his coffee, or that the shadow is of a dangerous assailant. The notions of justification and excuses are on the one hand, part of a meta-language or observer language used to describe their situation. From the standpoint of this meta-language it is appropriate to say that having good, albeit erroneous, reasons *is* the criterion for being justified. The person who is unreasonable in judgment, however, incorrectly believes that she has good reasons for acting. That person is unjustified. Clarity commends this account over one that says the actor who has good, if erroneous, reasons thinks she is justified but is not.

If it is appropriate to say that such mistaken behavior is nonetheless justified, it is necessary to distinguish these cases from such familiar cases of justification as privilege and self-defense.[42] Fletcher distinguishes harms from wrongs and commends a roughly utilitarian criterion for wrongs.[43] Privileged and self-defensive actions are immediately harmful, but not harmful on balance and therefore not wrong. Not only are the individual acts justified but so is the policy of encouraging persons to defend themselves and of training enforcement officers to use appropriate force to restrain dangerous offenders. Harm caused by justified mistake, on the other hand, is not the sort of harm that is bound inextricably to ultimate benefits. It is also not the vindication of personal rights and privileges.[44] If these features mark what is wrong, then it seems appropriate to use the phrases "justified act *tout court*" for the first kind of act and "justified wrong" for the second. At the same time we can reserve the term "excused act" (or "excused wrong") for

42 Thus we need two discrete classes of justified conduct, pure and simple justified conduct and what I call justified wrongs.

43 *See supra* note 7.

44 In other words, if justifications like self-defense and privilege are morally overdetermined, accommodating both a utilitarian account and an account in terms of the vindication of rights, the same cannot be said about so-called justified wrongs. Or perhaps a utilitarian argument is available but more remote, if one can establish that recognizing the defense of mistake does have long term benefit. I suspect that the benefit involved would be in some respects inseparable from whatever benefits are derived from a general sense that persons are treated fairly or justly. If that is true, then utilitarian accounts and accounts in terms of justice and rights are not as easily separable as one might suppose.

wrongs committed by persons who lack the ordinary resources of deliberation and control.

One caveat should be noted. The term "justified wrong" is potentially misleading. What is justified is the mistake and the action, but not the result. Dee is justified in thinking the white substance is sugar. She is not justified in killing Eldon. To say that she *is* justified in killing Eldon is to imply that she would be justified in killing him intentionally, and that is not true. Accordingly, neither the term "justification" nor the term "excuse" is fully satisfactory. Dee's mistake was justified and therefore we excuse the consequences.

II. The Criteria of Wrongness and the Defense of Necessity

The distinction and relationship between harms and wrongs deserve additional scrutiny. This can be done by reconsidering some of the limitations of a utilitarian account of the criminal defenses and then looking at other criteria for wrongness.

In the individual case of self-defense, the defender may in fact inflict more or as much harm on the attacker than the attacker originally intended or was likely to cause. The justifiability of the act does not depend on minimization of harm in the particular case. This does not mean, however, that standard cases of simple self-defense cannot be rendered understandable by a utilitarian account. All the utilitarian needs to argue is that harmful behavior is likely to be minimized overall by a policy of encouraging self-defense than by a different policy. Legal recognition of self-defense may, for example, discourage attackers who know that their intended victims are thus legally permitted to inflict harm on their attacker.

This revised utilitarian analysis may be criticized by those who would argue that empirical consequences should be irrelevant. One has a right, it will be said, to defend oneself even if defenders as a rule inflict more harm than attackers and even if attackers are not deterred by the legal recognition of the right of self-defense. Such an argument may be grounded on the notion of a fundamental right of self-preservation, represented by a basic moral requirement of respect for the physical and mental integrity of persons regardless of the consequences.[45] Accordingly, the recognition of self-defense

[45] I am making no assumption about the kind of theory of rights that lies in the background. In particular I am not claiming that there are universal rights derivable from human nature or that rights are traceable to a hypothetical social contract. The first kind of theory has recently been worked out by Alan Gewirth and the second by John Rawls. *See* A. Gewirth, Human Rights (1982); J. Rawls, A Theory of Justice (1971). The notion that a fundamental right is the right to be treated equally with all persons and

is morally overdetermined. Various theories of wrongness imply such recognition.

A more serious problem arises with what I have termed justified wrongs. A utilitarian may have trouble showing the moral basis of the defense of mistake of fact. The participants are clearly worse off as a result of the harmful and mistaken conduct than they would be if it had not occurred. If the utilitarian's concern, however, is with the consequences of punishing the conduct, he can argue in favor of exculpation on the grounds that harming the agent merely makes the situation worse. There may, however, be offsetting benefits from the punishment of justified wrongs. A policy of disallowing the defense of reasonable mistake may make persons more careful to investigate the grounds of their conduct.[46] To say that Flo had good reasons for her mistake is compatible with saying that we may require extraordinary care when the lives of innocent persons may be lost.[47]

The utilitarian has a harder time explaining the defense of mistake of fact than does the theorist who invokes justice and rights. It is a basic norm of criminal law that it is just to punish only those who have had an opportunity to shape their conduct to the demands of law,[48] only those who have acted purposefully to cause the sorts of harms that the law forbids or those who have failed to take expected precautions and care. Singling out for punishment persons who have acted innocently and with good reasons seems to flout a basic norm of justice, a right not to be punished without fault.

The treatment of mistakes within Fletcher's framework is significant. They are instances of wrongdoing both by utilitarian criteria, since society seeks to minimize such conduct, and by criteria of

with respect and concern is elaborated by Ronald Dworkin. *See* R. DWORKIN, TAKING RIGHTS SERIOUSLY (1977). There would seem to be two aspects to the recognition of such a right, a passive aspect (the right to expect others to respect one's integrity and autonomy) and an active aspect (the right to take action to see that one's autonomy and integrity are safeguarded).

46 To work out this argument in detail one would have to attend separately to the several kinds of mistake identified by Fletcher and work out the implications for each. *See* Fletcher, *supra* note 36. In this particular example it is hard to see what duty of care could have been imposed on the person.

47 *See supra* note 3, comment 2. This point puts in question the relationship between law and morality insofar as each may affect the other over time. By making persons strictly liable for certain kinds of conduct, or at least by disallowing particular defenses and imposing a high standard of care with punishment for those who fall short, the law may change the way the act is conceived morally. For example, by imposing severe penalties on drunk drivers and by making liable as accomplices those who contribute to drunkenness, the law may change moral attitudes. Accordingly, morality cannot be seen as a fixed and immutable set of norms to which the law simply may or may not conform.

48 *See* H. HART, *supra* note 25, at 158-85.

blame and retribution. Both criteria mark the boundaries of wrongdoing and thus the boundaries between justifications and excuses. Nonetheless, Fletcher concludes that even though a retributive response is appropriate in those cases, such acts are excused for humanitarian reasons because of the special situation of the actor.

Why does Fletcher say that most observers would seek retribution from actors like Dee and Flo? To be sure, observers and actors may regret such actions and actors may feel remorse, but feeling regret and remorse has little to do with retribution. (Regret over the outcome may even be appropriate in cases of pure self-defense.) It seems counterintuitive to argue first that certain acts are wrong and that retributive feelings are appropriate, and then to ask whether punishment is just and whether there are humanitarian reasons not to punish. This reasoning seems counterintutitive because judgments about wrongness and retribution are not independent from judgments about justice, but dependent on them. It is clear that it is just to exculpate Dee and Flo; it is much less clear that their conduct is "right" or how a relevant criterion for wrongness and rightness can be framed.

Fletcher's analysis is motivated in the following manner. First, the conclusion that acts of self-defense, etc., are not wrong is overdetermined.[49] It can be supported by utilitarian reasons or by reasons having to do with rights and just treatment. At this point it is not necessary to decide whether a utilitarian calculus of harm and benefit or intuitions about justice form a sufficient criterion for wrongness. When one comes to explaining excuses, however, it is necessary to explain why it is unjust to punish. This *seems* to suggest, as Fletcher argues, that the question of wrongness is sufficiently determined by utilitarian considerations, leaving questions of attribution and punishment to be decided on the basis of justice.

This conclusion, however, poses a dilemma. On the one hand, a utilitarian criterion for wrongness is unsatisfactory because it makes the rightness or wrongness of self-defense depend on an empirical calculation of net benefit. It does not allow us to distinguish wrongs from (net) harms to conclude that only some harms are wrongs.[50] On the other hand, in rejecting a utilitarian criterion for

---

49 *See supra* text accompanying note 45.

50 Throughout this article I ignore wrongful conduct that does not involve harm. Attempts to cause harm are of course the most obvious example of crimes that do not involve harm. Although each of the criminal defenses could also be raised against a charge of attempt, consideration of attempts would add nothing to my analysis. In his discussion of the relationship between wrongdoing and harm, Fletcher is correct that harm is not a necessary ingredient of wrongdoing, that acts intended to cause harm may

wrongness one cannot go so far as to say that only purposeful or negligent harm-causing is wrong, because this account is too narrow. It excludes innocent mistakes from the domain of wrongdoing. There is a need for a middle position, and Fletcher seems to aspire to one when he suggests that wrongs are those (net) harm-causings that are appropriately accompanied by a retributive feeling or demand.[51]

Such use of the notion of retribution produces an unstable theory. First, it appeals to intuitions about retribution that are uncertain. Does one really seek retribution from those who innocently and mistakenly cause harm? Secondly, it severs intuitions about retribution from intuitions about just treatment even though, conceptually, the sense of retribution seems to depend on the sense of justice as its clearest component.[52]

The implications of this analysis is that the notions of wrongdoing and retribution hover in a no-man's-land of concepts between two relatively clear notions, harm and justice. However problematic the details,[53] the utilitarian notion of a net general effect of greater benefit or greater harm is a determinable feature of many situations. Similarly, it is often clear what justice demands in regard to persons who harm even when the explanations of such intuitions vary and are disputable.[54] By comparison, the use of the term "wrong"

be punishable whether or not they succeed. RETHINKING CRIMINAL LAW, *supra* note 3, at 472-83. In *The Right and the Reasonable*, Fletcher restricts his analysis to acts that have succeeded. *See* Fletcher, *supra* note 1. I restrict my discussion here in the same way.

[51] Fletcher discusses the motivations for treating W (wrongdoing) as preceding R (determinations of responsibility) in *The Right and the Reasonable*. *See* Fletcher, *supra* note 1, at 958-60.

[52] *See* Morawetz, *Retributivism and Justice*, *supra* note 28, at 815-20. Among other things I suggest that the clearest relevant intuition of justice is that blameworthiness or desert is a necessary condition or a threshold for punishing. The retributivist would seem to hold that it is also a sufficient condition for punishing as well and that it is mandated by justice. Following Hart, I question this conclusion. *See also* H. HART, *supra* note 25.

[53] It is always easier to produce the data to be explained than to produce the explanation. Over a wide range of situations we know when the individual, another person, or society as a whole is better or worse off. We draw on knowledge of human satisfactions, desires, and needs; we are prepared to defend our conclusions and insights. But it is harder to explain and justify our knowledge of human nature, of benefit and harm, as well as our knowledge that some conclusions are seriously debatable and others are not. Attempts by utilitarians to identify the ingredients of judgments about benefit and harm have produced both disagreement over the particular analysis and skepticism over the possibility of giving any such analysis.

[54] *See supra* note 53. Attempts to formulate the principles of justice have met the same fate as attempts to clarify benefit, harm, and utility. In *Retributivism and Justice* and other forthcoming work, I suggest that some questions may be answered by noticing that intuitions about benefit and justice may be more closely related to each other than is generally assumed. *See* Morawetz, *supra* note 28.

seems unsettled, sometimes colored by utilitarian criteria and sometimes by considerations of justice.

The phrase "justified wrong" is useful in severing the criteria for justification from the criteria for a wrong. It is somewhat defective, however, in failing to capture the unsettled character of the notion of wrongful conduct. Regarding mistaken harm-causing as a kind of "justified wrong"[55] presupposes the utilitarian criterion that an act is wrong insofar as persons would be better off if acts of that kind did not occur. By this criterion privilege and pure self-defense are not instances of wrongs, while harmful mistakes are wrongs. The criterion for just punishment, involving as it does the fair opportunity to comply with the law, is a different moral standard and is not satisfied when those who make reasonable mistakes are punished.

Confusion over the criteria for wrongness affects the analysis of the defense of necessity or lesser evils. To plead necessity is to concede that one has caused a harm in violation of the letter of the law and to argue that one has done so only to avoid the alternative of bringing about an even greater harm. For example, one may be able to stop a forest fire only by trespassing and destroying private property by creating a firebreak, and he whose family is starving may be able to save them only by stealing food. Like privilege and self-defense, acts under the color of necessity involve deliberate choice and seem classifiable as justified acts *tout court*. They arguably involve socially approved conduct, conduct that may reasonably be encouraged.

Some commentators argue that necessity identifies the overarching concept of legal justification and includes privilege and self-defense as subcategories.[56] Assaulting one's attacker is said to be the lesser evil when compared with acquiescence. There are two problems with this argument. One is that self-defense applies even in situations in which harm to the attacker may be as great as the harm threatened. The second is that necessity is often applied when the actor must choose between two affirmative actions (as in the first example) while self-defense characteristically refers to the choice between action and acquiescence.[57]

Uncertainties about the necessity defense persist and they re-

[55] *See supra* text accompanying note 42.

[56] *See* Robinson, *supra* note 3, at 213-14; Morawetz, *Justification: Necessity*, in ENCYCLOPEDIA OF CRIME AND JUSTICE 959.

[57] This is only roughly true. In many necessity situations the actor must choose between letting a seriously harmful action happen (the forest fire sweeping across the landscape) and intervening to prevent it by bringing about evil (taking property to create a

flect uncertainty about the criteria of wrongness. Justification in the case of privilege and self-defense is morally overdetermined, supported and explained both by utilitarian theories and theories of justice. Is this so with necessity? Utilitarian theories again seem to be relevant. The necessity defense is an endorsement of the principle of minimizing harm in the particular case and, a fortiori, minimizing harm in general. Justice, however, is more problematic. The privileged acts of the police and the defensive acts of the would-be victim are justified at least in part because the person harmed has been an aggressor, has forfeited in part[58] her putative right to be respected and free of harm. The same cannot be said of the innocent victims of the necessary action. The man whose property is destroyed for a firebreak or the family swept away by the flood diverted from a town center to a park would seem to have the same rights as anyone else. Moral intuitions are most uncertain when we are required to count lives. Is it justifiable to kill one merely to save two?[59] And is it justifiable to kill one when it is merely probable that many others would otherwise die?[60] It seems obvious that a doctor would not be justified in sacrificing one healthy patient in order to transplant eight body parts into eight patients who would otherwise surely die, even if the would-be donor is uniquely compatible with the would-be recipients. The same doctor, it seems, could justifiably kill one person by steering his runaway car toward him if the *only* alternative were to drive into a crowd of eight pedestrians.

There seems to be no clear answer to this dilemma. It shows both that utilitarian intuitions have a major role in determining wrongness and that they tell us less than the whole moral story. If the doctor's actions in the first situation are clearly wrong, then wrongness has little to do with counting lives and much to do with

firebreak). Nonetheless, the context of the necessity defense is characteristically described as one in which the actor may choose a greater or lesser evil.

58 The aggressor has only forfeited these rights in part. The justification of self-defense extends only to a proportional response. The person who responds disproportionately, for example by killing an escaping felon who does not threaten violence or a thief who does not place the victim's person at risk, does not have a complete defense. *See* Robinson, *supra* note 1, at 216.

59 Our reliance on a consensus of intuition breaks down when lives are at stake. We have conflicting intuitions: that each life is of infinite value, that some lives are more valuable than others, that it is better to save more lives than fewer. We seem to be clear that taking lives is worse than taking property and we tend to have clear intuitions about situations in which we have to compare lesser harms. But only under cover of exigency do we permit persons to choose more lives over fewer and under that cover we may also put at grave risk many rescuers to save a single coal miner.

60 Some writers have thought that the distinction between killing and letting die is relevant, that taking a life is worse than allowing the taking of a life to happen. *See, e.g.*, J. Finnis, Natural Law and Natural Rights 100-33 (1980).

the rights of persons to safeguard their vital interests even when others may suffer. It is practicable for the would-be victim in the first case to call on the state to safeguard these interests, while it is not practicable to do so in the exigent second situation. This difference is in some way related to the fact that we can set rules for the protection of would-be victims in the first situation and can do nothing but leave matters to the actor in the second. The moral relevance of all this remains opaque, however. A theory that seeks to explain justification in terms of wrongdoing must in turn elucidate wrongdoing in terms of the underlying moral criteria of wrong and neither utilitarian criteria nor intuitions of justice are clear enough to be helpful.[61]

III. Understanding Duress

In the tripartite framework of justified harms (justified acts *tout court*), justified wrongs, and excused conduct (involving diminution or lack of control), the criminal defense of duress presents special difficulties of classification. Consider, for example, the case of Gerd who, held at gunpoint, is forced to use her technical skill to rewire a car so that it will explode when the ignition is turned. Like the person who is acting in self-defense, she is choosing to act to avert harm to herself. Like the person who acts from mistake, she is acting on the basis of good reasons and yet is acting in a manner that society does not encourage or approve. Like the person who is intoxicated or deranged, she may perhaps be said to lack the normal resources of control over her actions. The act committed under duress, therefore, seems in some respects like a justified act, in others like a justified wrong, and in still others like an excusable act.

Each of these analogies is problematic. Taking the last first, one finds conceptual difficulty in treating duress as an excuse. The guiding hypothesis here is that the threat of immediate harm (to oneself or to others)[62] takes away one's ordinary power and responsibility to control what one does. External coercion is analogized to

[61] The inquiry must be carried out on a metaethical level, with such questions as whether utilitarian (or consequentialist) analysis is the sort of analysis that will explain wrongness, whether an act can be wrong and justified, whether justifications are related to just dispositions of cases, whether there is a useful distinction between committing a wrong and simply acting wrongly, and whether there is an equally important distinction between calling an act or outcome wrong and saying that the actor acted wrongly. It seems to me unhelpful to dismiss the relevance of moral philosophy on the ground that persons have different moral convictions and that some persons are likely to be a good deal more idealistic than others. *See* Greenawalt, *supra* note 1, at 1904-07, 1927.

[62] Historically the defense of duress has been restricted in some periods and jurisdictions to threats to the actor and usually to threats to the actor or her family. The as-

inner derangement. One typical standard for duress is that the actor will be excused if she acted in response to pressures that a person with normal capacities of self-control could not be expected to withstand.[63] The idea is of a "will overborne." Acting under duress seems to be midway between controlling actions and being the unconscious agent of others (as if hypnotized).[64]

One difficulty with this account is that it presupposes a clearer theory of control and of the will than we really have. The actor under duress is surely aware of her choices and is choosing as deliberately as the person who acts under the pressures of self-defense and necessity. All are exigent situations. Yet in the case of such justifications as self-defense and necessity we do not claim to find an overborne will. These are situations of choice and control. These defenses are circumscribed by factors the actor is expected to take into account: self-defense is limited by the retreat restriction,[65] and necessity is limited by the requirement that the actor must choose the lesser evil.[66] The assumptions made about will, choice, and control in self-defense and necessity on the one hand and duress on the other seem inconsistent.

There are two options, to treat duress as an excuse but jettison the apparently arbitrary criterion for excuses, namely derangement causing lack of control, or to classify duress differently. Is duress a justified wrong? The mark of a justified wrong is that the actor has good reasons for acting, but at the same time takes actions that society (for utilitarian reasons) is anxious to discourage.[67] Persons acting under mistaken beliefs have good reasons and are morally

---

sumption has been that only these sorts of threats would be likely to coerce a person of reasonable resilience.

[63] *See* MODEL PENAL CODE, § 2.09 (Proposed Official Draft 1962).

[64] The conventional legal analysis of the situation of hypnosis is that one has not really acted at all. This situation is analogized to any other kind of automatism or reflex behavior. Thus duress seems to represent partial control, half-way between full control and no control. I suggest in the text that this is conceptually crude and inadequate. By Robinson's categorization, the situation of hypnosis would represent not a justification or excuse, but a failure to satisfy the elements of the offense. *See* Robinson, *supra* note 1.

[65] Even if threatened by deadly force, one may not respond with deadly force if (a) one can retreat in perfect safety, (b) one knows one can do so, and (c) one is not in one's own home. *See, e.g.*, MODEL PENAL CODE, § 3.04 (1)(b)(ii).

[66] A general way of expressing my disagreement with Fletcher is with regard to whether choosing the true lesser evil and choosing the apparent lesser evil are to be treated the same way and are to be regarded equally as justified conduct. By my analysis, they would both be justified because in both cases they would involve actions backed by good reasons. Fletcher would regard guessing incorrectly (in the case of an apparent lesser evil) as crucial, and the actor who guesses incorrectly could be excused but never justified. *See* Fletcher, *supra* note 1, at 971-77.

[67] *See supra* text accompanying note 42.

innocent. But can the same be said about those who act under duress?

In answering this question, one may get sidetracked by confusing good reasons for acting with moral reasons. Law does not require that people be particularly altruistic. The person who acts under an immediate and credible threat to himself is acting to avert that threat even at the cost of greater harm to other persons. Is this a good reason insofar as it warrants the claim that the actor was justified in acting as he did? The situation in a case of duress is radically different from that of mistake, in which the claim is genuinely one of moral innocence ("I had no reason to think that others would be harmed"). These reasons must be good reasons in quite a different sense from those that establish innocence, but they seem to be good reasons all the same.

It is clear that in nonexigent situations a preference for one's own interests and welfare becomes at some point monstrous and ceases to be a good reason. The sadistic killer for pleasure or the contract killer for money cannot claim to be justified by good reasons, because they appeal to a theory of personality and a scale of values that is generally rejected. It is important, nonetheless, to see that the claim of the person acting under duress is not altogether different. He too favors his own interest. A distinction between the cases is that the person acting under duress is seriously and imminently threatened, while the contract killer is not. What must be explained is *why* this difference means that the sadist or contract killer has no defense and the person acting under duress does. What are the moral as well as the legal limits of self-favoring? Understanding the criminal defense of duress depends not so much on understanding the will (and when it is overborne) as on understanding the morality of favoring the self.[68]

It can be argued, therefore, that harmful acts that are committed under duress could be called justified wrongs. They are neither excused acts, if the criterion for excusability is lack of control, nor justified acts, if the criterion for justifications is that society approves of such conduct (roughly for utilitarian reasons). Nonetheless, they are altogether different from mistakes, the other example of so-called "justified wrongs," in the conceptual problems they raise. In duress situations, one cannot say that the actor was *justified* in believing what he believed and therefore that the consequences of his ac-

68 *See, e.g.*, Williams, *Persons, Character and Morality*, in MORAL LUCK (1981); Williams, *Moral Luck*, in MORAL LUCK; Williams, *Utilitarianism and Moral Self-Indulgence*, in MORAL LUCK; Williams, *Internal and External Reasons*, in MORAL LUCK.

tions are *excused*.[69] If it is justifiable to act defensively when one reponds to threats, then the consequences must be *justified* as well. Duress, self-defense, and law enforcement, all of which involve responses to exigent situations, all present cognate problems of determining when the response to threats and danger is appropriate and defensible, when it is understandable if regrettable, and when it is beyond justification and toleration.

IV. Third Parties: Rights and Responsibilities

The concept of justified wrongs has implications for understanding the rights to act of third parties who interfere with justified or excused conduct. According to the widespread interpretation of these rights,[70] those who interfere with justified behavior may offer excuses but not justifications in defense of their behavior, while those who interfere with excusable behavior may be justified in their actions. If justified behavior is approved because it is right and contributes to the welfare of persons overall, then interference with such behavior (interference with the police, restraining those who act in self-defense) is not to be encouraged, merely excused. On the other hand, if persons act in harmful ways out of ignorance or because they are not in control, it is justifiable and socially desirable to prevent them from doing so.[71]

This account gives rise to certain anomalies. If Hal sees Ida struggling with Jo and goes to Ida's aid, the legal disposition of Hal's conduct will depend on whether he guesses correctly or not that Ida is being assaulted. If Jo, an undercover officer, is trying to arrest Ida and Hal interferes, Hal's conduct may or may not be excusable; the jurisdiction may or may not recognize the defense of mistake in such situations.[72] If, on the other hand, he guesses correctly that Jo is an assailant, he has a complete justification. Since

[69] *See supra* text accompanying notes 42-44.

[70] *See* Fletcher, *supra* note 1, at 971-77; Greenawalt, *supra* note 1, at 1918-27; Robinson, *supra* note 1, at 278-85. The litigation in *People v. Young* is instructive on this issue. 12 A.D.2d 262, 210 N.Y.S.2d 358 (1st Dept. 1961), *rev'd*, 11 N.Y.2d 274, 183 N.E.2d 319 (1962). The New York legislature's response is also instructive on this point. N.Y. Penal Law § 35.15 (McKinney 1975 & Supp. 1987).

[71] As I suggest *infra* at part III, it is difficult to accomodate these defenses (ignorance and mistake) within the confines of the standard conception of excuses as being defined by lack or diminution of control. Here I am bowing provisionally to the notion (which I reject elsewhere) that mistake is an excuse.

[72] Many jurisdictions implement a policy of discouraging the intervention of volunteers during arrests made by undercover police officers by disallowing the defense of excuse and thereby placing the helper at risk if he guesses incorrectly about an apparent assault. *See* S. Kadish, S. Schulhofer & M. Paulsen, Criminal Law and Its Processes 732-37 (1983).

some jurisdictions limit the availability of excuses but not of justifications in such cases, persons like Hal may bear a special risk when they choose to help. Arguably this is unjust.[73]

The analysis of justified wrongs eliminates such anomalies by implying that Hal is justified in either case. If Jo is simply enforcing the law, Hal has good reasons for intervening and, by committing harm, he carries out a justified wrong. If Jo is an assailant, Hal is justified as well. More generally, this analysis explains how someone who interferes with justified conduct can in turn be justified. Given discrepancies in reasonably available information and in the interpretation of contexts, the first person can have good reasons for acting in a way that is prima facie harmful and the second can have good reasons for trying to stop her.[74] Any problem of interpretation lies not with the idea that "justification" is being used in paradoxical or contradictory ways, but with the notion of good reasons. At what point does negligence, willful ignorance, or unreasonableness vitiate the claim of an actor that he acted on good reasons?

V. Judging Acts and Judging Actors

It is misleading to argue with Fletcher that justifications refer to generic characteristics of a situation, for example to whether it involves wrongdoing, and that excuses are determined by such personal characteristics of actors as lack of control. The distinction is sometimes described as a distinction between objective and subjective features, wrongdoing being objective and lack of control being

[73] *See supra* note 72. In these situations, the actor, if he guesses correctly, has a justification. Conversely, if the actor guesses incorrectly, he may be prosecuted on several possible grounds. The questionable basis for this policy is that erroneous interventions are more costly to society and are not outweighed by the benefits of voluntary assistance.

[74] By this method one can straightforwardly account for the counter-examples that Greenawalt offers to Fletcher. The case of People v. Young, 11 N.Y.2d 274, 183 N.E.2d 319 (1962)(reversing 12 App. Div. 2d 262, 210 N.Y.S.2d 358 (1961)), involves an intervention by a volunteer in a situation of plainclothes officers trying to make an arrest for disorderly conduct. The New York Court of Appeals held that one who goes to the aid of a third person "does so at his own peril," that he has no effective defense of honest mistake against a charge in this situation. *Id.* at 275, 183 N.E.2d at 319. The New York legislature finally codified such a defense in N.Y. Penal Law § 35.15. *See* Greenawalt, *supra* note 1, at 1919-21. Similarly, Greenawalt's counterexamples, see Greenawalt, *supra* note 1, at 1922, 1924, are effectively explained by the "good reasons" criterion for justifications. For example, Greenawalt conjures up two weak combatants, John and Mike, of which John is the attacker and Mike acts in self-defense, both with deadly weapons. Greenawalt says correctly that a strong third person (Arnold) who can keep each from harming the other would be justified in intervening. Arnold would thus have a justification for preventing a justified act (Mike's self-defense). If the "good reasons" approach is correct such examples should be easily anticipatable.

subjective.[75]

Both parts of the distinction are puzzling. What does it mean to say that wrongdoing is objective? If wrongdoing were the same as harmdoing, it could be argued that harmdoing has objective criteria. The two, however, cannot be identified.[76] If wrongdoing, on the other hand, is identified with unjustified harmdoing then the objectivity of the notion depends on the objectivity of the criteria for justification. These criteria, in turn, make reference to the motives and attitudes of the actor as well as to what the actor succeeded in doing. The necessity defense, for example, depends essentially on whether the actor reasonably believed that she had chosen the lesser evil. Self-defense is not available to every person who assaults a potential attacker but only to those who are aware of the attacker's intentions. The person who harms another not knowing or guessing that her victim would in turn have attacked her cannot plead self-defense when the victim's intentions are learned after the fact. Thus, the availability of justification defenses seems to depend on so-called subjective factors.

The suggestion that the determination of an excuse involves an essentially subjective assessment of the condition of the offender is also easily questioned. The dubious hypothesis about excuses is that they depend on abnormal subjective conditions and experiences. In fact, however, both excusable and inexcusable conduct have subjective dimensions and it is idle to suggest that one or the other situation is normal. The determination of the absence or the presence of excusing conditions and the determination of the presence or absence of justification are *all* "subjective" investigations. The main difference is that the subjective investigations relevant to justifications involve conditions pertaining to belief and the determinants of judgment, while investigations relevant to excuses involve the prevention or derangement of the process of judgment.[77]

---

75 *See* quotations, *supra* note 18. By "objective" I mean "determinable without reference to the state of mind of the actor" and by "subjective" I mean "determinable only by reference to the state of mind of the actor." This distinction differs from the usage of those who mean by an "objective" standard that, once the actor's state of mind has been ascertained, his conduct should then be measured against what the normal reasonable person would have done.

76 *See supra* text accompanying notes 42-45.

77 *Cf.* Greenawalt, *supra* note 1, at 1903.

> "Justification" is . . . used in relation to the reasons one puts forward for one's choices; an action is "justified" in this sense when one has defended it with sound arguments . . . . In epistimology, reference is made to "justified" belief about facts that is well-founded. What joins these various senses is the idea that to be justified is to have sound, good reasons for what one does or believes.

Greenawalt, *supra* note 1, at 1903. An excuse, on the other hand, involves, according to

A similarly defective characterization of justifications and excuses says that judgments about justifications are made at a higher level of generalization from judgments about excusable behavior. Thus, the statement that all law enforcement officers are justified in using necessary force to arrest or restrain dangerous offenders identifies a kind of justification by locating a general principle. Statements about excusable behavior, on the other hand, are said to pick out idiosyncratic, personal characteristics of the actor and are not generalizable.[78]

This distinction is hardly convincing. Why is the statement that Ida is involuntarily intoxicated any more idiosyncratic and personal than the statement that Jo is a police officer or that Kay believes that stealing food is necessary? In each case something said about Ida, Jo, or Kay distinguishes her from most persons and puts her in a limited class; in each case the statement substantiates a more general norm. The characteristic picked out for Ida (as the basis of an excuse) and for Kay (as the basis for justification) seems relatively situation-specific, bounded in time, but even this distinction is misleading. Ida's intoxication may extend over a series of situations as may Jo's perhaps temporary[79] status as a police officer. Certainly no clear rule emerges for distinguishing the personal characteristics or degree of generality relevant only to excuses and not to justifications.

VI. On Structured Analysis and Its Uses

What is to be gained by clarifying the distinction between justifications and excuses? Three questions must be distinguished.

(1) Given (a) that there is a distinction in moral usage between the concepts of justification and excuse, (b) that this distinction is

Robinson, "a disability causing an excusing condition. We say for example, that the actor is suffering from insanity, intoxication, subnormality, or immaturity." Robinson, *supra* note 1, at 211. Robinson goes on to say that there are two kinds of disabilities: long-term and short-term.

[78] *Cf.* Greenawalt, *supra* note 1, 1915.

> What does it mean to say that excuses are individual and justifications general? Roughly, the idea is that an excuse does not reach others who perform similar acts, but a valid justification would apply to anyone else in similar conditions. Exactly what this contrast amounts to is somewhat cloudy. In the broadest sense of "universalizability," common to discussions of moral philosophy, excuses as well as justifications are general: all persons with similar mental disturbances committing similar acts would have a similar excuse based on mental illness. The point must be that excuses, but not justifications, are based on personal characteristics or subjective attributes.

Greenawalt, *supra* note 1, at 1915.

[79] For example, one may be temporarily deputized for a particular occasion.

borrowed by the common law from ordinary language, and (c) that the so-called criminal defenses tend to be classified as justifications or excuses, what is the distinction? What coherence, incoherence, and sticking points are there in the categories as generally used?

(2) Can the answers to question (1) be used to turn hard cases into easy ones? Does the analysis of justification and excuses yield a single hard-edged distinction that allows one to classify with ease and without ambiguity those cases and situations which may otherwise seem problematic? Or does the anlaysis simply leave things better illuminated by showing why problematic cases are problematic?[80]

(3) Can this analysis be used for practical reform? Should legislators rewrite criminal codes using a reformed and clearer distinction? Should juries be instructed to give special verdicts stating whether they have found excuses or justifications relevant and decisive? Ought judges at least to instruct juries to think about the differences between excuses and justifications and distinguish clearly between them?[81]

This article addresses primarily the first question. The notion of justification is ambiguous, standing both for interventions that society wishes to encourage because they have socially desirable consequences and for acts done for good reasons. The second class can be said to encompass the first. By adopting the second conception, one can account for two kinds of justified behavior, behavior done for what are good reasons without regard to perspective (or from the perspective of society at large) and behavior done for what seem to be good reasons from the perspective of the actor.[82] The latter subcategory allows one to account (in very different ways) for mistake and duress, and for limitations on the defense of necessity.[83] It is important to see that requiring the actor to have good reasons from his perspective is not the same thing as requiring the actor to have reasons *tout court*. Accordingly, a mistake must be reasonable and the action that follows from it must be a reasonable response to the reasonably misunderstood situation. This is moral

[80] *See* L. WITTGENSTEIN, *supra* note 21, part I, § 124.

[81] Greenawalt, *supra* note 1, at 1900-02, is also concerned with the relation of theoretical and practical questions.

[82] This is likely to be misunderstood. As the text makes clear below, "good reasons from the perspective of the actor" does not refer to whatever the actor thinks are good reasons, but rather, to what are good reasons from the standpoint of society's modes of evaluating *and* are reasons guiding the actor.

[83] Mistake, necessity, and duress are discussed respectively *supra* in parts I, II, and III. The various limitations on the necessity defense are discussed in my article *Justification: Necessity*, *supra* note 56, at 958.

as well as cognitive reasonableness. The act of the person under duress must reflect a morally acceptable preference of self over others, or of some persons over others. I have adopted, with some trepidation,[84] the notion that excuses are best identified with diminished control through incapacity and with negligence.[85]

With respect to the second set of questions, this analysis explains why hard cases are hard, not how they can be made easy. The notions of a reasonable mistake and of a reasonable moral preference for self are notions about which people's opinions will continue to differ. Disagreement persists not only between persons with high moral standards and persons with lenient ones.[86] The point, for example, at which a medical mistake becomes negligent, the ways in which a reasonable mistake by a medical intern differs from what is reasonable in the performance of an experienced physician, must in the final analysis be decided case by case. Something, but not much, can be decided by anticipatory general rules. The same can be said about duress. The ways in which exigency and fear complicate human choice and compel leniency in deciding whether an actor had good reasons for yielding to threats are inevitably controversial.

The third set of questions is quite separate,[87] and encompasses a range of additional issues. One would have to know more than we do about the psychology of juries to know whether they would be helped or confused by analytical instructions on the justification/excuse distinction. This is a separate issue from the merits of the general verdict. As others have argued persuasively, there are good reasons for its retention.[88] Those reasons are not so much that persons have different moral convictions as that they have different conceptions of limits and endurance, of man's capacities for circumspection and deliberation, and so forth.[89] Defenders of the general verdict argue persuasively that agreement on guilt and exculpation can be reached without agreement about these conceptual

84 The notion of self-control and the limits of personal responsibility are explained in many ways and are the subjects of much disagreement. *See* S. HAMPSHIRE, FREEDOM OF THE INDIVIDUAL (1975); J. TRUSTED, FREE WILL AND RESPONSIBILITY (1984).

85 *See supra* parts I and III.

86 Greenawalt appears to think that the main relevant difference is between those who do and those who do not hold a perfectionist ethical code, those who stress what is mandatory and those who stress what is permissable. *See* Greenawalt, *supra* note 1, at 1904-05.

87 *See supra* note 81.

88 The merits of general and specific verdicts are discussed by Rohinson in Robinson, *supra* note 1, at 246-47, 290, and by Greenawalt, *supra* note 1, at 1900-01.

89 These uncertainties go to the heart of the distinction between justification and excuses. *See supra* part III.

boundaries. Additional issues are raised by such questions as whether criminal codes should reflect these categorical and conceptual distinctions, and whether judges' opinions should do so as well. These issues would take us beyond the scope of this article into the role of texts in legal interpretation.

Is a response only to the first set of questions worthless because it leaves legal practice unreformed?[90] A critic misunderstands philosophy and its applications if he looks for a quick fix.[91] An analysis responding to the first question does not leave *everything* untouched. The activity of thinking through the categories and their implications may purge inconsistency and nonsense from the discussion of these issues. Moreover, the goal of clarification is ambiguous. One can clarify concepts by describing their uses and showing how they are dependent on further concepts like that of "good reasons" or one can clarify by recommending different use with harder edges, rendering the concepts independent of such notions as "good reasons."[92] It is easy to get impatient with the first kind of clarification, with what J. L. Austin has called "linguistic phenomenology,"[93] and to condemn clarification because the second kind cannot be accomplished. The first is, however, a genuine alternative to capitulation in the face of the slogan that terms have "fuzzy edges."

The notion of good reasons for action helps one characterize a category of defenses one may call "justified wrongs." This in turn is a useful analytic tool for sorting criminal defenses, in particular the defenses of mistake, duress, and necessity. This analysis is relevant as well to puzzling questions about third-party interventions, for example how one actor can be justified in acting and another can be justified in interfering with that action.

Methodologically this article describes and takes a middle ground between positions taken by Greenawalt and Fletcher in their recent work on criminal defenses. Greenawalt questions whether conceptual analysis of justifications and excuses will yield any clarifi-

---

[90] Both Greenawalt and Fletcher seem to discuss the role of the investigation in relation to the possibility of reform.

[91] *See* T. MORAWETZ, WITTGENSTEIN AND KNOWLEDGE, ch. vii (1978). Wittgenstein argues that philosophy "leaves everything as it is." L. WITTGENSTEIN, *supra* note 21, at Part I § 124.

[92] Greenawalt seems to confuse the two senses of clarification when he says that "[a]ny definition of legal justification that is more specific than an open-ended reference to morally relevant factors is virtually certain to treat as justified some instances in which special factors would make the act only excused, at best, from a moral point of view." Greenawalt, *supra* note 1, at 1914-15.

[93] Austin, *A Plea for Excuses*, PHILOSOPHICAL PAPERS 130 (1961).

cation of difficult cases, whose difficulty he attributes to the fuzziness of the concepts and to the diversity of moral beliefs.[94] Fletcher, on the other hand, is Greenawalt's perfect foil because he seems to argue that both kinds of clarification can be accomplished at once, that structured thinking about these matters yields hard-edged categories and answers to hard questions.

The distinction between flat and structured thinking may be a chimera.[95] On the one hand, Fletcher's insistence that a determination about wrongdoing must precede a determination of blameworthiness for wrongdoing has the marks of a truism. At the same time, the notion that these are completely separable determinations is eroded by close analysis. The questions are easily separated when the wrong is palpable and the actor pleads some personal disability to control his conduct. The example of mistake, on the other hand, shows that there are multiple criteria for wrongness, and that they are inconclusive when the actor had good, morally defensible reasons but the result is one that society cannot approve. The criteria for wrongdoing and the criteria for the attribution of blame are neither identical nor wholly independent. We are comfortable separating the two notions when several alternative criteria of wrongdoing are satisfied, that is, when the classification is overdetermined.[96] That is not the case with mistake.

Does a concession that the two questions are not always independent and that more categories than two (justification *tout court*, excuse *tout court*) are needed make one a "flat" thinker?[97] No. One need not conclude that the punishability of actors and the admissibility of defenses is to be decided on an ad hoc, case by case basis, with appeal made only to the "reasonableness" of the conduct.[98] Instead, one may use the categories analyzed above and have conceptual reasons for using those categories. In part those categories are marked off by the presence and absence of good reasons for action and due care and thus they inevitably make reference to whatever standard of conduct society condones. In that sense, the reasonableness of conduct must always be at issue and the relevant standard is always in part "objective." The criminal defenses as a

94 *See supra* note 74.

95 *See supra* introduction and part I. The analysis I give seems to have the same density as that which Fletcher calls "structured" thinking, but it lacks the sharp edges. As I indicate in the text, one can use the criterion of "reasonableness" without succumbing to "flat" thinking, Fletcher to the contrary notwithstanding.

96 *See supra* text accompanying notes 24-28 and 44-48.

97 Fletcher, *supra* note 1, at 962-64.

98 *Id.*

general matter are about what one can and cannot reasonably expect persons to do and what standards one can expect them to understand and act upon. This will inevitably engender hard questions that vitiate any attempt to anticipate judgments with hard-edged concepts and to expunge "reasonableness" and its surrogates.

Name Index

Aristotle 38, 43, 249
Austin, John 222
Austin, J.L. 29, 65, 329

Bach, Johann Sebastian 253
Bellow, Saul 249
Bentham, Jeremy 62, 62
Berlin, Isaiah 255
Bickel, Alexander 80, 81
Brandt, Richard 64

Cooper, David 259, 260

Davidson, Donald 271, 272
Delgado, Richard 173
Derrida, Jacques 210, 211, 221
Dworkin, Ronald 3, 8, 10, 14–17 *passim*, 26, 30, 55, 65, 66, 67, 68, 70, 76–7 *passim*, 96, 126, 152, 153, 154, 159, 161–5 *passim*, 169, 184, 222, 223, 224–7 *passim*, 228, 239–45 *passim*, 247, 251–4 *passim*, 257, 260, 261, 273, 285

Einstein, Albert 43
Ely, John 159

Feinberg, Joel 263–5 *passim*, 295
Fish, Stanley 116, 187–90 *passim*, 225–7 *passim*, 228, 229, 235
Fiss, Owen 126, 159, 273
Flaubert, Gustave 275
Fletcher, George 303–5 *passim*, 306, 307, 309, 310, 315–17 *passim*, 324, 329
Frankfurter, Felix 80, 81
Freud, Sigmund 249

Gadamer, Hans-Georg 178
Gordon, Robert W. 166, 169, 230, 231
Greenawalt, Kent 305, 306, 329
Grey, Thomas 180, 191

Hart, H.L.A. 3, 13–17 *passim*, 26, 27, 28, 31, 55, 73, 96, 197–8 *passim*, 200, 201, 202–7 *passim*, 210, 216, 222, 223, 247, 248, 285, 290–92 *passim*, 295, 298
Holmes, Oliver W. 216, 222, 223
Hoy, David 180
Hume, David 247
Hyland, Richard 211–13 *passim*

Kant, Immanuel 101, 122, 249, 292
Kennedy, Duncan 171, 229, 230, 232–3, 265–8 *passim*, 269, 272
Kuhn, Thomas 97, 98, 99, 101, 102, 107, 124, 172

MacCallum, Gerald 256, 257
MacKinnon, Catherine 173, 187, 231, 272
Matsuda, Mari 173
Michelangelo Buonarroti 249
Mill, John Stuart 196, 247

Minow, Martha 185
Milton, John 249
Murphy, Jeffrie 294

Neurath, Otto 214, 215, 216, 236
Newton, Isaac 37, 44
Nozick, Robert 291

Perry, Stephen 208
Picasso, Pablo 249
Plato 122, 123

Quine, Willard V.O. 214
Quinton, Anthony 285–7 *passim*, 288, 290, 294

Radin, Margaret J. 192
Rawls, John 3, 5–7 *passim*, 23, 55, 64, 65, 67, 68, 70, 122, 123, 126, 239–42 *passim*, 245, 247, 261, 287–90 *passim*, 291, 294, 296
Raz, Joseph 151
Robinson, Paul 303, 306
Rorty, Richard 116, 181–7 *passim*, 188, 190, 191, 268, 269, 272, 273, 274

Schlag, Pierre 233–4 *passim*
Singer, Joseph 185, 186
Skinner, Quentin 213
Spelman, Elizabeth 185
Strawson, P.F. 33, 270

Taylor, Charles 256
Thucydides 215
Tolstoy, Leo 249
Tushnet, Mark 169, 178

Unger, Roberto 270, 272

Wasserstrom, Richard 75–7 *passim*
West, Robin 267, 272
Wittgenstein, Ludwig 27, 32–3 *passim*, 37, 42, 49, 50, 83, 84, 87, 88, 92, 101, 107, 115, 116, 117, 120, 135, 179, 180, 196, 201, 217, 218, 236
Wood, Gordon 215

For Product Safety Concerns and Information please contact our EU
representative GPSR@taylorandfrancis.com
Taylor & Francis Verlag GmbH, Kaufingerstraße 24, 80331 München, Germany

www.ingramcontent.com/pod-product-compliance
Ingram Content Group UK Ltd.
Pitfield, Milton Keynes, MK11 3LW, UK
UKHW021427080625
459435UK00011B/192

* 9 7 8 1 1 3 8 7 1 1 2 7 3 *